LIBRARY OF NEW TESTAMENT STUDIES

640

Formerly the Journal for the Study of the New Testament Supplement Series

Editor
Chris Keith

The Invention of the Inspired Text

Philological Windows on the Theopneustia *of Scripture*

John C. Poirier

t&tclark

LONDON • NEW YORK • OXFORD • NEW DELHI • SYDNEY

T&T CLARK
Bloomsbury Publishing Plc
50 Bedford Square, London, WC1B 3DP, UK
1385 Broadway, New York, NY 10018, USA
29 Earlsfort Terrace, Dublin 2, Ireland

BLOOMSBURY, T&T CLARK and the T&T Clark logo are trademarks
of Bloomsbury Publishing Plc

First published in Great Britain 2021

Library of Congress Cataloging-in-Publication Data
Names: Poirier, John C., 1963– author.
Title: The invention of the inspired text : philological windows on the
Theopneustia of scripture / John C. Poirier.
Description: London ; New York : T&T Clark, 2021. | Series: The library of New Testament
studies, 2513–8790 ; 640 | Includes bibliographical references and index. | Summary: "John
C. Poirier examines the "inspired" nature of the Scripture, as a response to the view that
this "inspiration" lies at the heart of most contemporary Christian
theology"– Provided by publisher.
Identifiers: LCCN 2020043642 (print) | LCCN 2020043643 (ebook) |
ISBN 9780567696731 (hardback) | ISBN 9780567696748 (pdf) |
ISBN 9780567696762 (epub)
Subjects: LCSH: Bible–Inspiration–History of doctrines. |
Bible–Criticism, interpretation, etc.–History
Classification: LCC BS480 .P6445 2021 (print) | LCC BS480 (ebook) |
DDC 230.1/3–dc23
LC record available at https://lccn.loc.gov/2020043642
LC ebook record available at https://lccn.loc.gov/2020043643

ISBN: HB: 978-0-5676-9673-1
     ePDF: 978-0-5676-9674-8
    eBook: 978-0-5676-9676-2

Series: Library of New Testament Studies, ISSN 2513–8790, volume 640

Typeset by Newgen KnowledgeWorks Pvt. Ltd., Chennai, India

To find out more about our authors and books visit www.bloomsbury.com
and sign up for our newsletters.

ἐγὼ ἦλθον ἵνα ζωὴν ἔχωσιν καὶ περισσὸν ἔχωσιν

Contents

Tables

Preface

The present study began as a 2010 conference paper. It took ten years for that mistake-ridden paper to give way to the more in-depth investigation that appears on the following pages. It has been an adventure in discovery the entire time.

As an independent scholar, I had much less interaction with others than an investigation of this sort normally involves, but I wish to thank Drs. Stephen Carlson and Edmon Gallagher for their feedback to the opening chapter. I also wish to thank Dr. Chris Keith and the editors at Bloomsbury for allowing a couple of mulligans.

Finally: I do not claim to be an expert in any of the remote reaches of the investigation, and I welcome any corrections or refinements of my work.

Easter 2020
Germantown, Ohio

Abbreviations

AB	Anchor Bible
ABD	David Noel Freedman (ed.), *The Anchor Bible Dictionary* (New York: Doubleday, 1992)
ABSA	*Annual of the British School at Athens*
AC	*L'Antiquité Classique*
ACSS	*Ancient Civilizations from Scythia to Siberia*
AJA	*American Journal of Archaeology*
AJEC	Ancient Judaism and Early Christianity
AJP	*American Journal of Philology*
ALGHJ	Arbeiten zur Literatur und Geschichte des hellenistischen Judentums
ANRW	Hildegard Temporini and Wolfgang Haase (eds.), *Aufstieg und Niedergang der römischen Welt: Geschichte und Kultur Roms im Spiegel der neueren Forschung* (Berlin: W. de Gruyter, 1972–)
APOT	R. H. Charles (ed.), *Apocrypha and Pseudepigrapha of the Old Testament in English* (2 vols.; Oxford: Clarendon Press, 1913)
ARG	*Archiv für Religionsgeschichte*
ARW	*Archiv für Religionswissenschaft*
AusBR	*Australian Biblical Review*
BabSup	Babesch Supplement
BAlt	Beiträge zur Altertumskunde
BBB	Bonner biblische Beiträge
BCCS	Brill's Companions to Classical Studies
BCHSup	Bulletin de Correspondance Hellénique Supplément
BETL	Bibliotheca ephemeridum theologicarum lovaniensium
BFPLUL	Bibliothèque de la Faculté de Philosophie et Lettres de l'Université de Liége
BHT	Beiträge zur historischen Theologie
Bib	*Biblica*
BibInt	*Biblical Interpretation: A Journal of Contemporary Approaches*
BJRL	*Bulletin of the John Rylands University Library of Manchester*
BJS	Brown Judaic Studies
BKP	Beiträge zur klassischen Philologie
BNP	Helmuth Schneider, Manfred Landfester, and Hubert Cancik (eds.), *Brill's New Pauly* (22 vols.; Leiden: Brill, 2002–11)
BRev	*Bible Review*
BSac	*Bibliotheca Sacra*
BTH	Bibliothèque de théologie historique
Byz	*Byzantion*

ByzZ	*Byzantinische Zeitschrift*
BZ	*Biblische Zeitschrift*
BZNW	Beihefte zur *ZNW*
C&M	*Classica et Mediaevalia*
CBQ	*Catholic Biblical Quarterly*
CChr	Corpus Christianorum
CEJL	Commentaries on Early Jewish Literature
CH	*Church History*
CJA	Christianity and Judaism in Antiquity
ClA	*Classical Antiquity*
ClQ	*Classical Quarterly*
ClR	*Classical Review*
CP	*Classical Philology*
CPSSup	Cambridge Philological Society Supplementary Volume
CRAI	*Critical Review of Books in Religion*
CRINT	Compendia rerum iudaicarum ad Novum Testamentum
CSEL	Corpus scriptorum ecclesiasticorum latinorum
DCLS	Deuterocanonical and Cognate Literature Studies
EBib	Etudes bibliques
ECF	Early Church Fathers
EKKNT	Evangelisch-Katholischer Kommentar zum Neuen Testament
EntAntCl	Entretiens sur l'antiquité classique
EpAn	*Epigraphica Anatolica*
EPRO	Etudes préliminaires aux religions orientales dans l'empire romain
EstBíb	*Estudios bíblicos*
EvQ	*Evangelical Quarterly*
ExpTim	*Expository Times*
FC	Fathers of the Church
FN	*Filología neotestamentaria*
FRLANT	Forschungen zur Religion und Literatur des Alten und Neuen Testaments
GRBS	*Greek, Roman, and Byzantine Studies*
HeyJ	*Heythrop Journal*
HistSci	Histoire des sciences
HSCP	*Harvard Studies in Classical Philology*
HTR	*Harvard Theological Review*
HUCA	*Hebrew Union College Annual*
ICC	International Critical Commentary
ICS	*Illinois Classical Studies*
IJCT	*International Journal of the Classical Tradition*
Int	*Interpretation*
ISBE	Geoffrey Bromiley (ed.), *The International Standard Bible Encyclopedia* (4 vols.; Grand Rapids: Eerdmans, rev. ed., 1979–88)
ITQ	*Irish Theological Quarterly*
JACErg	*Jahrbuch für Antike und Christentum*, Ergänzungsband

JBL	*Journal of Biblical Literature*
JEA	*Journal of Egyptian Archaeology*
JECS	*Journal of Early Christian Studies*
JewEnc	Isidore Singer (ed.), *The Jewish Encyclopedia* (12 vols.; New York: Funk and Wagnalls, 1901–6)
JHS	*Journal of Hellenic Studies*
JNES	*Journal of Near Eastern Studies*
JQR	*Jewish Quarterly Review*
JR	*Journal of Religion*
JRS	*Journal of Roman Studies*
JSHRZ	Jüdische Schriften aus hellenistisch-römischer Zeit
JSJ	*Journal for the Study of Judaism in the Persian, Hellenistic and Roman Period*
JSJSup	*Journal for the Study of Judaism in the Persian, Hellenistic and Roman Period*, Supplement Series
JSNTSup	Journal for the Study of the New Testament, Supplement Series
JSOT	*Journal for the Study of the Old Testament*
JSP	*Journal for the Study of the Pseudepigrapha*
JSPSup	*Journal for the Study of the Pseudepigrapha*, Supplement Series
JSRC	Jerusalem Studies in Religion and Culture
JTS	*Journal of Theological Studies*
KRI	Kenneth A. Kitchen, *Ramesside Inscriptions: Historical and Biographical* (Monumenta Hannah Sheen dedicata 5; 8 vols.; Oxford: Blackwell, 1970–90)
LCL	Loeb Classical Library
LNTS	Library of New Testament Studies
MH	*Museum Helveticum*
MnemSup	*Mnemosyne*, Supplement Series
MUSJ	*Mélanges de l'université Saint-Joseph*
NHMS	Nag Hammadi and Manichaean Studies
NICNT	New International Commentary on the New Testament
NovT	*Novum Testamentum*
NovTSup	*Novum Testamentum*, Supplements
NPNF	*Nicene and Post-Nicene Fathers*
NT	New Testament
NTL	New Testament Library
NTOA	Novum Testamentum et orbis antiquus
NTS	*New Testament Studies*
NTTSD	New Testament Tools and Studies
OCM	Oxford Classical Monographs
OECS	Oxford Early Christian Studies
OED	*The Oxford English Dictionary* (19 vols.; 2nd ed.; Oxford: Clarendon Press, 1989)
OT	Old Testament
OTL	Old Testament Library

OTM	Oxford Theological Monographs
OTP	James Charlesworth (ed.), *The Old Testament Pseudepigrapha* (2 vols.; Garden City, NY: Doubleday, 1983–5)
PhA	Philosophia Antiqua
Phil	*Philologus*
PhilSup	Philologus Supplements
PrÄ	Probleme der Ägyptologie
PRR	*Presbyterian and Reformed Review*
PW	August Friedrich von Pauly and Georg Wissowa (eds.), *Real-Encyclopädie der classischen Altertumswissenschaft* (Stuttgart: Metzler, 1894–)
QUCC	*Quaderni Urbinati di Cultura Classica*
RAC	*Reallexikon für Antike und Christentum*
RB	*Revue biblique*
RBén	*Revue bénédictine*
RE	*Realencyklopädie für protestantische Theologie und Kirche*
RechBib	Recherches bibliques
REG	*Revue des Études Grecques*
RevPhil	*Revue de philologie, de littérature et d'histoire anciennes*
RevThom	*Revue thomiste*
RGRW	Religions in the Graeco-Roman World
RhMP	*Rheinisches Museum für Philologie*
RHPR	*Revue d'histoire et de philosophie religieuses*
RHR	*Revue de l'histoire des religions*
RNT	Regensburger Neues Testament
RPP	Hans Dieter Betz, Don Browning, Bernd Janowski, and Eberhard Jüngel (eds.), *Religion Past and Present* (14 vols.; Leiden: Brill, 2006–13)
SAM	Studies in Ancient Medicine
SBLDS	SBL Dissertation Series
SBLMS	SBL Monograph Series
SBLSCS	SBL Septuagint and Cognate Studies
SBLTT	SBL Texts and Translations
SC	Sources chrétiennes
ScrCiv	*Scrittura e Civiltà*
SecCent	*Second Century*
SNTSMS	Society for New Testament Studies Monograph Series
SPhiloA	*Studia Philonica Annual*
STAC	Studien und Texte zu antike Christentum
StBibLit	Studies in Biblical Literature
StEphAug	Studia Ephemerides Augustinianum
StPatr	*Studia Patristica*
SVTP	Studia in Veteris Testamenti pseudepigrapha
Tait's	*Tait's Edinburgh Magazine*
TAPA	*Transactions of the American Philological Association*
TCH	Transformation of the Classical Heritage

TCSup	Trends in Classics Supplements
TDNT	Gerhard Kittel and Gerhard Friedrich (eds.), *Theological Dictionary of the New Testament* (trans. Geoffrey W. Bromiley; 10 vols.; Grand Rapids: Eerdmans, 1964–)
TRE	*Theologische Realenzyklopädie*
TSAJ	Texts and Studies in Ancient Judaism
TSK	*Theologische Studien und Kritiken*
TU	Texte und Untersuchungen
VC	*Vigiliae Christianae*
VCSup	*Vigiliae Christianae*, Supplement Series
WBC	Word Biblical Commentary
WTJ	*Westminster Theological Journal*
WUNT	Wissenschaftliche Untersuchungen zum Neuen Testament
ZNW	*Zeitschrift für die neutestamentliche Wissenschaft*
ZPE	*Zeitschrift für Papyrologie und Epigraphik*
ZWT	*Zeitschrift für wissenschaftliche Theologie*

1

Is "All Scripture … Inspired"? Toward a New Look at Θεόπνευστος in 2 Tim. 3:16

No passage has been more central to the church's understanding of Scripture than 2 Tim. 3:16. Christians routinely point to that verse as making the clearest and strongest claim for the Bible's inspiration. It comprises a "crucial piece of biblical self-testimony," as Mark Thompson (2012: 95) would have it. And yet, perhaps no words in the entire Bible have had more false implications read into them than the opening phrase of 2 Tim. 3:16. As nearly all those implications are based on a rendering of these words in a modern language, let us take the usual English rendering as representative of how this verse typically is read: "All scripture is inspired by God." From a strictly exegetical perspective, the corollaries hanging on these six English words are fewer and less far-reaching than the usual expansionist interpretation would have us believe. For many, there is more here than strict exegesis admits, and 2 Tim. 3:16 has served as the church's main proof text, not only for the idea of Scripture's inspiration but also for the (rather different) idea of its infallibility or inerrancy. Those who read infallibilist/inerrantist claims into these words do so on the basis of a preconceived system—a system that they consider (philosophically) basic to the theology of the New Testament.[1]

I use "expansionist" advisedly, as it is only in connection with *the Bible* that the word "inspired" tends to be connected so directly with the notions of infallibility and inerrancy.[2] The tendency to do so, of course, is more pronounced among Evangelicals and Fundamentalists. We read in Harold Lindsell's *The Battle for the Bible*, for example, that "inspiration involved infallibility from start to finish"[3]—the former somehow

---

[1] A number of scholars call out the "deductive" nature of the usual reading of 2 Tim. 3:16: readers typically begin with a preconceived notion of what Scripture's alethiological, epistemological, and/or formal profiles should be, and they "deduce" those profiles from the words of 2 Timothy—see Abraham (1981: 16–17), Trembath (1987: 8–46), and Farrow (1987: 16).

[2] "Infallibility" is not consistently defined. Some use it synonymously with "inerrancy." A seeming majority use it to guarantee the truth of all that Scripture says about a circumscribed area of doctrine. Scott (2009a: 149), on the other hand, seems to view infallibility as a sort of logical anteroom to inerrancy: "We say that Scripture *cannot* contain any error (i.e., is *infallible*) and therefore *does not* contain any error (i.e., is *inerrant*)."

[3] Lindsell (1976: 31). As Trembath (1987: 139 n. 13) notes, for Lindsell "infallibility" and "inerrancy" are synonymous. On the straits created by Lindsell's defense of inerrancy, see Allert (2007: 162–3).

is held to imply the latter.[4] Yet, as the word "inspired" is used in everyday speech—applied to an assortment of things besides Scripture—the thought of a resulting *inerrancy* or *infallibility* scarcely enters the picture. (We are still discussing the *English* word "inspired"—we will get to the Greek term behind it soon enough.)[5] When the author of a story or poem speaks of being "inspired" to write, no one thinks to test the author's claim to inspiration by fact-checking the story's or poem's claims (see Barr 1973: 16–17). And that is not only because we normally allow the word "inspired" to refer to a momentary fit of genius. There have been many, in fact, specifically claiming (with all earnestness) to be "inspired" *by God* to write,[6] but in their case the fact-checking that might win or lose the reader's approval seldom goes beyond testing the author's *central point*.

The question therefore arises: if we routinely allow claims of divine inspiration in *non-scriptural* writings to stand (at least as tenable) in the face of a fallible literary canvas, why do the rules of engaging the notion of inspiration change so dramatically when it comes to Scripture? The answer, of course, is found in what I said above: the word "inspired" in English translations of 2 Tim. 3:16 is seldom allowed to function innocently. Instead it has served as the means for smuggling a whole system of ideas into the Bible. On the one hand, if I say *I'm* inspired, no one thinks I'm claiming to be inerrant. On the other hand, if Scripture claims to be inspired, then the claim to inerrancy is (supposedly) loud and clear. The rules are clearly flexible,[7] and that flexibility creates a blind spot for those holding to inerrancy, regarding the logical fit of inerrancy within their doctrine of Scripture.

The name of Benjamin Warfield is always among the first mentioned in any discussion of the inspiration of Scripture, especially as that doctrine is made to undergird the notion of inerrancy. William Abraham (1998: 313–14) notes, however, that Warfield was quite willing to admit that inspiration played *no necessary role* within

---

[4] Scott (2009b: 197) tries to show that 2 Tim. 3:16's (supposed) claim to inspiration *does* logically imply inerrancy:

> Two qualities are predicated of "all" writings (i.e., their complete text) that properly belong in the category of "Scripture" ... : (1) that it is inspired ("breathed out by God"), and (2) that it is profitable for teaching, reproof, correction, and training. ... The sense of the passage is that the first leads to the second. That is, it is precisely because Scripture is inspired by God that all of it is profitable in various ways. Now nothing erroneous can be profitable for teaching. And certainly an erroneous statement cannot provide correction. So embedded in the logic of this passage is the teaching that Scripture, being inspired, is entirely without error.

This is curious reasoning, to say the least. Scott seems to assume that "*all* scripture" refers to Scripture in all its atomic propositional bits, rather than in its extent as a corpus. Given that the author of 2 Timothy is probably responding to opponents who dispensed with parts of the Old Testament, it is more likely that he is defending the extent of the scriptural corpus.

[5] Ward (2002: 277–8) protests that Warfield's use of "inspiration" is sensitive to matters of philology and that it does not allow Abraham and Trembath to infer a one-for-one correlation between θεόπνευστος and the English term that serves as its placeholder. My argument, however, intends to show that the English term has been mishandled and then to ask what the Greek term actually means.

[6] I do not automatically doubt such claims.

[7] Abraham (1981: 71) expresses the collapse of logical categories involved in the latter in terms of those who fail "to distinguish inspiration from speaking or dictation."

the theology of the New Testament. Thus Warfield (1893: 208–9) could write in a way unimaginable for most inerrantists today:

> Were there no such thing as inspiration, Christianity would be true, and all its essential doctrines would be credibly witnessed to us in the generally trustworthy reports of the teaching of our Lord and of His authoritative agents in founding the Church, preserved in the writings of the apostles and their first followers, and in the historical witness of the living Church. (See Barr 1977: 265)[8]

To my mind, these words express almost perfectly the inessentiality of the Evangelical doctrine of biblical inspiration. But was this really *Warfield*, the celebrated watchdog of Princeton Orthodoxy, saying these things? It was indeed Warfield, but only, it seems, as he was caught in a lapse of his real intellectual and religious commitments. As Abraham (1998: 314) notes, Warfield immediately (within the same essay) "proceeded to turn this [disclaimer] on its head by insisting that giving up inspiration would entail giving up the evidence on which our trust in Scripture rests." In Warfield's (1893: 210) words, the inspiration of Scripture is "an element of the Christian faith ... which cannot be rejected without logically undermining our trust in all other elements of distinctive Christianity by undermining the evidence on which this trust rests."[9] Warfield's response to his own streak of methodological honesty was to totalize the mischief in doubting the New Testament's word in any one instance. If we should mistrust the doctrine of inspiration as laid out for us in the New Testament, he argues, we cannot trust what Scripture tells us of any doctrine of the faith: "The human mind is very subtle, but with all its subtlety it will hardly be able to find a way to refuse to follow Scripture in one of the doctrines it teaches without undermining its authority as a teacher of doctrine" (Warfield 1893: 207). David Kelsey (1975: 22) summarizes Warfield's move at this point by characterizing inspiration as "logically dispensable" but "methodologically basic."

Today this "slippery slope" argument is more likely to elicit a smile than a gasp of horror,[10] but it is worth noting that the terms it lays down are entirely agreeable to the present book's argument. The pages that follow do not attempt to dismiss the doctrine of inspiration *in spite of* Scripture's supposed claim, but rather to show that Scripture really *makes no such claim* in the first place. Warfield (1893: 185) writes that the doctrine of inspiration "is based wholly upon an exegetical fact." I aim to

---

[8] A somewhat similar argument had appeared already in Irenaeus, *Adv. haer.* 3.4.2 (see Minns 2010: 137). In fact, it is not unlikely that Warfield was inspired by Irenaeus. Cf. Jowett (1860: 351):

> If the term inspiration were to fall into disuse, no fact of nature, or history, or language, no event in the life of man, or dealings of God with him, would be in any degree altered. ... Therefore the question of inspiration, though in one sense important, is to the interpreter as though it were not important; he is in no way called upon to determine a matter with which he has nothing to do.

[9] As Gnuse (1985: 24) notes, "The doctrine of inspiration was the starting point for Warfield's theology, and he felt that other doctrines could not be believed unless the authority of Scripture was undergirded by a firm understanding of inspiration."

[10] On the "slippery slope" argument, see Barr (1973: 15).

show that the facts (both exegetical and historical) are quite otherwise. To his credit, Warfield (1893: 181) appears explicitly to accept these terms of engagement: "If a fair criticism evinces that this is not the doctrine of the Biblical writers, then of course it has 'destroyed' the doctrine which is confessedly based on that supposition."[11]

Returning to the slippery slope, one wonders why the witness of the apostles and their first followers so quickly lost its sparkle for Warfield. Why does Scripture need to be inspired in order to be trustworthy in its central commitments?[12] Is the truth true only when it's inspired?[13] As early as the seventeenth century, Jean Le Clerc (1690: 29–31) registered the same complaint about the slovenliness of certain habits of thought surrounding the supposed inspiration of Scripture:

> People believe commonly …, first, that the sacred Historians were inspir'd with the Things themselves: And next, that they were inspir'd also with the Terms in which they have express'd them. In a word, that the holy History was dictated word for word by the holy Spirit, and that the Authors, whose Names it bears, were no other than Secretaries of that Spirit, who wrote exactly as it dictated.
>
> As to what concerns the Inspiration of Historical Matters of Fact, I observe, First, That they suppose it without bringing any positive Proof, and that consequently a Man may with good reason reject their Supposition. They say only that if it were not so, we could not be perfectly certain of the truth of the History. But, beside that, a Consequence cannot undeniably prove a Fact; and that it may happen that one cannot disprove a Consequence, although that which is pretended to be prov'd thereby be not true; I affirm that it is false, that we cannot be perfectly certain of the main substance of a History unless we suppose it inspir'd. …
>
> … To relate faithfully a matter of Fact, which a Man has seen and well observed, requires no Inspiration. The Apostles had no need of Inspiration to tell what they had seen, and what they had heard Christ say. There needs nothing for that but Memory and Honesty.

In fairness to Warfield, it needs to be said that the *truth* of the Gospel and the trustworthiness of Scripture for "all other elements of distinctive Christianity" are two different things. Strictly speaking, therefore, he is not being inconsistent. But he *is* positing an epistemic guarantee where it is unnecessary—even gratuitous. If the

---

[11] Scott (2009a: 132) similarly writes, "Our understanding of what Scripture says about itself can be corrected only if the meticulous exegesis of its relevant didactic statements yields a superior understanding of them."

[12] Abraham (1998: 315) writes,

> Aside from the dubious assumption that the witnesses teach their own inspiration in the sense required and enunciated by Warfield, the problem with [his] construction [of an inspirationist doctrine] is that it is unconvincing. … It is not essential to the general reliability of a witness that the witness be infallible or absolutely, 100 per cent reliable. All that is required is that the witness be overall reliable; a single mistake does not negate that general reliability; otherwise we could not rely on any witness, for no witness is completely reliable.

[13] Cf. Jowett (1860: 351): "Rigid upholders of the verbal inspiration of Scripture, and those who deny inspiration altogether, may nevertheless meet on the common ground of the meaning of words."

witness of the apostles was epistemically sufficient for the first believers, why should it suddenly become insufficient once the New Testament arrived? In other words, if we concede the need for a "formal" principle,[14] why must that principle seek its epistemic basis in the *canon* as opposed to, say, the *Gospel*? This is the central question, I believe, that inerrantists and infallibilists must face. But there is also the related question of what Warfield means by "all other elements of distinctive Christianity." If we grant that he is not contradicting himself, those elements must be *other than* those found within the Gospel message per se. Presumably they include matters of ethics, liturgy, and church polity. (For some inerrantists, they extend even to matters of science.)[15] Here the question facing inerrantists is whether they have sufficiently distinguished the Gospel core (viz., that which is guaranteed by the apostolic witness) from what we might call "adiaphora" (viz., those things that are less important than a proper understanding of the Gospel).

That Warfield should view inspiration as "logically dispensable" but "methodologically basic" (to use Kelsey's words) reveals a certain lack of coordination, in Evangelical theology, between the *scopes* of the "formal" and "material principles." Why should the "formal principle" trace, in outline, the entirety of Scripture—the entirety, that is, in both extent and detail—while the "material principle" traces only the bounds of the Gospel message, as preserved in a few places within Scripture? If the Gospel message was efficacious even *before the latest parts of Scripture were written*, why should it now be tethered to a formal principle involving *all* of Scripture?

1 "All Scripture Is θεόπνευστος"

When we move to consider the Greek word in 2 Tim. 3:16 usually translated as "inspired by God," things improve only slightly. This improvement consists of the fact that many embrace the habit of rendering θεόπνευστος in the form of a (supposed) literal calque, in that references to the "God-breathed" nature of Scripture have become a staple within bibliological discussions. This increased somewhat in 1973, when the NT portion of the *New International Version* first appeared, with its now famous rendering: "All Scripture is God-breathed ... ."[16] Unfortunately, this move to speak in

---

[14] I concede this need only for the argument at hand. It is not clear to me why we should admit a formal principle for our understanding of how Scripture relates to the Gospel.

[15] Harris (2008: 126) notes, "Since Warfield's time, a very high expectation of factual accuracy has come to distinguish American from British accounts of inerrancy." See Achtemeier (1980: 108).

[16] Some even use the rather handy term "theopneustic"—as perfect a placeholder for the Greek term as we could imagine, but this term was once more common than it is today. Its popularity in earlier times was perhaps owed to the influence of Louis Gaussen's book *Theopneustia* (French original: 1840; English: 1841). (Abraham gives a date of 1888 for the English debut of Gaussen's book [1981: 18], but Stewart [2003: 216 n. 2] notes that the first English edition appeared in 1841, and the dates he lists show that there had been no less than ten editions or reprintings prior to 1888.) Stewart characterizes the 1888 reprint of the English version of *Theopneustia* as the beginning of a period of rediscovery: "*Theopneustia* had lived just long enough to be re-discovered by a new generation, which felt the dangers of irreverent biblical criticism in a way akin to the anxieties of the long-deceased author" (228). Stewart writes, "When Louis Gaussen's *Theopneustia* came from the Paris printing presses in 1840, it was as though readers in the English-speaking world had been primed to expect it" (215).

terms of Scripture's "God-breathed" quality has usually served only to strengthen the preconceived system. To say that Scripture is "God-breathed" has become, for many, only a way of bolstering the (presumed) claim that God was the *author* of Scripture. Thus, Louis Gaussen (1841: 24–5) wrote, in a book nearly programmatic for Evangelical bibliology in the late nineteenth and early twentieth centuries, that 2 Tim. 3:16 implied an almost rapturous conveyance of the divine through the authors of Scripture:

> Their word, [Scripture] assures us, is *theopneustic;* their book is of God. Whether they record mysteries antecedent to creation, those of futurity more remote than the return of the Son of Man, the eternal counsels of the Most High, the secrets of the heart of man, or the deep things of God; whether they describe their own emotions, speak of things from recollection, or repeat what has been noted by contemporaries; whether they treat of genealogies, or extract from uninspired documents; their writing is inspired; what they pen is dictated from on High—it is always God who speaks, who relates, ordains, or reveals by their instrumentality, and who, for this purpose, employs, in various degrees, their personality.[17]

Edward J. Young (1957: 123), former OT professor at Westminster Theological Seminary, similarly tied the claim about Scripture's *theopneustia* to a need to view Scripture as divinely authored, extending God's authorial control to all of Scripture's alethic aspects: "The Bible, according to its own claim, is breathed forth from God. To maintain that there are flaws or errors in it is the same as declaring that there are flaws or errors in God Himself."[18] This presumed connection between the claim to *theopneustia* and Scripture's supposed God-authored nature forms the basis for the ages-old convention of referring to Scripture as the "word of God." This habit, in turn, led to the widespread assumption that Scripture's many references to God's "word" should be read as comments on the theological nature of Scripture itself—a development reflected in the title of Young's book: *Thy Word Is Truth.* The scriptural verse (Jn 17:17; cf. Ps. 119:160) from which that book takes its title applies the label "thy word" to words of prophetic utterance, but in Young's mind, and in the minds of many other Evangelicals, that verse says something about Scripture itself. The claim that "the Bible *is* God's word" became a rallying point against the liberal threat of supposing that the Bible merely "contains" God's word.[19]

The problem with referring to Scripture as the "word of God," of course, is that that convention is wholly out of keeping with how Scripture itself uses that term. Scripture uses "word of God" or "word of the Lord" in two ways: as a reference to prophecy (e.g., "the word of the LORD came to Elijah the Tishbite, saying …")[20] or as a reference to

---

[17] Abraham (1981: 18) quotes this passage in a later translation than the one I use here.
[18] Quoted in Trembath (1987: 139 n. 15).
[19] Cf. the lively exchange between Abraham Kuyper and J. H. Gunning, exemplified in these competing formulas. See Heslam (2000: 33–4).
[20] See Gen. 15:1, 4; Exod. 9:20–21; Num. 3:16, 51; 11:23; 15:31 (cf. 22:38; 23:5, 16); 24:13; 27:14; 36:5 (cf. Deut. 8:3; 18:20–22; 33:9); Josh. 1:13; 8:27 (cf. 14:10; 1 Sam. 1:23); 1 Sam. 3:1, 7, 21; 9:27; 15:10, 23, 26; 2 Sam. 7:4 (cf. 25); 12:9 (cf. 23:2); 23:11 (cf. 1 Kgs 2:4); 1 Kgs 2:27; 6:11 (cf. 8:26; 12:15); 12:22, 24; 13:1, 2, 5, 9, 17–18, 20–21, 26, 32; 14:18; 15:29; 16:1, 7, 12, 34; 17:2, 5, 8, 16, 24; 18:1, 31; 19:9; 21:17, 28; 22:5, 19, 38 (cf. 2 Kgs 1:16); 2 Kgs 1:17; 3:12; 4:44; 7:1, 16; 9:26, 36; 10:10, 17; 14:25

the apostles' preaching (= the Gospel).[21] The phrase "word of God" *never* appears as a reference to Scripture itself. As James Barr (1973: 21) notes, the conceit of so referring "belonged too much to the world of systematic theology, of dogmatics, and had too little contact with the world of actual biblical scholarship."

Those who refer to the Bible as the "word of God" are usually quite sure they do so advisedly, but the passages to which they appeal refer only to the *prophetic* aspect of the scriptural words they quote, rather than to their *scriptural* aspect per se. James W. Scott (2009a: 140), for example, claims that the identification of Scripture itself as "the written word of God" is

> repeatedly taught by Scripture itself, most commonly whenever the NT introduces an OT quotation with such words as "God said" (e.g., 2 Cor 6:16) or "the Holy Spirit says" (e.g., Heb 3:7), especially when God is not the speaker in the OT passage (e.g., Acts 13:37, quoting Ps 16:10). "The word of God," to which Heb 4:12 refers, includes the Scriptures (along with God's spoken words), as is clear from the repeated statements in the previous verses that God has spoken the words of Scripture.

The difficulty with Scott's argument is that every one of these NT references to the Old Testament appeals to a prophetic passage (2 Cor. 6:16 refers to Lev. 26:12; Heb. 3:7 refers to Ps. 95:7–11). Scott thinks that Ps. 16:10 (quoted in Acts 13:37) stands out as a passage in which "God is not the speaker," but the NT writers clearly did not regard it so: David was widely viewed as prophetically inspired in his (supposed) authorship of the Psalms, and Ps. 16:10 was especially dear to the early Christians as a prophecy of the Christ event. (See Poirier 2014.) The string of OT passages that are quoted in the verses leading up to Heb. 4:12 are similarly prophetic in form.

(cf. 19:21); 20:4, 16, 19; 23:16; 24:2; 1 Chron. 11:3, 10; 12:23; 15:15 (cf. 16:15); 17:3 (6, 23); 22:8 (cf. 2 Chron. 6:17; 10:15); 2 Chron. 11:2, 4; 12:7; 18:4, 18; 30:12; 34:21; 35:6; 36:21–22; Ezra 1:1 (cf. Neh. 1:8; Ps. 17:4); Pss. 33:4, 6; 56:4, 10 (cf. 89:34; 103:20; 105:8); 105:19 (cf. 107:20; 119:9, 11, 16–17, 25, 28, 42–43, 49, 65, 67, 74, 81, 89, 101, 105, 107, 114, 160, 162, 169); 130:5; 138:2; 147:15, 18–19); Prov. 30:5; Isa. 1:10; 2:1, 3; 5:24; 9:8; 16:13; 24:3; 28:13–14 (cf. 30:12); 37:22; 38:4; 39:5, 8; 40:8 (cf. 45:23; 55:11; 66:2); 66:5; Jer. 1:2, 4, 11–13; 2:1, 4, 31 (cf. 5:13); 5:14; 6:10; 7:1–2; 8:9; 9:20; 10:1; 11:1; 13:2–3, 8, 12; 14:1; 16:1; 17:15, 20; 18:1, 5; 19:3; 20:8; 21:1, 11 (cf. 22:1); 22:2 (cf. 4), 29; 23:17 (cf. 18), 28 (cf. 29, 36); 24:4; 25:3; 26:1; 27:1, 18; 28:12; 29:20, 30; 30:1; 31:10; 32:1, 6, 8, 26; 33:1, 19, 23; 34:1, 4 (cf. 5), 8, 12; 35:1, 12; 36:1, 27; 37:6 (cf. 17); 39:15; 40:1; 42:7, 15; 43:8 (cf. 44:1, 16); 44:24, 26; 46:1, 13; 47:1; 49:34; 50:1 (cf. Lam. 1:18); Ezek. 1:3; 3:16 (cf. 17); 6:1, 3; 7:1; 11:14; 12:1, 8, 17, 21 (cf. 25), 26 (cf. 28); 13:1–2; 14:2, 12; 15:1; 16:1, 35; 17:1, 11; 18:1; 20:2, 45, 47; 21:1, 8, 18; 22:1, 17, 23; 23:1; 24:1, 15, 20; 25:1, 3; 26:1; 27:1; 28:1, 11, 20; 29:1, 17; 30:1, 20; 31:1; 32:1, 17; 33:1 (cf. 7), 23, 30; 34:1, 7, 9; 35:1; 36:1, 4, 16; 37:4, 15; 38:1; Dan. 9:2 (cf. 10:1); Hos. 1:1; 4:1; Joel 1:1; Amos 3:1 (cf. 4:1; 5:1); 7:16; 8:12; Jon. 1:1; 3:1, 3; Mic. 1:1; 4:2; Zeph. 1:1; 2:5; Hag. 1:1, 3; 2:1, 10, 20; Zech. 1:1, 7; 4:6, 8; 6:9; 7:1, 4, 8; 8:1, 18; 9:1; 11:11; 12:1; Mal. 1:1; Mt. 4:4; 15:6 (cf. Mk 7:13; Lk. 1:38; 2:29); Lk. 3:2; 5:1; 8:21; 11:28; 22:61; Jn 10:35; 17:6, 14, 17; Rom. 9:6; 1 Thess. 4:15; 1 Tim. 4:5; Heb. 4:12; Rev. 1:2, 9; 20:4.

21 See Acts 4:29, 31; 6:2, 4, 7; 8:4, 14, 25; 10:44; 11:1, 16, 19; 12:24; 13:5, 7, 44, 46, 48–49 (cf. 14:3); 14:25; 15:35–36; 16:6, 32; 17:13; 18:5, 11; 19:10, 20; 1 Cor. 14:36; 2 Cor. 2:17; 4:2; Gal. 6:6; Eph. 6:17 (cf. Phil. 1:14; Col. 1:5); Col. 1:25 (cf. 4:3); 1 Thess. 1:8; 2:13; 2 Thess. 3:1; 2 Tim. 2:9 (cf. Tit. 1:3); Tit. 2:5; Heb. 6:5; 13:7; 1 Pet. 1:23, 25; Rev. 6:9; 20:4. See Schlier (1960); Baird (2002: 50–5); Pahl (2009).

1.1 The Present Study

Inerrantists and infallibilists are not the only target of this study. An improper understanding of θεόπνευστος has claimed other victims as well, and some of them, in an effort to avoid the blunders of the inerrantists, have wound up in a still worse place.

A commitment to reading 2 Tim. 3:16 in a way that brackets its theological reception threatens to unwind the view many people have of the Bible—or at least their belief that the Bible claims to be the same thing *they* claim it to be. And here we get to the real burden of this book: What does 2 Tim. 3:16 really claim about the Bible? If we consult an English version, we are met with the claim that Scripture is "inspired." Our normal way of thinking about inspiration—that is, the concept attached to a particular English word—fleshes this out in one of two ways: *verbal* inspiration and *epistemic* inspiration. But how secure is that rendering? What if θεόπνευστος doesn't mean the same thing we mean by "inspired"?

We should, of course, welcome the attempt to get in touch with the etymological profile of θεόπνευστος. But etymology does not provide game-ending moves—while it often provides helpful indicators of what a term *likely* means, the real clues to a word's meaning are revealed by philology. If we want to know what the author of 2 Timothy meant by θεόπνευστος, we need to try to see how other writings, contemporary with 2 Timothy, used that word.

The main part of this book consists of a detailed philological investigation of the word θεόπνευστος, but we eventually will move on to the question of whether any sort of doctrine of the inspiration of Scripture is set out or implied *anywhere* within Scripture itself. Might it be, as Helmut Koester (1995: 19) writes, that such a doctrine "has no support in the Bible"?[22]

2 Is θεόπνευστος Passive or Active?

Before considering the broader semantic aspect of θεόπνευστος, we must attend to matters of (grammatical) voice—as these matters have directed the discussion to a large extent. Is it true that θεόπνευστος is passive in form, as so often assumed—that is, that it is a passive verbal adjective? How did such an assumption take root, and does it have a basis in Greek morphology?

In a detailed attack on Hermann Cremer's view that θεόπνευστος has an active sense (viz., "God-breathing," in the sense of "redolent with God"), Warfield argued that translators must give the word a passive sense wherever they find it—that the noun(s) it modifies is/are the *recipient(s)* of the action denoted by the term's verbal root. That is, he claimed that the sense of θεόπνευστος is "God-inspired" (or "God-spired," as he preferred to express it [see below]) and not "God-breathing."[23] Among his arguments for a passive sense, Warfield appealed to features of the word's form, which

---

[22] Koester is characteristically forthright: "Christians who want to follow the teachings of the New Testament about the Holy Spirit should discard the doctrine of the inspiration of Scripture."

[23] On Warfield's interaction with Cremer's view, see Burkhardt (1988: 24–5).

(he claimed) support a passive sense. The result of his case has been that, over the past century, many students of the Greek NT text have labored under the impression that θεόπνευστος *must* be passive, simply because it ends in -τος. Even published guides to the Greek New Testament promote this understanding of the matter. Unfortunately for those students and published guides, however, the arguments put forth in support of that view are lacking in force. There are, in fact, plenty of verbal adjectives ending in -τος that are active in sense—as Warfield himself recognized.

Whereas Cremer had insisted that θεόπνευστος has an active sense (viz., Scripture is theopneustic because it imparts the Spirit),[24] Warfield argued that θεόπνευστος is primarily a passive term: Scripture is theopneustic in that it is verbally inspired (or "spired") by God. Warfield begins with a nod to the consensus view (viz., θεόπνευστος = "God-breathed") as found in the lexicons of Schleusner, Robinson, and Thayer-Grimm and in the first two editions of Cremer's own lexicon.[25] He then introduces Cremer's subsequent adoption of an active sense, as found in the third edition of his lexicon (1883). Interestingly, Warfield admits that at one time he had accepted Cremer's active-sense rendering, so his lengthy discussion of that view would appear to be the fruit of personal repentance.[26]

What was Warfield's argument? Rather than compare θεόπνευστος with other compounds formed with -πνευστος, Warfield chose, for his field of comparanda, words beginning with θεο- and ending in -τος. His claim was that active meanings were meaningfully scarce[27] within that compass of terms: "[The] few exceptional cases cannot avail to set aside the normal sense of this compound, as exhibited in the immense

---

[24] Cremer (1880: 746) writes, "scheint γραφὴ θεόπνευστος nicht wol 'von Gottes Geist eingegeben' im Sinne der Vulgata heissen zu können; vielmehr würde es mit solchen Begriffen, wie hier γραφὴ, Sibyll. 5, 308, Quelle, verbunden s. v. a. 'göttlichen Geist atmend' bedeuten nach jenem naheliegenden Übergang der passive in active Bedeutung, wie er in ἄπνευστος, εὔπνευστος vorliegt, schlecht, gut beatmet = schlecht, gut atmend." A similar view is found in Bengel (1742: 879): "non solum dum scripta est, Deo spirante per scriptores; sed etiam, dum legitur, Deo spirante per scripturam, & scriptura Ipsum spirante."

[25] See Schleusner (1819: 1.1058); Robinson (1836: 370); Thayer (1889: 287); Cremer (1866: 231; 1872: 282). It might be noted that Warfield accessed Robinson's work through the 1872 printing of the 2nd edition (orig. 1850), in which θεόπνευστος was defined as "*God-inspired, inbreathed of God*" (333). In the original 1836 edition, θεόπνευστος was defined as "*God-inspired, given from God.*"
    Cremer's understanding of what θεόπνευστος implies for the reading event is not very different from some descriptions of the so-called doctrine of illumination.

[26] Warfield (1900: 192) writes, "The present writer, after going over the ground under Prof. Cremer's guidance, too hastily adopted his conclusion in a paper on 'Paul's Doctrine of the Old Testament' published in *The Presbyterian Quarterly* for July, 1899 [read '1889']." (Warfield should have written "1889" rather than "1899.") Warfield wrote in his 1889 article:

> Paul was not concerned here with how the Scriptures originated, he was concerned with what they are; his mind was less on their genesis than on their nature. And the fact that they are repletively filled with God, and breathe out God to the hearer, forms the better preparation for the exhibition of their usefulness in making the man of God perfect. (396).

See van Bemmelen (1987: 238–9).

[27] Warfield (1900: 118–19) counted eighty-six such headwords in the sixth edition of Liddell-Scott, out of which some seventy-five are indisputably passive in sense:

> The eleven instances that remain, as in some sort exceptions to the general rule, include cases of different kinds. In some of them the verbal is derived from a deponent verb and is therefore passive only in form, but naturally bears an active sense: such are θεοδήλητος (God-injuring), θεομίμητος (God-imitating), θεόσεπτος (feared as God). Others may possibly be really passives, although we prefer an active form in English to express the idea

majority of the cases of its occurrence. If analogy is to count for anything, its whole weight is thrown thus in favor of the interpretation which sees in θεόπνευστος, quite simply, the sense of 'God-breathed' " (Warfield 1900: 119).[28] Warfield represented the one-sided profile of this philological data set as indicating a rule of word-formation, and in this he has been enlisted as an authority on the matter ever since.[29] Unfortunately, Warfield's rule has more to do with the limited availability of adjectival notions applying divine agency in an active sense. How often can one ascribe divine agency *in an active sense* to an object other than God? Let us consider, for example, the words θεοκατάρᾱτος, θεοκέλευστος, and θεόκλητος. That these three words all have exclusively passive meanings in the Liddell–Scott lexicon (respectively, "accursed of God," "ordered by God," and "sung by gods") is owed to the fact that one would be hard pressed to imagine how an active-sense understanding for any of these words could ever be applied to anything. It is the difficulty of such a construction lending itself to active meanings that determines the trend. That difficulty, in itself, cannot be used to close off the possibility of an active meaning in the rare (but *real*) instance in which it might be conceptually feasible.

Warfield argued as though all Greek adjectives, or at least a certain class of them, must be formally committed to either the passive or active voice—thus his ill-conceived search for a "law of word formation." (Why Greek morphology should be more restrictive than English morphology is nowhere explained.) In this way he assumed that even those -πνευστος words that Liddell–Scott lists as functionally active are really formally passive. He writes, for example, that " ἄπνευστος, εὔπνευστος, ... from 'ill- or well-breathed' came to mean 'breathing ill or well' " (Warfield 1900: 114)—that is, these terms (Warfield alleged) didn't originally have an active sense but rather developed one over time. Unfortunately, he lists no evidence that ἄπνευστος (etc.) originally meant "ill-breathed" (etc.) but simply assumed this to be the case. (Both Cremer and Heinrich Ewald [on whom Cremer had relied] conceded too much to the line of thinking that Warfield [1900: 114–15] would come to promote, in that both assumed the primary meaning of any word formed with -πνευστος to be passive, and the active sense reflected in its actual use to be an outworked conceptualization of what

---

involved: such are, perhaps, θεόκλυτος ("God-heard," where we should rather say, "calling on the gods"), θεακόλλητος ("God-joined," where we should rather say, "united with God"), θεόπρεπτος ("God-distinguished," where we should rather say, "meet for a god"). There remain only these five: θεαίτητος ("obtained from God"), θεόθυτος ("offered to the gods"), θεορράστος and the more usual θεόρροττος ("flowing from the gods"), and θεοχώρητος ("containing God"). In these the relation of θεός to the verbal idea is clearly not that of producing cause to the expressed result, but some other: perhaps what we need to recognize is that the verbal here involves a relation which we ordinarily express by a preposition, and that the sense would be suggested by some such phrases as "God-asked-of," "God-offered-to," "God-flowed-from," "God-made-room-for."

[28] This same argument can be found in Pesch (1906: 3–4); Piñero (1988: 148). But cf. Artola (1999).

[29] Artola (1999: 65 n. 11) writes, "El argumento decisivo en favor del pasivo es el paralelismo con otras expresiones en que entra el componente θεός, como parte primera, y con sentido pasivo en el adjetivo verbal que le sigue: θεόγνοστος, θεόδοτος θεοκίνητος θεόπεμπτος." Farkasfalvy (2006: 741) writes, "Grammatically, it would be possible to attribute to [θεόπνευστος] an active meaning: 'every Scripture is breathing God.' However, such words made up with the noun *theos* and a participle derived from a noun would have usually a passive meaning: every Scripture 'breathed by' or 'inspired by God.'"

the passive meaning entails in a given instance.)[30] This left Warfield a clear path by which to argue that θεόπνευστος means "God-breath*ed*" in 2 Tim. 3:16, as the account of how an active sense arose with words like ἄπνευστος and εὔπνευστος implies that the passive sense was still implicitly there within the word—not quite dormant—even when used in an active sense. Warfield (1900: 117) writes,

> Ewald ... has already taught us to look beneath the "active" usage of εὔπνευστος and ἄπνευστος for the "half-passive" background, and it may equally be found in the other cases; in each instance it is a state or condition at least, that is described by the word, and it is often only a matter of point of view whether we catch the passive conception or not.[31]

Thus Warfield (1900: 117) "fully accord[s] with Prof. Schulze ... when he says that all words compounded with -πνευστος have the passive sense as their (presumed) original implication, and the active sense, when it occurs, is always a derived one."[32] This implied, for Warfield (1900: 116), that the passive sense of θεόπνευστος is still implicitly operative within 2 Tim. 3:16—as if Scripture can only use words according to their earliest meanings. In other words, if the point of 2 Tim. 3:16 is to say that Scripture is "pervaded by God, full of His Spirit" (= Cremer's and Ewald's position), then Scripture obtained that state by first being "God-breathed."

There are two general responses to make to Warfield's argument. First, it needs to be said that Cremer's and Ewald's concession that a passive sense is (somehow) primary in words like ἄπνευστος and εὔπνευστος is philologically groundless. There is no compelling reason to think that the active sense obtaining in those words is derivative of a previously obtaining passive sense. Second, even if Cremer's and Ewald's concession *were* correct, that would not imply that the active-sense meaning that this study attributes to 2 Tim. 3:16 is imperiled. In all this, I think it is safe to say

---

[30] Warfield (1900: 117) writes,

> We still read in Schmiedel's Winer: "Verbals in -τος correspond sometimes to Latin Participles in -*tus*, sometimes to adjectives in -*bilis*" and then in a note (despite Ewald's long-ago protest), after the adduction of authorities, "θεόπνευστος, *inspiratus* (2 Tim. iii. 16; passive like ἔμπνευστος, while εὔπνευστος, ἄπνευστος are active)." To these Thayer-Grimm adds also πυρίπνευστος and δυσδιάπνευστος as used actively and δυσάναπνευστος as used apparently either actively or passively. (117)

> See Ewald (1855: 88–9). Three years later, Ewald (1858: 91–4) continued with a discussion "Über den ausdruck θεόπνευστος von h. Schrift."

[31] Warfield (1900: (117–18 n. †) writes,

> The rare word εὔπνευστος might equally well express "breathing-well" quasi-actively, or "well-aired" passively; just as ἄπνευστος is actually used in the two senses of "breathless" and "unventilated": and a similar double sense belongs to δυσάναπνευστος. Ἔμπνευστος does not seem to occur in a higher sense; its only recorded usage is illustrated by Athenaeus, iv. 174, where it is connected with ὄργανα in the sense of wind-instruments: its cognates are used of "inspiration." Only πυρίπνευστος [*sic*] = πυρίπνους = "fire-breathing" is distinctively active in usage: cf. ἀναπνευστος, poetic for ἄνπνευστος = "breathless."

[32] "Schulze" refers to "Prof. Dr. L. Schulze, of Rostock" who published "an adverse criticism of Dr. Cremer's reasoning, ... in the course of a review of the eighth edition of the *Lexicon*" (Warfield 1900: 93). See Schulze (1896: 253).

that Warfield exemplifies what James Turner (2014: 142) recently called "a distinctive American species of speculative philology ... not defined by any consistent theory of language but instead by reliance on conjecture rather than research, by entanglement in theological polemics, and by recurrence to philosophical problems."

Words formed from verbs ending in -τος share a number of features that suggest they are not participles at all, at least not in the sense of -μενος words. They are better called "verbal adjectives"—as in our usage above. The fact that they cannot be linked to agentival clauses is one indication that we are not dealing with participles purely and simply. And the fact that words like ἄπνευστος ("unbreathing" [= "breathless"]) and πυρίπνευστος ("fire-breathing") are better rendered with an active construction should be warning enough that the rules of grammar do not predetermine that θεόπνευστος must be passive in meaning.[33] The availability of active meanings for words formed from -πνευστος was shown long ago by Thayer-Grimm (1889: 287) *Greek-English Lexicon of the New Testament*, which compares θεόπνευστος with ἄπνευστος, εὔπνευστος, πυρίπνευστος, and δυσδιάνευστος (which are "used ... actively"), and with δυσάναπνευστος (which is "appar. either act. or pass"). Adjectives ending in -τος thus are morphologically equivocal with respect to whether the voice of the action subsumed by the adjective is passive or active. This equivocality sometimes causes words of this form to be *alternately* passive or active, according to the writer's intention—and so we find Liddell–Scott (1940: 792) defining θεόφαντος as *"revealed by God or revealing God."* Many participants in the debate over θεόπνευστος have understood this well enough, but there is a danger of -τος words being classified as full-fledged participles of the sort that Blass-Debrunner-Funk (1961: 3) confines to the passive voice. It appears that -τος adjectives are *not* always passive in form. They are better compared with English adjectives ending in *-al* or *-ic*, and there should be nothing strange about finding some writers using θεόπνευστος with a passive sense, and others (perhaps from a different era) using it with an active sense. In this regard, Warfield's argument from a so-called "law of word formation" is misguided. The only law of word formation governing an aspect of voice within this class of adjective is that there shall be no such law: voice is supplied by context. As A. T. Robertson (1934: 1095, cf. 157–8) noted, "We must not overdo" the "perfect passive idea" inhering in the earliest Indo-Germanic form: "Strictly this pro-ethnic *-tos* has no voice or tense and it never came to have intimate verbal connections in the Greek as it did in Latin and English."[34]

---

[33] Tronci (2014: 476) writes,

   With respect to the *-tó-* forms which are traditionally translated by means of past participles, scholars notice that they may have a passive or an active value: *thetós* "placed, set" vs. *rhutós* "flowing" (...). This difference may depend on the syntactic structures in which the related verb forms occur: verb forms occurring in intransitive structures appear to be related to active *-tó-* forms, whereas verb forms occurring in transitive structures give rise to passive *-tó-* forms.

   (I owe this reference to Stephen C. Carlson.) See Bishop (1892: 171–99, 329–42, 449–62); Ammann (1956).

[34] Cf. Winer (1892: 96–7): "Verbals in τος (...) correspond in signification, sometimes to the Latin participle in *tus*, as γνωστός *notus*, σιτευτός *saginatus*, ἀπαίδευτος (*untrained, awkward*) cf. θεόπνευστος *inspiratus*; sometimes to adjectives in *bilis*, as ὁρατός, δυσβάστακτος, ἀνεκτός, ἀκατάσχετος, ἀκαταπαυστός, ἀνεκδιήγητος, ἀνεκλάλητος; sometimes they have an active meaning (...), as ἄπταισος *not stumbling*, i.e. not sinning (certainly, however, not ἀλάλητος Rom. viii. 26)."

I shall have to revisit these matters when discussing Tertullian's translation of θεόπνευστος with "divinitus inspirari."

3 Beyond the Warfield–Cremer Debate: The Semantic Question

Warfield rang in the twentieth century with a spirited defense of the traditional understanding of θεόπνευστος. His article on "God-Inspired Scripture" (1900) is still hailed by many as a tour de force of philological investigation.[35] As we saw above, that article is essentially a sustained critique of Cremer's argument that θεόπνευστος has an active sense (viz., "all scripture is inspiring"), and the long-lasting effect of Warfield's argument has been that Cremer's view is now in near total eclipse.[36] In the preceding section, we showed several problems with Warfield's argument.

But there is more to our understanding of θεόπνευστος than the question of voice. What might we say about the word's semantic domain? Hardly anyone has seriously questioned whether the term's root meaning has to do with inspiration. In fact, scholars supporting the traditional understanding of θεόπνευστος have usually been quite sure about how to move from the word's etymological valence to its actual meaning as employed. For example, William Cunningham (1878: 360) assured his readers that the term's "etymological meaning ... is very plain, and quite sufficient to bring out and to establish the general idea attached to it."[37] But the range of possible images and associations that the traditional rendering fails to find within the term's etymology is

---

Unfortunately, Winer writes that "there can be no doubt" about the passive sense of θεόπνευστος in 2 Tim. 3:16, "though several derivatives of the same class have an *active* signification, as εὔπνευστος, ἄπνευστος" (96 n. 1).

[35] Abraham (1981: 15) writes, "There is little doubt but that Warfield did more to shape recent Evangelical thinking on inspiration than any other theologian. ... Most of the arguments advanced by Conservative Evangelicals owe an enormous debt to his way of approaching the subject." Abraham (1998: 313) elsewhere writes, "In the essays related to inspiration Warfield's mind was like a steel trap." See Kelsey (1975: 17–24). Stewart (2003: 233) writes, "Warfield ... was a New Testament exegete before he turned his hand to dogmatic theology—and in consequence, his treatment of inspiration had been marked by great exegetical care."

[36] So, rightly, Mounce (1982: 566). Boda (2011: 42 n. 53) claims that the meaning "God breathing" is "now generally accepted." This is so out of keeping with my own encounters with scholarship that I cannot imagine where Boda gets his information. Even the scholars he names as holding this view (Collins, Towner) argue explicitly against it. See Collins (2002: 264); Towner (2006: 589).

[37] The strength of the assumption that θεόπνευστος means "inspiration" is shown by the regularity with which scholars attempt to illuminate its meaning by reference to passages about inspiration that *do not even use the word!* For example, an entry on θεόπνευστος in Moulton and Milligan's *The Vocabulary of the Greek Testament* (1929: 287) reads as follows: "*Syll* 552[12] (ii/B.C.) opens a decree in connexion with the Parthenon at Magnesia with the words θείας ἐπινοίας καὶ παραστάσεως γενομένης τῶι σύμπαντι πλήθει τοῦ πολιτεύματος εἰς τὴν ἀποκατάστασιν τοῦ ναοῦ—a divine 'inspiration and desire' which has impelled the people to arise and build to the glory of Artemis." In a similar vein, Vawter (1972: 8) writes that θεόπνευστος "comes ... from the philosophico-religious vocabulary of classical Greece and of Hellenism, where it applied to the ecstatic *mantis* possessed by an alien ... spirit (μαντικῆς ἐνθέου, so Plato, *Tim.* 71E)." Vawter is perhaps showing his reliance on a similar statement in Schweizer (1964: 454). Contra Vawter's (and Schweizer's) implication, θεόπνευστος never appears in such a context.

startling. If we wish to settle the question of what θεόπνευστος means in 2 Timothy or elsewhere, we need to enlarge on the territory covered by its usual rendering. The way to do that is simple, but somehow it has escaped the debate over θεόπνευστος.

Warfield's 1900 article not only strikes at greater exhaustiveness and precision in the philological task, but it also calls for reconsideration of the basic meaning of θεόπνευστος. To his credit, Warfield recognized that the traditional rendering of θεόπνευστος as "inspired" cannot be made to fit the contexts uncovered by his philological investigation. To try to force the traditional rendering into these contexts would serve up some bizarre notions, like "inspired ointments" (in the *Testament of Abraham*) or "inspired sandals" (in Nonnus' *Paraphrase of the Gospel of John*). Warfield's solution (1900: 121) is creditable in that it is at least partly sensitive to the demands of philology: he enlists the biblical image of God breathing into Adam as a warrant for associating θεόπνευστος with the *divine act of creation*: "To a Hebrew, at all events, the 'breath of God' would seem self-evidently creative; and no locution would more readily suggest itself to him as expressive of the Divine act of 'making' than just that by which it would be affirmed that He breathed things into existence."[38] This gave a new understanding of θεόπνευστος that ultimately served the same bibliological end as the traditional inspirationist understanding: "Everywhere the word appears as purely passive and expresses production by God" (Warfield 1900: 410). Scripture, on this view, was still inspired, but now its inspired status was to be inferred from the prior claim that it was "produced by God's creative breath" (Warfield 1900: 119). Warfield's adjustment to the traditional understanding of the argument from 2 Tim. 3:16 stood to be a win–win situation for the Evangelical cause—more so, perhaps, than most Evangelicals realize—as it is manifestly more honest to infer inerrancy from the divine *production* of a text than from the divine *inspiration* of a text.

The problem with Warfield's solution, however, was that this new understanding of θεόπνευστος made tolerably good sense within the context of 2 Timothy 3, but it did not make sense at all in several of the other occurrences of θεόπνευστος. Douglas Farrow (1987: 89–90) writes,

> The adjective θεόπνευστος or God-breathed *appears* to be an appropriate construct for attaching the formation of the very words of Scripture to God himself. That, in fact, is just how the word is often understood, with obvious ramifications for the nature and application of the doctrine of inerrancy. But upon examining its other early occurrences, this thought is nowhere to be found. In the Plutarch reference it qualifies certain dreams; in Pseudo-Phocylides the reference is to "the speech of theopneustic *wisdom*;" in the fifth book of the Sibyllines it refers to streams (the sources of the Kyme which serve the sibyl?) and to all theopneustic things (μέγαν γενετῆρα θεὸν πάντων θεοπνεύστων); in the Testament of Abraham it modifies "ointments" (and, as Warfield observes, to some extent parallels the accompanying phrase σινδόνι θεοϋφαντῷ "God-woven burial cloth").

---

[38] According to Warfield (1900: 114), "There is ... nothing in the word θεόπνευστος to warrant the *in-* of the Vulgate rendering: this word speaks not of an '*in*spiration' by God, but of a 'spiration' by God." See Ward (2002: 269).

Thus, Warfield's applications of this new understanding of θεόπνευστος often make for strange *literary* readings. When he writes, for example, that "the rivers that water the Cymean plain are God-breathed (Sibyll. v. 308)" (Warfield 1900: 113), the reader, armed with Warfield's claim that "God-breathed" means "divinely created," can only wonder why the divine creation of the river(s) near Cyme is relevant to the sense of the text. Farrow (1987: 90) continues,

> In his only partially successful endeavor to prove the purely passive sense of θεόπνευστος, Warfield in fact demonstrates in his own interpretation of these passages that the word maintains a certain ambiguity and may also be translated "God-provided," "God-pervaded," or simply "divine." This is evident in looking at specifically Christian and later usages as well. Consider, for example, Nonnus's paraphrase of John 1:27, where he refers to Christ's sandals as theopneustic.

Warfield's suggestion to interpret θεόπνευστος in light of the creation narrative was on the right track, but his unwillingness to let go of his Evangelical commitments in the area of bibliology caused him to approach the biblical image of divine breathing at an oblique angle. Where in Scripture does in-spiration[39] (or *spiration*) as such *create*, in the sense of "produce," as opposed to merely animate?[40] The imagery and *notion* of creation in the Bible are not monolithic. On the one hand, there is the creation of inanimate objects, including the world, the heavenly expanse (together with the greater and lesser lights), the sea, and so on. The consistent mechanism by which these are created is said to be God's *word*. On the other hand, there is creation in the sense of imbuing humans and animals with life. Here the consistent mechanism is that of God's *inbreathing*. Obviously the distance between these two ways of talking about creation should be respected by any later terminology based on the creation narrative. It should hardly seem possible for a biblical writer to use the imagery associated with the creation of inanimate objects to convey the sense of giving life, and vice versa. And yet Warfield tries to adopt the imagery of God's *breathing* as a cipher for creation in the sense of *production*.[41] Clearly a better approach would be one that associates God's breathing with the same range of creative activity with which we find it associated in Scripture—that of giving life.

In other words, whereas Warfield continually spoke of the "breath of God" as "creative," he should have spoken of it as "life-giving." That would have represented a more accurate understanding of both the word θεόπνευστος and the biblical image standing behind it. The vivificationist association of God's breathing into things is far and away the most prominent use of this image throughout the Old and New Testaments (Gen. 2:7; Job 33:4; Wis. 15:11; cf. Job 27:3; Isa. 42:5; Ezek. 37:5–10; Acts 17:25; 2 Macc. 7:23; 2 Esd. 16:61 [see below]). In keeping with the OT use of

---

[39] On the hyphenated term "in-spiration," see the section below on " 'Inspired' vs. 'In-spired.'"

[40] Scott (2009b: 188) objects to A. T. B. McGowan's use of the word "spiration" on the grounds that it "is a very obscure word" and because "in theological usage, *spiration* already refers to the mode of the Spirit's procession within the Trinity."

[41] Austin (1981: 77) argues similarly to Warfield, appealing to a supposed parallelism between "the images of the breath of God and the word of God", as found, e.g., in Ps 33:6; 147:18. This relies on a minority use of "breath" as the expiration that accompanies speaking.

the *theopneustia* image, describing something as "theopneustic" most likely would indicate that it is characterized either as "living" (= "God-breathed") or as "life-giving" (= "God-breathing"). When we make this adjustment to our use of the biblical creation narrative, the philological data fall perfectly in line.

The point of the following chapters is to show that this alternative to the inspirationist understanding of θεόπνευστος, in spite of having been all but forgotten since the early centuries of the Common Era, enjoys far better philological support than the traditional understanding of θεόπνευστος.[42] In fact, this vivificationist understanding of the word better accounts for *all* the philological data that precede the third century CE. This study also seeks to establish that the inspirationist understanding of θεόπνευστος, in spite of its universal acceptance through most of church history, did not arise until the time of Origen.[43] The word was not unpacked in terms of inspiration until the Alexandrian church fathers (under Origen's influence) mistakenly read 2 Timothy through the lens ground by the Philonic understanding of the nature of Scripture.[44] Translators who automatically assign an inspirationist understanding to θεόπνευστος in 2 Tim. 3:16 can therefore be said to be in thrall to an Origenist innovation.

According to the understanding of 2 Tim. 3:16 argued below, the description of Scripture as "God-breathing" denotes that Scripture possesses a *life-giving* aspect. The question then arises: In what sense might Scripture be said to be life-giving? The answer (once again) is simple and is at once suggested by one of the New Testament's most consistent claims about the Old Testament: Scripture conveys the life-giving *Gospel*.[45] The sort of vivification conveyed by 2 Timothy's use of θεόπνευστος is probably very close to the notion of "breathing incorruption" in a famous passage from Irenaeus (*Adv. haer.* 3.11.8):

> There can be neither more nor fewer gospels than there are. As there are four regions of the world in which we live, and four principal winds, and as the church is spread over all the land, and has for a column and support the Gospel and the Spirit of life; consequently it has four pillars, breathing incorruption from every side and giving life to humans (πανταχόθεν πνέοντας τὴν ἀφθαρσίαν, καὶ ἀναζωπυροῦντας τοὺς ἀνθρώπους). From this it is manifest that the Logos is the artificer of all, who sits above the cherubim, and encompasses everything, when manifest to men gave us the fourfold Gospel, encompassed by one Spirit. (Author's translation)

---

[42] As we will see below, this view has been preserved in the way most scholars have translated *Sib. Or.* 5.406. It is strange that a vivificationist rendering in that instance has not led to a renewed investigation of the general sense of θεόπνευστος.

[43] I should state my agreement with Warfield (1893: 198) when he writes, "The assertion in the term 'theopneustic' in such a passage as II Tim. iii. 16 … cannot be voided by any construction of the passage; and the doctrine taught in the assertion must be understood to be the doctrine which that term connoted to Paul who uses it, not some other doctrine read into it by us."

[44] As I discuss later in this study, book 4 of Origen's *De Principiis* clearly demonstrates the influence Philo had on the Alexandrian Christians' understanding of the nature of Scripture.

[45] It is ironic, therefore, that Warfield (1889: 406) should write that the Bible "is precious because it is a life-quickening book."

We shall have occasion to revisit this passage later. For now it suffices to say that Irenaeus, who draws on 1 Tim. 3:15 for the "pillar and ground" reference (cf. also *Adv. haer.* 3.1.1), appears also to allude to the imagery and connections found in 2 Tim. 3:15–16.

In what follows, I argue not only that this is a neglected possibility for understanding θεόπνευστος but also that it is the *only* interpretation that fits the term's philological profile for the period in question, and that it is by far the best interpretation for making sense of 2 Timothy.

3.1 The Wording and Meaning of 2 Tim. 3:16 in the Latin Tradition

So far I have discussed both the English and the Greek aspects of a proper understanding of 2 Tim. 3:16's claim for Scripture's *theopneustia*, but much of the change in how that verse was read was abetted by, and encapsulated in, a corresponding change in how a certain *Latin* term was understood. The Latin Vulgate of 2 Tim. 3:16 used *divinitus inspirata* to render θεόπνευστος, but what does it *mean* by *inspirata*? If we search for other appearances of *inspir-* within the Vulgate, we attain a mixed field of meanings. On the one hand, we are met with several verses in which *inspir-* refers to God's *vivificationist* inbreathing:

Gen. 2:7 Formavit igitur Dominus Deus hominem de limo terræ, et inspiravit in faciem ejus spiraculum vitæ, et factus est homo in animam viventem.	Gen. 2:7 καὶ ἔπλασεν ὁ θεὸς τὸν ἄνθρωπον χοῦν ἀπὸ τῆς γῆς καὶ ἐνεφύσησεν εἰς τὸ πρόσωπον αὐτοῦ πνοὴν ζωῆς καὶ ἐγένετο ὁ ἄνθρωπος εἰς ψυχὴν ζῶσαν	Gen. 2:7 then the LORD God formed man from the dust of the ground, and breathed into his nostrils the breath of life; and the man became a living being.
Job 32:8 Sed, ut video, spiritus est in hominibus, et inspiratio Omnipotentis dat intelligentiam.	Job 32:8 ἀλλὰ πνεῦμα ἐστιν ἐν βροτοῖς πνοὴ δὲ παντοκράτορός ἐστιν ἡ διδάσκουσα	Job 32:8 But truly it is the spirit in a mortal, the breath of the Almighty, that makes for understanding.
Acts 17:25 nec manibus humanis colitur indigens aliquo, cum ipse det omnibus vitam, et inspirationem, et omnia:	Acts 17:25 οὐδὲ ὑπὸ χειρῶν ἀνθρωπίνων θεραπεύεται προσδεόμενός τινος, αὐτὸς διδοὺς πᾶσι ζωὴν καὶ πνοὴν καὶ τὰ πάντα·	Acts 17:25 nor is he served by human hands, as though he needed anything, since he himself gives to all mortals life and breath and all things.
Wis. 15:11 quoniam ignoravit qui se finxit, et qui inspiravit illi animam quæ operatur, et qui insufflavit ei spiritum vitalem.	Wis. 15:11 ὅτι ἠγνόησεν τὸν πλάσαντα αὐτὸν καὶ τὸν ἐμπνεύσαντα αὐτῷ ψυχὴν ἐνεργοῦσαν καὶ ἐμφυσήσαντα πνεῦμα ζωτικόν.	Wis. 15:11 because they failed to know the one who formed them and inspired them with active souls and breathed a living spirit into them.

Ecclus 4:11 (4:12) Sapientia filiis suis vitam inspirat: et suscipit inquirentes se, et præibit in via justitiæ.	Sir. 4:11 ἡ σοφία υἱοὺς αὐτῆς ἀνύψωσεν καὶ ἐπιλαμβάνεται τῶν ζητοῦν των αὐτήν.[46]	Ecclus 4:12 (Latin [Douay–Rheims]) Wisdom inspireth life into her children, and protecteth them that seek after her, and will go before *them* in the way of justice.

On the other hand, we also find *inspirati* being used in 2 Pet. 1:21 to refer to the inspired nature of the prophecies found within Scripture:

2 Pet. 1:21 Non enim voluntate humana allata est aliquando prophetia: sed Spiritu Sancto inspirati, locuti sunt sancti Dei homines.	2 Pet. 1:21 οὐ γὰρ θελήματι ἀνθρώπου ἠνέχθη προφητεία ποτέ, ἀλλὰ ὑπὸ πνεύματος ἁγίου φερόμενοι ἐλάλησαν ἀπὸ θεοῦ ἄνθρωποι.	2 Pet. 1:21 because no prophecy ever came by human will, but men and women moved by the Holy Spirit spoke from God.

Here, in this single (but very visible) instance, *inspir-* is used with the sense of epistemic or verbal inspiration commonly assumed by later bibliologies. Of the remaining passages that feature *inspir-*, two relate the violence of the Lord's rebuke, while the final one, as the focus of this study, is included here for the sake of completeness:

2 Sam. 22:16 Et apparuerunt effusiones maris, et revelata sunt fundamenta orbis ab increpatione Domini, ab inspiratione spiritus furoris ejus.	2 Sam. 22:16 καὶ ὤφθησαν ἀφέσεις θαλάσσης καὶ ἀπεκαλύφθη θεμέλια τῆς οἰ κουμένης ἐν τῇ ἐπιτιμήσει κυρίου ἀπὸ πνοῆς πνεύματος θυμοῦ αὐτοῦ.	2 Sam. 22:16 Then the channels of the sea were seen, the foundations of the world were laid bare at the rebuke of the LORD, at the blast of the breath of his nostrils.
Ps. 18:15 (17:16) Et apparuerunt fontes aquarum, et revelata sunt fundamenta orbis terrarum, ab increpatione tua, Domine, ab inspiratione spiritus iræ tuæ.	Ps. 18:15 (17:16) καὶ ὤφθησαν αἱ πηγαὶ τῶν ὑδάτων καὶ ἀνεκαλύφθη τὰ θεμέλια τῆς οἰκουμένης ἀπὸ ἐπιτιμήσεώς σου κύριε ἀπὸ ἐμπνεύσεως πνεύματος ὀργῆς σου.	Ps. 18:15 Then the channels of the sea were seen, and the foundations of the world were laid bare at your rebuke, O LORD, at the blast of the breath of your nostrils.

[46] In the conventions of Ben Sira scholarship, the Greek text presented here represents "GrI," while the Latin is usually held to be a translation of "GrII."

2 Tim. 3:16 Omnis Scriptura divinitus inspirata utilis est ad docendum, ad arguendum, ad corripiendum, et erudiendum in justitia:	2 Tim. 3:16 πᾶσα γραφὴ θεόπνευστος καὶ ὠφέλιμος πρὸς διδασκαλίαν, πρὸς ἐλεγμόν, πρὸς ἐπανόρθωσιν, πρὸς παιδείαν τὴν ἐν δικαιοσύνῃ.	2 Tim. 3:16 All scripture is theopneustic and is useful for teaching, for reproof, for correction, and for training in righteousness,

My point in showing the duplicity of the Vulgate's use of *inspir-* is to expose the roots of the English term's primary signification: the etymological roots of both the Latin *inspir-* and the English "inspire" clearly allow for the notion of a *vivificationist* inbreathing, but the overwhelming dominance of the English term's association with an external bolstering (or overriding) of one's noetic and/or artistic abilities effectively removes the *vivificationist* understanding of the term from the minds of today's readers. This confusing state of affairs began already within the Vulgate. The Greek text provides little justification for using the same term in rendering 2 Tim. 3:16 and 2 Pet. 1:21, but the Vulgate helped to ensure that these verses would come to be read as making equivalent claims about Scripture.

The Vulgate, of course, hails roughly from the fourth century, so we should not be surprised to find it supporting notions that Origen may have caused to pass into general circulation. It would be helpful if somehow we could see how the Vulgate's forebears rendered 2 Pet. 1:21, but the sources are silent: The Old Latin text did not include 2 Peter, and neither does Tertullian ever discuss that book.[47]

3.2 Cremer's and Warfield's Philological Databases

As the present study is philological in method, it is worth noting which sources Cremer and Warfield used in their respective arguments.

Cremer's revisionist understanding of θεόπνευστος first appeared in an article on "Inspiration" that he wrote for the second edition of the Schaff–Herzog *Real-Encyklopädie* (1880).[48] He subsequently transferred that understanding to the third edition of his own *Biblisch-theologisches Wörterbuch der Neutestamentlichen Gräcität* (1883 [s.v. "θεόπνευστος"]), replacing the more traditional understanding that he had expressed in the first two editions (1866[1], 1872[2]).[49] Cremer (1880: 746) noted that the use of "inspiration" as a stand-in for the concept conveyed by θεόπνευστος is derived from the Latin Vulgate of 2 Tim. 3:16 (*omnis scriptura divinitus inspirita …*), and he

---

[47] That the Latin version of 2 Peter presents a post-Origen snapshot of terminology is suggested by the fact that *adspiro* (*aspiro*) was the preferred Latin term, among pagans of the time, for poetic inspiration. See Ziolkowski (1990: 26–7). Frisius (2011: 13) notes, "There is little evidence that Tertullian knows 2 Peter, and he never specifically indicates that he is referencing this book."

[48] See Cremer (1880).

[49] Cremer (1866: 231; 1872: 282). As Warfield (1900: 91 n. *) notes, "The chief differences between the *Herzog* and *Lexicon* articles are found at the beginning and end—the latter being fuller at the beginning and the former at the end."

questioned the sufficiency of the Latin as a guide to NT philology.[50] The philological evidence that others had cited in support of rendering θεόπνευστος as "divinely inspired," Cremer claimed, simply is not there: the use of θεόπνευστος in a passage of Plutarch (*De placit. phil.* 5.2 [*Mor.* 904.2]), for example, almost certainly comes from the hand of a copyist, covering over an earlier appearance of θεοπέμπτους.[51] Other instances of θεόπνευστος are better translated with a passive meaning as "mit Gottes Geist begabt." This revisionist understanding, Cremer claimed, is "unzweifelhaft" in *Sib. Or.* 5.406 and in two passages from *Vita Sabae* 16.[52] Cremer also claimed that the active-sense understanding of θεόπνευστος fits the context of 2 Tim. 3:16 better than the usual (passive) rendering. He noted a particularly happy fit with τὰ δυνάμενά σε σοφίσαι in v. 15, and with ὠφέλιμος πρὸς διδασκαλίαν, πρὸς ἐλεγμόν, πρὸς ἐπανόρθωσιν, πρὸς παιδείαν τὴν ἐν δικαιοσύνῃ in v. 16. He did not deny that θεόπνευστος ever was understood to mean "divinely inspired" (in the sense usually read into that word today), but he suggested that this use of the term reflects a design taken over from Alexandrian Jewish or pagan tradition (Cremer 1880: 747). Cremer's philological database, therefore, consisted of Plutarch (which he rejected as corrupt), the fifth *Sibylline Oracle*, and the *Vita Sabae*.[53]

In his 1889 article on "Paul's Doctrine of the Old Testament," Warfield's (1889: 395–6) philological database for θεόπνευστος included "one passage in Plutarch" ("probably corrupt," as Cremer also held), *Sib. Or.* 5.308, two uses of the term in the *Vita Sabae*, one in Nonnus' *Paraphrase of the Gospel of John*, and "only a single other early passage": Pseudo-Phocylides' *Sentences* 121. Although he speaks as if this list of witnesses is complete, his failure to mention the second passage in the *Sibylline Oracles*, and the other three in Nonnus, would suggest that he did not intend this as a sort of final account. Indeed, his language in his passage is confusing, as he uses the expression "only … single other early passage" immediately following a mention of the fifth-century work by Nonnus and of the sixth-century *Vita Sabae*, which would imply that all of Clement's and Origen's (etc.) uses of the word are also "early." Perhaps he intended "other" to signal a back reference to the previously named Pseudo-Plutarch and the *Fifth Oracle*. Warfield (1889: 394) writes, "With the one not very certain exception of the fifth Sibyl, which was probably written by a Jew of the second century, [θεόπνευστος] occurs nowhere where it might not possibly have been derived from our present passage."

In his 1900 article on "God-Inspired Scripture," Warfield was more circumspect in his wording and more thorough in his philological task. His database had grown a little as well, given the publication in 1892 of a text of the *Testament of Abraham* (James 1892). Warfield began his philological investigation in that study by discussing the two occurrences of θεόπνευστος in the fifth *Sibylline Oracle*—the first of which is found in an oracle against (Aeolian) Cyme—an oracle that, as Warfield (1900: 105) tells us, "skillfully brings together all that we know of Cyme."

---

[50] Quoted in translation in Warfield (1900: 91).
[51] As Warfield (1900: 94–5) notes, however, Cremer, in attributing to Wyttenbach the priority of θεόπεμπτος, had misrepresented him. See Wyttenbach (1797: 650).
[52] See Cremer (1880: 746).
[53] The *Vita Sabae* is too late for our purposes and will not be discussed in this study.

The second occurrence of θεόπνευστος in the fifth *Oracle* appears in a lament over the destruction of the Jerusalem Temple—the place where "the great Father-God of all theopneustic things" was worshipped (Warfield 1900: 106). Warfield then turned to the use made of θεόπνευστος in *Pseudo-Phocylides*. Here too he found a connection with a supposed creative aspect: "Wisdom is conceived as theopneustic, in a word, because wisdom itself is thought of as coming from God" (Warfield 1900: 107).[54] (He was innocent of the claim that the verse from *Pseudo-Phocylides* is a late gloss.) Warfield (1900: 107–8) next turned to the use of θεόπνευστος in the *Testament of Abraham*—a text unknown to Cremer—where he took the description of Abraham's burial ointments as theopneustic to denote their "God-provided" nature. He then moved forward to Nonnus of Panopolis's fifth-century paraphrase of the Fourth Gospel, in which (in one of four appearances of the word in that work) John the Baptist describes Jesus's sandal as theopneustic. He took this to mean that the sandal "partook of the divinity of the divine Person whose property it was" (Warfield 1900: 108). Warfield also discussed three later instances in which θεόπνευστος is used as a description of certain men. These he recognized as requiring a somewhat different understanding of the word than that which he held to be its primary meaning. In connection with the word's appearance in an inscription found at Bostra, for example, he noted that "it is difficult to understand the word in this connection as expressing simple origination by God" (Warfield 1900: 109).[55] And in connection with the *Vita Sabae*'s reference to a "caravan of all theopneustics, of all his christophers," he finds it necessary to attribute "a secondary and derived sense" of θεόπνευστος, although he maintains that there "should still cling a flavor of the idea of origination" (Warfield 1900: 109).

4 The Philological Profile in Pre-Alexandrian Sources

Before determining whether a vivificationist rendering fits the context of 2 Timothy, we must consider the term's philological profile in other writings, to see if it lends itself to that rendering as decisively as its etymology suggests. This will take us beyond Cremer's and Warfield's databases. This is due to the fact that we have more texts from late antiquity than were known in Cremer's and Warfield's day, to the need to include alternate spellings, and to the existence of search tools that Cremer and Warfield never could have imagined.[56]

At the center of both Cremer's and Warfield's cases are a number of instances in which θεόπνευστος appears in other sources—Jewish, Christian, and Greco-Roman.

---

[54] Warfield (1900: 94) writes,

> There seems to be pretty good positive reason for supposing the Pseudo-Phocylidian poem to be in its entirety a Christian production. … Its relation to the *Teaching of the Apostles* has caused the subject to be reopened, and we think has brought it to at least a probable settlement in favor of [Joseph] Scaliger's opinion that it is the work "ἀνωνύμου Christiani."

[55] The Bostra inscription is too late for our purposes and will not be discussed in this study.

[56] Trembath (1987: 6) dismisses the possibility of learning what θεόπνευστος really means:

Table 1.1 *TLG* results

Witness	Century	Occurrences
Manetho Hist.	3 BC	1×
Oracula Sibyllina	2 BC–AD 4	2×
Novum Testamentum	AD 1	1×
Testamentum Abrahae	AD 1	1×
Pseudo-Phocylides Gnom.	AD 1/2	1×
Aelius Herodianus et Pseudo-Herodianus Gramm. et Rhet.	AD 2	1×
Papias Scr. Eccl.	AD 2	1×
Vettius Valens Astrol.	AD 2	1×
Clemens Alexandrinus Theol.	AD 2–3	4×
Origenes Theol.	AD 2–3	48×[a]
Physiologus	AD 2/4	1×
Pseudo-Plutarchus Biogr. et Phil.	p. AD 2	1×
Gregorius Thaumaturgus Scr. Eccl.	AD 3	2×
Hippolytus Scr. Eccl.	AD 3	1×
Methodius Scr. Eccl.	AD 3–4	1×

[a]Our discussion of Origen will show that this figure is inflated by duplicate data.

As Cremer's case involves separating earlier sources from those influenced by a later Alexandrianizing of the term, he treated them as a block before turning to the use of θεόπνευστος in Clement of Alexandria, Origen, and so on. Warfield, seeking to answer Cremer point for point, kept to this same organizing principle and indeed sharpened it somewhat. As my own view accepts Cremer's assumption that the Alexandrians' use of the term represents a watershed for how it came to be popularly understood, I also will discuss the pre-Origenist uses of θεόπνευστος as a block.[57]

We must begin by determining which instances of θεόπνευστος properly belong to the period preceding Origen. This involves making a number of adjustments to the list generated by a simple search of the *Thesaurus Linguae Graecae* database (hereafter *TLG*). Table 1.1 shows all those witnesses in the *TLG* containing θεόπνευστος and dated by the *TLG* to the third century CE or earlier.[58] Witnesses appearing in the first column are given according to the *TLG*'s nomenclature, and dates in the second column are given (nomenclaturally) exactly as by the *TLG*.

> We do not [know the real meaning of the word], in spite of the staggering amount of attention it has received over several generations. *Theopneustos* is a *hapax legomenon:* it occurs only here in the Bible, and only rarely outside it. Thus we have extremely little to go on in order to discover what the author of 2 Timothy intended by the word, and not nearly enough to justify its use as a critical factor in inspiration discussions.

The case set out in this book should show Trembath's skepticism to be unjustified.

[57] My own view is that the major shift in meaning began with Origen. Cremer posited a shift beginning with Clement.

[58] All references to the indications of the *TLG* are based on a search conducted on April 14, 2010.

Unfortunately, the dates supplied by the *TLG* are in several instances open to doubt, especially in the case of dubious texts, or in the case of framing narratives for fragments.[59] As Luci Berkowitz and Karl Squitier (1990: xxv) explain, the *TLG* can sometimes present results under the wrong chronological heading, due to the difficulty of separating a quoted fragment from the words that frame it:

> Often, it is simply not feasible or, for that matter, justifiable to attempt to separate *ipsissima verba* from surrounding testimonia, especially when the text in question is prose rather than poetry; in far too many cases, such a separation is at best artificial and at worst misleading. Over the years, the TLG's efforts to isolate *ipsissima verba* have met with exasperation when the fine line between quoter and quoted is stretched so thin as to render a distinction meaningless, if not altogether impossible to achieve.

Three of the works appearing in our search results are affected by this technical glitch: Manetho, Aelius Herodianus, and Papias. None of these works belongs on the list of pre-third-century witnesses to the term θεόπνευστος, as that word appears in each case in a work broadly assigned to the head-name, but in a portion written by a later collector of words. Manetho wrote in the third century BCE, but θεόπνευστος occurs in "Manetho[TLG]" only in the framing narrative written by Manetho's eighth-century epitomator, George Syncellus: "Thus Panodorus contends to show that Egyptian writings against God and the theopneustic scriptures are (really) in harmony with them."[60] The *TLG* also lists the grammarian Aelius Herodianus as a source for θεόπνευστος, but the word actually appears in the words of Herodianus' seventh-century CE epitomator Georgius Choeroboscus, and not in the original words of the Herodianic *On the Inflections of Names*.[61] Its appearance in the *TLG* is due to the database's failure to differentiate between a fragmentary source and the narrative framing the fragment. The *TLG* similarly lists Papias as a witness for θεόπνευστος, but the word appears only in the framing narrative of Andrew of Caesarea's sixth-century commentary on Revelation (which quotes an otherwise lost text of Papias).[62]

---

[59] Berkowitz and Squitier (1990: xix n. 24) write, "Information regarding dates in the [*TLG*] *Canon* is drawn from a variety of sources, including the standard lexica, biographical dictionaries, encyclopedias, and literary histories as well as modern publications that address specific chronological problems." They mention two relevant works as having been "particularly useful": Geerard (1974–87), and LaRue, Vincent, and St.-Onge (1985).

[60] Frag. 2 of Manetho's *Aegyptiaca* (§5) (author's translation). Panodorus was a late fourth/early-fifth-century Egyptian monk who sought to harmonize Egyptian and Christian writings.

[61] Choeroboscus refers to ὁ θεόπνευστος ὁ ἰατρός (in Lentz 1867: 2.655 line 2), which Lentz takes as a reference to the author of Acts, and on which grounds he emends a reference to Ἀκύφας to Ἀκύλας (655 n. 1). On Herodianus *On the Inflections of Names*, see Lentz (1867: 1.cviii); Dyck (1993: 789).

[62] The *TLG* refers to "fragment 5" in Funk, Schneemelcher, and Bihlmeyer (1970: 134–7). (Cf. Lightfoot 1898: 532.) The fragment begins with περὶ μέντοι τοῦ θεοπνεύστου τῆς βίβλου and then lists Papias and others as witnesses to Revelation's "trustworthiness" (τὸ ἀξιόπιστον). In fact, this is Andrew's second use of θεόπνευστος in the prologue to his Revelation commentary. See Constantinou (2008: 2.11); more generally: Diekamp (1938: 161–72). On Andrew of Caesarea's commentary, see Aune (1997: li); Hernández (2011: 185–7).

Table 1.2 First revision of *TLG* results

Witness	Century	Occurrences
Oracula Sibyllina	2 BC–AD 4	2×
Novum Testamentum	AD 1	1×
Testamentum Abrahae	AD 1	1×
Pseudo-Phocylides Gnom.	AD 1/2	1×
Vettius Valens Astrol.	AD 2	1×
Pseudo-Plutarchus Biogr. et Phil.	p. AD 2	1×
Clemens Alexandrinus Theol.	AD 2–3	4×
Hippolytus Scr. Eccl.	AD 2–3	1×
Origenes Theol.	AD 2–3	48×

This appearance of the word in "Papias" belongs to the sixth century rather than to the second century.

Θεόπνευστος also appears in one stream of the Greek versions of the *Physiologus*, but it is a late stream, which cannot be brought anywhere near the date that most scholars assign the *Physiologus* (viz., the second century CE), and the reading preserved in this stream is explicable only by the co-opting of this text by Christians. (There is more going on here than meets the eye, so I discuss the *Physiologus* in more detail later in this study.) We may also delete Gregory Thaumaturgus and Methodius from the chart, on the grounds that they postdate Origen. (While we're at it, we can change the date on Hippolytus to "A.D. 2–3" and move him ahead of Origen.) These qualifications neatly reduce our field of genuine examples of pre-Origen uses of θεόπνευστος to a handful. The list up to and including Origen appears in Table 1.2.

This still is not the full story, however, as a failure to consider the uses of the word's alternate form θεόπνους would represent a serious lacuna. A *TLG* search turned up three (purported) occurrences of the word in pre-Origenist sources—one in a fragment of Numenius (preserved by Porphyry), one in *Poimandres* (= *Corp. Herm.* 1), and one in the *Cyranides*. To this we also can add two inscriptional uses of the word, not registering in the *TLG* but dating from the early third century: one found in a nymphaeum in Laodicea and the other on a Roman-era platform that once stood in front of the Great Sphinx of Giza. In this study, I argue that Numenius, *Poimandres*, and the two inscriptions all use θεόπνους in a vivificationist sense, but that the *Cyranides*, which may or may not use θεόπνους in a vivificationist sense, features our word only in a later stream of the textual tradition—the phrase in question having materialized as a copyist's marginal note. (The argument against the relevance of the *Cyranides* is too convoluted to present in just a few sentences. I discuss it more fully when I discuss the *Physiologus*.) This brings the adjusted results shown in Table 1.3.[63]

---

[63] The most complete list of θεόπνευστος and θεόπνους texts appearing in a NT commentary is probably that found in Marshall (1999: 793 n. 83, 794 n. 84), which, of the non-Christian texts we will examine, omits only the inscription at the Laodicean nymphaeum. Unfortunately, Marshall never thinks to question that the word in question means "God-inspired."

Table 1.3 Second revision of *TLG* results

Witness	Century	Occurrences
Oracula Sibyllina	2 BC–AD 4	2×
Novum Testamentum	AD 1	1×
Testamentum Abrahae	AD 1	1×
Pseudo-Phocylides Gnom.	AD 1/2	1×
Vettius Valens Astrol.	AD 2	1×
Pseudo-Plutarchus Biogr. et Phil.	p. AD 2	1×
Numenius Phil.	AD 2	1× (θεόπνοος)
Corpus Hermeticum	AD 2?/4	1× (θεόπνους)
Clemens Alexandrinus Theol.	AD 2–3	4×
Hippolytus Scr. Eccl.	AD 2–3	1×
Great Sphinx of Giza	AD 3	1× (θεόπνους)
Laodicean Nymphaeum	AD 3	1× (θεόπνους)
Origenes Theol.	AD 2–3	48×

The traditional, inspirationist understanding of θεόπνευστος appears to have had a tight hold on modern lexicography regarding the general use of the word, both in and beyond the New Testament. The powerful influence of this understanding is shown by the regularity with which θεόπνευστος/θεόπνους is translated in inspirationist terms whenever it appears in noncanonical works, including a number of pre-Alexandrian works in which the context clearly points away from such a rendering. All the translators of the works that we will be examining had an opportunity to set the record straight on θεόπνευστος's philological profile, but in nearly every instance they squandered that opportunity by adopting the inspirationist understanding found in the lexicons. In some instances, the vivificationist meaning of the term is so obvious from the context that the translator's feeling of confliction must have been rather heavy.

In the chapters that follow, I discuss what θεόπνευστος/θεόπνους means within the texts listed in the final chart presented above. I also discuss what it means in a few sources not included in the final chart: the *Physiologus*, the *Cyranides*, and Nonnus of Panopolis's *Paraphrase of the Gospel of John*.

4.1 "Inspired" vs. "In-spired"

To avoid confusion throughout this book and to sharpen our understanding of how the traditional understanding of 2 Tim. 3:16 came to have such an overwhelming influence, there is a matter of clerical housekeeping to which we must attend. The confusion to be avoided is that which threatens from the different understandings of the English words "inspire" and "inspiration." The *Oxford English Dictionary* (= *OED*; 1989: 7.1036–37 [*s.v.* "inspiration," "inspire"]) divides the fields of meaning for each of these words into two domains: "I. Literal (physical) senses" and "II. Figurative senses." The meanings most commonly tied to the words "inspired" and "inspiration" today are those found in the second domain. In fact, the *OED* includes the divine inspiration of Scripture (in the traditional sense) as a marked example of "inspiration" denoting a "special immediate action or influence of the Spirit of God (or of some divinity or supernatural being) upon the human mind or soul." And yet the understanding of θεόπνευστος found in every pre-Origenist use of the word hangs pendant from a notion found in the *first* domain of the *OED* entry for "inspiration." The *OED*'s first definition of "inspiration" (which it lists as "*Obs. rare*") is "The action of blowing on or into." Obviously, it might lead to confusion if I were to argue at length against an "inspirationist" understanding of θεόπνευστος, only to offer in its place a meaning that invokes an alternative definition of the English word "inspiration."

To avoid this complication, I will use the spellings "inspire" and "inspiration" when referring to the traditional (*OED*'s "figurative") understandings of those words, but I will use the spellings "in-spire" and "in-spiration" when referring to the act of breathing on or into a person/thing. Hopefully, the hyphens in the latter pair of terms will facilitate a more etymologically focused reading of the words in question.

2

Pre-Origen Uses of Θεόπνευστος

This chapter will look at six pre-Origen uses of θεόπνευστος: two in the fifth *Sibylline Oracle*, and one each in the *Testament of Abraham*, the *Anthologies* of Vettius Valens, Pseudo-Plutarch (Aetius), and the *Sentences* of Pseudo-Phocylides.

1 *Sibylline Oracles* 5.308

The *Sibylline Oracles* are largely the product of (Egyptian) Judaism.[1] Although they are modeled on the sibylline books of the Romans, and although some of the material included in them probably began in a pagan context, the literary design and the redactorial voice are those of a Jew (see Barclay 1996: 216–28; Paget 2007: 188–9; Stoneman 2011: 190–8; cf. Collins 1998).[2] The books also include Christian interpolations to varying degrees.

We will be considering one of the more extensively studied *Oracles*: the fifth. This work is an important witness for the meaning of θεόπνευστος, not least because the word appears there twice. As I argue below, there are clear indications, in both passages, that the word refers to the giving of life.[3]

The fifth *Sibylline Oracle* is a collection of 531 hexameter verses[4] of harsh judgment against an assortment of Greco-Roman cities.[5] Scholars do not agree on how to divide the book along source-critical seams or on how much was penned by the final editor—at most, there is broad agreement that some material originated shortly after the

---

[1] Collins (1972: 35–55; 1974) has long argued that they were written by the Jewish community at Leontopolis. Cf. the doubts in Gruen (1998: 283–4 n. 158).

[2] Davila (2005: 188 n. 17) is not convinced that *any* of the extant *Sibylline Oracles* can be shown "with any confidence" to be Jewish. See Gager (1972). On the pagan context of some of the material, see Bloch (2011: 159–65). On the *Sibylline Oracles* more generally, see Romagnoli (2014: 220–6).

[3] The *Sibylline Oracles* were enthusiastically received by Christian writers. Felder (2002: 366 [cf. 370–1]) finds them "quoted or alluded to in 22 different patristic texts." See Hooker (2007: 438–45, 446–9, 453–7)—cf. also Weiland (1935: 65–76); Demougeot (1952); Thompson (1952); Guillaumin (1976); Ogilvie (1978: 28–33); Goodman (1986: 650–1); Bartelink (1993). On the figure of the sibyl in the *Shepherd of Hermas*, cf. Carlini (1985); O'Brien (1997); Dronke (1990).

[4] Per the translation in Collins (1983).

[5] On *Sibylline Oracle* 5, see Geffcken (1902a: 22–30); Teyssèdre (1990); Felder (2002); Woschitz (2005: 866–75).

first revolt against Rome, that some must be dated a few decades later (to the early second century CE), and that nothing in the book indicates a date later than the rule of Hadrian.[6] Stephen Felder (2002: 374) suggests a way to understand how the two main strata of material were combined into the work that survives today. He dates the anti-Roman stratum relatively late, but identifies another stratum comprised of earlier bits. The older material was used, he suggests, "to compensate for technical weaknesses and to lend authenticity to the newer document."[7] We might add that the older material was selected or reshaped in the service of the work's chauvinism. As John Collins (2014: 207) points out, the book "has nothing good to say about any people except the Jews."[8]

In *Sib. Or.* 5.308–14, θεόπνευστος appears in the first line of an oracle against Cyme:

Foolish Cyme, with her theopneustic νάματα.
dejected at the hands of unjust and lawless gods and men,
will no longer go forth to such a height,
but will remain, a corpse, in Cymean νάματα.[9]
And then they will cry out in unison, awaiting evil.
The difficult people and disagreeable tribe of the Cymeans,
Having a sign, will know wherewith it has toiled. (Author's translation)

It is important to note that this Cyme is the city of that name on the southwestern coast of Asia Minor—part of the original Aeolian *dodekapolis* (Hošek 1974: 189; see Herodotus, *Hist.* 1.149–50)—and not the Italian city that was famous as the home of the sibyl, nor the Euboean island locale with that name. The traditional rendering of θεόπνευστος has caused some interpreters to infer redactorial confusion between Aeolian Cyme and Italian Cyme(/Cumae) or at least to comment that

---

[6] Collins (1986: 122–3) writes that the "bitterness of complaint" about the Temple's destruction (esp. in vv. 398–413) suggests a date shortly after that event. Monaca (2008: 26) gives a date range of 80 BCE–130 CE. See Momigliano (1992: 731–2); Goodman (1986: 643–5). Some recent studies on Egyptian Judaism contend that the revolt of 117 CE was quashed so effectively that literary production from that quarter ceased altogether, for an extended period, suggesting that works like *Sibylline Oracle* book 5 were written earlier (e.g., Kerkeslager 2006: 53–68 [esp. 62–67]). But see now the qualifications about our knowledge of the post-117 period in Ilan (2016: 203–24).

[7] See Simon (1983: 226–7). On the reuse of earlier material (not wholly aligned with the editor's views), see Potter (1990: 134–5).

[8] The anti-Roman sentiments in the fifth *Sibylline Oracle* appear to have, as their corollary, a preference for the Parthians. See van Henten (2000: 14–15); Felder (2002: 383). Kocsis (1962) has argued that the *Sibylline Oracles* (esp. books 3 and 5) reflect an attitude of Eastern chauvinism vis-à-vis the West (= Romans). But cf. Erho (2009: 52–3). On the positive portrayal of the Jews in the fifth *Sibylline Oracle*, see Woschitz (2005: 872–3).

[9] Collins (1983: 400) rendered the last two words in line 311 as "swelling streams," based on a conjectural emendation from Lanchester (1913: 405). *Sib. Or.* 5.308–14 is numbered as 5.307–13 in Alexandre (1841: 210). Alexandre translates these lines as "Cuma antem demens, cum plenis numine lymphis, / Sævorum manibus sceleratorumque virorum" (211). The Greek wording in Alexandre's line 308 differs slightly: "Ἐν παλάμῃσι θεῶν ἀνδρῶν [τ'] ἀδίκων καὶ ἀθέσμων." Greek texts can also be found in Friedlieb (1852); Rzach (1891); Geffcken (1902b); Gauger (1998) (revised edition of Kurfess 1951).

Italian Cyme(/Cumae) seems (to them) a better fit.[10] (See below.) A more correct understanding of how θεόπνευστος functions in this passage will show that such expedients are unnecessary.

This is one of the passages with which Benjamin Warfield dealt in his discussion of θεόπνευστος.[11] Although he made a number of salient points, he ultimately missed the passage's literary design. Warfield (1900: 105) pointed out that most translators have rendered θεόπνευστος as "inspired": "It has been customary to understand by 'the theopneustic streams' mentioned, some streams or fountains in the neighborhood known for the presumptively oracular powers of their waters." Indeed, J. Floyer (in the William Whiston edition) had rendered θεόπνευστος as "inspired" (Whiston 1715: 2.69), as did Milton S. Terry (1899: 130 [his v. 414]), and so also the team of Alfred Canon White and Mariana Monteiro (1905: 135). Valentin Nikiprowetzky (1987: 1127) rendered it "inspirés," H. N. Bate (1918: 108) "oracular," Jörg-Dieter Gauger "begeisterten" (1998: 143), and H. C. O. Lanchester (1913: 403) "inspired of God." Warfield rightly disagrees with this line of interpretation: if "Cyme" had referred to the Italian city of that name (rather than the Asian city)— and if θεόπνευστος meant "inspired"—the rendering might make sense, as Italian Cyme(/Cumae) was home to the most famous of the sibyls. Warfield's rejection of this rendering is ostensibly based on geography, but it probably had as much to do with how the idea of an *inspiring* stream or fountain could play into the view he was combatting—that is, Hermann Cremer's active-sense meaning. Warfield (1900: 105–6) writes,

> There does not seem to have been preserved any notice of the existence of such oracular waters belonging to Cyme, and it makes against this assumption that the Cymeans, like the rest of the Ionians and Æolians, were accustomed to resort for their oracles to the somewhat distant Branchidæ, in the south. It appears much more likely, then, that the streams adverted to are natural streams and stand here only as part of the rather full and very exact description of the town—the reference being primarily to the Xanthus and to it as an element merely in the excellence of the situation. In that case "theopneustic," here too, would seem to mean something akin to "God-given," or perhaps more broadly still "divine," in the sense of specially excellent and desirable.[12]

---

[10] Alexandre (1841: 210) asks, "An a poeta confusæ sunt?" (These words are not found in Alexandre 1869, which abridges the notes.) Collins (1983: 400 n. k3) writes, "The inspired streams suggest the Sibylline shrine at Cumae in Italy, but the context favors the Cumae in Asia." Schweizer (1964: 453 n. 1) thinks it "not quite certain whether the ref. is to Campanian or Aeolian Kyme." He is led to this confusion by the assumption that νάμασι θεοπνεύστοις describes "substantially the sources of Kyme which serve the sibyl" (454). A similar confusion besets Bate (1918: 108 n. 308). See Nikiprowetzky (1987: 1127 n. *ad* v. 308).

[11] Geffcken (1902a) took the appearance of this word as proof of the passage's Jewish pedigree.

[12] The Cymeans' practice of consulting the Branchidae (viz., the oracle at Didyma) is gleaned from the infamous Paktyes incident (on which, see below). In point of fact, at the time the fifth *Sibylline Oracle* was written, Cyme was sending consultations to the oracle at Claros. (See Ferrary 2005: 742, 749, 757, 758; Busine 2005: 60.)

Unfortunately, Warfield's reading scarcely represents an improved sensitivity to the literary clues in the text. Warfield is right not to pursue the (supposed) streams as bearing mention for their own sake—the reference to Cymean νάματα was part of a running trope in this part of the oracle (e.g., Hierapolis and Tripolis would be addressed in similar terms a few lines further [vv. 320–1]). But he misses the fact that the sibyl uses θεόπνευστος in describing the νάματα's continuing state, in pointed opposition to the use of "dead." The fuller context of the verse bears this out, as line 311 refers to Cyme as "a corpse" lying in "Cymean νάματα." Θεόπνευστος thus refers, not to the supposedly divine source of the water (as Warfield supposed) but to the life-giving properties of the νάματα in which (or beside which) Cyme lies dead.[13] In other words, θεόπνευστος is being used in ironic anticipation of the mention of Cyme's drowned corpse. Thus the term works here with a manifestly vivificationist sense.[14]

The background of Aeolian Cyme might illuminate two aspects of the sibyl's choice of words. First, addressing Cyme as "the fool" recalls the fact that the city was regularly the butt of jokes: Strabo invokes the Cymeans' legendary stupidity, manifest in their long-standing failure to impose harbor dues (*Geography* 13.3.6; cf. Herodotus, *Hist.* 8.130; Purcell 2005: 207–8),[15] while the *Philogelos* preserves more than twenty jokes aimed at the Cymeans' dim-wittedness.[16] Second, it is possible that the sibyl's reference to Cyme's failure to be a "life-giving" (θεόπνευστος) city is intended to recall Herodotus' well-known account of the Cymeans' failure to provide refuge for Paktyes against his Persian assailants (*Hist.* 1.154–57), in clear violation of accepted principles regarding the treatment of refugees (see Schlesinger 1933).[17] The judgment of death which the sibyl serves against Cyme fits with the hardships the Cymeans purportedly endured for failing to fulfill their obligation to a refugee.[18] This, of course, comports with my suggested rendering of θεόπνευστος as "life-giving": as Cyme withheld its life-giving protection from Paktyes, so also death is dealt in its own νάματα.

That the sibyl intends an allusion to the Paktyes affair is far from certain. Given the temporal remoteness of that affair, it might seem an unlikely key for understanding the

---

[13] Streams have always been identified as sources of life. Cribiore (1995: 105) writes, "Eustathius repeatedly says that rivers were called κουροτρόφοι because life is brought about by wetness and they are bringing life, see e.g. *Comm. Il.* 4.274.20, κουροτρόφοι … ἐνομίζοντο οἱ ποταμοὶ διὰ τὴν ὑγρότητα." (Eustathius wrote in the twelfth century, but the sentiment has always been widespread.) See Stovell (2013: 462).

[14] The literary effect has seemingly escaped the notice of translators. For example, although Collins (1983: 400) discerns the vivificationist sense of θεόπνευστος in *Sib. Or.* 5.406 (see below), he unhelpfully renders it as "divinely inspired" in 5.308.

[15] Kaletsch (2003: 1050) inexplicably discusses Strabo's remarks on Cyme's stupidity in a section on *Italian* Cyme/Cumae.

[16] On Cymeans as the butt of jokes (esp. those collected in the *Philogelos*), see Hošek (1974: 195–6 n. 42); Ragone (2006: 133–49). Ragone names *Sib. Or.* 5.308–14 (esp. the reference to "Cyme the fool") as first among ancient parallels to the *Philogelos*' collection of jokes about Cyme's stupidity (141). See Pulci Doria (1996).

[17] According to Herodotus, the Cymeans consulted the Branchidae (viz., the Apolline oracle at Didyma), who (twice) instructed them to surrender the refugee. After doing so, they learned that the oracle's instructions were intended to teach a lesson to the Cymeans, who should have known better than to question the duty of harboring a refugee. See Hošek (1974: 189–90); Brown (1978); Parker (1985: 313); Auffarth (1992: 204 [cf. 216 n. 80]); Eidinow (2007: 260 n. 52); Greaves (2012: 197–8).

[18] The history of Cyme is a dismal tale of defeat—see Hošek (1974); Lagona (1993a; 1993b).

text. But such an allusion is far from necessary for a vivificationist understanding of θεόπνευστος.[19]

1.1 An Allusion to Nymph-Caused Drownings

In the foregoing, I adopted Warfield's translation of νάματα as "streams" only when commenting directly on his view. I otherwise left it untranslated, as the correct rendering is open to question. While there are streams in the vicinity of Cyme (viz., the Hermus, Caicus, and Xanthus), a νᾶμα can also be a spring, and there is reason to believe that the author of *Sib. Or.* 5.308 had the latter in mind.[20] (Warfield [1889: 395] himself once used "fountains" in speaking of the Cymean νάματα.) Whether νάματα means "streams" or "springs" depends in part on whether the operative idea in vv. 309–10 is the same as that in vv. 308 and 311. If the operative idea in all four lines is the same, then "theopneustic streams" is as good a rendering as any—the "godless, unjust and lawless men" might then be those responsible for the corpse lying "in Cymean streams." But if the ABB'A' structure of these four lines is structured around two *distinct* ideas (viz., A–A' vs. B–B'), it makes better sense, from a lexical point of view, to translate νάμασι θεοπνεύστοις as "theopneustic *springs*" (v. 308) and νάμασι κυμαίοισι as "Cymean *springs*" (v. 311). The idea behind such a rendering is that the source of water is called θεόπνευστος for the same reason that the spring water in Porphyry's *On the Cave of the Nymphs* is called θεόπνοος. As I discuss Porphyry later in this study, it suffices to note that his use of θεόπνοος almost certainly refers to the fecundating effect that the water in Homer's nymph cave (*Od.* 13.102–12) has on the women who ritually bathe in it. This, in turn, suggests that the νάματα in lines 308 and 311 might be springs—that is, that the waters in line 308 might be *theopneustic* springs associated with a nymph cult (or perhaps with an Artemision), while the waters in line 311 (ironically) possess a death-dealing aspect. On the other hand, it was also widely held that spring waters could be transported (by aqueduct) and retain their life-giving properties. In that case, "stream" is as good a rendering as any. That reading, however, leaves us bereft of a ready context for understanding the finding of a corpse within (or near) the νάματα.[21]

The strength of reading *Sib. Or.* 5.308–14 in the light of Porphyry's text lies in two factors: (1) the correspondence between applying θεόπνευστος to water in one text, and applying θεόπνοος to water in the other, and (2) the fact that spring-fed pools associated with nymphs *were also widely associated with accidental drownings*—such as that apparently depicted in v. 311. The case for (1) is manifest. I present the case for (2) in what follows.

---

[19] Brown (1978: 74) suggests that Herodotus' account stems from a Miletian point of view, "intended to put the oracle in a favorable light," and that perhaps another version was in circulation "in which Apollo did not take such a high moral position."

[20] Ballentine (1904: 81) similarly objects to the translation of νᾶμα as "rain" in a supplication addressed to nymphs (in *Orphic Hymn* 51.17–18), noting that "spring" makes better sense. For references to the Hermos river, see Testimonia 26, 28, 34, in Engelmann (1976: 153–5).

[21] See the discussion of the Sibyllist's "use of pagan myth" in Lightfoot (2007: 203–19).

The evidence that drownings were attributed to nymphs is extensive. The well-known story of Hylas' abduction by nymphs features prominently within this body of evidence. The myth's three principal Greek retailers were Apollonius Rhodius (*Arg.* 1.1153–1362, esp. 1207–8), Theocritus (*Id.* 13), and Nicander of Colophon (summarized in Antoninus Liberalis 26), but the myth is also preserved in Propertius (1.20), Valerius Flaccus (*Arg.* 3.481–740, 4.1–57), the Orphic *Argonautica* (629–57), and a number of other sources, including Callimachus and Dracontius.[22] According to the myth, as the boy Hylas dipped his pitcher in a wooded pool to fetch water[23] for his master Heracles, a nymph put her arm around his neck to pull him near for a kiss, causing the boy to fall into the water, never to be seen again.[24] Hylas' abduction was memorialized at Kios (the story's setting), with sacrifices and a ritual search at an annual festival in the boy's honor.[25]

The Hylas myth was widely depicted on friezes and other art pieces (e.g., see Oakley [1990: 575–6]; Türk [1895: 74–97]; de Vos [1997: 68]) and served as a model for more allegations of abduction by nymph(s), some mythical in their own right and some intended to explain the real drowning deaths of loved ones. For example, a similar tale was told of another good-looking youth, Bormos, who, like Hylas, was snatched away by nymphs while dipping his pitcher into a pool of water (see Athenaeus, *Deipn.* 14.619–20). (Sourvinou-Inwood [2005: 128–9] is not convinced that Bormos was abducted, as she interprets the reference to his "nympholepsy" along alternative lines.)[26] Bormos was memorialized by the peasantry of Bithynia similarly to Hylas at Kios (see Himmelmann-Wildschütz 1957: 26 n. 6; Pouilloux 1982: 102; Sourvinou-Inwood 2004; Romano 2009; Ondine Pache 2011: 165).

It is sometimes claimed that the lethal aspect of interacting with nymphs came to the fore relatively late,[27] but Theocritus, already in the third century BCE, refers to nymphs

---

[22] The full range of evidence for Hylas is discussed in Türk (1895), while literary references receive a more recent treatment in Mauerhofer (2004). See Mastonarde (1968); Huxley (1989); Campbell (1990); Effe (1992); Bernsdorff (1994); Köhnken (1996); Muth (1998: 137–44); Sourvinou-Inwood (2005); Heerink (2007); Fantham (2009). David Petrain (2000) argues that Cornelius Gallus composed an elegy for Hylas. On variations in the Hylas myth (*apud* Antoninus Liberalis, Dracontius, Apollonius Rhodius, Valerius Flaccus, Theocritus, and Propertius), see Murgatroyd (1992). See Hani (1974); Borgeaud (1979: 161–3, 178–80); Sourvinou-Inwood (2005: 69–70). On nymphs in Apollonius Rhodius, see Bacchielli (1995). Most versions of the myth feature multiple nymphs, while Apollonios has only one.

[23] As Zenobius (6.21) tells the story, Hylas had gone hunting rather than searching for water.

[24] Valerius Flaccus has it that the boy voluntarily stayed with the nymphs because he found love there.

[25] Sourvinou-Inwood's (2005: 329–59) monograph, seeking to explain the tale of Hylas as a foundation myth, concentrates on the ritual memorials related to the tale.

[26] Sourvinou-Inwood explains Bormos' disappearance as the wandering of a mantic under the influence of a possessing nymph.

[27] In the words of Nock (1961: 301), "latterday Neraids are usually terrifying and capricious and not *faciles Nymphae.*" Larson (2001: 62) writes, "As the centuries passed, the more sinister and disturbing aspects of nymph beliefs in classical Greece were selected for emphasis." Bachvarova (2009: 302–3) writes,

> While there is little reference to the dangerous powers of nymphs in Classical Greek sources, in the later tradition the dangers for men who consort with nymphs become a prominent feature of stories about them; in modern Greek folklore their descendants, the *neraides*, are extremely dangerous, luring children and young women to their death in wells and carrying off young men.

as "goddesses terrible for country folk" (δειναὶ θεαὶ ἀγροιώταις [13.44]). We should not allow a claim for the nymphs' increasing maliciousness over time to obscure the regularity with which they were blamed for drowning deaths at an earlier date.[28] When a river or spring-fed pool claimed the life of a child, it was frequently alleged (viz., on funerary inscriptions) that nymphs had seized the child in order to gain a playmate (see Sourvinou-Inwood 2005: 109). (Abduction by nymph was not always sexually motivated [see Redfield 2003: 316–17; Baert 2016: 48].)[29] From Hermoupolis (Egypt), a well-known second-century CE grave inscription laments the young Isidora, who, upon drowning, was transformed into a nymph (see Larson 2001: 191–3; Michaeli 2009: 52). Arthur Darby Nock (1961: 304–5) notes that attributing a child's death to a nymph served as "a ground of consolation" on epitaphs: "Kaibel, *Epigr. Gr.* 570 begins by reproaching Pluteus for unrighteously carrying off a little girl and then bids the bereaved parents to desist from lamentation, '*So believe in the old myths* (presumably that of Hylas); *your fine child was carried off for her charm by the Naiades, not by death*'" (see Kaibel 1878; Larson 2001: 70). Jennifer Larson (2001: 70) notes the prevalence of abduction myths within "a cosmopolitan, probably widespread funerary tradition," exemplified in the first- or second-century CE epitaph of a 2-year-old: "The spring nymphs snatched me from life."[30] Nock (1961: 299–301) discusses an inscription from the Hauran (south of Damascus), in which it is said that "nymphs and nereids receive [a certain] Onezathe." According to Servius, the Egyptians combined the nymphs' fondness for children with a native mythology about the Nile, and children were purposely "given to the nymphs" as an offering during a festival for the river god. This idea neatly combines the Greek notion that drowning led to one's defection to the world of the nymphs with the Egyptian notion that drowning in the Nile conferred immortality (see Larson 2001: 191).[31] As Sourvinou-Inwood (2005: 109) notes, "These stories may have been perceived by some as simple metaphors for death, inspired by abduction myths like the myth of Hylas, and by others as expressing something more, at least a hope of something more."[32]

A second category of drowning is the one we examined in the model of Hylas' death: the idea of nymphs seizing humans for erotic purposes. This version of the abduction myth involved both children and adults.[33] The children were desired by the nymphs, while adult males paid the price for their seduction. Here we might consider the story of Daphnis, who, after pledging his love to a nymph, gave himself up by

---

[28] Vian (1974: 47–8) traces the Hylas myth to a Hesiodic exemplar.

[29] Nymphs were not the only female divinities who abducted men—see Lefkowitz (2002). On abductions by nymphs, see Connor (1988); Larson (2001: 66–71); Ondine Pache (2011: 155–81).

[30] For the epitaph of the 2-year-old, see *Inscriptiones graecae* 14.2067. Cf. also *Anth. Pal.* 7.170; *Corpus inscriptionum Latinarum* 6.29195 (1862–); Cumont (1942: 401–3 n. 3).

[31] Cf. Wild's (1981: 98–9) discussion of "apotheosis by drowning in the Nile."

[32] An epigram attributed to Posidippus or Callimachus tells of a young boy who fell into a well, attracted by his reflection, and who was pulled out just before he died, "defil[ing] not with death the dwelling of the Nymphs" (trans. Paton 1970: 97 [no. 170]).

[33] Mention should be made of Hermaphroditus (see Ovid, *Meta.* 4.285–388)—his tale does not end in a drowning tragedy, but it shows the predatory designs of nymphs at springs. The story is celebrated in a now famous poem on "The Pride of Halicarnassus," inscribed at Salmacis. For the text of the poem, see Isager (1998). See also Lloyd-Jones (1999); Sourvinou-Inwood (2004); Gagné (2006).

"going to the stream," which probably (but not uncontroversially)[34] means that he drowned (Theocritus, *Id.* 1.140).[35] The duplicitous nature of water appears to play a role here. According to Charles Segal (1974b: 4):

> "Sacred water" [in Theocritus, *Idyll* 1.69] partakes of the ambiguity of this mythicized natural world. As the haunt of Nymphs, it is life-giving and points back to the refreshing springs by which Thyrsis and the Goatherd sing (12, 22). But to the herdsman embattled against Aphrodite it shows its destructive side. To that ambiguity of water corresponds an ambiguity within this mythical world as a whole.[36]

In a similar way, Callimachus says that the goatherd Astacides was carried away by a nymph and was now "holy" (viz., he had died [*Ep.* 22]).[37] Mythology thus spilled over into real life, providing explanations for drowning deaths.

There are two more categories of nymph-related drownings which we cannot detail here (viz., four in all): nymphs might drown humans as punishment for crimes or they might do so purely out of mischief, as when the nymphs in Menander's *Dyskolos* (late third century BCE) are blamed for Knemon falling into a well.[38] (Knemon survives [see Menander, *Dyskolos* 444–5; Ondine Pache 2011: 157].)

Returning to *Sib. Or.* 5.308–11, it is worth noting that these four categories of nymph-related drownings might bear on the text in two ways, depending on how one views the relation of the BB′ lines (vv. 309–10) to the AA′ lines (vv. 308, 311). If the drowned corpse of *Sib. Or.* 5.311 lies dead out of recompense for the Cymeans' stupidity, then the text might have the third category of nymph-related drowning in view—such as drowning as punishment. It is also possible, however, that BB′ does not inform AA′ quite so directly, and that the point of linking the drowned corpse with the theopneustic waters of line 308 was simply to press the irony behind the contrasting images: the same nymph-related waters that *brought life* to the brides who bathed in it (viz., by making them fruitful in childbearing) brought death to others. Either way, we are faced with the distinct possibility that the corpse of *Sib. Or.* 5.311 was the victim of

---

[34] Some interpret "the stream" as referring to the river of Hades, making "going to the stream" figurative for dying in general. Cf., e.g., Lawall (1967: 25–6) ("The stream is simply the stream of Death" [25]); van Erp Taalman Kip (1987). This view appears to figure in Mills's (1963: 6) translation: Daphnis "crossed over the stream."

[35] On the phrase "going to the stream" as a reference to drowning, see Ogilvie (1962: 109–10); Segal (1974a: 23–5; 1974b: 1–11); White (1977). See also Larson (2001: 293 n. 68). Ogilvie (1962: 109) considers it "inescapable" that Daphnis drowned: "Why ask the nymphs why they had abandoned their post and were absent when Daphnis died unless to insinuate that if they had been present they could have saved Daphnis? And the only death which water-nymphs can prevent is death by drowning." See Theocritus, *Id.* 1.66–69. See Schmidt (1968).

[36] Regarding the danger of watery settings, cf. Segal (1974a: 38).

[37] According to an epigram attributed to Callimachus: "A nymph from the mountains carried off Astacides the Cretan goat-herd, and now Astacides is holy. No more, ye shepherds, beneath the oaks of Dicte shall we sing of Daphnis, but ever of Astacides" (trans. Paton 1970: 281 [no. 518]). See Nock (1961: 304); White (1977: 579); Larson (2001: 70).

[38] Rose (1956: 65–6) downplays the mischief of the nymphs, but admits "it was well to avoid offending them."

a nymph, an ironic situation given the widespread characterization of nymph-haunted springs and streams as *life-giving*. In view of this explanation, θεόπνευστος is the term that drives the irony home.[39]

Although these accounts of Hylas' death suggest a possibly significant parallel to the imagery of *Sib. Or.* 5.308–14, especially in the light of that myth's place within Greco-Roman culture, it is not the story of Hylas but rather that of *Daphnis* that presents the closest parallel. One obvious detail that makes Daphnis a nearer parallel is the presence of a dead body. Hylas' abduction left no bodily trace of the boy. He became *immortal*, not dead. Daphnis' story, on the other hand, corresponds more closely to the use of nymph abduction as an explanation for drowning deaths. The suggestiveness of the Daphnis tragedy is especially noticeable in Theocritus' version of the story. Segal (1974a: 22) writes,

> Water is not only the element in which Daphnis meets his death; it is also akin to the life-giving water of the Hesiodic tradition, for the opening of the *Idyll* gives a complex and sophisticated formulation to the archaic association of water and poetic creativity.
>
> This ambiguity of water parallels the ambiguity of the *locus amoenus* which it adorns and refreshes. Such *loci* are frequently the haunt of deities who may be either friendly or destructive or both by turns.[40]

The advantage of interpreting the sibyl's judgment on Cyme in terms of a nymph-related drowning is that the aspect of irony is ready-to-hand: nymph-haunted waters are related to a life-giving force, while the nymphs themselves were known to deal death to wrongdoers by means of that same water. Should we suppose that second-century readers would have recognized the nymphological context that drives this irony? Given the universality of these myths in literary and monumental remains, I suggest the answer is "yes."

Admittedly, this is not the only explanation that fills the bill, as the elements of a life-giving/death-dealing contrast in watery ordeals are also present in other contexts. The nymphological setting of a given water source's life-giving properties is ultimately still operative, but the nymphs in these other contexts are there mentioned (if at all) only to identify the water as sacred. One such context is that of a loose relation of different ways in which sacred waters reveal the guilt of sinners and criminals. Ramsay MacMullen (1981: 58) has called attention to the belief that a sacred spring or river "scalded or melted away the flesh of the perjurer" (see Achilles Tatius, 8.12.8–9;

---

[39] To be sure, certain elements in some versions of the nymph-abduction myth would not serve the Sibyllist's purpose. For example, Ausonius' version of the Hylas myth depicts the boy as "luxuriating in his death" (as Kay puts it), and it would not suit the Sibyllist's point to make death a reward. (See Kay's [2001: 277] commentary on epigram 106. Kay's epigram 106 = Combeaud's epigram 110, while Kay's epigram 107 = Combeaud's epigram 111. See Combeaud 2010: 416–19).

[40] Segal (1974b: 10–11) elsewhere writes, in connection with Theocritus' description of Daphnis' death, "Water is a unifying symbol of whatever is alive and vital in this pastoral world. It is a symbol both of the life-giving aspects of nature and of the vital energies on which the poet draws. ... Yet the powers of nature can be dangerous: Pan can be 'bitter' (17), and water can bring death as well as life."

Philostratus, *Vita Apol.* 1.6). And an invitation from the Pythia bids the "pure in mind" to "come … to the precinct of the pure god, after touching your hand in the stream of the nymphs," but warns that no amount of water will cleanse the wicked who presumed to approach the same "pure god" (*Greek Anthology* 14.71).

2 *Sibylline Oracles* 5.406–7

In his explication of the fifth *Oracle*'s second use of θεόπνευστος, Warfield comes close to expressing the vivificationist meaning that I argue was the term's general meaning in the period before Origen. Due to his focus on the passive- versus active-sense dimensions of the term, however, he fails to register that he has exchanged an inspirationist understanding for one lying nearer the vivificationist field.

Θεόπνευστος appears in the last line of the following passage:

> *Sib. Or.* 5.397–407
> The desired temple has been long extinguished by you,
> when I saw the second temple thrown down,
> soaked in fire by an unclean hand,
> the ever-budding house, the watchful temple of God
> made by holy ones and hoped
> by their soul and body to be ever imperishable.
> For no one unburied praises a god of obscure clay,
> nor did a clever sculptor make one from stone,
> nor worship an accoutrement of gold, a deception of souls.
> But they honored the great God, begetter of all that is theopneustic,
> with majestic sacrifices and holy hecatombs. (Author's translation)

According to Warfield's (1900: 106) translation, *Sib. Or.* 5.406–7 refers to men "ador[ing] in sacrifices, with pure and noble hecatombs, the great Father-God of all theopneustic things."[41] Warfield (1900: 107) claims that θεόπνευστος here means "creature." A rendering of "living things" or "breathing things" would have been nearer the mark—thus Bate (1918: 112) translates it as "the great father of all to whom He gives breath," Lanchester (1913: 405) as "the great Father of all within whom is the breath of God," Collins (1983: 402) as "the great God, begetter of all who have God-given breath," and Nikiprowetzky (1987: 1133) as "le père de tous ceux qui ont reçu le souffle divin." Warfield (1900: 106) notes that Alexandre had translated this as "Qui caelestis vitam pater omnibus afflat," and Terry (in his first edition [1890: 149 (v. 525)]) as "the God and mighty maker of all breathing things." (Terry ill-advisedly changed

---

[41] *Sib. Or.* 5.406–7 is numbered as 5.405–6 in Alexandre (1869: 184). Alexandre translates these lines as "Sed qui cælestis vitam pater omnibus afflat, / Hunc unum coluere sacris purisque hecatombis" (185). The Greek wording in Alexandre's line 406 differs slightly: "Ἐν θυσίαις ἐγέραιρον καὶ ἁγίαις ἑκατόμβαις."

this to "God [o]f all things God-inspired" in his second edition [1899: 136 (v. 546)].) Jörg-Dieter Gauger (1998: 143) translated θεόπνευστος as "gottbeseelt."

Warfield's attempt to flatten θεόπνευστος into a designation of divine origination *simpliciter* fails to grasp the true sense in which the word is used. His emphasis on creatureliness speaks to his desire to tie the word's normal meaning to the idea of *origination*. (This was in keeping with his general approach to θεόπνευστος, beginning about 1900, or slightly earlier.) Bate and Collins, on the other hand, correctly understood the use of θεόπνευστος in the passage: the oracle basically calls God the "God of the living" (cf. Mt. 22:32 // Mk 12:27 // Lk. 20:38) in a way that highlights the fact that he is the source of life.[42]

3 The *Testament of Abraham*

The *Testament of Abraham* is a Jewish pseudepigraphon extant in two recensions—one long and one short—dubbed "A" and "B" respectively. The story in both recensions is that of an extraordinarily long-lived Abraham who finally must give up his life. Our focus is on rec. A, as that is where θεόπνευστος appears. The work almost certainly was composed in Greek (see Turner 1955; Delcor 1973: 32), although it is also extant in Coptic, Arabic, Ethiopic, Slavonic, and Romanian (see Denis 1970: 31–9; Allison 2003: 9–11).

In rec. A, Abraham refuses to comply with God's determination that he has reached the end of his days, and the author presents a series of amusing scenes of how Abraham's refusal plays out. Most scholars locate rec. A's composition in Egypt, based on a number of hints, not least of which are the supposed Egyptian elements in the judgment scene of chs 11–13.[43]

A once lively debate over which recension represents an earlier form of the work has mostly subsided, with the weight of opinion now fixed in favor of rec. A. In the past couple of decades, a new argument supporting this view has taken center stage, based on the (supposed) presence of a redactorial direction indicator in the *Tendenz* of

---

[42] In connection with the *Sibylline Oracles*, Warfield (1900: 94) is forced to admit that most scholars assign the θεόπνευστος passage to a Jewish author, but he is satisfied simply to register a range of doubt on the question, as if the traditional rendering of θεόπνευστος should be given the benefit of a doubt. (Warfield names "Bleck, Lücke, Grförrer, Ewald, Hilgenfeld, Schürer.") He seems to argue that, if *Sibylline Oracle* book 5 and Pseudo-Phocylides can be shown (in the relevant sections) to have been shaped by Christian [?] hands—citing "pretty good positive reason for supposing the Pseudo-Phokylidian poem to be in its entirety a Christian production"—then Cremer's dismissal of θεόπνευστος as "hellenistic" is undermined. (He does not consider the term's connectedness with Alexandria to threaten its suitability as a prescriptive concept for a Christian concept of Scripture: "Perhaps if we cannot call it a purely Christian term or yet, with Dr. Cremer, an exclusively Hellenistic one, we may venture to think of it, provisionally at least, as belonging to Alexandrian Greek" [103].) But that, of course, would not be an automatic conclusion, for if the words in question are Christian and not Jewish, that would not mean they are not "hellenistic." (The idea that the New Testament is free of "hellenism" was once common—e.g., cf. Friedrich 1964: 714.)

[43] Turner (1984: 221) writes, "Everything points to Egypt as the probable provenance of the book." See James (1892: 76); Delcor (1973: 67–9); Schmidt (1976); Munoa (1998: 123–6); Allison (2003: 32–3); Woschitz (2005: 478). Davila (2005: 204; cf. 203–4) finds ch. 13 "replete with Christian terminology." See Lee (2012: 93–4). On the judgment scene in the *Testament of Abraham*, see Reiser (1997: 123–9).

rec. B. To wit: scholars have increasingly come to see in rec. A a satirical, even comedic work, and to see in rec. B (correspondingly) a lack of comprehension or sympathy in relation to rec. A's satirical mode. Jared Ludlow (2002a: 29), for example, refers to "unmistakable comic elements" in rec. A, Lawrence Wills (1995: 254) characterizes the work as "lampoon[ing] the credulous genres beloved by many others," and Erich Gruen (2002: 187) writes that "the humor in this text is deliberate and persistent."[44] Ludlow's (2002a: 33) character sketch of the archangel Michael in rec. A presents a sample of this humor:

> Michael had to use the pretense of needing to relieve himself to leave Abraham's house and ascend to God to refuse his mission. He had to ask God how he could eat Abraham's banquet. He wept with his human counterparts at the drop of a tear, and knelt in prayer at Abraham's suggestion to raise the sinners Abraham had killed. Thus despite being the chief archangel, Michael repeatedly had to ask God how to proceed, seemed to be ignorant of some capabilities of angelic beings, and was beholden to the human Abraham's requests. In the end, after all these comic blunders, he failed in his mission and was replaced by Death.[45]

Rec. A's characterizations of Abraham and Death also appear to be spoofs on what those figures normally represent (cf. Ludlow 2002b: 11–12). In light of this view of rec. A, most scholars now recognize in rec. B an attempt to grapple *unapprovingly* with elements in rec. A that are not characteristic of serious hagiography (cf. Ludlow 2002b; 2005; Allison 2003: 23; Mirguet 2014).[46] Dale Allison (2003: 23), in fact, has collected a number of remarks from manuscript margins revealing a sharp reserve on the part of early readers toward rec. A's comic elements.

The tendentiousness of rec. B's attempt to put a straight face on the work shows through in enough places to suggest that the arc of development runs (at least) roughly from rec. A to rec. B.[47] I use the word "roughly," because a number of scholars continue

---

[44] Nickelsburg (1976b: 87) states that the author of the *Testament of Abraham* "has created a veritable parody of the biblical and traditional Abraham." Wills (2011: 142) refers to the work as a "satirical novella" as opposed to an "ideal novella."

[45] Dean-Otting (1984: 177) notes that the motif of the tour of the universe can be found in *4 Ezra* and *Pistis Sophia*, but that there the tour is given *after* the death of the individual. It may be that Abraham's insistence on receiving the tour *before* he dies is meant to be comical. Doran (1986: 288) wonders whether "heavenly tours" are "being parodied" in the *Testament of Abraham*. Scholars have noted that several aspects of this tale of Abraham seem to be modeled on a similar tale about Moses (cf. Denis 1970: 35; Loewenstamm 1986; Chazon 1985–6). Allison (2003: 24–5 [cf. 388]) lists the parallels "between RecLng. and traditions about the death of Moses." Of particular interest are the words "angels bury his body" (*T. Abr.* 20.11), with parallels in Philo, *Vit. Mos.* 2.291; Tg. Ps.-Jn. on Deut. 34:6; *Deut. Rab.* 11:10.

[46] This view appears also in Reed (2009: 209). Delcor (1973: 13–14) writes, "L'attitude du patriarche vis-à-vis du décret divin, en particulier, constitue une ligne de demarcation qui les rend totalement opposées dans leur ton et nous ne croyons pas que pareil changement ait pu se faire sans transition, surtout si là où s'opéra ce changement, une de nos deux recensions s'était déjà répandue."

[47] As Ludlow (2002a: 27) writes, both recensions contain elements parodying the testamentary genre, but rec. B contains them "most likely because it was drawing upon Recension A as a source." See Mirguet (2010: 264). On Christian elements in rec. B, see Heide (2012: 3–4, 40–1). MacRae (1976) argues for the Coptic *Apocalypse of Paul*'s dependence on rec. B or on a shared tradition. (The Coptic *Apocalypse of Paul* is found in a fourth-century codex in the Nag Hammadi library.)

to see signs of lateness in rec. A's vocabulary. Nigel Turner (1955: 222) judged rec. A's language to be "virtually medieval," although he thought an earlier edition from no "later than the third century A.D." might have existed.[48] Allison (2003: 16) lists ninety-three words and phrases that one "must ... suspect ... of being Christian and/ or medieval," yet he remains convinced that rec. A, for the most part, is older than rec. B. This is an arrangement many scholars now concede: rec. A represents an early version in form and substance, but its language was partly updated after a few centuries.

Another argument for the priority of rec. A is associated with George Nickelsburg and Ludlow. These scholars note that details in rec. A often serve a clear narrative purpose, while the same details in rec. B serve no corresponding narrative purpose. In rec. A, for example, Abraham's request for a tour of the world is "one of a series of procrastinations and refusals to die" (Nickelsburg 1976b: 89), while in rec. B it merely prolongs the story. And when the Abraham of rec. A refuses to follow Michael, the narrative payoff is that God is forced to send Death to do Michael's appointed task. In rec. B, Abraham never refuses to follow Michael, so Death's appearance is unprovoked and unnecessary (Nickelsburg 1976b: 90–1; see Ludlow 2002a: 152–80; Allison 2003: 13–14). As Ludlow (2002a: 119–20) notes, the crafter of rec. A built up a "'cause-effect' type plot ... to show Abraham's cunning and stubbornness advancing the events of the story," while rec. B "seems to have more disconnected episodes ... because it adapted these events from Recension A but without the same narrative context."[49]

Apart from the elements of refitted vocabulary, rec. A is usually dated to the first or second century CE (see Denis 1970: 36–7). A number of scholars are confident that the text has been at least partly Christianized.[50] Those who suppose this happened at the work's formative stage are forced to push its writing toward the latter two-thirds of this timeframe. Some interpreters, however, are less convinced of a Christian overlay[51] and place the text in the first century. Martha Himmelfarb (2009: 17), in fact, refers to a *scholarly consensus* for a first-century date.[52] Whether she speaks advisedly, there is the matter of the work's possible dependence on the gospel of Matthew, a writing that could scarcely be much earlier than 80 CE.[53]

---

[48] The apparent lateness of rec. A's language once led to a greater diversity among scholars' views of the priority issue. This shows up clearly in several essays in the 1976 volume *Studies on the Testament of Abraham*—see esp. Kraft (1976). Nordheim (1980: 142) argues that rec. B is nearer the original—see also Schmidt (1986). On the language of the *Testament of Abraham* (rec. A), see Delcor (1973: 28–32).

[49] Allison (2003: 20) lists sixteen places where rec. B "seems secondary" to rec. A.

[50] Allison (2003: 19) argues that the "Christian contribution" to rec. A. is more than "superficial," and that ch. 20 "is rather Christian from beginning to end" (30; cf. 386).

[51] Reed (2009: 210) writes, "Overtly Christian material [in the *Testament of Abraham*] is minor in scope and incidental to the plot and main themes."

[52] On the date of the *Testament of Abraham* (rec. A), see Jansen (1980: 200). Kerkeslager (2006: 67 n. 92) apparently dates the work later: he lists it as a work of "uncertain" date from "the renewed Jewish communities in Egypt and Cyrenaica"—communities whose renewal he places in the third century CE.

[53] Cf. *T. Abr.* (A) 11.3 with Mt. 7:13. On rec. A's apparent reliance on Matthew, see Pennington (2007: 120–4). Fishburne (1970) has argued for Paul's reliance on *T. Abr.* (A) 13.11–13, but others trace the dependence in the other direction (Allison 2003: 277–9, 287, 291; Davila 2005: 204). Martin (1999: 141) argues that 1 Peter knows the *Testament of Abraham*. Davila (2005: 199–207) thinks it likely that the *Testament of Abraham* is extensively christianized, and he is followed in

3.1 The Meaning of θεόπνευστος

The word θεόπνευστος appears toward the end of rec. A. Abraham has finally died, and a great company of angels[54] sets out to anoint his body:

> 20.10 καὶ εὐθέως παρέστη Μιχαὴλ ὁ ἀρχάγγελος μετὰ πλήθους ἀγγέλων· καὶ ἦραν τὴν τιμίαν αὐτοῦ ψυχὴν ἐν ταῖς χερσὶν αὐτῶν ἐν σινδόνι θεοϋφάντῳ·
> 20.11 καὶ μυρίσμασι θεοπνεύστοις καὶ ἀρώμασιν ἐκήδευσαν δὲ τὸ σῶμα τοῦ δικαί ου᾽ ἕως τρίτης ἡμέρας τῆς τελειώσεως αὐτοῦ· (Schmidt 1986: 166)[55]

> 20.10 And immediately Michael the archangel stood beside him with multitudes of angels, and they bore his honorable soul in their hands in divinely woven linen, 20.11 And they tended the body of the righteous one with theopneustic ointments and perfumes until the third day after his death. (Author's translation)[56]

Nearly everyone who has looked into the matter notes that translating θεόπνευστος as "inspired" does not fit the context, and we are met with an array of guesses as to how the author used the term. Francis Schmidt (1986: 167) renders θεόπνευστος as "d'une senteur divine." G. H. Box (1927: 36) neutralizes the term by rendering it as "exquisite." W. A. Craigie (1896: 201), Michael Stone (1972: 55), E. P. Sanders (1983: 895), and Annette Yoshiko Reed (2013: 1695) all render it simply as "divine." Allison (2003: 382) settles on "divinely-smelling." He explains as follows:

> θεόπνευστος … matches the θεοῦφαντος of the previous verse and carries something close to its usual sense, "divinely inspired"; cf. *Sib. Or.* 5:308, 407; Ps.-Phoc. 129 (an interpolation); 2 Tim 3:16. If Abraham's soul is wrapped in a heavenly garment, his body is enveloped in ointments made in heaven. One is reminded of the hagiographical motif of a supernatural odor attending the death or burial of a saint; cf. Antonius the Hagiographer, *Vit. Symeonis Stylitis* 28; *Dorm. BMV* 48; Vatican Gr. 1982, ed. Wenger, p. 230; Cyril of Scythopolis, *Vit. Joannis Hesychastae* 17; Gregory the Great, *Dial.* 4.15–17, 28; John of Thessalonica, *Dorm. BVM* A 23, ed. Jugie, p. 396; etc. (Allison 2003: 401)[57]

Mathias Delcor (1973: 172) makes a somewhat odd remark about the word in question: "θεόπνευστος absent de la LXX prend ici le sens d''ange', qui semble unique dans la grécité." His actual translation, however, remains in line with the established tradition: "Avec des parfums divins et des aromates, ils oignirent le corps du juste

---

this view by Bauckham (2009: 123 n. 70). Allison (2003: 38–9) argues against NT knowledge of the *Testament of Abraham*.

[54] The theme of angels performing funerary duties in the absence of human attendants appears in a number of pseudepigraphic texts. E.g., cf. *LAE* 40.1–2 (see Arbel 2012: 68–9, 83).

[55] The text printed in James (1892) is identical (apart from the accents), except for the inclusion of Abraham's name.

[56] Sanders (1983: 895) supplied "Abraham" where I supply "one," as he followed the Greek text from Stone (1972: 54).

[57] For additional examples of a supernatural fragrance at a saint's death, see Atchley (1909: 109–10); Nir (2004: 38, 42).

Abraham jusqu'au troisième jour après sa mort." Nigel Turner (1984: 421) translates θεόπνευστος as "divinely-scented" (cf. Allison), while Kaufmann Kohler (1895: 590-1) paraphrases the passage as saying that Abraham's body was "anointed with paradisiacal incense." It is worth noting that Warfield (1900: 107-8) did not attempt to fit the word "inspired" into this context—he claimed that a meaning "not far from 'God-given'" or "God-provided" makes the most sense. But we should want to ask Warfield and some of the others cited above: Why would ointments and herbs (of all things) be described as theopneustic, especially if the point of that description is simply to signify their divine origin? That a word meaning "divine" should be used in this context should not surprise us, but is θεόπνευστος really such a word? In what way are the ointments and herbs imagined (even if only figuratively) to be "God-breathed" or "God-breathing"? Under these presumed meanings, the term seems to fit the application rather poorly.

3.2 Theopneustic Ointments

In spite of the primary witnesses he gives for illustrating the suggested "hagiographical motif," there are problems with Allison's claim for "something close" to the "usual sense" of θεόπνευστος as "divinely inspired." Among other things, this rendering leaves an important contextual clue out of its account: the reference in the text to "three days," and the connection between that three-day period and the "*theopneustic* ointments and perfumes."[58] While the pairing of θεόπνευστος with θεόφαντος is indeed notable, the function of the former term in this context more likely has to do with the well-known motif of a three-day waiting period after the soul's release from the body. If the soul is allotted three days in which it might return, then Abraham's body obviously must be preserved for three days against the effects of death (see Delcor 1973: 62, 173-4). What better preservative than heavenly "life-giving" ointments? The key detail is not that the ointments are administered by angels, but rather that they are administered for three days, and three days *only*.[59] The ointments evidently are not regular burial ointments, nor are they *unguentaria*.[60] They are something no longer required after "the third day," when there is no more need to preserve the body from decay.[61]

A well-known example of the body being preserved from decay so that its spirit might return to it appears at the beginning of Plato's presentation of the myth of Er in book 10 of the *Republic* (613e–621d). Plato relates that Er's corpse was preserved

---

[58] Kohler's (1895: 590–1) paraphrase inexplicably cuts the connection: he states that Abraham's body was "anointed with paradisiacal incense, and after three days buried *under the tree of Mamre*." The reference to "three days" is missing from a pair of Greek manuscripts (G and J), as well as from the Romanian version. See Gaster (1893: 225–6).

[59] On the three-day waiting period, see Box (1927: 36–7 n. 4); Allison (2003: 402).

[60] Although I say these are not regular burial ointments, it is unnecessary to suppose that their preservative function differs from that of ointments regularly applied shortly after death. On the use of burial ointments and *unguentaria*, see *Lev. Rab.* 18.1; *Eccl. Rab.* 12.6; Safrai (1987: 776); McCane (2003: 31–2, 48–9); Hachlili (2005: 479–83). The precise role of unguentaria is still unknown—see Anderson-Stojanović (1987: 116). See Allison (2003: 400).

[61] Mirguet (2010: 272) refers to the "lavish care" given Abraham's body as exceptional, but fails to account for the three-day period.

for twelve days, while his spirit was visiting the heavenly realm.[62] Although the other slain bodies from the battlefield were all in a state of decay ten days after the battle, Er's body showed no signs of decay, and indeed his spirit returned to his body as it lay on his funeral pyre:

> Er, the son of Armenius, by race a Pamphylian … once upon a time was slain in battle, and when the corpses were taken up on the tenth day already decayed, was found intact (ἀναιρεθέντων δεκαταίων τῶν νεκρῶν ἤδη διεφαρμένων, ὑγιὴς μὲν ἀνῃρέθη), and having been brought home, at the moment of his funeral, on the twelfth day as he lay upon the pyre, revived, and after coming to life related what, he said, he had seen in the world beyond. (Plato, *Republic* 614b [trans. Shorey 1980: 491–3])

In the 1940s, Grace Harriet Macurdy (1942) noted numerous points of similarity between the *Testament of Abraham* and the myth of Er—so numerous and remarkable are the similarities, in fact, that one is tempted to posit the former's direct reliance on the latter.[63] While such reliance is entirely possible, Macurdy (1942: 226) doubted it: she wished "not … to imply that the derivation was direct and that the writer of this apocalyptic portion of the [*Testament of Abraham*] was acquainted with the *Republic* … at first hand."

Robert Kraft mentions a detail from Homer's *Iliad* that roughly parallels the thought found in the *Testament of Abraham*, although it intriguingly forms a closer parallel to my reading of the text than to the usual way of reading it. He points out that Apollo, following Zeus' orders, personally prepared the body of the fallen Sarpedon before giving it into the hands of Sleep and Death (*Il.* 16.667–84). These preparations included washing the body in river water, anointing it with ambrosia, and clothing it in "immortal vesture" (16.670, 681—see Kraft 1976: 63).[64] As Kraft notes, this further parallels the way Apollo and Aphrodite preserve Hector's fallen body from decomposition, even when Achilles is determined to destroy it utterly (*Il.* 23.185–91). The idea of using ambrosia as a funerary ointment is known from the *Iliad*. Aphrodite anointed Hector's dead body with *ambrosial* rose oil (ῥοδόεντι δὲ χρῖεν ἐλαίῳ / ἀμβροσίῳ [*Il.* 23.186–87]),[65] so as to preserve the body from damage when it is dragged behind Achilles' chariot. And Thetis pours ambrosia and nectar into the nostrils of the deceased Patroclus' nostrils, to prevent decomposition of the body (*Il.* 19.37–39). Doukaina Zanni compares this to Artemis' action of applying ambrosia to the head of the sacrificed Iphigenia (= Iphimede), "[so that her] flesh would be

---

[62] Dean-Otting (1984: 203) briefly compared our pseudepigraphon's Abraham with Plato's Er. See Nickelsburg (1976a: 27). On the myth of Er, see Morgan (2000: 201–10).

[63] Mihai (2010: 574) lists a number of characters from Greek narratives whose disembodied souls receive tours of the heavenly regions: "Strepsiades, Cleonymus, Er the Pamphylian, Empedotimus, the king of Aristotle, Timarchus and Thespesius."

[64] Von Bothmer (1981: 66–7) writes that "the conceit, the lifting of a naked, despoiled body [of Sarpedon] by Sleep and Death, initiates an artistic tradition that can be followed through the scenes of the dead Meleager straight to the deposition of Christ." See Roscher (1883: 59).

[65] On ambrosial rose oil, see Roscher (1883: 40).

steadfast forever" (Hesiod, *Catalogue of Women* frag. 19 line 23 [trans. Most 2007: 69]; see Zanni 2008: 395).

The idea that the spirit cannot return to its body *unless* that body had been preserved from corruption also parallels what we find in Jewish sources: the body's lack of decay is what makes it possible for the spirit to return. The advantage of *this* point of comparison, of course, lies in the three-day period of nondecay commonly assumed in Jewish and Christian contexts (see below), while the period of nondecay in Plato's myth is much longer.[66] The Er legend is thus illustrative, but not necessary, for understanding what takes place in the *Testament of Abraham*.

That the body must remain in reanimable condition for a three-day period is implied in a number of Jewish and Christian sources. In his discussion of this *Testament of Abraham* passage, Allison (2003: 401) lists seven Jewish and Christian texts that support the notion of a three-day embargo against bodily decay: (1) in the *Testament of Job*, Job's body remains unburied for three days (52.1–2; 53.7),[67] (2) in the *Apoc. Zeph.* 4.7, it takes the angels three days to escort the ungodly to their final abode, (3) in *Dormition of the Blessed Mary* 48, the angels sing for three days after the death of Mary, (4) in *David, Symeon, and George of Lesbos* 9, the titular David says he will depart "after the third day," (5) *Semachot* 8.1 recommends a three-day period of examining a grave to insure that the interred body was really dead, (6) according to *Gen. Rab.* 100.7, the soul tries, for three days, to reenter the body (cf. *y. Moʾed Qatan* 3.5; *Lev. Rab.* 18.1; Kraemer 2000: 83; Poirier 2014), and (7) in *4 Bar.* 9.12–14, a (heavenly) voice of warning held off burial, predicting the soul's reanimation of the body, which happened as promised "after three days." Naturally the impressiveness of these seven parallels is uneven (e.g., [2] is hardly as significant as [5], [6], or [7]), but together they say something rather firm about a shared belief.[68] Allison's list of parallels can easily be expanded. That the soul might return during an initial three-day period is supported, for example, by Eve's falling "as if dead" for three days in the Adamic pseudepigrapha (see Stone 2002: 20). That idea also informs at least three NT references to circumstances surrounding a given individual's death: (1) Jesus's purposeful procrastination in visiting Lazarus's entombed body to a time beyond the three-day window of opportunity, apparently to increase the miraculousness of Lazarus's revivification,[69] (2) the three-and-a-half-days-dead status of the "two witnesses" in Revelation 11,[70] and (3) the New Testament's reference to Christ's

---

[66] There is evidence in Plutarch *Lyc.* 27.2 that a twelve-day period was perhaps not so exceptional for a Greco-Roman context: Lycurgus "set apart only a short time for mourning, eleven days; on the twelfth, they were to sacrifice to Demeter and cease their sorrowing" (trans. Perrin 1914: 287).

[67] Allison notes that this is "consistent with Greek practice." It was standard Greco-Roman practice for the body to lie in state the first day and to be carried out of the house before sunrise on the third day. See Cicero, *De leg.* 2.66; Rohde (1925: 165); Kurtz and Boardman (1971: 144–6).

[68] Kraemer (2000: 126) writes, "Whatever the accepted law [concerning the mourning ritual], the prominence of those positions that seek to mark and protect the three days ritually is unmistakable."

[69] The text implies a significant difference between raising a body four days dead and raising a body only two days dead. In fact, the onlookers' warning that Lazarus's body has begun to stink seems to be tied to the supposition, on their part, that Jesus had waited too long.

[70] As with Lazarus, the miraculousness of the witnesses' revival is tied to their having remained dead longer than three days.

resurrection "on the third day" as a fulfillment of Scripture (1 Cor. 15:4), taking Ps. 16:10 as the passage Paul has in mind.[71] Allison (2003: 402) further notes that the soul's three-day stay near the body of the deceased "was a common belief in Byzantine Christianity, and it is also attested in Zoroastrian sources (e.g. *Hadhokht Nask* 2:3–20; *Vendidad* 19:28; *Menog i Khrad* 2:114)" (see Freistedt 1928: 53–72). It is worth noting Israel Knohl's (2008: 150–1) reconstruction of the phrase "after three days, live" in the so-called *Vision of Gabriel*, although that reconstruction has been challenged.

Thus the "theopneustic" ointments that the angels administer "until the third day" appear to function as "life-giving" preservatives to keep Abraham's body in good repair, in case his soul should return to it. Θεόπνευστος therefore bears a vivificationist sense. It is worth noting, however, the disparity between how, on the one hand, *Sib. Or.* 5.407 (see above) and Porphyry's *De antr.* 10 (see below) use θεόπνευστος/θεόπνοος to denote the giving of life in terms of initial ensoulment and how, on the other hand, the *Testament of Abraham* uses that term to describe an ointment that merely keeps the body in animable condition. The former refers to a force that directly animates, while the latter refers to a force that preserves the body *for the possibility* of animation. As the former use is more widely established, it would appear either that the latter is meant in a less literal sense or that its true meaning in that context actually invokes the idea of the body's readiness for ensoulment. It should also be noted, however, that the notion of anointing a corpse with a "life-giving" ointment comports perfectly with the references we noted in Homer and Hesiod regarding an embalming medium. Thus the use of θεόπνευστος as a reference to a life-giving aspect also makes perfect sense without appealing to the tradition of a three-day embargo against decay.

The *Testament of Abraham* clearly does not use θεόπνευστος to denote the idea of verbal or epistemic inspiration. A meaning having to do with the special *life-giving* properties of the ointments and herbs—properties like those associated with ambrosia—makes far better sense.

---

[71] This last reference might require a word of explanation. As Hill (1967) argues, the literary design Paul has in mind is most likely found in reading Ps. 16:10 (= LXX Ps. 15:10 ὅτι οὐκ ἐγκαταλείψεις τὴν ψυχήν μου εἰς ᾅδην οὐδὲ δώσεις τὸν ὅσιόν σου ἰδεῖν διαφθοράν ["that you will not leave my soul in Hades or allow your holy one to see decay"]) through the lens of the idea we have been considering. See Poirier (2014). For Christ to be raised "after three days" (as 1 Cor. 15:4 states) fulfills the promise in Ps. 16:10 (cited according to its septuagintal version in Acts 2:27 and 13:33) that God will "not allow his holy one to see decay"—that is, "after three days" is interpreted not so much as "*not less than* three days," but rather as "*not more than* three days." (A similar "no more than" emphasis appears in Jesus's reference to rebuilding the "Temple" in three days [Mt. 26:61 // Mk 14:58; Jn 2:19].) Note that, in antiquity, the expression "after three days" (Mt. 27:63; Mk 8:31) was normally construed as a period *less than* 72 hours. Cf., e.g., Drabkin's (1950: xix–xx) explanation of Caelius Aurelianus' language in medically prescribing changes to one's regimen: "an important element of time is the *diatritus* (διάτριτος), which I have rendered '(end of a) three-day period,' though more exactly, by our method of counting, it represented the termination of a period of two full days."

4 Vettius Valens's *Anthologies*

The term θεόπνευστος is used by the astrologer Vettius Valens (120 CE–*ca.* 185 CE) in the final book of his *Anthologies*. This work is the longest astrological guidebook to survive from the ancient world, but it is also the most inaccessible astrological text in terms of its technical aspect and displays a very large vocabulary.[72] Valens' text cast a long shadow over the science of astrology and was in continual use until the Renaissance.[73] It consists of eight books filled with some 130 actual horoscopes—most belonging to the upper crust of society (see MacMullen 1971: 109–10)—used to illustrate principles and procedures, along with a book of random notes on the science of horoscope-casting in general. The word θεόπνευστος appears in this ninth book.

To determine the date of Valens' writing, O. Neugebauer and H. B. van Hoesen (1959: 176–9) present a series of tables on the terminal years of the persons discussed in Valens' casuistry. (Valens' lasting contribution to astrology lay in relation to the birth-hour's effect on longevity. See King 2004: 666–7.) According to their analysis, the *Anthologies* was probably published in sections, beginning in the early 150s CE. A presumption that one or two later cases were interpolated leads to a publication date for the latest sections in the 170s CE. A more purist presumption that all the cases are original (but that Valens perhaps slowed his research in the last decade or so) leads to a date in the 180s or 190s CE.[74] Mark Riley (1987: 235 n. 1), for one, is of the view that Valens lived into the 180s.

The word θεόπνευστος appears in the preface to the final book of the *Anthologies*: "For not everything humans attain is wholly corruptible and wretched, but there is wrought in us something divine and theopneustic" (οὐ γὰρ φθαρτὰ πάντα καὶ μοχθηρὰ ἔλαχον οἱ ἄνθρωποι, ἔστι δέ τι καὶ θεῖον ἐν ἡμῖν θεόπνευστον δημιούργημα [*Anth.* 9.1.37 (Greek text from Pingree 1986: 317)]).[75] The longer passage is as follows:

> For not everything humans attain is wholly corruptible and wretched, but there is wrought in us something divine and theopneustic. The incorruptible and all-pervading air around us streams temporary immortality into us at appointed and fixed times. As the divine Orpheus says:
> "The soul of man takes root in the aether."
> And elsewhere,
> "By drawing in air, we harvest the divine soul."
> elsewhere,
> "The immortal and undecaying soul is given by God."
> elsewhere,
> "The soul, of all things, is immortal, the body mortal." (Author's translation)

---

[72] On Vettius Valens' language and vocabulary, see Warning (1909).

[73] Cramer (1954: 190) writes, "Next to Ptolemy's[, Valens'] writings … have been copied wholly or in part more often than those of almost any other astrologer of antiquity." See Pingree (2001); King (2004: 668). Pingree (2001: 10) notes that Valens was a source mentioned in Rhetorius' (sixth- or seventh-century) *Compendium*.

[74] See Neugebauer (1954). See the discussion of Valens in Cramer (1954: 185); Gundel and Gundel (1966: 216–21); von Stuckrad (1996: 82–4); Komorowska (2004); Beck (2014); Lloyd (2018: 282–5).

[75] Θεόπνευστον is found there on line 15 and in Kroll (1908: 330 line 19).

The way Valens contrasts having a theopneustic element within oneself with being "wholly corruptible and wretched" suggests that θεόπνευστος has something to do with incorruptibility. And so we see that Valens uses θεόπνευστος to begin a brief discussion on the immortality of the soul/spirit. Valens supports his view with four brief quotations from "the divine Orpheus," all of them expressing, in so many words, what the third quotation says explicitly: "The immortal and undecaying soul is given by God" (see Festugière 1932: 120–7). It is the Stoic aspect of this divine gift of the "life-giving spirit" that the word θεόπνευστος expresses in this context.[76]

Valens was not the only astrologer to express these views. Manilius promoted a similar mixture of astrology and Stoic philosophy:[77]

> For I shall sing of God, silent-minded monarch of nature, who, permeating sky and land and sea, controls with uniform compact the mighty structure; how the entire universe is alive in the mutual concord of its elements and is driven by the pulse of reason, since a single spirit [or *breath*] dwells in all its parts and, speeding through all things, nourishes the world and shapes it like a living creature. (*Astronomica* 2.60–66 [trans. Goold 1977: 87–9])

This paean to the life-giving divinity touches the same themes as Valens' quotations from "the divine Orpheus"—the most important, for our purposes, being that of vivification itself.

Thus Valens' use of θεόπνευστος supports the vivificationist meaning found in other pre-Origenist writings. Although he spent part of his life in Alexandria (and perhaps wrote the *Anthologies* there [see Komorowska 2004: 15, 18]), the verbal-inspirationist meaning of θεόπνευστος had not yet arisen there or was unable to overcome Valens' association of that word with an older, vivificationist meaning. This supports the claim that a vivificationist understanding of θεόπνευστος enjoyed exclusive rule before Origen co-opted the word to denote the verbal inspiration of Scripture. It also suggests that a vivificationist understanding held sway beyond Jewish and Christian contexts.

A word of speculation might be in order as to why Valens used the spelling otherwise associated with Jewish and Christian writings (θεόπνευστος), and not the one associated with Greco-Roman writings (θεόπνους). It would probably be wrong to suppose that the divide between the spellings always lined up with the divide between groups of writings, but it is worth noting, in this connection, that Valens was clearly aware of Jewish and Christian tradition.[78]

---

[76] On the "purer Stoicism" of Valens' system, see Cumont (1912: 170).

[77] Klauck (2003: 243) writes that "the close connection made in [Manilius'] work between traditional astrological ideas and Stoic philosophy is possibly Manilius' own achievement." If so, then it may be that Manilius' "achievement" was taken over and perfected by Valens.

[78] Kroll (1906: 152) lists a number of Greek terms that Valens shares with the Septuagint and New Testament, including the term θεόπνευστος. Warning (1909: 32) writes, "Legentibus imprimis tanta verborum antiquorum copia notabilis est, sed qui numerum verborum eorum, quae apud ceteros Alexandrinae aetatis scriptores occurrunt—veluti ea quae Helbingius e LXX vel Nägeli e copia

5 Pseudo-Plutarch, *Placita Philosophorum*

One of the more important appearances of θεόπνευστος for Warfield's overall argument is in the so-called *Placita Philosophorum*, a doxography of cosmological (books 1–3) and anthropological material (books 4–5). Although not penned by Plutarch, this doxography was passed down as part of his *Moralia* (at 904.2). Θεόπνευστος appears there (in 5.1.2) in a passage purporting to represent (or perhaps derive from) the medical writer Herophilus (*ca.* 335 BCE–280 BCE). Warfield (1900: 104) renders the passage as follows: "Herophilus says that theopneustic dreams come by necessity, but natural ones from the soul's imagery of what is fitting to it and its consequences."[79] There has been a lengthy (and curious) tradition of supposing that θεόπεμπτος (= "God-sent") originally stood in the text, with that word figuring almost universally in scholarly references to this passage (not least in Cremer's [1880: 6.746] discussion of θεόπνευστος),[80] but Warfield argues convincingly that the originality of θεόπνευστος is certain (see below), and that this appearance of the word exemplifies how it was understood about the time 2 Timothy was written. He also claims that this establishes that θεόπνευστος was known outside Christian circles.

Falsely attributed writings typically postdate the lives of those to whom they are attributed, but while the final form of the *Placita Philosophorum* might postdate Plutarch, much of the material it contains certainly *predates* him. (Whether this appearance of θεόπνευστος belongs in our survey is not a matter of the *Placita Philosophorum*'s proper placement, but of the text-critical dimensions of the word's use.) The work came to be associated with Plutarch sometime after his death.[81] According to the tradition history worked out by Hermann Diels (1879) in the nineteenth century (and more recently affirmed, in large part, by Jaap Mansfeld and David Runia [1997]), the *Placita Philosophorum* reworks an earlier (perhaps fuller) doxography which left its traces in a number of other writings as well.[82] Diels outlined this tradition history by tracing the original doxography (which he called the *Vetusta Placita*) to the first century BCE.[83] His goal was to reconstruct the source of the material found in this section of Plutarch's *Moralia*, on the basis of its shared wording with Stobaeus and Theodoret (as parallel

---

verborum Pauli apostolic affert—cum Valentis comparabit, apud eos non minorem numerum esse inveniet." In this connection, Leicht (2011: 279–80) wonders whether the references to the Sabbath in *Anth.* 1.10 might be authentic (*contra* Pingree). On Abraham's reputation as an astrologer, see Feldman (1993: 187, 214).

[79] Parenthetical glosses removed.

[80] See the text cited in Bluhme (1906: 52); Pease (1923: 572 n. *ad* line 1); Dodds (1951: 124 n. 28); Kessels (1969: 414).

[81] Although this passage is now regularly assigned to "Pseudo-Plutarch," Warfield treats the passage as genuinely Plutarchian, but allows for either view. The question of whether the author should be identified as Pseudo-Plutarch has little bearing on the basic text's chronology, as the true author of the text worked at least as early as Plutarch (first–second century CE), and possibly even a century earlier. Ziegler (1951: 880) argues that the *Eclogae* was published under Plutarch's name because it was found among his papers after his death.

[82] See the chapter on "The Sources for Aëtius: Ps.Plutarch and His Tradition" in Mansfeld and Runia (1997: 121–95) and the stemma showing Mansfeld and Runia's refinements of Diels (328).

[83] See the chart in Diels (1879: 249). Diels dates the *Vetusta Placita* on the basis of the latest philosopher it mentions: Xenarchus of Seleucia (*ca.* 80/75 BCE to *ca.* 1 CE). See Mansfeld and Runia (1997: 319).

branches in the tradition), and with Pseudo-Galen (as a pendant branch).[84] Diels found cause, however, to posit a common ancestor of these works, more recent than the *Vetusta Placita*. The *Placita Philosophorum* he dates to about 150 CE, shortly before its quotation (about 177 CE) in a work by Athenagoras (Diels 1879: 64–6; see Mansfeld and Runia 1997: 124–5). Thanks to Theodoret, we know it to be a work by someone named "Aetius" (see Mansfeld and Runia 1997: 77).[85]

5.1 The Genuineness of the θεόπνευστος Reading

Whether θεόπνευστος stood in the *Vetusta Placita* is impossible to tell, but the chronological profile of the word's other uses suggests it did not.[86] (We are much better prepared to meet that word in a second-century CE writing than in something from the first century BCE.) We are seeking, however, to identify the reading originally found in the *Placita Philosophorum*, and not the ultimate source of that reading.[87] The first question before us is whether to stand with Cremer and take θεόπεμπτος as the original reading of the second-century CE text, or with Warfield, and read θεόπνευστος. Warfield devotes considerable space to debunking Cremer's contention that θεόπνευστος is textually suspect: he emphasizes that θεόπεμπτος is not found in *any* extant manuscript of the *Placita Philosophorum* but appears only in two manuscripts of a later work that used this text as a source—that is, the Pseudo-Galenic *Historia Philosophiae*.[88] Notwithstanding the actual shape of the manuscript tradition, Cremer (1880: 184) had argued, on Daniel Wyttenbach's supposed authority, that θεόπεμπτος originally stood in the text and that θεόπνευστος was introduced by a later Christian scribe. Warfield (1900: 95–6) showed, however, that Cremer had misread Wyttenbach and that the latter, in fact, did *not* support the θεόπεμπτος reading (see Wyttenbach 1797: 650).

Warfield's argument is that we need to give the manuscript tradition its due and that the θεόπεμπτος reading really has nothing going for it: *every* manuscript reads θεόπνευστος.[89] There is perhaps room to wonder whether Warfield is right to make Wyttenbach's *non*-acceptance of that reading sound like a text-critical argument. After all, Christian scribes under the spell of a later Alexandrian understanding of the term

---

[84] See the stemma for Diels's source theory in Mansfeld and Runia (1997: 4). Cf. the stemma in Diels (1879: 40). Mansfeld and Runia (1997: 4) note that Diels's view of Pseudo-Galen as dependent on Pseudo-Plutarch was anticipated by Francesco Patrizi in 1571. But cf. Kessels (1969: 414), who seems to assume that Pseudo-Galen is *not* dependent on Pseudo-Plutarch.

[85] On Aetius, see Dorandi (1989).

[86] I say this in spite of Mansfeld and Runia's (1997: 189) claim that the author of the *Placita Philosophorum* "never takes the trouble to paraphrase a longer text in his own words; he either transcribes or excises."

[87] The copy of the *Placita Philosophorum* found in the third-century CE Antinoopolis papyri has a lacuna at this point. See Barns and Zilliacus (1960: 78).

[88] This matter represents another change of mind for Warfield: eleven years earlier, he had argued that the text of "Plutarch" is "probably corrupt, and the true reading is perhaps θεοπέμπτους" (Warfield 1889: 395).

[89] For a discussion of the manuscripts of the *Placita Philosophorum*, see Mansfeld and Runia (1997: 173–5).

could have changed the text.[90] But shouldn't we (with Warfield) demand at least a *hint* of evidence that that happened? As I try to show below, Warfield's argument gets the better of the text-critical debate.

According to Warfield (1900: 95–6), his predecessors privileged the speculative θεόπεμπτος reading to a degree inconsistent with its merits:

> Wyttenbach has transferred [Christian Daniel] Beck's note on τῶν ὀνείρων τοὺς μὲν to θεοπέμπτους. It is this clause and not θεοπέμπτους that Beck professes to have got out of the Moscow MS. and Galen: θεοπέμπτους he presents merely as a pure conjecture founded on the one consideration that θεοπνεύστους has a flavor of Christian scribe about it; and he does not venture to put θεοπέμπτους into the text. ... The reading θεοπέμπτους was merely a conjecture of Beck's, founded solely on his notion that θεοπνεύστους was a purely Christian term, and possessing no diplomatic basis whatsoever. Accordingly it has not found its way into the printed text of Plutarch: all editions, with one exception, down to and including those of Dübner-Döhner (Didot's *Bibliotheca*) of 1856 and Bernardakis (Teubner's series) of 1893 read θεοπνεύστους.[91]

Having (rightly) called out an earlier generation's inattention to detail, Warfield (1900: 96) turns to the "new face … put on the matter" by Diels's *Doxographi Graeci* (1879: 15), which advances the θεόπεμπτος reading on the grounds of its (supposed) use by Pseudo-Galen. This amounts to an admission, on Warfield's part, that there is more to Cremer's position than sheer speculation and misreading. Diels (like Beck) found cause for reading θεόπεμπτος in Pseudo-Galen, but Warfield (1900: 97) would have none of this "excursion into 'higher criticism'":

> The key to the situation, with Diels, lies in the reading of the Pseudo-Galen: for as an excerpt from the [Pseudo?-] Plutarch the Pseudo-Galen becomes a valuable witness to its text, and is treated in this case indeed as a determinative witness, inasmuch as the whole MS. transmission of [Pseudo?-] Plutarch, so far as known, reads here θεοπνεύστους. Editing θεοπέμπτους in Pseudo-Galen, Diels edits it also, on that sole documentary ground, in [Pseudo?-] Plutarch.

Warfield contends that Diels unfairly made it appear that the θεόπεμπτος reading represents the whole of the Pseudo-Galenic manuscript tradition, when in fact it is attested in only two manuscripts. Warfield (1900: 99) then aligns the difficulty (as he sees it) of affirming a minority reading in Pseudo-Galen with the difficulty (as he sees it) of allowing Pseudo-Galen's reading to correct the Plutarchian manuscript

---

[90] Warfield (1900: 101) claims θεόπνευστος is "a rare word and one suggested to a dull or inattentive scribe by nothing." But the word can hardly be called "rare" in the time when Christian copyists busied themselves with classical texts (like Plutarch), and the thesis of its substitution has little need to posit "a dull or inattentive scribe." Warfield further argued that the substitution of θεόπνευστος for θεόπεμπτος would not support Cremer's larger argument regarding θεόπνευστος but rather would show that scribes regarded the terms as synonymous.

[91] It might be noted that Holtzmann (1880: 440) accepts the θεόπνευστος reading.

tradition: "Which is most likely,—that θεοπνεύστους in the [Pseudo?-]Plutarch originated in the pious fraud of a Christian scribe?—or that θεοπέμπτους in the text of Pseudo-Galen edited by Diels originated in the error of a careless scribe?" He objects that Diels's view of matters is beset by the "unlikelihood" that a scribe would deliberately change the text: "deliberate corruption of texts is relatively rare and not to be assumed without good reason" (Warfield 1900: 99).

Admittedly, there are a few problems with Warfield's reasoning on this score—some of them unsurprising for the time in which he wrote. The contention that "deliberate corruption of texts is relatively rare" sounds particularly hollow in the light of today's text-critical sensibilities.[92] Still, if we are honest with Warfield's complaints about Diels's proceeding, we must admit he makes some excellent points, particularly where it matters most. On the grounds of accepted text-critical principles, the θεόπνευστος reading has a much stronger case than the θεόπεμπτος reading. (This appears to be recognized by Heinrich von Staden [1989: 386], who prints θεοπνεύστους in his collection of Herophilean fragments.) The deciding factor, in my view, is that positing the priority of θεόπεμπτος would require θεόπνευστος to have crept into *two* manuscript traditions independently—that is, into both Pseudo-Plutarch and Pseudo-Galen.[93] (That is, unless we imagine a scribe of the Pseudo-Galen tradition restoring θεόπεμπτος on the grounds of its presence in [now lost] manuscripts of Pseudo-Plutarch.) It will not do to assign this occurrence of θεόπνευστος a late date on the basis of Diels's forced view, and the fact that θεόπεμπτος appears only as a minority reading in a source-critically *pendant* work presents weighty grounds for affirming the lateness of the reading. Although Warfield stands in the minority with his acceptance of θεόπνευστος, the evidence is clearly on his side. We must make sense of the text as we have it.

5.2 The Meaning of θεόπνευστος in Pseudo-Plutarch

I referred above to a "first question" we must answer, and so it follows that there is a second question. That question has to do with the function (or meaning) of θεόπνευστος in Pseudo-Plutarch.

As noted already, Warfield translates the passage in which the term appears as follows: "Herophilus says that theopneustic dreams come by necessity, but natural ones from the soul's imagery of what is fitting to it and its consequences." Warfield assumes that, for Herophilus, the former type of dream differs from the latter by dint of its (supposed) inspired nature. Unfortunately, however, he fails to discuss the sequential thoughts in the continuation of Herophilus' view in the Pseudo-Plutarch passage. The full Herophilean excerpt refers not to two categories of dream but to *three*.[94] John Dowel's (1909: 176) translation, on the other hand, ends this portion of text with a

---

[92] See esp. the examples discussed in Ehrman (1993).
[93] John Lydus' use of Pseudo-Plutarch in *De mensibus* (sixth century CE) appears to know the θεόπεμπτος reading, while Psellus, in his apparent use of Herophilus in the Διδασκαλία παντοδαπή, knows the θεόπνευστος reading. See Mansfeld and Runia (1997: 168–71).
[94] Some say it refers to *four* categories.

semicolon, continuing the sentence with Herophilus' remark on those dreams that (in Warfield's terms) are both theopneustic and natural:

> Herophilus, that dreams which are caused by divine instinct have a necessary cause; but dreams which have their origin from a natural cause arise from the soul's forming within itself the images of those things which are convenient for it, and which will happen; those dreams which are of a constitution mixed of both these have their origin from the fortuitous appulse of images, as when we see those things which please us; thus it happens many times to those persons who in their sleep imagine they embrace their mistresses.[95]

Although there are aspects of Dowel's rendering that we will question below, it is clear that this continuation of Pseudo-Plutarch's text presents a difficulty for Warfield's view. In what way can the impulse behind a "God-inspired" dream be combined with that of a "natural" dream to explain the physiological reaction that other ancients ascribed to the mischief of a succubus[96] (viz., the nocturnal emission)? To put it more bluntly: What part of a *wet dream* is divinely inspired? It would appear that Warfield can make his interpretation work only by being selective in his use of Herophilus' words—by hiding from his readers the troubling implications of his suggested rendering.

As far as I know, Warfield is the only commentator who simply ignores Herophilus' third category of dream, but he is hardly alone with the problems created by his interpretation of θεόπνευστος. Those who read θεόπεμπτος instead of θεόπνευστος are stuck in the same rut, which is a need to explain how a wet dream can be a mixture of a divinely inspired (or "god-sent") dream with some other category. Our revisionist understanding of θεόπνευστος, however, allows us to make perfect sense of Herophilus' use of θεόπνευστος: if we suppose that "theopneustic" dreams are not inspired but rather "life-giving" in some respect, perhaps as diagnosing or fulfilling a physiological need, we begin to see how the combination of this class of dream with the "natural" dream can result in the type of erotic dream described in the continuation of this text. Herophilus was a medical writer, and he theorized according to the Hippocratic tradition—albeit with occasional departures from that tradition. As such, he was heir to the view that dreams revealed the causes of bodily diseases and discomforts. A similar claim for the diagnostic value of the dream can be found in Cicero (*De div.* 2.69.142 [see Cox Miller 1994: 46]).[97] In fact, the view that some dreams were symptomatic—laden with symbols that revealed health problems—underlay everything medical writers said about dreams: they considered the soul to be the body's most able diagnostician and depended upon dreams to reveal what should be done to restore health. The soul's presumed ability to reveal bodily conditions was based on the widespread view that sleep turned the soul inward and allowed it privileged access to

---

[95] Dowel's translation begins in medias res because the passage builds on remarks by Democritus and Strato.

[96] Perhaps Herophilus' purpose was to demythologize the phenomenon.

[97] On dreams in Cicero generally, see ten Berge (2013). On "the concept of self-healing nature," see Bartoš (2015: 267–70).

information about the body—including not only those bits of immediate diagnostic value but also information about the future.[98]

This view of the soul as an almost transcendent informant could be found already in pre-Platonic times, in a Pseudo-Hippocratic writing called *On Regimen*, in which the soul "becomes its own mistress" during sleep (see Dodds 1951: 119).[99] Pliny writes that sleep "is nothing but the retreating of the soul into its own midst" (*Hist. nat* 10.98.211 [trans. Rackham 1940: 426]). Cicero writes that "the soul is at its best" when the body is asleep, "because it is then freed from the influence of the physical senses and from the worldly cares that weigh it down" (*De div.* 1.51.115 [trans. Falconer 1923: 349 (see Cox Miller 1994: 44)]).[100] (Scholars usually trace the connection between dreams and the active soul to Pindar [frag. 131b; see Palm 1933: 67; Kessels 1978: 199].) *On Regimen* 4.88 interprets the dream images generated by the freewheeling soul's privileged knowledge in order to prescribe changes to a patient's diet and exercise regimen:

> Such dreams as repeat in the night a man's actions or thoughts in the day-time, representing them as occurring naturally, just as they were done or planned during the day in a normal act—these are good for a man. They signify health, because the soul abides by the purposes of the day, and is overpowered neither by surfeit nor by depletion nor by any attack from without. But when dreams are contrary to the acts of the day, and there occurs about them some struggle or triumph, a disturbance in the body is indicated, a violent struggle meaning a violent mischief, a feeble struggle a less serious mischief. As to whether the act should be averted or not I do not decide, but I do advise treatment of the body. For a disturbance of the soul has been caused by a secretion arising from some surfeit that has occurred. (Trans. Jones 1979: 423–5)[101]

---

[98] Cicero writes, "Plato's advice to us is to set out for the land of dreams with bodies so prepared that no error or confusion may assail the soul. … When, therefore, the soul has been withdrawn by sleep from contact with sensual ties, then does it recall the past, comprehend the present, and foresee the future" (*De div.* 1.30.62 [trans. Falconer 1923: 293–5]). Winkler (1990: 25–6) notes that the phrases "the dream says" and "the soul says" appear to be interchangeable in Artemidoros. Bartoš (2015: 201–3) argues that viewing the soul's activity in *On Regimen* should not be taken in an overly "Orphic," "Pythagorean," or "Platonic" manner. The futurist vision obtaining in some dreams is accepted also by the Stoic Posidonius (cf. von Arnim 1903–24: 3.157 [no. 605]).

[99] Dodds (1951: 133 n. 102) writes,

> That dreams can be significant symptoms in illness is recognised elsewhere in the Hippocratic corpus (*Epidem.* 1.10, II.670 L.; *Hum.* 4, V.480; *Hebd.* 45, IX.460). In particular, anxiety dreams are seen to be important symptoms of mental trouble, *Morb.* 2.72, VII.100; *Int.* 48, VII.286. Aristotle says the most accomplished physicians believe in taking serious account of dreams, *div. p. somn.* 463ᵃ 4. But the author of περὶ διαίτης carries this essentially sound principle to fantastic lengths.

See Palm (1933: 43–96); Hulskamp (2016). *On Regimen* is usually dated to the fourth century BCE. See the assorted views listed in Holowchak (2002: 137 n. 6). (See Oberhelman 1993: 128–9.) For other references to dreams in the Hippocratic corpus, see Hippocrates, *Prorrh. I* 5; *VM* 10; *Epid. I* 23.

[100] On the wandering soul, see Palm (1933: 62). To add confusion: sometimes divinely inspired dreams *were* diagnostic, as often with dreams received by incubation. See the discussion of the diagnostic dreams Aelius Aristides received from Asclepius, in Temkin (1991: 184–8). On therapeutic incubation, see now Renberg (2017).

[101] On the role of dreams in medicine, see Lloyd (2003: 54–9, 213–15).

On Regimen goes on to break down the varieties of dreams "contrary to the acts of the day" and to prescribe adjustments to one's regimen on their basis (cf. Rufus, *Medical Questions* 5). For example, dreams of fighting, wanderings, or "difficult ascents" are said to indicate a stray secretion "opposed to the [body's] circuit," and the recommended action against this secretion is "to take an emetic, to reduce the flesh, to walk, to eat light foods, and after the emetic to increase food gradually for four days" (*On Regimen* 4.93 [trans. Jones 1979: 445–7]). The remedies (as in all the Hippocratic writings) always center on changes to the regimen (and not on drugs or surgery). Bodily health is a matter of keeping one's humors (yellow bile, phlegm, black bile, and blood) in harmony (see Temkin 1991: 12–13; Holowchak 2002: 129–30; Boudon-Millot 2009: 625–32). A bevy of dream interpretations from Galen's *On Diagnosis from Dreams* illustrates this approach in a striking way:

> The dream can indicate for us the condition of the body. For example, if someone sees a conflagration in a dream, he is troubled with yellow bile. If he sees smoke or mist or deep darkness, he is troubled with black bile. A thunderstorm, on the other hand, indicates an excess of cold moisture, while snow, ice, and hail indicate cold phlegm. (Trans. Oberhelman 1983: 43–5; see Boudon-Millot 2009)

5.3 Making Sense of the Passage

A number of ingredients in Herophilus' threefold classification of dreams support a vivificationist rendering of θεόπνευστος. As these ingredients all involve technicalities of the Greek wording, it will help to have that wording before us for reference. Here is the text of *Placita Philosophorum* as presented by von Staden (1989: 386):

> Ἡρόφιλος τῶν ὀνείρων τοὺς μὲν θεοπνεύστους κατ᾽ ἀνάγκην γίνεσθαι, τοὺς δὲ φυσικοὺς ἀνειδωλοποιουμένης τῆς ψυχῆς τὸ συμφέρον αὐτῇ καὶ τὸ πρὸς τούτοις ἐσόμενον, τοὺς δὲ συγκραματικοὺς ἐκ τοῦ αὐτομάτου κατ᾽ εἰδώλων πρόσπτωσιν, ὅταν ἃ βουλόμεθα βλέπωμεν ὡς ἐπὶ τῶν τὰς ἐρωμένας ἐχόντων ἐν ὕπνῳ γίνεται.[102]

Diels's stemma shows the text of Pseudo-Galen (*Historia Philosophiae* 106) to be dependent on Pseudo-Plutarch, but it is sometimes argued that Pseudo-Galen has a superior reading with respect to certain details. For that reason, I also present von Staden's (1989: 386) text of Pseudo-Galen:

> Ἡρόφιλος τῶν ὀνείρων τοὺς μὲν θεοπέμπτους κατ᾽ ἀνάγκην γίνεσθαι, τοὺς δὲ φυσικοὺς εἰδωλοποιουμένης τῆς ψυχῆς τὸ συμφέρον αὐτῇ καὶ τὸ πάντως ἐσόμενον· τοὺς δὲ συγκριματικοὺς αὐτομάτως κατ᾽ εἰδώλων πρόσπτωσιν, ὅταν ἃ βουλόμεθα βλέπωμεν· ‹ὡς ἐπὶ τῶν› φιλούντων γίγνεται τὰς ἐρωμένας ἐρώντων ἐν ὕπνοις.[103]

---

[102]   Cf. the critical text in Diels (1879: 416).
[103]   Cf. the critical text in Diels (1879: 640). Cf. also the text in Kühn (1830: 321).

Any attempt to understand Herophilus must make sense of the phrase κατ' ἀνάγκην. Warfield translated it as "by necessity," while Dowel translated it as "have a necessary cause." This approach falls in line with earlier Latin renderings: Guillaume Budé (1510: xxxii) had translated κατ' ἀνάγκην as "e necessitate esse" and Wyttenbach (1797: 650) as "necessario fieri." J. F. Dobson (1925: 32 n. 76), working from Pseudo-Galen, translated it as "inevitably." While none of these translations is wildly off the mark, the way in which they might help us understand the occurrence of what these scholars think is a "divinely inspired" (or "God-sent") dream is far from clear. In what sense is the giving of an inspired dream "necessary" or "inevitable"? A. H. M. Kessels (1969: 417) thinks that κατ' ἀνάγκην "probably means that the human being has no part in it as to [the dreams'] origin; in other words, they are sent from outside, from the gods." The difficulty of rendering κατ' ἀνάγκην as "by necessity" or "inevitably" has not escaped notice. P. H. Schrijvers (1977: 22–4), for example, notes that the sentence is so constructed as to imply that κατ' ἀνάγκην marks a point of contrast with the "physical" dream (ὄνειροι φυσικοί), but that the sense in which a "God-inspired" or "God-sent" dream might be deemed "necessary" does not straightforwardly represent such a contrast. In fact, Schrijvers (1977: 24) argues, it makes better sense to say that the second dream category is the one given by necessity, all the more so since the pursuit of a divinely inspired dream (e.g., through incubation) involves preparatory tasks: "On peut se demander si l'expression κατ' ἀνάγκην doit être rendue plutôt d'après la physique et la métaphysique aristotélicienne par 'selon nécessité', les rêves θεόπεμπτοι étant des faits nécessaires et constants, non pas contingents, ou bien plutôt, en correspondance avec la catégorie Empirique αὐτοσχέδιος πεῖρα, par 'par contrainte' (de la part de l'homme)." Carlo Brillante (1990: 79) is able to explain the combination of divine inspiration with necessity by reminding us of the Eastern belief that even the gods were subject to astral determinism, but it is not clear why qualifying divine inspiration in this way should be relevant for taxonomic purposes.

On the other hand, if we take Herophilus to be discussing dreams that are "life-giving" (rather than "inspired") by virtue of the diagnoses they afford, then κατ' ἀνάγκην begins to make sense. The fourth definition for ἀνάγκη in *Liddell-Scott* (1940: 101) outlines the word's frequent denotation of "*bodily pain, anguish.*" Dreams in this category might then be "life-giving" in relation to the sort of bodily distresses and diseases signaled by this side of κατ' ἀνάγκην's semantic range. On these terms, it is not clear whether the preposition κατά brings the dream into relation with the "bodily pain" as that for which "life" is needed or whether it denotes the pain as that which gives rise to the dream's symbolism. What *is* clear is that κατ' ἀνάγκην makes sense on the terms of a vivificationist rendering of θεόπνευστος. In that case, a more wooden rendering would perfectly express the medical writer's view of diagnostic dreams: "according to [the body's] *need.*" Herophilus would then be presenting an understanding of diagnostic dreams similar to what we find in *On Regimen*: fluid and thermal imbalances manifest themselves in a patterned way through dreams.[104]

---

[104] Jaeger (1961: 27) writes, "The doctor's duty is to restore the secret proportion when it is disturbed by disease. In health, nature herself produces that proportion, or else she herself *is* the right proportion."

If the understanding argued here is correct, Herophilus' three types of dreams all fall under Arthur Lennig's larger category of "Innentraum."[105] We may describe Herophilus' three categories as follows: (1) the "life-giving" (θεόπνευστος) dream, (2) the "natural" (φυσικός) dream, and (3) the "mixed" (συγκραματικός) dream. The life-giving dream is the diagnostic dream, providing the doctor with insights for adjusting the patient's regimen. The mechanism for this sort of dream is the soul, which gains access to the body's status every night during sleep and relays that status to the mind via dreams. The natural dream also has the soul for its mechanism, but it manifests either the soul's cravings or the knowledge of the future it gains through its nightly wanderings.[106] The mixed dream is both a manifestation of the soul's cravings *and* a curative/corrective for the body's imbalances.[107] The ancients believed that an excess of semen was detrimental to one's health (see Lucretius, *De rerum natura* 4.1030–36; cf. Galen, *On Diagnosis from Dreams* 6 [Kühn 1823: 834; see Boudon-Millot 2009: 630–1]) and (correlatively) that nocturnal emissions were nature's means of regulating an aspect of health.[108] The wet dream therefore exemplifies a mixture of the first two dream categories by both

---

[105] See the discussion of "Außen- und Innentraum" in Lennig (1969: 33–7). Cf. Schrijvers's (1977) categories: "endogenous" vs. "exogenous." Cf. Cox Miller's (1994: 42) categories: "psychological" vs. "theological."

[106] Dreams could predict the future without being divinely inspired. Galen writes,

> It has been our experience that certain matters are prophetically foreshadowed by the soul. Therefore the diagnosis of the body on the basis of dreams that have their impulse from the body itself becomes no easy task. For if it were necessary to base our interpretations of dreams only on what we do and think each day, it would not be difficult to suppose that whatever dreams are not of actions and thoughts [during our waking-states] will have their source in the body. But since we concede that some dreams are also prophetic messages, it is not easy to say how these dreams are to be distinguished from those which originate in the body. (*Diagnosis from Dreams* [Kühn 1823: 832], translation from Oberhelman 1983: 44–5)

[107] Dodds (1951: 124 n. 28) writes that "a dream of one's beloved is not a 'mixed' dream in … any … sense," but it would appear he didn't consider all the possibilities. Harris (2009: 266) explains the "mixed" nature of this type of dream as containing "elements of involuntariness, like the first category ('by necessity') and elements of voluntariness like the second ('forms for itself')." Von Staden (1989: 307) understands a "mixed" dream to be one that combines the "external agency" of the god-sent dream with the "internal stimulus" of the natural dream. Giulio Agostini (2009: 100) writes that these dreams are "mixed" because "while the causes of the first category are only internal and those of the second category are only external, in this third category there is both an internal cause, desire, and an external one, the desired image."

[108] Lucretius writes, "when the seed first penetrates / The racing tides of youth, as time matures it, / Meet with a wandering image from some body / That tells of lovely face and rosy cheeks, / And this excites the parts swelling with seed, / And so, as if the act were being performed, / They pour a great flood out and stain their clothes" (trans. Melville 1997: 129). Galen writes, "the hungry will dream of eating insatiably and men full of sperm [τοῖς σπέρματος πλήρεσιν] will imagine that they are having sexual intercourse" (*On Diagnosis from Dreams* [translation from Oberhelman (1983: 45–6)—Greek text from Guidorizzi 1973: 104]). See Schrijvers (1977: 19 n. 13). Cf. Oberhelman (1993: 143). Other ancient writers took a dimmer view of the nocturnal emission, as Caelius Aurelianus (fifth century CE), for whom it was generally a manifestation of desires (*Chronic Diseases* 5.80), but sometimes "a prelude to a coming attack of epilepsy, insanity, or any other disease" (5.83–84 [trans. Drabkin 1950: 961]). See Rousselle (1988: 6). Alexander of Tralles (*Therapeutica* 11.7) and Pedanius Dioscorides (*De materia medica* 3.132.2) both prescribe the white water lily (*nymphaia alba*) to combat nocturnal emissions, and Pedanius claims that cultivated lettuce (*lactuca sativa*) will do the same (2.136.1–3). See Puschmann (1963: 496–9); Beck (2005: 150–1).

ridding the body of excess semen (making it "life-giving") and fulfilling the sexual urge (making it "natural" as well).

One advantage of this line of interpretation is that the advent of θεόπνευστος's post-Origenist career (viz., as an *inspirationist* term) can help explain the alternative wording we find in Pseudo-Galen. The fact that two Pseudo-Galen manuscripts read θεόπεμπτος instead of θεόπνευστος makes sense on the presumption that θεόπνευστος later came to mean "god-inspired": a copyist simply swapped the term before him or her for the inspirationist term preferred by other dream theorists (e.g., Aristotle [*De div. in somno* 463 b 13], Artemidorus [*Oneirocritica* 16.3.7], Philo [*De somniis*]).[109] (A similar interchange between θεόπνευστος and θεόπεμπτος can be found among manuscripts of the *Alexander Romance*.)[110] And Pseudo-Galen's use of συγκριματικός instead of συγκραματικός, if the former has the meaning Max Wellmann attributes to it (see below), can be explained as a response to the problem that an inspirationist construal of the first category poses for the third category. (As we saw above, the problem lies with Pseudo-Plutarch's use of the wet dream as an example of the "mixed" [συγκραματικός] category—an example difficult to square with an inspirationist aspect.) The copyist's substitution of συγκριματικός for συγκραματικός takes care of that problem in a strikingly convenient way. It should also be noted that an inspirationist construal of the first dream category leaves Herophilus' taxonomy without a *diagnostic* category of dream, which would be supremely odd for a leading medical writer.[111] (Why else would a medical writer discuss dreams?) This loss of the diagnostic category might have contributed to the rise of the συγκριματικός reading as well. The reasoning behind such a development does not seem to be reversible: to posit (with Wellmann [1924–25: 70–2], Dodds [1951: 124 n. 28], C. A. Behr [1968: 174–5 n. 11], and others)[112] that συγκριματικός was the original reading in Pseudo-Plutarch would leave us at a loss to explain the rise of the συγκραματικός reading—except, of course, as a simple confusion of letters. This discussion of συγκριματικός, however, assumes a definition for the word that is, in fact, open to question. (See below.)

---

[109] On the god-sent dream in Artemidorus, see Renberg (2017: 4). Cf. the full Greek title of Philo's *On Dreams*: Περὶ τοῦ θεοπέμπτους εἶναι τοὺς ὀνείρους. As Warfield (1900: 100 n. †) writes, "The superficial parallelism of Philo with what is cited from Herophilus is close enough fully to account for a scribe harking back to Philo's language—or even for the compiler of the Pseudo-Galen doing so."

[110] Θεόπεμπτος is found in mss. KVLγ of the *Alexander Romance*, while θεόπνευστος is found in mss. BA. See Bergson (1965: 38).

[111] Von Staden (1989: 307) notes the lack of a diagnostic category in the usual interpretation of Pseudo-Plutarch, but he does not address the strangeness of this conclusion.

[112] Kessels is one of those touting Wellmann's case for reading συγκριματικός instead of συγκραματικός in Pseudo-Plutarch. (So also Oberhelman 1993: 136.) The above considerations, however, put us in a position to answer his three "considerable difficulties" for the συγκραματικός reading. "Firstly," Kessels (1969: 418) asks, "what has been mixed together?" Answer: the principal aspects of the "life-giving" and "natural" dream categories. "Secondly," he asks, "how are we to explain ἐκ τοῦ αὐτομάτου, which seems to mean almost the same as κατ' ἀνάγκην?" Answer: the former phrase refers to the automatic creation of the "natural" dream, while the latter refers especially to bodily pains and imbalances. "And thirdly," he asks, "what about κατ' εἰδώλων πρόσπτωσιν?" Answer: the phrase means something like "according to visions near at hand" (viz., not exogenic). (As Kessels himself notes, "The words ἐκ τοῦ αὐτομάτου κατ' εἰδώλων πρόσπτωσιν have nothing to do with the divine, but rather suggest a mechanical automatism" [419].) Cf. Brillante (1990: 84).

The (laudable) presumption that one of Herophilus' three dream categories was *diagnostic* has spurred a lot of creative parsing of his words. Kessels (1969: 416–17), for example, would find a diagnostic function in the second category, interpreting ἀνειδωλοποιουμένης τῆς ψυχῆς τὸ συμφέρον αὐτῇ καὶ τὸ πρὸς τούτοις ἐσόμενον as describing a single aspect of a dream (as opposed to two subcategories of the φυσικός dream), and taking the seemingly futurist aspect of πρὸς … ἐσόμενον as a reference to physiological normalcy, rather than as a reference to knowledge about the future. (Admittedly, Kessels underargues this position, as it would fit with the reasoning found in *On Regimen* 4.89–90.) The problem with this reading is that it is based on a misunderstanding of what it means to call a dream φυσικός: according to Kessels, if Herophilus had intended a reference to predictive dreams, "he would have called them rather ψυχικοί than φυσικοί." Schrijvers (1977: 14–15) points out that Kessels appears to read the term φυσικός too much through the lens of the modern English term "physical."[113] Wellmann and his followers, as noted above, interpret the third dream category as diagnostic, reading συγκριματικός instead of συγκραματικός, taking the former in the sense of "organisch" (Wellmann 1924–25: 70–2), "constitutional" (Behr 1968: 174–5 n. 11), or "instinctive" (Winkler 1990: 33).[114] Schrijvers (1977: 16), however, argues that συγκριματικός more likely means "compound"—such that its meaning really is not far from συγκραματικός:

> Le sens de "constitution, structure anatomique," qui se recontre dans des textes médicaux, n'est au fond rien d'autre que l'emploi technique de la désignation générale de τὸ σύγκριμα = *res composita*. A cause des arguments et des faits susmentionés, l'interprétation par Wellmann de l'expression ὄνειροι συγκριματικοί doit être rejetée à notre avis de même que les différentes interprétations de la classification hérophiléenne, qui, sur ce point, ont été fondées sur lui. (Palm, Blum, Behr, Kessels)[115]

For those holding out an expectation that Herophilus' dream classification should include divine causation as one of its types, it should be pointed out that that category of dream is not as universal among dream theorists as some studies make it appear. *On Regimen* indeed includes "divine" dreams within its threefold system, but it is the only Hippocratic writing that unambiguously refers to such.[116] Steven Oberhelman (1983: 40) notes that our fragments of Galen's *On Diagnosis from Dreams* make "no

---

[113] Schrijvers (1977: 21) writes of Kessels: "Son étude souffre généralement du fait que de façon trop exclusive il a considéré le sujet dans la perspective des théories anciennes sur les rêves, sans tenir compte de la personne et de l'oeuvre du médecin Hérophile."

[114] Winkler's rendering is not a direct translation.

[115] Schrijvers writes, "La classification des rêves fait voir elle-aussi cette tripartition favorite et l'explication la plus simple et la plus évidente du terme συγκριματικοι est à notre avis celle de 'composés', ce qui implique que le sens est à peu près synonyme de celui de συγκραματικοι = 'mixtes'" (17). Cf. Dobson (1925: 32 n. 76).

[116] Harris (2009: 243–4) writes, "[*On Regimen*] seems to be atypical of the Hippocratic corpus, in that it allows that *some* dreams are of divine origin—whereas it is clear that around 400 BC most medical writers saw dreams in largely naturalistic terms."

mention of divine dreams and only grudgingly allowed some dreams to be mantic prognostications by the soul."

6 The *Sentences* of Pseudo-Phocylides

In the early centuries of the Common Era, a Jew or a Christian composed a wisdom poem in the name of Phocylides, a well-known Miletian poet from the sixth century BCE.[117] (The consensus position has been that the author was Jewish, but Jonathan Klawans [2017] recently presented an argument for Christian authorship.)[118] Scholars usually date the work to the first century BCE or the first century CE, but in the following pages I argue that it might have been written as late as the second century CE.

Θεόπνευστος appears in v. 129: "But speech of the theopneustic wisdom is best" (τῆς δὲ θεοπνεύστου σοφίης λόγος ἐστὶν ἄριστος). Some readers might be surprised that I enlist this passage as evidence for θεόπνευστος's pre-Origenist career, as nearly every edition or translation of the work dismisses v. 129 as inauthentic—presumably late (e.g., see Lincke 1903: 172–3; Farina 1962: 43–4 n. 56; Van der Horst 1978: 201–2; Derron 1986: cvii; Thomas 1992: 191; Wilson 1994: 115 n. 148; 2005: 155–6).[119] Most commentaries point out that the verse does not appear in two important tenth-century manuscripts (M and B), nor in Joannes Stobaeus' fifth-century quotation of vv. 125–30 (Stob. 3.3.28). Scholars also regularly claim that the verse interrupts the sequence of thought. (It is sometimes conjectured that an interpolator composed it on the basis of the preceding verse's use of λόγος and the following verse's use of σεσοφισμένος [e.g., Van der Horst 1978: 202; Thomas 1992: 190].) In describing the verse's supposedly dubious status, Pieter van der Horst twice uses the word "clumsy": once (1978: 202) to characterize the (supposed) interpolator's feat and once again (1985: 579 n. b) in judgment of the verse's wording.[120]

Before I attempt to settle the issue of the verse's authenticity, I should address what θεόπνευστος meant for its author. (The reason for doing so will become clear soon enough.) Considered in isolation from the verse's context, both the inspirationist and vivificationist renderings are plausible, as it is easy to envision wisdom as something imparted by divine inspiration, and it is equally easy to view it as life-giving in its effects.[121] Contextual considerations, however, weigh

---

[117] On Pseudo-Phocylides, see Gilbert (1984: 313–16); Mack and Murphy (1986: 395–6).

[118] At one time scholars commonly assumed that Pseudo-Phocylides' use of θεόπνευστος derived from the hand of a Christian. In the nineteenth and early twentieth centuries, there were those who argued that the entire book was written by a Christian, even if some of the source material was pre-Christian. E.g., Harris (1885: 21–6) was sure that the *Sentences* was in part a rewriting of the *Didache*. According to Harris, "Ps. Phocylides can only by extremely rough criticism be divested of sentiments which are either Christian or differ very slightly therefrom" (26). (See the response to Harris in Funk 1887: xxi–xxii.) Cf. Bernays (1856: xv–xvi); Harnack (1886: 105). There were also those, like the more recent Derron (1986: cvii), who took the presence of θεόπνευστος to indicate a Christian gloss in an otherwise Jewish work. But cf. Bergk (1882: 2.99); Van der Horst (1978: 201–2).

[119] Walter (1983: 187) writes, "Vers 129 fehlt in M und B sowie bei Stobaios; und schließlich steht Vers 36 zwar in den ältesten Handschriften M und B, er fehlt aber in LPV; und der Umstand."

[120] Diehl (1950: 101) also brackets v. 129, citing the verse's omission from "M B Stob."

[121] Nickel (1833: 19) translates: "Aber das herrlichste Wort ist das Wort der göttlichen Weisheit."

in favor of the latter rendering. Several passages make it clear that wisdom, for Pseudo-Phocylides, is a matter of rational reflection on the created order. It is *not* acquired by means of inspiration—esoteric or otherwise—a notion that might have been at home in a more mystical writing. The notion that wisdom is life-giving, moreover, is very much a traditional Jewish thought, recalling Prov. 3:18's reference to wisdom as a "tree of life" (cf. Prov. 8:35; 9:6; 13:14; Eccl. 7:12; *4Q185* 2.11–13; von Rad 1972: 172; Murphy 1996: 28–9; Collins 1997: 183).[122] It can be found throughout Jewish and Christian wisdom writings and fits particularly well with the understanding of wisdom promoted by Pseudo-Phocylides. A close parallel with the imagery of *Sentences* 129, in fact, can be found in the Latin version of Sir. 4:12 (= Greek Sir. 4:11 numerically), rendered in the Douay-Rheims version as "Wisdom inspireth life into her children, and protecteth them that seek after her, and will go before *them* in the way of justice" (*sapientia filiis suis vitam inspiravit et suscipit exquirentes se et praeibit in viam iustitiae*).[123] It is not unlikely, in fact, that Pseudo-Phocylides knew this verse in the form of its presumed Greek *Vorlage* (GrII). (See below.) Nor is it unlikely that *Sentences* 129 is directly dependent on the expression preserved in Lat Sir. 4:12.[124]

Although the *Sentences* was passed off as the product of the pagan Phocylides, its brand of wisdom is decidedly (but not explicitly) Jewish. The majority of its verses are apparently based on scriptural passages, although their wording is disguised to preserve the ruse of Phocylidean authorship. One of the more convincing explanations of its ultimate purpose, in fact, sees it as a rigged exemplar for the conceit that the pagans stole their wisdom from Moses and other Jewish figures (see esp. Wilson 2005: 4).[125] (This would explain why the author attributed the work to a revered figure from the sixth century BCE.) Moreover, Ben Sira appears to have been especially prominent within Pseudo-Phocylides' working canon: Walter Wilson lists Ben Sira more times than any other biblical book in his chart of suggested scriptural echoes in the *Sentences*.[126] If the supposed interpolator of v. 129 understood the original writer's purpose, as well as the importance of Ben Sira as a source for that writer, it would not be unexpected to hear an echo of Lat Sir. 4:12's Greek *Vorlage*.

---

[122] Von Rad (1964: 845) writes, "In all its varied forms OT wisdom has only the one goal of offering man life, or, in its own words, of leading him on the way of life." On *4Q185*, see Harrington (1996: 35–9). See Burkes (1999: 254–7).

[123] *The Holy Bible Translated from the Latin Vulgate* (1914: 716). Latin text from Fischer, Gribomont, Sparks, and Thiele (1975: 1034). Nolland (1989: 346) writes, "The idea of 'children of Wisdom' is implied by Prov 8:32; Sir 4:11, and analogous formations are well known in Semitic idiom (in the NT cf. Luke 16:8; John 12:36; 1 Thess 5:5; Eph 5:8)." See Legrand (2011: 228). See the apparatus in Thiele (1992: 255).

[124] Lat Sir. 4:12 is a more likely source for *Sentences* 129 than is Wis. 7:24–25, as suggested in Krauss (1906: 10.255–56).

[125] Kirk (2016: 134) writes that "*Pseudo-Phocylides* opens with a sapientialized Decalogue."

[126] Wilson (2005: 17–18) lists some thirty-two Sirachic passages behind twenty-five Pseudo-Phocylidean *logia*, noting that the former's influence on the latter was often "indirect." A similar listing of the *Sentences*' possible OT and NT contacts can be found in Beltrami (1908). Cf. Goram (1859: 98–9).

6.1 Was v. 129 Original to the *Sentences*?

Wilson (2005: 155) pronounced v. 129 "spurious," and most scholars agree with that judgment. But how strong is the case for that view?

In the preceding section, I referred to the "supposed interpolator" of v. 129, as it is *not* clear, in spite of universal opinion, that the verse is secondary. Previous scholarship's failure to see how the verse functions within the work's argument stems from the difficulty of making sense of the passage on terms of the traditional inspirationist understanding of θεόπνευστος. The verse only "disrupts the continuity of vv. 128 and 130," as Van der Horst would have it, if we assume it refers to wisdom as an *inspired* commodity.[127] If we render θεόπνευστος as "life-giving," v. 129 no longer puts a strain on the sense of the passage. In fact, we not only arrive at a familiar way of talking about wisdom, but we find the verse agreeing with, and adding substance to, the author's larger argument:

> Pseudo-Phocylides, *Sentences* 122–31
> Do not become mad in your mind through your boasting.
> Practice speaking the right word, which will greatly profit everyone.
> Speech is for humans a tool sharper than iron.
> God allotted a tool to each creature; the ability to fly
> to birds, speed to horses, and strength to lions;
> to bulls self-growing horns and stingers to bees
> he gave as a natural defense, but to humans speech as a protection.
> [But the speech of theopneustic wisdom is best.]
> Better is a wise person than a strong one.
> Wisdom guides lands and cities and ships. (Author's translation)

If we render θεόπνευστος as "life-giving," v. 129 suddenly makes sense, both as a development of v. 128b and as a resumption of the line of thought we find in v. 123. The speech of "life-giving wisdom" is the highest or most effective form of man's "protection" (= speech [v. 128 (cf. Aristotle, *Pol.* 1.1.10)]), and it fulfills the injunction of v. 123: "Practice speaking the right word, which will greatly profit everyone." A corrected understanding of θεόπνευστος makes all the difference. Van der Horst (1978: 202), supposing the verse to be a later gloss, suggested it "may be a product of Byzantine sophialogy." On the terms of a vivificationist understanding of θεόπνευστος, however, its sophialogy could not be made to fit any better with what we might expect from the original Pseudo-Phocylides.

In light of our newfound understanding of the earliest uses of the word θεόπνευστος and the way its meaning changed in the third century CE, it is now easier to explain the verse's omission than its addition. The common assumption that θεόπνευστος means "inspired" in this context has caused difficulties for scholars' readings of the passage, and the same difficulties would have been faced by Christians attempting to read

---

[127] Van der Horst's rendering is typical. Cf. Feuling's (1879: 16) rendering: "man hath God-inspired speech."

the passage in the wake of Origen's resignification of that word. Suddenly a passage that made perfect sense as a reference to wisdom's life-giving aspect was read very differently—as a claim that wisdom was *inspired*. Most attentive readers, I presume, would have found a (supposed) reference to wisdom's inspired aspect out of line with the work's (Sirachic) sophialogy.[128] It is easy, therefore, to understand why a copyist might have marginalized the verse, or excised it from the text.

And what shall we say about the commonly cited manuscript evidence for excluding this verse? Although the *Sentences* is extant in numerous manuscripts—Pascale Derron (1980; 1986: lxxxiii n. 1) listed some 157 of them in a 1980 inventory (adding two more in 1986)[129]—scholars usually reduce the key witnesses to a mere five:

Parisinus suppl. gr. 388 (M), f. 75ᵛ–80ʳ (10th c.)
Oxoniensis Baroccianus 50 (B), f. 371ʳ–375ʳ (10th c.)
Parisinus suppl. gr. 690 (P), f. 247ʳ–248ᵛ (12th c.)
Laurentianus 32, 16 (L), f. 321ʳ–322ʳ (13th c.)
Vindobonensis phil. gr. 321 (V), f. 222ᵛ–224ʳ (13th–14th c.)[130]

Scholars typically give the manuscript evidence for including or excluding contested passages in the *Sentences* almost entirely in terms of what these five comparatively early manuscripts say about the matter, with an occasional reference to an "inferior" witness. The first two manuscripts in the list are usually taken to represent an "Italian" family of witnesses (although that designation has recently been questioned [see below]), while the last three are taken to represent a "Byzantine" family.

A brief comparison of the reasons for excluding v. 129 with the reasons for excluding certain other verses is instructive. In his 1978 commentary, Van der Horst placed the following verses in square brackets, to indicate their contested status: 31, 36, 37, 87, 116–17, 129, 144, 145, 146, 155, and 218.[131] He gave the following reasons for bracketing these verses:

v. 31: "only one inferior ms. contains it" (Van der Horst 1978: 135)
v. 36: "identical with v. 69b. Either both vv. are to be retained or v. 36 has to be athetized since 3 important mss. (L, P, V) omit it" (Van der Horst 1978: 137)[132]

---

[128] Reiterer (2008: 215–16) writes, "According to Gr, wisdom is not a gift, which one receives without one's own effort. The disciple has himself to strive for wisdom. Sira struggles for it, as in a war he fights for it: διαμεμάχιται ἡ ψυχή μου ἐν αὐτῇ (Sir 51:19a)." See Marböck (1971: 93–6; 1976); Schnabel (1985: 28). Cf. the view of wisdom in Wis. 7:22; 8:5–6. See Mattila (2000: 486).

[129] Two of Derron's listed items (nos. 43 and 44 in Derron 1980) appear under the same cover.

[130] These dates are as given in Van der Horst (1985: 567). Van der Horst claims that only this "limited number are valuable," the five on which Young based his edition—see Young (1998: 2.566). Mss. M, B, P, L, and V are listed in Derron (1980 112, 89, 115) (dated there as eleventh–twelfth century), 43, and 156, respectively. A minority of scholars allow that ms. B was a late ninth-century writing—e.g., Borovilou-Genakou (2002: 252). Ronconi (2007: 146–7) suggests that M may have been copied in the eleventh century. See Ronconi (2007: 91–131) on ms. B more generally, and 133–47 on ms. M.

[131] Van der Horst treats vv. 116–17 as a single *logion*, but 144, 145, and 146 as three separate *logia*, although their text-critical profiles are identical.

[132] In Van der Horst (1985), there are no brackets around v. 36. See below.

v. 37: "V. 37 is in only one ms. (…) and interrupts (with v. 36) the coherence
between vv. 35 and 38" (Van der Horst 1978: 138)

v. 87: "given in only two inferior mss" (Van der Horst 1978: 173)

vv. 116–17: "Both verses … occur in only one ms. (V)" (Van der Horst 1978: 195)

v. 129: "its omission by two important mss. (M, B) and by Stob. (III 3, 28, where
vv. 125–30 are quoted without v. 129) …" (Van der Horst 1978: 201)

v. 144: "only in one ms., V" (Van der Horst 1978: 209)

v. 145: "again only in ms. V" (Van der Horst 1978: 210)

v. 146: "again only in ms. V" (Van der Horst 1978: 211)

v. 155: "found in only one ms. (V)" (Van der Horst 1978: 217)

v. 218: "in only one ms. (V)" (Van der Horst 1978: 252)

The text-critical profile of v. 129, it should be noted, compares favorably with the other
contested verses. Of the eleven *logia* listed above, no less than six appear *only* in ms. V
(vv. 116–17, 144, 145, 146, 155, and 218). Another *logion* appears in "only one inferior
ms." (v. 31), and yet another in "only two inferior mss." (v. 87). Verse 37, Van der Horst
tells us, "is in only one ms.," but we are not told which one, nor are we told whether
that manuscript is "important" (viz., one of the five listed above) or "inferior." This
leaves only two sets of brackets: those for vv. 36 and 129. Van der Horst placed v. 36
in brackets in 1978, because "3 important mss. (L, P, V) omit it," but he saw fit to
remove those brackets, seven years later, from the *OTP* presentation of the *Sentences*.
Apparently he had changed his mind in favor of the verse's authenticity, in spite of its
absence from three "important" manuscripts.

This leaves only v. 129. This verse is missing from mss. M and B (Derron 1986: cvi–
cvii),[133] and it is also missing from Stobaeus' quotation of vv. 125–30 in his *Anthology*
(fifth century CE). (Contrary to how this omission is usually described, the hiatus of
words begins two words prior to the beginning of v. 129 and ends two words prior
to the end of that verse, with ὅς standing in place of the omitted material.) It is with
respect to this last claim—that regarding the text of Stobaeus—that the scholars' tale
about the manuscript evidence really starts to unravel. Virtually all scholars of Pseudo-
Phocylides report that Stobaeus omits v. 129 in his quotation of vv. 125–30 (*Anth.*
3.3.28). By this, they signal their reliance on the edition by Curt Wachsmuth and
Otto Hense (1884–1912 [Hense 1894: 203]). In point of fact, several manuscripts of
Stobaeus *include* v. 129,[134] and most printed editions and translations of Stobaeus also
include the verse.[135] Today's scholars' preference for the shorter reading appears to be

---

[133] The supposition of an Italian provenience was based on the work of Irigoin (esp. 1969; cf.
1975: 435–6; 2000: 590–4) and on further work by Canart (1978: 141) and Cavallo (1980: 167–8).
See also Canfora (1995: 124–5). This provenience has come under fire during the past decade, as
Ronconi (2007: 113, 123, 133, 144–7; 2005: 296–9, 326–8, 350–3), Migoubert (2003: 406–7), and
others have promoted a return to the Byzantine provenience argued by Browning (1963). See also
Carlini (1997: 121 with n. 1).

[134] Somewhere along the way, Stobaeus' long, cumbersome text was split into two works: the
Anthology's first two books came to circulate as the *Eclogae*, while the last two came to circulate as
the *Florilegium*.

[135] A number of older editions of Stobaeus are missing (most of) *Sentences* v. 129—e.g., Trincavelli
(1536: *ad loc.*); Gesner (1543: 24)—but Gesner (1557: 96 and 1609: 57) include the longer reading,
as do Gaisford (1822: 92); Meineke (1855: 73).

based on the place given it in Wachsmuth and Hense. To be sure, Mansfeld and Runia (1997: 199) have argued that reliance on "Wachsmuth" is generally justified,[136] but in light of the foregoing, there is reason enough to be cautious about accepting the shorter reading.

Assuming (as Wachsmuth does) that the hiatus of words in the Stobaean manuscript tradition is original, how should we judge the manuscript evidence for both Stobaeus and Pseudo-Phocylides? Derron (1986: cvi) refers to "le télescopage des vers 128–29" in Stobaeus—a happy choice of words, as the wording found in the shortened version of Stobaeus is clearly an adaptation of a longer wording. It is difficult to tell whether the hiatus in Stobaeus goes back to the original penning of the *Anthology* or was created later. It has usually been surmised that Stobaeus was not a Christian, as he fails to include any Christian works in the collection he creates for his son's education (see Campbell 1984). Mansfeld and Runia, however, judge a first name of "Johannes" problematic for such a view.[137] If Stobaeus was a Christian, we could easily imagine the problem he might have had with what appeared to be an inspirationist view of wisdom in Pseudo-Phocylides. As S. Luria (1929; cf. Hahm 1990: 2939–40) has shown, Stobaeus regularly rounded the edges, so to speak, of the passages he excerpted, so as to refashion them into complete sense units.[138] He was quite capable of omitting any line that threatened the semantic integrity of a reading. In that case, those manuscripts that include the longer wording represent a scribal correction.[139]

6.2 The Date of v. 129

If we are to posit that the Greek *Vorlage* of Lat Sir. 4:12 was known to Pseudo-Phocylides, then presumably the chronological aspects of such a schema should not pose a difficulty. We should want to know two things in particular: When was the Greek wording behind the Latin version of Sir. 4:12(11) first available to someone like Pseudo-Phocylides, and when was the *Sentences* written?

How early should we date the expression preserved in Lat Sir. 4:12 (*sapientia filiis suis vitam inspiravit et suscipit exquirentes se et praeibit in viam iustitiae*)?[140] It is widely

---

[136] Mansfeld and Runia write (1997: 203), "We are in fact most fortunate to have had such a competent and conscientious editor."

[137] Mansfeld and Runia (1997: 197) write, "Because the last author he quotes is Themistius and all Christian writers have been rigorously excluded, it has been surmised that he must have been a pagan author. But the grounds for such a view must be questioned. It is in our view quite likely that he was a Christian, if only on account of his name." See Runia (2011: 846). For the more usual view, cf., e.g., Hahm (1990: 2938): Stobaeus "appears to have been an immensely learned non-Christian scholar of the early fifth century A.D."

[138] Hahm (1990: 2943) writes of a "tendency on the part of both the compilers of gnomological anthologies and also the scribes who copied them to treat the texts to some degree as their own property."

[139] Hahm (1990: 2941) writes, "The copyists in the gnomological tradition, apparently feeling less obligation to preserve the received text of a gnomologium than that of a surviving classical author, were prone to fix the errors that they found by altering the text."

[140] Kearns (2011: 55) writes, "The time and place of origin of the Latin *Sirach* were the same as for the Old Latin version in general: pre-Cyprian, in Roman North Africa." Thielemann (1893; 1894) argued for an early third-century date. De Bruyne (1929) argued for the period 150 CE to 200 CE.

known that Jerome did not regard Ben Sira as scriptural, so he did not translate the book anew. Thus there is little difference between the text of the *Vetus Latina* and that of the Vulgate (see Forte 2011: 202).[141] (The principal difference between the two consists in the fact that the latter includes the grandson's prologue and chs 44–50, while the former does not.) This allows us to presume that our expression is at least as old as the *Vetus Latina* of Ben Sira, and older still, if we presume a continuity of expression between the Latin text and its Greek *Vorlage*. (See below.)

Ben Sira has its own distinctive text-critical problems, stretching across versions in four languages, created by an abundance of additional stichoi in the Latin and Syriac versions, and by a similar expansionist tendency in certain Greek manuscripts.[142] Only a few aspects of these problems can now be reduced to a consensus view, but we can be reasonably certain that the expression in Lat Sir. 4:12 goes back to a Greek form (see Thiele 1997)[143] and that that form existed as early as the late second century CE. We know this because it appears to have been known to Clement of Alexandria: "ἡ σοφία, φησὶν ὁ Σολομών, ἐνεφυσίωσε τὰ ἑαυτῆς τέκνα" (*Strom.* 7.16).[144] There is also the well-known argument from order, based on the Latin text's agreement with the order of material in the extant Hebrew and Syriac texts, and its *dis*agreement with the order of material in the extant Greek. According to Maurice Gilbert (2008: 4–5; cf. Legrand 2011: 216),

> If the Latin version of Ecclesiasticus has the same order of … chapters as in Hebrew and in Syriac, it must be concluded that the Greek manuscript which was used by the Latin translator was different from the archetype of all the Greek manuscripts still extant. What was the date of this archetype with the inversion of some chapters? … It was certainly done before the first half of the 4th century, because the uncial manuscripts *Vaticanus* and *Sinaiticus* already have the inversion. It is impossible to give an earlier date, because today we do not yet have any previous Greek papyrus comprising the chapters in question. It is generally accepted that the inversion was done during the 3rd century. Then the Greek manuscripts used by the Latin translator were anterior, and if the Latin version was done, as de Bruyne suggested, during the second half of the 2nd century, this Greek manuscript used by the Latin translator has to be dated earlier.

---

[141] Cf. the discussion of the *Vetus Latina* in Smend (1906: cxviii–cxxix).

[142] Scholars mark the existence of a manuscript tradition containing additional stichoi with the designation "II," so that the original Hebrew form of Ben Sira would be "HebI," while a (conjectured) Hebrew form with the sort of expansions that characterize the Latin text would be "HebII." Thus scholars speak in terms of "HebI," "HebII," "GrI," "GrII," "LatII," and "SyrII." HebII and GrII are conjectural, based on the Latin and Syriac versions, and on the additional stichoi *sometimes* found in Greek manuscripts (cf. esp. Codex 248).

[143] Herkenne (1899: 9) gave four supports for the Latin text's derivation from the Greek: (a) the Latin sometimes leaves Greek terms untranslated and matches Latin to Greek terms on the basis of morphology, (b) the Latin sometimes shows a misunderstanding of the Greek, (c) departures can be explained by changes to the Greek, and (d) errors in the Greek text are sometimes retained. See Gilbert (2008: 2); Kearns (2011: 56–7); Winter (2012: 252).

[144] On Lat Sir. 4:12 and Clement, *Strom.* 7.16, see Ziegler (1964: 277–80). Ziegler argued that the same text lies behind Tertullian, *Scorp.* 7.1, but Bauer (1965: 85–9) argued, in response, that Tertullian was echoing Prov. 9:2.

Whether this Greek "expanded text" (= GrII) goes back to a conjectured Hebrew "expanded text" (HebII) is immaterial for the question at hand.[145] What *is* material is the fact that the Latin text appears to witness an older Greek text than do all the extant Greek manuscripts.[146] By Thierry Legrand's (2011: 218) count, the Latin version of Ben Sira contains about 20,150 words, of which some 2400 (or 11–12 percent) represent expansions relative to the text of the GrI recension.

Lest there be a misunderstanding: I am not trying to establish that θεόπνευστος stood in the Greek text of Ben Sira. I am only making the case for a pre-third-century CE date for *Sentences* 129. Although I have suggested that the *Sentences* of Pseudo-Phocylides knows the Greek *Vorlage* of Lat Sir. 4:12, the fact that Pseudo-Phocylides used θεόπνευστος does not prove that a lost Greek form of Ben Sira also used the word. (Clement's wording [if it really echoes Ben Sira] suggests otherwise.) Ben Sira easily could have used some other Greek expression for wisdom's life-giving quality. The combination of the Latin wording with the wording found in Clement, however, suggests that the image of insufflation was a component of this lost Greek text.

So what date should we assign the *Sentences*? Van der Horst (1978: 81–2) refers to a "growing consensus" for dating it between 200 BCE and 150 CE, but thinks the most probable range of dates is between 30 BCE and 40 CE.[147] He opines that "another dating should probably have to be earlier, not later" (Van der Horst 1978: 82 n. 9), but his reason for resisting a later date is hardly convincing: he argues that anti-Jewish actions during the reign of Caligula (37–41 CE) cooled Jewish–pagan relations in a way that would have dissuaded the sort of program attempted in the *Sentences*.[148] I am not so sure. Persecution that is massively deadly in scope can do that sort of thing, but persecution that is disruptive on a lesser scale often amounts to opportunities to regroup and redouble. I have already signaled my agreement (albeit tentative) with Wilson's understanding of the *Sentences* as an exemplar for Jewish one-upmanship over pagan culture. Painful dealings with pagan forces might actually move one to concoct a slate of Phocylidean thefts from Jewish tradition. Derron's (1986: lxvi) contention that a post-first-century date is betrayed by a lack of Christian influence on the writing is similarly weak (cf. Susemihl 1892: 644 n. 64; Klawans 2017).

We should perhaps answer another argument for dating the *Sentences* to the pre-Destruction period, which sees in vv. 100–103 an allusion to the practice of ossilegium—that is, of exhuming the deceased after a year in order to place the bones in an ossuary: "Do not dig up the grave of the deceased, nor expose to the sun / what may not be seen, lest you stir up the divine anger. / It is not good to dissolve the human frame; / for we hope that the remains of the departed will soon come to the light (again)" (Van der Horst 1985: 577). Since most ossuary inscriptions date between 30 BCE and 70 CE, a passage censuring ossilegium might give the impression of a date

---

[145] Gile (2011: 248) argues against the view that most of the additions from GrII, LatII, and SyrII originated from a Hebrew text.

[146] As Kearns (2011: 56) points out, the Latin text has a lot of commonalities with family 248 among the Greek manuscripts: the Latin contains 33 of some 150 additional stichoi found in family 248. See Segal (1934–5: 109–10).

[147] On the date of the *Sentences*, see Van der Horst (1985: 567); Derron (1986: li–lxvi).

[148] Derron (1986: lxv) reproduces Van der Horst's reasoning with respect to an Alexandrian scenario.

before the First Revolt.[149] Levi Rahmani (1994: 21–5) notes, however, that ossilegium actually continued until at least the third century CE.

We already know that Pseudo-Phocylides was greatly influenced by Ben Sira. The question is: Which *recension* of Ben Sira did he know? If our chronological arguments are sound, the *Sentences* was written in the second century CE, or slightly earlier.[150] The combination of this dating with our argument for a second-century or earlier Greek exemplar for Lat Sir. 4:12 makes it entirely possible that Pseudo-Phocylides knew the expression now found in Lat Sir. 4:12 and to have mined its imagery for *Sentences* 129. Such a date fits comfortably, of course, with the vivificationist understanding of θεόπνευστος found in other works. Should it be decided that the *Sentences* could not have been quite so late, we will have to reckon with the possibility that v. 129 is an interpolation. In that case, however, we still should presume it to have crept into the manuscript tradition rather early—probably in the second or third century. Either way, Pseudo-Phocylides should be considered yet another witness to the vivificationist understanding of θεόπνευστος in pre-Origenist times.

---

[149]   Niebuhr (2008: 475) calls vv. 100–102 a "supposed reference" to ossilegium.
[150]   A second-century date was suggested in Dieterich (1893: 190).

3

Pre-Origen Uses of Θεόπνους

This chapter will look at all the known pre-Origen uses of θεόπνους (an alternate spelling of θεόπνευστος): the fragment of Numenius preserved in Porphyry's *On the Cave of the Nymphs*, the *Poimandres*, a Roman-era inscription in front of the Great Sphinx of Giza, and an inscription from a nymphaeum in Laodicea on the Lycus.

1 Fragment of Numenius, from Porphyry's *On the Cave of the Nymphs*

Numenius of Apamea is our first exemplar for the spelling θεόπνους—or, in this case, θεόπνοος.[1] Today we can access his work only through fragments preserved by later writers, including Clement of Alexandria, Origen, Eusebius, and other representatives of the Christian intelligentsia, as well as pagan writers like Porphyry, Proclus, and Macrobius.[2] The fragment that concerns us was preserved in a late-third-century writing by Porphyry, entitled *On the Cave of the Nymphs*.[3] Nothing in the text suggests that Porphyry understood θεόπνοος differently from how Numenius meant it, but his use of the word counts more directly toward Numenius' second-century understanding of the word than of how it was understood in his own day. The relevant passage reads as follows:

---

[1] As Johnson (2013: 276 n. 104) notes, this is apparently the first use of the form θεόπνοος in Greek literature.

[2] The fragments of Numenius are gathered in Thedinga (1875) (cf. 64 [frag. 35]); Nauck (1886) (cf. 63); Leemans (1937) (cf. 104 [frag. 46]); des Places (1973) (cf. 81 [frag. 30]); Guthrie (1987) (cf. 37 [frag. 35]). See Saffrey (1975). On the date of Numenius, see Dodds (1960: 11); des Places (1973: 7); Frede (1987: 1038–9). John Dillon (1996: 362, 379–80) argues that Cronius, an oft-mentioned contemporary of Numenius (see Brisson 2004: 71–4), was the recipient of a letter by Lucian in 165. On Numenius' philosophy, see Frede (1987); Merlan (1970: 96–106); Baltes (1975); Dillon (1996: 361–79); Whittaker (1978); Culianu (1981); O'Meara (1989: 10–14); Kenney (1992); Alt (1993: 29–42, 101–8, 130–47, 204–11; 2006: 31–4); Edwards (2010).

[3] Most scholars date *On the Cave of the Nymphs* later than 262 CE, the year Porphyry was admitted into Plotinus' circle. It is sometimes argued that the writing must be later than the seemingly less Plotinian *Homeric Questions*—see esp. Schrader (1880: 349). Lamberton (1986: 110 [cf. 108–10, 318–24]), however, argues the possibility of an earlier date. Edwards (1996: 88) suggests that *On the Cave of the Nymphs* is "perhaps among the first fruits of [Porphyry's] maturity."

For they ["the ancients"] held that souls settled upon the water which was theopneustic, as Numenius says, and therefore the prophet said "The Spirit of God was moving upon the face of the waters," and therefore the Egyptians depicted all their daimons standing not on dry land but all on a boat—the sun and the rest—and these are construed as the souls descending into genesis and hovering over the water. (*De antr.* 10 [Author's translation])[4]

Scholars usually describe Numenius as a Middle Platonist or a Neopythagorean. John Dillon (1996: 378) counts several additional strands of thought in Numenius, including Hermetic, Gnostic, Zoroastrian, and Jewish. His knowledge and appreciation of Jewish texts and theology was exceptional among pagan philosophers and might have a bearing on his use of θεόπνοος.[5] As a follower of Plotinus, Porphyry is generally labeled a Neoplatonist.[6] His *On the Cave of the Nymphs* is an extended allegorical interpretation of a Homeric passage describing a cave near Phorkys' harbor on Ithaca (see *Od.* 13.102–12), explicitly based on an earlier work by Numenius.[7] It is not known

---

[4] The Greek text was published in Duffy et al. (1969); Simonini (1986); Lardreau (1989).

[5] Numenius' knowledge of Jewish writings and theology is widely celebrated—see Gager (1972: 63–9); Edwards (2010: 117). It is possible, however, that that knowledge was mediated by secondary sources. Cf. Edwards (1990: 68). On Numenius in Jewish and Christian contexts, see Sterling (1993: 108–10) and the sources listed in Lyman (2003: 215 n. 24). See the discussion of "Numenius and Alexandrian Judaism" in Quispel (1992: 7–10). On Numenius' use of the Old Testament, see Cook (2004: 36–41, 167–8). On the biblical tradition in Numenius and Porphyry, see Zambon (2002: 196–204). Things often said about Porphyry's supposed appreciation for Jewish tradition perhaps stand in even greater need of qualification than things that have been said about Numenius. One frequently reads of the great respect Porphyry gave to the Jews—for example, Johnson (2013: 282) writes of his "overt sympathies for the Jews and their way of life." See Van der Horst (2010: 71). Beatrice (2009) recently argued, however, that Porphyry was less appreciative of Jewish thought than usually held. See Cook (2012); Johnson (2013: 275–6); and the discussion of "the Greeks as plagiarists" in Johnson (2006: 128–42).
    We should also note Puech's (1934: 754) often cited suggestion that Numenius was *Jewish*, which Dillon (1996: 378–9) appropriately calls "misguided."

[6] Brisson (2004: 71) writes, "Numenius's point of reference was Plato, but a Plato inseparable from Pythagoras." See Puech (1934: 768); van Winden (1959: 105); Dillon (1996: 378); Winston (1993: 145–6); Kingsley (1995: 328–9); Joost-Gaugier (2006: 40–1); Turner (2006: 31–4). On the relation of Numenius to Plotinus, see Phillips (2002: 235–47).

[7] Niehoff (2011: 150) thinks that *On the Cave of the Nymphs* "strongly resembles" Philo's *Legum allegoriae*. See Berthelot (2012: 165–71) (but cf. Lamberton [1986: 75]; Zambon [2002: 182–3]; Gaston [2009: 575]).
    On the original Homeric account of the cave of the nymphs, see Weinberg (1987: 32–34); Byre (1994); Zusanek (1998: 16–29); Larson (2001: 24–5); Ondine Pache (2011: 115–21). On nymphs in Homer more generally, see Malkin (2001). Porphyry records that Cronius questioned the historicity of the cave on Ithaca, but that he (Porphyry) had confirmed its existence by a passage in Artemidorus of Ephesus (*De antr.* 4). (Strabo likewise expressed doubts about points of Homer's geography of Ithaca [*Geography* 10.2.10]. On the debate over Homer's knowledge of geography, see Mark [2005: 161–78].) On Porphyry's stance regarding the historical reality of the cave, and its immateriality to the point of the allegory, see Tate (1934: 111). Karivieri (2010: 427–8) notes that a cave at Vari seems to have been modeled on "the Cave of Plato," esp. as recreated by Porphyry. There have been many attempts to identify the original cave in Homer's *Odyssey*. Lord Rennell of Rodd (1932–3: 15) claimed that a cave called "Marmarospelia" on modern Ithaca is Homer's cave: Marmarospelia

    has the two entrances referred to, one facing the north wind, accessible to men; the other facing the south wind, a wide aperture at the far end of the vaulted roof, the way only of immortals who walk the air. ... You descend, as the text indicates, on entering to a lower level

which of Numenius' works Porphyry used, but it is widely recognized (on the basis of Proclus, *In Rep.* 2.96) that Numenius had written a commentary on the myth of Er in Plato's *Republic*. Robert Lamberton (1983: 4) suggests that this commentary could be found in a work called *On the Secrets in Plato* (see Dillon 1996: 364; Puech 1934: 748).

As Lamberton (1983: 6) notes, the Homeric text serves for Porphyry "as a pretext for the elaboration of a vast amount of lore about the symbolism of stone, of caves, of bees, and so forth."[8] (Félix Buffière [1956: 419] described Porphyry's work as "un catéchisme symbolique.")[9] The passage from Homer describes a double-entry cave associated with a local nymph cult, and Homer's readers plied the passage with considerable ingenuity.[10] Porphyry, in reliance on Numenius, read Homer's description of the cave through the lens of Plato's myth of Er and unpacked a number of supposed allusions to a Platonizing myth of the γένεσις of the world and of the souls within it.[11] The alignment of the cave's two entrances along a north–south axis, which Homer had differentiated as separate entries for humans and gods, becomes in Porphyry's hands a symbol of the cosmogonic narrative: "When a cave is double, like the one with two entrances that Homer describes, they used to consider it symbolic not of the noetic but rather of the sensible cosmos, and likewise the cave under consideration, because its 'water flows incessantly,' would not be a symbol of the noetic hypostasis, but rather of material existence" (*De antr.* 10 [trans. Lamberton 1983: 27]).[12] Porphyry evidently takes the "ever-flowing water" (ὕδατ' ἀενάοντα) of *Od.* 13.109 as a symbol of human generateness—which he then unpacks in terms of *ensoulment*. In this way, Porphyry explained the attribution of life-giving qualities to spring water in terms of an anthropogonic narrative.

How does θεόπνοος function in this passage? Most translators have tried to stay in line with the lexicons, but a few have ventured beyond those bounds. Lamberton's rendering is typical—the SUNY-Buffalo translation (Duffy et al. 1969: 13) renders θεόπνοος as "divinely inspired," Laura Simonini (1986: 51) as "divinamente ispirata," and Kenneth Guthrie (1987: 37 [frag. 35]) as "divinely inspired." More than 250 years

---

by a rough rock stair. ... The steady drip which formed the stalactites also hollowed out the "mixing-bowls" on the rock shelves. The cavern is still haunted by the wild bees.

Cf. *Odyssey* 13.105–6 (quoted in *De antr.* 1): "Within are kraters and amphoras / of stone, where bees lay up stores of honey" (trans. Lamberton 1983: 21). Waterhouse (1996: 303–4, 315) argues either for a different cave or for a composite of two caves (she is not clear on the point), on the basis of tripods found in the so-called Polis cave. See Benton (1934–5); Heurtley (1939–40); Elderkin (1940); Fraser (1941).

[8] On bees as souls in *On the Cave of the Nymphs*, see Ransome (1937: 106–7); Giuman (2008: 36). On bees as souls more generally, see Roscalla (1998: 28–9).

[9] See the discussion of *On the Cave of the Nymphs* in Praechter (1910: 122–8); Meredith (1985); Weinberg (1987: 35); Berthelot (2012: 165–71). On Numenius' interpretation of Homer, see Whittaker (1993); Edwards (1994: 73–4). On Porphyry's interpretation of Homer, see Pépin (1966). On Neoplatonist allegorizing in general, see Chastel (1975).

[10] Aristotle, for his part, found an intensification of ornament in this passage. See Fletcher (1964: 117).

[11] Buffière (1956: 442–4) argued that Numenius was trying to reconcile Homer's and Plato's views of the soul. See Lamberton (1986: 319–22).

[12] On the idea of soul gates, see Reiche (1993: 174–6). On the two entrances in Numenius (= Capricorn and Cancer), cf. Proclus, *In Rep.* 2.128.26–131.14. See Lamberton (1986: 66–9).

ago, Lucas Holstein (in Gesner and van Goens 1765: 11) translated ἡγοῦντο γὰρ προσιζάνειν τῷ ὕδατι τὰς ψυχὰς θεοπνόῳ ὄντι as "Quas aquæ, quæ divino spiritu fovetur, assidere putabant."[13] These scholars all translated according to what they thought θεόπνευστος/θεόπνους meant in Numenius' day, but there are clear indications within the text that θεόπνοος meant "life-giving."[14] Not only does θεόπνοος correspond to the "living" quality of Homer's ὕδατ' ἀενάοντα (*Od.* 13.109)—the only type of water with which naiads were associated (see below)—but Porphyry uses the term as a more powerful load-bearing device in his argument: the description of the water as θεόπνοος is connected with the belief that "souls settled upon the water."

To understand the connection between the cave's theopneustic waters and the descent of souls into γένεσις, it helps to consider the ritual purpose of the waters within the cult of nymphs, beginning with Porphyry's own description of what took place in the cave near Phorkys' harbor. Nymph caves were widespread in the Mediterranean world, and the mythology behind them enjoyed an active subscription for well over a millennium.[15] One prominent type of nymph—called a "naiad"—was always connected with water, including rivers, fountains/springs, (nonstagnant) backwoods pools, or cave waters.[16] (Porphyry connects the naiads specifically with waters "out of which streams 'flow' [νάουσι]" [*De antr.* 8 (trans. Lamberton 1983: 26)].) These naiads were invoked for their favors as patrons of marriage and procreation, and spring-fed pools in the caves were regarded as a means of curing barrenness.[17] (Sallustius writes that "the nymphs preside over generation" [*On the Gods and the World* 4 (trans. Murray 1951: 204)].) Women bathed in the pools as a preparatory ritual in a wedding rite[18]—to ensure their ability to bear children. Thus the waters were thought to have a fecundating effect.[19] Numenius' description of the cave waters as θεόπνοος expresses this belief in the waters' life-giving properties and uses it as the

---

[13] The same rendering appears in part 2 of Hercher (1858: 90).

[14] Lamberton (1986: 55) expresses a degree of uncertainty about Porphyry ever quoting Numenius directly (although I may be reading him too strongly), which perhaps would suggest (for him) that the word θεόπνοος was supplied by Porphyry.

[15] For an annotated list of nymph caves, see Amandry (1984: 404–8). On nymph caves, see Wace and Thompson (1908–9); Levi (1923–4); Faure (1961–2); Mitford (1980: 261–3); Ustinova (2009: 55–68); Wagman (2011). On the cult of nymphs in general, see van Straten (1976). See also the sources cited in Sourvinou-Inwood (2005: 103). In parts of Greece, nymph mythology lasted even until modern times—see the tales collected in Horton (1929).

[16] On the association of nymphs with water, see Ovid, *Meta.* 2.238–39; Ballentine (1904); Blümel (1950); Lacroix (1953); Carnoy (1956); Tusa (1993). Parker (2011: 75) writes, in connection with votive reliefs to the nymphs, that "rivers embodied for the Greeks in cultic terms … the fructifying power of moisture, the source of life itself." For a popularizing collection of ancient tales about springs, many of which feature nymphs, see Smith (1922).

[17] Muthmann (1975: 37 [see 77–112]) writes, "Als Numina der fruchtfördernden und heilkräftigen Wasser erfüllten die Nymphen die Funktionen von Fruchtbarkeits-, Geburts- und Heilgöttinnen." See Oakley and Sinos (1993: 15). On nymphs as symbols of fecundity, see Santa Cruz (2007: 84–7).

[18] On marital rites at nymphaea, see Ginouvès (1962: 265–82); Settis (1973: 685–8). See Muthmann (1975: 94–5); Gagné (2006: 6–7). Marchetti (1995: 237) writes, "Les nymphes, omniprésentes dans la mythologie … symbolisaient universellement l'union des hommes et des femmes." See Dowden (1989: 102, 104–5).

[19] The waters of the Nile were considered esp. fecundating—causing women to bear twins, triplets, and quadruplets. See Solinus 1.51; Pliny, *Hist. nat.* 7.3.33; Leclant (1994); Wild (1981: 95–6).

basis for an anthropogonic allegorical reading. Porphyry alludes to this function of the cultic waters a little later in *On the Cave of the Nymphs*:

> [§12] ... Thus souls coming into γένεσις are Naiad Nymphs and so it is the custom to call brides "nymphs" [νύμφαι] as well, since they are being married for childbearing [γένεσις], and to pour over them water drawn from springs or streams or everflowing fountains. For souls that have been initiated into the material world and for the deities that preside over γένεσις, the cosmos is both holy and pleasing, though by nature it is shadowy and "murky": that is why these beings are considered to be misty and to have the substance of mist or air. For the same reason an appropriate temple for them on earth would be a "pleasant grotto," a "murky" one, in the image of the cosmos in which souls dwell as in the greatest of temples. The cave is likewise appropriate for nymphs that preside over the waters since it contains water which "flows unceasingly." [§13] Thus let us say that the cave in question is dedicated to souls and to the nymphs of the realm of the more fragmented powers that preside over flowing streams and springs and are called Pegaean Nymphs (Spring Nymphs) and Naiads for that reason. (Trans. Lamberton 1983: 28–9)[20]

Thus Bonnie MacLachlan (2009: 207) refers to Porphyry's allegorizing of the water's theopneustic effect as a development of the "purpose" that a Euripidean scholion attributes to the "lustral bath"—that of "confer[ring] upon the bride and groom the fecundating powers of water."[21]

In her book on *Greek Nymphs*, Jennifer Larson discusses the role of water in the cult of the nymphs, including its life-giving effect in the prenuptial ritual, which she associates more generally with the healing power of water in Greco-Roman cults.[22] She writes, "The primary purpose of the maiden's bath is fecundating: all the river deities, including the river gods and their offspring, the nymphs, aid in conception as well as in nurturing children after birth" (Larson 2001: 111; see Connor 1988: 180; Dowden 1989: 123; Bachvarova 2009: 291). Although Porphyry does not refer to Numenius in §§12–13, it can scarcely be doubted that the argument he earlier attributed to Numenius drew upon the water's power to bless newlyweds with children.[23]

---

[20] Only "living" (viz. flowing) water, it was widely assumed, could be life-giving (viz. possess healing properties, etc.). On the desire for "ever-flowing" springs, see Ballentine (1904: 86–7). See Halm-Tisserant and Siebert (1997: 898–9). Cf. the importance of "living" water in early Christian baptismal liturgy and in rabbinic strictures on water to be used in a *mikveh*—see Jenson (2011: 132–4). On life-giving water in Greco-Roman literature, see Stovell (2013: 472–5).

[21] The scholion in question comments on Euripides' *Phoenissae* 347—cf. Ginouvès (1962: 421–2). See Ballentine (1904: 100–1); Borthwick (1963: 231–7). Cf. Cumont and Cumont (1906: 171). On prenuptial rites associated with nymphs, see Costabile (1991). See Andò (1996: 52–4, 63–5); Redfield (2003: 111). There is some doubt as to whether the groom's lustration (as owned by MacLachlan) bears the same purpose as that of the bride—see Ginouvès (1962: 422 n. 4). See Halm-Tisserant and Siebert (1997: 896–7).

[22] On the healing powers of water associated with nymphs, see Strabo, *Geography* 8.3.32; Pausanias 5.5.11; 6.22.7; Larson (2001: 158–9, 178, 188, 196, 200, 224). On nymph caves as centers of healing, see Larson (2001: 229). See Gow and Page (1965: 2.415); Cole (1988); Speyer (2015: 11–12).

[23] It is worth noting Ervin's (1959: 156–9) argument that a connection between nymphs and the blessing of progeny lies behind local myths associated with the Athenian Hill of the Nymphs. The

While most translators and lexicographers have rendered θεόπνοος along the same lines as Lamberton, Simonini, Holstein, and the SUNY-Buffalo team—that is, in deference to the term's presumed inspirationist valence—a minority of translators appear to realize that an inspirationist rendering does not fit the logic of Porphyry's argument. In 1789, the latter-day Neoplatonist Thomas Taylor (1789: 2.282) published a translation of *On the Cave of the Nymphs*, in which he rendered θεόπνοος as "nourished by a divine spirit"—a rendering that arguably captures some of the sense of a life-giving force.[24] (Unfortunately [and inexplicably], Taylor [1823: 177] mis-revised his translation of θεόπνοος, some thirty years later, to "inspired by divinity.")[25] More recently, Édouard des Places (1973: 80 [frag. 30]) translated the relevant phrase as "qu'anime un souffle divin." Menahem Stern (1980: 444 [no. 456b]) translated the phrase as "which is divinely animated." Presumably the nearness of the allusion to Gen. 1:2 helped Stern with his choices. Catherine Tihanyi, while translating the first volume of Luc Brisson's *Sauver les Mythes* into English, gave Porphyry's use of the word a vivificationist rendering. There she presented, in lieu of an English translation of des Place's French rendering (as used by Brisson), a "slightly modified" version of the SUNY-Buffalo translation. Where the SUNY-Buffalo committee had rendered θεόπνοος as "divinely inspired," Tihanyi (Brisson 2004: 72) substituted the wording adopted by Stern: "divinely animated." Did she recognize that her rendering better suited the logic of Porphyry's account (or of Brisson's original French)?[26] At any rate,

---

cult of nymphs in some places combined with the cult of Artemis or (possibly) Parthenos—see Braund (2007: 195); Makarov and Ushakov (2009: 254–5).

The second half of the remains of lines from Aeschylus' play *Semele* gives several clear indications of the nymphs' connection with nuptials and with the bearing of children. Lines 16–30 are spoken by Hera, disguised as a begging princess:

Infallible nymphs, glorious goddesses, for whom I collect alms,
life-giving daughters [παισὶν βιοδώροις] of the Argive river Inachus,
who attend upon all mortal act[ivities,]
[…] and we[ddings] with their happy music,
and [… maidens (?)] new to the bed of wed[lock],
white [… e]yes (?) [they are (?)] kindly,
light … […] … of the eye … […]
For modesty is pure and is by f[ar] the be[st] adorner of a bride,
and a rich crop of children are born to those whom [they]
25 come to meet in propitious mood, w[ith] a plea[san]t spirit,
goddesses who come in two ways, … [… and also (?)]
harsh, hateful, and […]
in their approach; many women … […]
[…] … of a wedded husba[nd …]
[…] and with … headbands […]
(Aeschylus, Fragment 220a [trans. Sommerstein 2008: 231]).

[24] Raine and Harper (1969: 296) narrow the range of possible dates for Taylor's actual work of translation to the period 1787–9.
[25] Both Critchley (2005: 227 n. 137) and Uždavinys (2009: 236) wrongly imply that Taylor's (1823) translation is a reprint of his 1792 translation. The two translations, in fact, are very different. (Warfield [1900: 101 n. †] appears to have known only the 1823 rendering.)
[26] Brisson's (1996: 102) original version contained des Place's rendering: "sur l'eau qu'anime un souffle divin."

Tihanyi's rendering represents a step in the right direction—a direction that had been indicated already two centuries ago by Taylor.[27]

2 *Corpus Hermeticum* 1.30

The *Corpus Hermeticum* is a collection of seventeen or eighteen[28] loosely connected tractates, gathered in the name of a third- and fourth-century Hermetic cult.[29] Most of the tractates expressly refer to Hermes, but *Poimandres* (= *Corp. Herm.* 1) is among the exceptions.[30] While the cult behind the *Corpus Hermeticum* worshipped a pagan god, there are traces of Jewish influence, especially in the two earliest tractates—*Corp. Herm.* 1 and 13.[31] The corpus as a whole bears the imprint of Egyptian influence and almost certainly was written in Egypt (see Derchain 1962; Daumas 1982; Fowden 1993; Kingsley 1993).[32]

In *Corp. Herm.* 1.30, θεόπνους once again refers to the giving of life—this time, in a soteriological sense, not far removed from the understanding that obtains in 2 Timothy. As with many of the examples of θεόπνευστος/θεόπνους discussed elsewhere in this book, a predisposition to see the idea of "inspiration" in this word has led generations of translators to misunderstand the word, as well as the passage in which it appears.

Admittedly, an uncritical reading of *Corp. Herm.* 1.30 might allow θεόπνους to pass for something like prophetic inspiration. I present the passage here with the relevant phrase untranslated:

---

[27] If these scholars appear to be on the cusp of realizing θεόπνοος means "life-giving," we find an even nearer approach to that position in Gager's (1972: 66) remarks on this passage: "The key [to Numenius' reasoning] seems to be the verbal connection between the *theopnous* in Numenius' system and the *pneuma theou* of Gen. 1:2." See Gager (1973: 104–5). Unfortunately, Gager squanders this gain by keeping the term θεόπνοος at a distance from Numenius' reference to the genesis of souls: Numenius, he tells us, "interpreted *pneuma theou* in one of two ways: either the *pneuma* represents the souls themselves as they rest on the water, or, more probably, the spirit borne over the water explains how and why the water was *theopnous*." By all appearances, the inspirationist understanding of θεόπνοος kept Gager from seeing the more direct connection between the "God-breathing" aspect of the water and the souls it generates.

[28] The number depends upon the edition at hand.

[29] Although editions of the *Corpus Hermeticum* disagree on the numbering of the tractates, *Poimandres* is placed first in every edition after (but not including) Everard (1650). Some early modern editions apply the name "Poimandres" to the entire *Hermetic Corpus* and look upon the tractates as *chapters*, as of a single work. Scott (1924–36: 1.17) rightly remarks, "This is much as if one were to call the New Testament as a whole 'the Gospel according to St. Matthew.'"

[30] *Corp. Herm.* 3 and 7 are also exceptions. See Chlup (2007: 152 n. 47). Some translations gloss the text to look like a dialogue between Poimandres and Hermes.

[31] Jewish elements lie near the surface in *Corp. Herm.* 1, 3, and 7. On the Jewish elements in the *Poimandres*, see Philonenko (1975; 1979); Pearson (1981); Camplani (1993: 381–3); Lahe (2011: 222–8, 247–51); Wikander (2013: 589–90). See also the discussion of "Esoteric Jewish influence on Hermes" in Quispel (1992: 10–11). In spite of the Jewish elements, it would be quite impossible to identify the author as a Jew, as did Bestmann (1885: 263) and Jansen (1977: 162). On the Hermetica and the Old Testament, see Cook (2004: 49–52). On the echoes of Genesis in *Poimandres*, see Kroll (1928: 139, 142, 148–9).

[32] But see the discussion of Reitzenstein's "Egyptomania" in Zielinski (1905–6: 27–30).

I recorded the beneficence of Poimandres within myself, and I exulted in being filled with what I wished. For the sleep of the body became the sobriety of soul, and the closing of the eyes true vision, and my silence was made pregnant with the good, and the birthing of the word became the progeny of good things. This happened to me because I took from my mind that which is of Poimandres, that which is of the word of authority, θεόπνους γενόμενος τῆς ἀληθείας ἦλθον. Therefore, I give praise to God the father from my soul and with all my might. (Author's translation)

The phrase θεόπνους γενόμενος τῆς ἀληθείας ἦλθον[33] has been rendered in various ways over the years—more often than not, along the lines adopted by Brian Copenhaver: "I have arrived, inspired with the divine breath of truth." At times the phrase has been rendered as a sentence complete in itself, and at other times it has been made part of a longer sentence.[34] Table 3.1 gives an indication of how translators have dealt with this phrase.[35]

Most of these renderings take θεόπνους as representative of divine inspiration, referring explicitly either to being "God-inspired" or simply to being "inspired" (e.g., du Preau, de Foix Candalle [1574, 1579], Everard, Chambers, Scott, Dodd, Newbold, Mead, Cartlidge and Dungan, Segal, Layton, van den Broek and Quispel, Copenhaver, Holzhausen [1994, 1997], Salaman et al., Barnstone).[36] Some renderings take a less committal approach, rendering θεόπνους in terms of spirit-filling (Ficino, von Metternich, Schultz, Festugiére, Haardt/Hendry, Foerster/Hall, Tröger [perhaps], Büchli, Portogalli, Vigna and Tondelli, Eckart, Vatri, Ramelli, Miller [perhaps], Scarpi),[37] but even then an inspirationist sense enters through the back door by rendering τῆς ἀληθείας as a genitive of content (viz., "θεόπνους *with* the truth" or "filled with the divine breath *of* truth") rather than as a genitive of agency (viz., "θεόπνους *by* the truth").[38] The only translation to render τῆς ἀληθείας agentively ("by the truth," etc.) is

---

[33] Greek text as found in Parthey (1854: 17); Reitzenstein (1904: 338); Scott (1924–36: 1.130); Scarpi (2009: 1.46).

[34] See Holzhausen (1994: 68 n. 260).

[35] References for Table 3.1: Ficino (1505: 8a); Benci (1548: 15); du Preau (1557: 11(a)); de Foix Candalle (1574; 1579); Everard (1650: 33); von Metternich (1706: 15); Tiedemann (1781: 21); Parthey (1854: 17); Ménard (1866: 14); Chambers (1882: 15); Mead (1906: 2.19); Schultz (1910: 68); Scott (1924–36: 1.131); Dodd (1935: 178); Newbold (1940: 199); Nock and Festugiére (1945: 1.17); Haardt (1971: 176); Hall (1972: 334); Tröger (1973: 116 n. 66); Jansen (1977: 157); Cartlidge and Dungan (1980: 250); Segal (1986: 22); Büchli (1987: 163); Layton (1987: 458); van den Broek and Quispel (1991); Copenhaver (1992: 7); Holzhausen (1994: 79; 1997: 21); Portogalli (1997: 23); Eckart (1999: 41); Nebot (1999: 98); Vatri (2000: 47); Salaman et al (2000: 24); Vigna and Tondelli (2000: 42); Barnstone (2003: 510; 2005: 573); Ramelli (2006: 89); Miller (2009: 126); Scarpi (2009: 1.47). For a list of editions and translations of the *Corpus Hermeticum* prior to the 1600s, see Faivre (1995: 184–5). See also Ebeling (2007: 51–7, 118–21).

[36] Fr. Pfister (1959: 981) does not provide a translation, but he may be added to those who assume θεόπνους means "inspired."

[37] Gager (1972: 65 n. 120) commends Festugière's rendering for "retain[ing] the literal meaning of the two components in *theo-pnous*."

[38] Tiedemann avoids the difficulty (unacceptably) by ignoring θεόπνους altogether, a tactic repeated 199 years later by Cartlidge and Dungan. In a double-asterisked footnote, Tiedemann asks who thinks ("wer denkt") that θεόπνους does not refer to inspiration.

Table 3.1 Select renderings of θεόπνους γενόμενος τῆς ἀληθείας ἦλθον in *Corp. Herm.* 1.30

Year	Translator	Rendering
1505	Marsilio Ficino	"Unde ipse divino afflatus spiritu: veritatis cōpos effectus sum."
1548	Tomasso Benci	"Onde che io confortato da'l Divino Spirito, fui fatto chiaro de la verità."
1557	Gabriel du Preau	"Estant doncques inspiré de l'esprit divin, ay sceu & cogneu l'entiere & parfait verité de toutes choses, …"
1574	Francois de Foix Candalle (1)[a]	"Unde Divinitus veritate afflatus veni."
1579	Francois de Foix Candalle (2)	"… dont ie suis venu divinement inspiré de verité."
1650	John Everard (working from a Latin base)	"… whereby I became inspired by God, with the Truth."
1706	Wolf Freiherr von Metternich (alias "Alethophilus")[b]	"Göttlich bin angeblasen / und der Wahrheit theiihafftig geworden …"
1781	Dieterich Tiedemann	"Von ihm mit der Wahrheit angehauft, bin ich gekommen, …" [In footnote (**): "Θεοπνους, wer denkt hieben nicht an die Inspiratien?"]
1854	Gustavus Parthey	"… unde ipse divino afflatus spiritu, veritatis compos effectus sum …"
1866	Louis Ménard	"… ainsi, par une inspiration divine, je possédai la vérité."
1882	John David Chambers	"…whence becoming God-inspired, I arrived at the truth"
1906	G. R. S. Mead	"… by whom being God-inspired I came unto the Plain of Truth."
1910	Wolfgang Schultz	"Denn gottbegeistert drang ich bis zu dem Kreise der Wahrheit …"
1924	Walter Scott	"… whereby, becoming God-inspired, I attained to the abode of Truth."
1935	C. H. Dodd	"Wherefore being inspired by God I arrived at the truth."
1940	William R. Newbold	"… whence I have become inspired and have come to the Circle of the Truth."
1945	A.-J. Festugiére[c]	"Et me voici donc, rempli du souffle divin de la vérité."
1971	Robert Haardt/J. F. Hendry	"So I became full of the divine breath of truth, and have come (to you) …"
1972	Werner Foerster/S. G. Hall	"I have come, filled with truth by God's Spirit."
1973	Karl-Wolfgang Tröger	"Hier bin ich also (wörtlich: ich bin gekommen), erfüllt vom göttlichen Hauch der Wahrheit."
1977	H. Ludin Jansen	"Durch Gott eingeblasen und der Wahrheit teilhaftig, bin ich aufgetreten."
1980	David R. Cartlidge and David L. Dungan	"I came to men because I was divinely inspired."
1986	Robert A. Segal	"Being divinely inspired by the truth, I came."
1987	Jörg Büchli	"Ich bin gekommen, von Gottes Geist mit Wahrheit angefüllt [geworden]."
1987	Bentley Layton	"Divinely inspired with truth, I came …"
1991	R. van den Broek and G. Quispel	"Door goddelijke inspiratie van waarheid vervuld, …"
1992	Brian P. Copenhaver	"I have arrived, inspired with the divine breath of truth."

Table 3.1 continued

Year	Translator	Rendering
1994	Jens Holzhausen (1)	"Ich gelangte dahin, von der göttlichen Wahrheit inspiriert zu werden."
1997	Jens Holzhausen (2)	"Von der göttlichen Wahrheit inspiriert, bin ich hier angekommen."
1997	Bianca Maria Tordini Portogalli	"Sono venuto dunque pieno del soffio divino della verità."
1999	Karl-Gottfried Eckart	"Hier bin ich, gottbegeistert durch die Wahrheit."
1999	Xavier Renau Nebot	"Y he regresado nacido dal soplo divino de la verdad."
2000	Giuseppe M. Vatri	"Eccomi qui, dunque, riempito dal soffio divino della verità."
2000	Clement Salaman, Dorine van Oyen, William D. Wharton, and Jean-Pierre Mahé	"I have come, divinely inspired by the truth."
2000	Pierre Dalla Vigna and Carlo Tondelli	"Dunque, sono venuto, spinto dal soffio divino della verità."
2003/2005	Willis Barnstone	"I became god-inspired, … and came with the truth." / "I became God-inspired, … and came with the Truth."
2006	Ilaria Ramelli (following Festugière)	"Sono dunque venuto dopo essere stato investito dal divino soffio della verità."
2009	Maria Magdalena Miller	"Vom Geiste angehaucht stieg ich zur Sphäre der ewigen Wahrheit empor."
2009	Paolo Scarpi	"Ed ecco, sono venuto, spinto dal divino soffio della verità."

ᵃThis translation was reprinted in Rossel (1585).
ᵇVon Metternich's translation was based on an earlier Dutch translation.
ᶜIn Nock and Festugiére (1945).

Segal's, but by combining that rendering with "divinely inspired," it seems to draw on a more modern understanding of "inspiration" (*qua* fructifying thoughts). The prejudice against combining a non-inspirationist rendering of θεόπνους with an agentival rendering of τῆς ἀληθείας does not spring from considerations of grammar but from the force of habit—namely, the habit of associating θεόπνευστος/θεόπνους with verbal or epistemic inspiration. Thus the above table reveals a presumption, seemingly on the part of everyone who has tried to translate this passage (with the possible exception of Miller), that θεόπνους must refer to divine (verbal or epistemic) inspiration in some way. Some of the translators, in fact, gloss the text in order to give a smooth inspirationist rendering—thus Scott, Newbold, and Mead refer not to arriving at (the) truth per se but rather to arriving at the "abode," "circle," or "plain" of truth.[39] Dodd

---

[39] Newbold follows Reitzenstein's (1904: 338) emended Greek text—Reitzenstein had inserted ‹ἐπὶ τὸν κύκλον› between θεόπνους γενόμενος and τῆς ἀληθείας ἦλθον. Newbold passed away in 1926 and could not have known Dodd's suggested emendation, and most likely knew nothing of Scott's rendering. (Clark published Newbold's translation in 1940 with his widow's permission.) It should be noted that Miller similarly makes recourse to "Sphäre der ewigen Wahrheit," but with better results. Scott (1924–36: 1.130) includes a parenthetical ellipsis at this point in his Greek text. He

(1935: 178 n. 2) makes an equivalent move by calling for the insertion of μέχρι within the phrase τῆς ἀληθείας ἦλθον. Given the (groundless) assumption that τῆς ἀληθείας cannot be a genitive of agency, the introduction of these facilitating glosses makes good sense, as it surely is more likely, in the context of *Poimandres*, that "truth" refers (in a quasi-technical sense) to religious truth rather than to merely correct information and to *the* truth in the sense of the "true faith."[40] If we take θεόπνους in a vivificationist sense, however, we open ourselves to the possibility that τῆς ἀληθείας is a genitive of agency. We can also allow "truth" to refer to religious truth (= "Truth"), without emending the text.

Microcontextually considered—bracketing everything before and after §30—θεόπνους could refer to either inspiration *or* vivification. When we widen our lens beyond §30, however, the evidence becomes one-sided in favor of a vivificationist meaning. Not only are there no other references to inspiration in this tractate—indeed the awakening of gnosis in those who have νοῦς ("mind") appears to be a matter of *teaching* rather than of prophetic inspiration—but the whole of the writing deals with a sort of personal salvation explicitly defined in *vivificationist* terms.[41] Soteriological references to "life" or "immortality" (or to the avoidance of "death") appear in §§6, 18, 19, 20, 21, 28, 29, and 32.[42] In fact, rendering the phrase in §30 in vivificationist terms, and reading it together with the sentence immediately preceding it ("This happened to me because I was receptive of mind"), creates a parallel with the thought expressed in §21: "If you learn that you are from light and life and that you happen to come from them, you shall advance to life once again" (trans. Copenhaver 1992: 5). The tractate's closing sentence completes the parallelism: "For this cause I believe, and bear witness, I go to Life and Light" (1.32).

The pairing of the theme of life with that of light (see Cox 2007: 294) is often said to be suggestive of Philo and the Fourth Gospel (Dodd 1935: 133–6),[43] but, as Rudolf Bultmann (1948: 14, 24–6; cf. 1964: 841–2) noted, the mutual association between these terms is more widespread (see Wlosok 1960: 249; DeConick 1996: 73–74; Choufrine 2002: 69–70). Alfred Loisy (1921: 89) had noted a similarity between *Poimandres* and

---

offers Reitzenstein's interpolation in the apparatus, along with a conjecture of his own: "Fortasse ‹ἐπὶ τὸ πεδίον› τῆς ἀληθείας." Mahé (1987: 292) rightly complains, "[Scott's] English translation is based upon texts that are often distorted by arbitrary corrections."

[40] Thus Everard, Scott, Newbold, and Mead capitalize "Truth." Cartlidge and Dungan avoid the problem of how to render τῆς ἀληθείας simply by ignoring it. One might say that *Poimandres* uses "the truth" in a way that parallels its use in the Pastoral Epistles. See 1 Tim. 2:4; 2 Tim. 3:7; Murphy-O'Connor (1968); Thiselton (1980: 412–13).

[41] See the discussion of "salvation in *Poimandres*" in Cox (2007: 303–8). Festugière (1948: 11, 23) correctly notes that a "doctrine" of salvation appears only in *Corp. Herm.* 1, 4, 7, and 13. See Copenhaver (1992: xxxvii). Mahé (1978: 38–41) compares *Poimandres*'s eschatology to that of the Nag Hammadi *Discourse on the Eighth and Ninth*. See Holzhausen (1994: 46–7 n. 158); DeConick (1996: 73–9, esp. 79); Moreschini (2006).

[42] Dodd (1935: 134) notes elements of a vivificationist soteriology elsewhere in the *Corpus Hermeticum*: "The author of *Corp.* XI. says that it is the ἔργον of God 'to make life, soul, immortality and change'. ... Again, in *Corp.* XII. life and immortality are 'parts' of God, and the κόσμος, the πλήρωμα of life, is His image (§§ 21, 15)."

[43] Dodd notes that the pairing of life and light is "equally important" in *Corp. Herm.* 13, "which depends on the Poimandres" (133 n. 2). See Klein (1962: 84–107); Holzhausen (1994: 46–9). Most scholars today do not explain the contacts between the *Corpus Hermeticum* and the Fourth Gospel through the independent use of tradition. See Braun (1955); Evans (1993: 72–5).

the Fourth Gospel with respect not only to the pairing of light and life but also to a third theme: *truth* (see Lagrange 1924: 483).[44] The passage from §30 that lies at the center of our investigation represents the narrator's actions in response to Poimandres' offer of life—life (*qua* salvation) consequent on the communication or realization of truth.[45] It thus appears that the phrase in question (θεόπνους γενόμενος τῆς ἀληθείας ἦλθον) is intended to relate a conversion experience of some sort.[46] Θεόπνους denotes a vivificationist experience for the author, and the best translation of θεόπνους γενόμενος τῆς ἀληθείας ἦλθον would be along the lines of "I was (divinely) made alive by the truth, I came [to give praise, to testify, etc.]."[47] "*The* truth," in this formulation, stands for the message preached.

The question of *Poimandres'* date has a bearing on our investigation. Although a few scholars make *Poimandres* contemporary with Origen, most date it to the second century, while a minority (mostly of a bygone generation) date it to the first. Most of the best arguments for a second-century date were presented by Dodd (1935: 201–9) more than eighty years ago.[48] He established a *terminus post quem* by affirming Scott's argument that *Poimandres* must postdate the hybridizing of Platonism and Stoicism, a development he traces to Posidonius in the first century BCE (Dodd 1935: 201). For a *terminus ante quem*, Dodd (1935: 202) refers to the alchemist Zosimus' apparent knowledge of *Poimandres*.[49] (He mistakenly gives an *early*-third-century date for Zosimus' *floruit*. Zosimus was active at the *end* of the third century and the beginning of the fourth.) To narrow this range of dates, Dodd (1935: 202) offers several considerations, of which the following are perhaps the most astute: (1) the lack of any reference to Hermes within *Poimandres* may indicate that it "was written before the emergence of a definitely Hermetic school, for which Hermes

---

[44] On the comparison between the Fourth Gospel and the *Poimandres*, see Groff (1897: 74).

[45] It is perhaps significant that life, light, and truth are brought into collocation within a Marcosian baptismal formula preserved by Irenaeus (*Adv. haer.* 1.21.3). See Hoffmann (1903: 298); Bousset (1973: 63–4).

[46] Willoughby (1929: 206) writes, "Hermetism, too, had its baptism and the Trismegistic prophet, like John the Baptist, summoned men to 'Repent and be baptized!' These cult remains are so indigenous to this literature and are handled with such naïve sincerity that the student cannot regard them as literary fictions." See Zielinski (1905; 1906); Kroll (1928); Tabor (1981: 90 n. 49). See the discussion of "Hermès missionnaire" in van den Kerchove (2012: 34–9). Hadas (1972: 145) notes a congruence between Paul's preaching in Athens (*apud* Acts) and the message of the *Poimandres*, the *Odes of Solomon*, and the *Sermon of Peter*, in that all these texts include "the four motifs of correcting ignorance …, worshiping God not through material representation but in spirit …, calling for repentance …, and referring to resurrection …."

[47] Note the similarity to Segal's rendering. Holzhausen (1994: 68 n. 260) regards the placement of ἦλθον as a problem. On the "call to preach" in *Poimandres*, see Fowden (1993: 158–9). See also McGuire (1986: 354).

[48] Dodd presented these arguments mostly in response to Reitzenstein's first-century date. (A first-century date was also held by Philonenko 1975: 204.) Reitzenstein had argued that the *Shepherd of Hermas* was dependent upon *Poimandres*—an argument based on erroneous assumptions about the meaning of the name "Poimandres." See Dodd (1935: 203). On the debate over the meaning of "Poimandres," see the reviews and proposals in Marcus (1949); Jackson (1999).

[49] At the end of *Final Count*, Zosimus tells his sister Theosebeia to take refuge in "Poimenandres" and to receive baptism "in the mixing bowl" (a reference to *Corp. Herm.* 4)—see Berthelot (1887–8: 2.245); Festugière (1950: 1.368 lines 1–4); Fowden (1993: 33, 125–6); Mertens (2002: 172); Fraser (2004: 136–7, 141–4).

Trismegistus must be the source of all teaching of this kind."[50] (Garth Fowden's [1993: 33] claim that Poimandres instructs "none other than Hermes Trismegistus himself" is based on a "canonical" reading of *Poimandres* [*qua* Hermetic tractate], rather than on a documentary reading.)[51] (2) Dodd (1935: 202–3) notes that the hymn at the end of *Poimandres*—surely written (he claims) "as part of the tractate"— is included in a third-century collection of Christian prayers: "The papyrus … affords evidence that the tractate was known to a Christian reader before the end of the third century. To allow for such a writing becoming current in Christian circles we should probably have to put its composition some considerable time before A.D. 300" (see Nock and Festugière 1945: 1.xxxvii).[52] (3) Dodd approvingly cites an argument made by Scott with regard to *Poimandres'* nearness to the thinking of some second-century philosophers. According to Scott (1924–36: 2.8), the writer bearing the greatest resemblance to *Poimandres* is Numenius (see Kingsley 1995: 333).[53] (4) Dodd (1935: 209) notes a similarity in thought between *Poimandres* and Valentinus' writings (*ca.* 130–140 CE) and suggests (albeit in the absence of any real argument) that the former is likely somewhat earlier than the latter. On the basis of these considerations, Dodd suggests a date in the early second century but does not rule out the late first century.[54]

From my point of view, a date in the mid- to late second century looks more plausible than Dodd's early-second-century date, especially given the similarity with Numenius. It must also be said that an early-third-century date cannot be ruled out. Dodd's mistake in dating Zosimus to the early third century may have been a factor in his preference for the early second century, and adjusting his date range fifty years *later* does no violence to the time lag he posits between *Poimandres* and Zosimus.[55] An early-third-century date for *Poimandres* does not pose a difficulty for the thesis that Origen changed the meaning of θεόπνευστος during the same period. Even the mid-third-century date argued by Büchli would not pose a difficulty,[56] as we could hardly expect all vivificationist uses of the term to cease as soon as Origen began using it with an inspirationist meaning.

---

[50] The same argument appears in Edwards (1992: 57 n. 10). Philonenko (1975: 209) appears to see an internal link between *Poimandres* and Hermetism in his suggestion that the use of the *trishagion* in *Corp. Herm.* 1.31 is (intentionally?) evocative of "Le Trismégiste."

[51] Fowden's decision to read Hermes into *Poimandres* calls to mind Ralph Cudworth's criticisms of Isaac Casaubon's homogenization of the hermetic tractates in the early seventeenth century (on which, see Assmann 1997: 84–85). See Zielinski (1905: 323).

[52] The Christian prayer that incorporates the hymn from *Poimandres* is found in *P. Berol.* 9794—see van Haelst (1976: no. 722).

[53] Dodd (1935: 204) is content to look upon Numenius and the author of *Poimandres* as representative of "parallel developments." See Denzey Lewis (2013: 109).

[54] Mahé (1987: 289) argues for a late-first-century or early-second-century date, on the grounds that the allusions to the Jewish liturgy in *Corp. Herm.* 1.31 require a continuing presence of Jews in Alexandria. I cannot see why such allusions could not have been made after 117 CE.

[55] Haenchen (1965: 377) also dates *Poimandres* to the late second century. Ferguson (2003: 314) writes that *Poimandres* is "second century at the earliest." See van den Kerchove (2011: 80).

[56] Büchli (1987) argues that *Poimandres* is strongly influenced by Christian thought. See Windisch (1918); Lagrange (1924).

3 Inscription at the Great Sphinx of Giza

Θεόπνους appears in an early-third-century inscription that once adorned a platform in front of the Great Sphinx of Giza. The inscription was discovered in late 1817 or early 1818[57] by Giovanni Battista Caviglia, the famous Genoese mercantile-captain-*cum*-archaeologist, who was in the employ of Henry Salt,[58] the British consul general in Egypt. While Caviglia conducted the dig, Salt (an accomplished artist) drew maps and perspective drawings, and wrote an account, all of which were intended for a dig report of some sort.[59] A significant portion of Salt's prepared report had to do with Greek inscriptions found on one of the Sphinx's forepaws, or on or near a pair of platforms situated on two broad stairways in front of the Sphinx. In Salt's own words:

> On a stone platform, at the top of the steps, was a small building (…), which, from its construction, and from various inscriptions found near it, seemed to have been a station (…), whence the emperors, and other persons of distinction, who visited the Pyramids, could witness the religious ceremonies performed at the altar below. An inscription on the front of it was much worn. (Quoted in Vyse 1940–2: 3.112)[60]

These inscriptions express reverence toward the Sphinx as a cult object and celebrate the presentation of offerings in the forecourt of the complex. They also advertise the care and interest that Roman emperors took in preserving the Sphinx.[61] Among the

---

[57] The dates commonly assigned to Caviglia's discovery of the porch between the forepaws (and of its inscriptions) vary from 1816 to 1818. The year 1818 is given in the intended title of Salt's account, but he begins his account by referring to a six-month period of Caviglia's activity in late 1817 and early 1818 (in Usick and Manley 2007: 56). (Maspero [1893: 259] gives a date of 1818.) A date of 1818 would force us to assume that Salt's account was written almost as soon as things transpired, given that it is heavily quoted in *Quarterly Review* for 1818. (An earlier account in the *Quarterly Review* that same year [Barrow and Young 1818], based on information from Salt, made no mention of the stairway or the platform yielding Θεόπνους.) On the other hand, Caviglia (1837a: 707) claims (doubtless through an intermediary) that he "exposed to view the north and east sides of the Andro-Sphinx" in 1817 and refers to "the antiquities which I found in the year 1817" and to the "monuments which I had brought to light in the years 1817, 1820, 1821, 1836, and 1837" (1837b)—nowhere mentioning the year 1818. Vyse (1940–2: xii), who worked with Caviglia some twenty years later, refers to the latter's "excavations at the Sphinx in 1816." Birch (1852–3: 27) also maintained that Caviglia's discoveries took place "probably in 1816." Hassan (1953: 13) gives 1816 as the year "Captain Caviglia commenced to excavate the Sphinx." Zivie-Coche (2002: 112) gives a date of 1817. On Caviglia's work on the Sphinx, see Lehner (1991: 32–4, 269–75).

[58] Caviglia's excavation at the Sphinx was underwritten by Salt and "two or three other gentlemen" (Barrow and Young 1818: 418). See Bosworth (1974–5: 87).

[59] We are indebted to Usick and Manley for publishing Salt's account, but their discussion of the inscription presents conflicting information about its original location. In one part of Salt's account, he mentions inscriptions found on the "2d digit" of the paw, including the inscriptions represented by "Sketch 38 a.b.c" (in Usick and Manley 2007: 66). The problem is created by Usick and Manley's (2007) purported correction of Salt's "Sketch 38" to "Sketch 48," as "Sketch 48" includes our inscription, which was *not* found on the paw, but rather (as explicitly indicated on Salt's sketch) "on the front of the lower small edifice on the platform facing the sphinx" (9, 45). (The edifice no longer stands.)

[60] The platforms are usually understood to be *viewing* platforms, although fellow Giza explorer Giovanni Belzoni (1822: 1.216) saw them as altars. On the inscription on the platform, see Zivie-Coche (2002: 104); Usick and Manley (2007: 66–7).

[61] It was Rome's policy, when in Egypt, to do as the Egyptians do. See Heinen (2007: 193–4).

royalty who visited the Sphinx and left inscriptions were Nero, Hadrian, Antoninus Pius, Verus (Antoninus' son), Marcus Aurelius, and Septimius Severus.[62]

The inscription on the platform looking directly down on the sphingian forecourt bears our next example of the word θεόπνους, while the inscription on the other platform helps us date *both* inscriptions: the latter features the name "Septimius Severus" (reigned 193–211 CE) and an erased reference to Severus' son, Geta.[63] (Geta was executed by his brother Caracalla in 211 CE, and his name and image were erased throughout the Empire [see Varner 2004: 168–84].)[64] As the platforms are parallel in design, we can assume their inscriptions stem from the same imperial reign.[65]

Salt's drawings included the θεόπνους inscription. Salt's own publication of the dig never materialized, but the inscription appeared on a plate in the appendix volume of Howard Vyse's *Operations Carried on at the Pyramids of Gizeh in 1837* (1840–2: 3.Plate F), some fifteen years after Salt's death.[66] (Although Vyse had Salt's facsimile drawing of the inscription available to him, he appears to have passed it up for an alternative rendering.)[67] A number of scholars have attempted to reconstruct the inscription on the basis of his plate, including Antoine-Jean Letronne (1842–48: 2.484), August Boeckh (1828–77: 3.1188 [no. 4700b]), George Kaibel (1878: 428 [no. 1016]), Étienne Bernand (1969: 521), and Jean-Yves Carrez-Maratray (1993).[68] Letronne (1842–8: 2.484) presented what may be the earliest reconstruction in 1848:

Ἥδε κυρεῖ πάντων σφίγξ, ἡ καὶ Θεῖον ὅραμα·
χῶμα γὰρ ἀγνοέεις ὕψος Θ' ὅπερ ἔπλετο τῇδε·
φάσματος εὐέργοιο (?) νοήσεις κόσμον ἅπαντα
ἱερὸν, ὡς ἐφύπερθε πρόσωπον ἔχει τὸ Θεόπνουν,
γυῖα δὲ καὶ δέμας οἷα λέων, βασιλεὺς ὅ γε Θηρῶν
..... κεν τὸ Θέαμά τις ἀτρεκέως γε νοήσει
ταῖς ....

62 On royal visitors to the Great Sphinx in the Greco-Roman period, see Hassan (1953: 119–25). See Hawass (1998: 27).

63 According to *Historia Augusta Sept. Sev.* 17.4, Severus visited Memphis, Memnon, the Pyramids, and the Labyrinth. On Severus' visit to Egypt, see Birley (1999: 132–9). Bowersock (1984: 30) doubts Letronne's view that Septimius Severus tried to restore the upper half of the Sphinx. On the dates suggested for Septimius Severus' visit to Memphis, see Platnauer (1918: 122) ("sometime probably about March, 201"); Hasebroek (1921: 119) (dated 199/200 CE); Halfmann (1986: 21–2) (dated 200 CE); Birley (1999: 139) (in 200 CE); Spielvogel 127 (dated Spring 200 CE). See esp. Halfmann (1986: 21); Rowan (2012: 77–82).

64 On the *damnatio memoriae* in general, see Hedrick (2000: 89–130). Krüpe (2011) somehow misses the erasure of Geta's name at the Great Sphinx. Russell (1831: 118) long ago took the odd view that Severus erased Geta's name from the inscription in front of the Sphinx "probably ... by his own hand."

65 Bernand (1969: 521) gives the inscription a date of "Époque impériale avancée, d'après la provenance et la forme des lettres."

66 Some of Salt's maps and drawings were published (with parts of his account) by Vyse, while others remained unpublished until Usick and Manley (2007).

67 Owing to the inscription's faintness at the time of discovery, Salt's drawing left much to be desired. Not only was the transcription lacunose but Vyse (1840–2: 3.188) noted that "the characters [on the inscriptions] do not appear to have been accurately copied." The inscription appears to have been lost during Émile Baraize's excavations (1925–36), when the stairway was removed.

68 The inscription is often discussed as "no. 130," the number assigned it in Bernand (1969).

.... ἐκ τῆς Θεότητος·
ἐσθλῆς αὐτὰρ ἐγώγε Θέας ἀπιὼν ἐχάραξα.

For our purposes, Letronne's reconstruction is helpful—the letters that concern us in line four were a bit misrepresented in Salt's transcription, but the corrections needed to read that part of the inscription are now scarcely in doubt: ὡς ἐφύπερθε πρόσωπον ἔχει τὸ θεόπνουν.

The inscription as a whole describes the Sphinx—its leonine body ("king of the beasts"), its lordship over all, and its divine aspect. Line four fits this scheme, describing the Sphinx as having a theopneustic face. What does θεόπνους mean in this context? Carrez-Maratray flattens the term into a bare reference to divinity, translating πρόσωπον ἔχει τὸ θεόπνουν as "il possède un visage sacré."[69] To his credit, Letronne (1842–8: 2.485) recognized that θεόπνους has something to do with animation by the imparting of divine breath, but he took the Sphinx's face to be the object animated rather than the one animating: "Πρόσωπον τὸ Θεόπνουν est remarquable, au lieu de ἀνδροπρόσωπον, ἀνθρωπόμορφον, ἀνθρωποφνῆ ou βροτόμορθον (qui aurait pu entrer dans le vers); mais Θεόπνους, *animé du souffle de Dieu*, est bien plus beau." (Letronne [1842–8: 2.485–86] saw that an inspirationist interpretation of θεόπνους cannot apply in this context, but that makes it all the more surprising that he should posit, *on the basis of that word*, that the inscription was probably written by a Christian.)[70] Christiane Zivie-Coche (2002: 109) gives a similar interpretation: "he has a holy visage enlivened by divine breath."[71] But this last interpretation seems off the mark, given its context. Why refer to the animation of the face alone?

It is more likely, in my view, that θεόπνους refers to the face's ability to give life *to others*—or, rather, that the face represents someone with that power. We need only to consider why the epigraphist singled out the *face*. Why not describe the whole statue as theopneustic? It is possible, of course, that the reference to the face is connected with its being the locus of the deity's inbreathing, but it is more probable, in my view, that the face's theopneustic aspect is connected with its identification with the ruler of Egypt. It has long been held that the face on the Sphinx represents that of Chephren, the Fourth-Dynasty pharaoh who ordered its construction (see Hawass [1995: 227];

---

[69] Carrez-Maratray (1993: 151) discovers an acrostic "ΗϹΦΙΓΞ" in an alternative reconstruction of the Sphinx epigram and argues that the words *"par en haut"* il possède un visage sacré" are an allusion to "plus ou moins sibyllines au principe même de l'acrostiche."

[70] Birch (1852–3: 32–3) accepts Letronne's identification of the epigraphist as "probably a Christian." Letronne perhaps labored under the misconception—still prevalent in some circles—that the Apostle Paul coined the word θεόπνευστος.

[71] Zivie-Coche's translation (2002: 116) appears to be based on that of Bernand (1969: 521), who translates as follows:

> Il a tout en partage, ce sphinx qui est aussi un spectacle divin. En effet, si l'on remarque son corps et la hauteur qu'il a, on remarquera tout ce qui fait l'ornement d'un prodige combien sacré: par en haut, il possède un visage sacré, animé du souffle de dieu, mais il a les membres et la stature d'un lion, le roi des animaux. Vision effrayante! Mais si l'on remarque exactement... le surnom d'Héphaistos ... sa divinité ... En quittant cette belle vue, moi, j'ai gravé ces vers.

Lehner [2002]; Zivie-Coche [2002: 36–40]).[72] And there is an abundance of evidence (also well known) that rulers of Egypt were regularly ascribed the ability to bestow life (see Bultmann 1964: 840).[73]

In point of fact, "giver of life" was one of the most common epithets awarded the pharaohs. In the Abydos inscription, engraved in a temple of Seti I during the reign of Ramesses II (Nineteenth Dynasty), construction-project officials extol the Pharaoh with a profusion of epithets, among them the identification of Pharaoh as Khnum, "... who gives breath to every person (nose) / who vivifies the entire Ennead" (translation from Spalinger 2009: 30).[74] A few lines further, Pharaoh is identified as "the breath of our nostrils." The image of Pharaoh as the dispenser of life was central in formulations about his dealings with subjects and conquered foes. (The phrase could also denote the freeing of prisoners [see Capart, Gardiner, and van de Walle 1936: 190 n. 2].) David Lorton assembled a catalog of "juridical terminology" based on the image of giving or denying breath, stretching across the reigns of numerous pharaohs. He lists dozens of occurrences of *ṯ3w n 'nḫ* ("breath, air (of life)"), connected with the reigns of Hatshepsut, Thutmosis III, Amenophis II, Thutmosis IV, Amenophis III, Amenophis IV, Tutankhamun, and Horemhab (Lorton 1974: 136–8). He notes, "When these examples are considered together, it is clear not only that they are based upon the religious use ... but also that the usage of *ṯ3w n 'nḫ* is extended to indicate something which the king says (thus *ṯ3w* 'breath'), this apparently being appointment to office and/or the granting of land or an income" (Lorton 1974: 138). Shlomit Israeli (1998: 276 [cf. nn. 34–42]) lists a number of different forms of requests for "breath"/"life" that a defeated foe might make of Pharaoh: "Breath! Breath!" (e.g., *KRI* 5.47.10); "Give us the breath to our nose!" (e.g., *KRI* 5.37.3); "Breath! Breath! ... Give us the breath of your ability to give!" (e.g., *KRI* 5.317.14/15–16); "Give us the breath!" (e.g., *KRI* 5.34.13); "Give us the breath of your ability to give!" (e.g., *KRI* 5.9.8); "*Give* us the breath!" (e.g., *KRI* 5.20.7); "May you give us the breath of your ability to give" (e.g., *KRI* 5.47.8); "Breath is in your arm. Yours is the life. It is according to that which you have commanded that we breathe it" (e.g., *KRI* 5.86.10–11); "Breath is in your arm ... your father, Amon, has placed us beneath your feet forever" (e.g., *KRI* 5.81.3–4).[75] The hero of the *Tale of Sinuhe* (Twelfth Dynasty) praises Pharaoh with similar words: "... the air of heaven is breathed at your order. / ... / One lives by the air which you give. / Ra, Horus and Hathor love these, your noble nostrils!" (B 234–9 [translation from Bárta 2003: 26]).

---

[72] For a dissenting view, see Stadelmann (2001). That the Sphinx represents a king was suspected at least as early as Salt's interpretation of Caviglia's discovery of pieces of the Sphinx's beard. See Usick and Manley (2007: 65). On the sphinx as the image of the king, see Zivie-Coche (2006: 56–8). Pieces of a Fourth-Dynasty sculpture found at Abu Rawash reveal otherwise lost details of the Great Sphinx's appearance. See Jordan (1998: 80).

[73] Eyre (1976: 106) writes that "the connection between breath and life is ... basic to the Egyptian concept of existence."

[74] See the remarks on this passage in Assmann (1999: 534–5). The text of the Abydos inscription is presented in Maspero (1867). Cf. the translation in Breasted (1906: 108).

[75] These forms are often augmented with "reasons" and "additional remarks," some of which make further reference to breathing (277–8). Cf. Thraede (1986: 715). Lorton (1974: 144) notes that the expression also appears in the Amarna Letters, probably in reference to Egyptian practice.

David Silverman (1995: 56), commenting on a scene in which the royal children ask their father to restore Sinuhe's breath (B 275), notes that "the power to give breath to the breathless … is well-attested in scenes found in temples and tombs," except that, in those scenes, we find a deity giving breath to a king.[76] Similar wording also appears in the immediate vicinity of our θεόπνους inscription, on the hieroglyphic tablet found between the Sphinx's front legs, which refers to Thutmosis IV (Eighteenth Dynasty) as "the giver of life" (see Vyse 1940–42: 3.115).[77]

4 Nymphaeum at Laodicea on the Lycus

A final use of θεόπνους lies in an early-third-century inscription at Laodicea in Asia Minor. The inscription was found in the ruins of a Severan-era nymphaeum at the center of town, sometimes called the "Fountain of Caracalla."[78]

The nymphaeum was excavated from 1961 to 1963 by a team from Laval University, led by Jean des Gagniers.[79] Their work established the building's early-third-century date, primarily on the basis of decorative elements (see, e.g., Ginouvès 1969: 85 n. 1, 89 n. 1, 92 n. 2). The nymphaeum featured two fountains and a basin and was fed by an aqueduct[80] that brought water from a spring five miles to the south (in modern Denizli). (See Meinardus 1974: 132; Yamauchi 1980: 141–2; Sperti 2000: 74–8.) A large statue of Isis (or of an Isiac priestess) adorned the nymphaeum.

For the official dig volume, Louis Robert was assigned the task of interpreting the inscriptions, which included three metrical fragments—all on white marble. Robert assumed that the fragments were pieces of a single inscription. His main clue to the inscription's basic nature comes from fragment C (see Robert 1969: 336–8 [cf. plates CXIV–CXV]; Peek 1972: 256–7). He gives the letters of the fragment as follows:

- - - PO - - - -
- - ΣΘΕΟΠΝΟ - - -
- - ΥΝΑΠΟΘΕΙΝΑ - -

The second line of the fragment appears to feature our word: "… ς θεόπνο …." Drawing on the inspirationist sense he assumes θεόπνους has in Porphyry (= fragment of Numenius) and in *Poimandres*, Robert (1969: 337) found a reference to a prophecy,

---

[76] Murray (1970: 160) notes an Egyptian priestly view of kings as those "who discovered the necessities of life."

[77] Lepsius (1849: series 1, table 30) included a depiction of the granite stele and the chapel between the forepaws among his Egyptological tables. See Jordan (1998: 89, 100–1).

[78] The nymphaeum is no. 47 in Richard's (2012: 271–2) catalog of nymphaea and fountains.

[79] See the discussion of "le nymphée de Laodicée et les nymphées romains," in Ginouvès (1969: 136–67). According to Richard (2012: 8), "the publication on the so-called Fountain of Caracalla at Laodikeia by J. des Gagniers and R. Ginouvès marked the first significant achievement towards a global classification of monumental fountains throughout the Roman Empire." Archaeologists have uncovered other nymphaea in Laodicea as well—see Şimşek (2007: 141–66).

[80] On the Laodicean aqueduct, see Ramsay (1895–7: 1.48–49); Weber (1898); Bean (1971: 255–6); Huttner (1997: 100–1).

or to an office of prophesying: "Il est probable que θεόπνους s'applique au prophète d'Apollon Pythien."[81] The presumption that the inscription refers to something oracular then becomes the test bed by which Robert (1969: 337) interprets other words in the inscription, and so, accordingly, the words σκιόεν τέμ[ενος] ("sanctuaire ombragé") in fragment A become a reference to the Temple of Apollo at Claros, and the word πρέσβυς at the beginning of fragment B becomes a reference to "l'ambassadeur sacré" who traveled to the oracle as a representative of Laodicea.[82] Robert (1969: 337) finds enough clues of this nature to conclude that the three fragments are "les morceaux d'un oracle": "Il est probable que θεόπνους s'applique au propheté d'Apollon Pythien."

Robert interpreted the appearance of θεόπνους in what was probably the only acceptable way known to him: as a reference to *inspiration*. Armed with this assumption, Robert then "uncovered" a context in which to make sense of the appearance of θεόπνους. From the famous oracle in Claros, he counted twenty-five references to "prophets" from Laodicea. It is one of these prophets of Apollo, he suggests, whose inspiration is indicated by the word θεόπνους.[83] In order to locate the inscription at a high point in Laodicea's involvement with the Clarian Apollo, Robert dated it several decades earlier than the nymphaeum itself, conjecturing that it had been moved to the nymphaeum after it was built. (Robert [1969: 337–8 (cf. 306–7)] even identifies the prophet [!]: Lucius Antonius Zeno Aurelianus.) This served to align the date of the inscription with the period that Robert (1954: 7) elsewhere called "la grande vogue de l'oracle" at Claros.

Although others have welcomed Robert's understanding of the nature of the inscription (e.g., Peek 1972: 260; Corsten 1997: 134–6), his position has some evident weaknesses. (See below.) He drew on what he supposed θεόπνους meant for Porphyry and for the author of *Poimandres*, but how would he have interpreted this inscription if he had a more reliable philological profile for the word? How might he have read the inscription differently if he had been open to a vivificationist sense for θεόπνους?

As noted above, Robert inferred that σκιόεν τέμενος must be a reference to the temple of Apollo at Claros. (He built his case partially on Laodicea's long history of supplying prophets for that temple.)[84] But A. R. A. van Aken (1951: 272) reminds us

---

[81] Joannae Robert (in Stauber and Merkelbach 1996: 32), in a summary of Louis Robert's argument, calls θεόπνους "ein religiöses Wort," and thus not surprising in an oracle.

[82] Robert (1969: 336–7) writes, "Le morceau A porte, à la fin de la ligne 3, l'amorce du *pi* qui se plaçait avant le ρεσβυς du morceau B. … Le πρέσβυς est alors l'ambassadeur sacré, le *théopropos*, qui vient consulter l'oracle au nom de sa cité. L'adjectif ἄριστος ou un mot composé avec lui se rapporte à ce délégué." On delegations of θεοπρόποι to the oracle at Claros, see Busine (2005: 40–7); Dana (2011: 58–65). Ferrary (2005: 728, 734–6, 741) discusses the chronology of Laodicean delegations to the Clarian oracle. He lists memorials for Laodicean visits to Claros for the years 128/9, 129/30 or 130/1, 131/2, 132/3, 133/4, 136/7, 139/140, 141/2, 143/4 or 144/5, 146/7, 147/8, 148/9, 149/150, 150/1, 153/4, 155/6, 174/5, 175/6, 184/5, along with scattered references that could not be precisely dated (745–60). See Huttner (2013: 139–40, 201–3). See the discussion of "Géographie de la clientèle de Claros" in Busine (2005: 59–69). The inscriptions listing the Laodiceans who traveled to Claros are nos. 18–21 in Şahin (1987: 67–9). On the practice of traveling to oracles, see Harland (2011: 9–11). On *hymnodoi*, see the studies listed in Rogers (2012: 367 n. 38). Cf. Lane Fox (1987: 177–8). On the popularity of the Apollo cult in Laodicea, see Picard (1922: 696–7); Huttner (1997: 98–9; 2013: 44–8). On the oracle at Claros, see Levin (1989: 1628–37). See Stoneman (2011: 96–7).

[83] Robert (1969: 298–303) discusses these Clarian inscriptions. The prophets to whom he refers were envoys to the Apolline oracle at Claros (discussed more broadly in Robert 1969: 289–309).

[84] See Robert's (1969: 298–303) discussion of these prophets.

that "the primary meaning of the 'nymphaeum' … is of a religious nature: sanctuary of nymphs,"[85] and so it would be perfectly natural to read σκιόεν τέμενος as a reference to the nymphaeum itself. An inscription from the time of Constantius in neighboring Hierapolis supports this reading. That inscription, discovered in the theatre, celebrates the civic beneficence of a certain Magnus. Among his listed contributions, we read of how, "with his splendid wisdom, he made the city a sanctuary of the Nymphs (νυμφῶν τέμενος)" (translation from Huttner 2013: 307). The reference to Magnus making the whole city a sanctuary, of course, should not be unpacked too literally. It probably meant that Magnus contributed in grand fashion to the building and/or upkeep of the city's nymphaea, or to the construction or repair of the *castellum aquae* that distributed water to the nymphaea.[86] Although the term "sanctuary of nymphs" is here applied to the whole city, it was obviously interchangeable, on a more literal level, with the nymphaea.

Three years after Robert published his transcription and reconstruction of the three metrical fragments, Werner Peek (1972: 256) offered an improved reading of fragment C (see Corsten 1997: 134–6). According to Peek, Robert's reconstruction of συναποθεῖναι from []ΥΝΑΠΟΘΕΙΝΑ[] is by no means secure. Peek (1972: 256) questions the leftmost letter (Υ) in Robert's transcription and offers an alternative reading: "die Abbildung auf Taf. 114 unten völlig klar erkennen, daß vielmehr [τ]έκνα ποθεινά auf dem Stein steht (die rechte obere Gabel wäre für Υ auch viel zu lang)." The reconstructed words τέκνα ποθεινά should be translated as something like "desired children." Although Peek failed to recognize it, this is a dead giveaway that the inscription deals with the religious function of the nymphaeum in which it was found, as the whole purpose of identifying a nymphaeum's waters as "life-giving" was to advertise their fecundating effect. Peek's revisionist reading (in spite of his continuing support for Robert's view of the inscription as oracular in nature) actually provides striking confirmation of the nymphological reading that I am propounding. According to the inscription, women who wanted children were best served using the facility's water for their prenuptial bathing rituals.

---

[85] As Aupert (1974: 119 [see 119–21]) points out, the *Suda* defines a νυμφαῖον as a νυμφῶν ἱερόν, "et c'est le terme dont use également Libanius (XI, 202)." Ginouvès (1969: 165–6) writes,

> Les expressions qui désignent certain nymphées, "sanctuaire des Nymphes," "temple des Nymphes," les statues des divinités qui les ornaient et les consacraient, certaines dédicaces de fontaines aux Nymphes et à Aphrodite, ou à Déméter, l'existence de fêtes religieuses en l'honneur de sources, invitent au moins à supposer que le Nymphée n'était pas seulement un bâtiment public comme les autres,—dans la mesure où, jusqu'aux derniers temps de l'Antiquité, s'est conservée, à des niveaux et avec des qualités différentes, une réelle vénération pour les eaux et pour les grottes d'où elles jaillissent: *nullus enim fons non sacer*.

[86] Huttner (2013: 308) deems it unlikely that a man of Magnus' station "actually established a pagan sanctuary" in Constantius' day and that therefore "the verse must be understood metaphorically as a reference to the water supply or the public baths in Hierapolis." On the nymphaea in Hierapolis, see Ferrero (1987); Campagna (2006: 387); Dorl-Klingenschmid (2006: 382). The ruins of Hierapolis feature the largest nymphaeum yet found in Asia Minor: the Tritons' Nymphaeum—its length listed alternately as 65 m (Campagna) or 63 m (Richard). Richard (2012: 113) lists the "basin capacity" of the Tritons' Nymphaeum in Hierapolis as 353 m³.

Needless to say, the word πρέσβυς (in fragment B) is amenable to a range of scenarios. The dignitary in question could easily have been credited with some aspect of the nymphaeum's construction or upkeep.

4.1 Nymphaea as Religious Facilities

A failure on the part of many scholars to recognize the religious function served by the nymphaeum may have contributed to Robert's and Peek's inability to discern the inscription's true referents. In an earlier period, the typical nymphaeum architecturally imitated the grotto whose religious function they emulated. The purpose of imitating natural grottoes was to preserve those aspects of the grotto setting that were amenable to the nymphs to whom the nymphaea was consecrated.[87] By the second century CE, however, nymphaea became more grandiose structures—especially in Asia Minor, where seemingly every civic-minded populace arranged for an imposing fountain house to celebrate the local aqueduct and the city it served (see Aicher 1993: 341).[88] René Ginouvès (1969: 136–67) provides a detailed comparison of the Laodicean nymphaeum's architectural features with other types of nymphaeum throughout the contemporary Roman world. Some nymphaea even featured "fragments de stalactites et de rocailles" (Ginouvès 1969: 143), and nymphaea in general were often accompanied by gardens. The nymphaeum's distance from the spring that fed it did not affect its religious function. The nymphs apparently approved of the civil engineers' efforts, and the fact that some of the populace used a nymphaeum's water in a purely recreational manner did not preclude its continuing importance for the community's religious regimen.[89] Although they served as part of a town's water works, nymphaea were not the secularized facilities that some scholars imagine them to have been. Their religious associations and functionality remained intact.[90]

---

[87] *Orphic Hymn* 51 (line 5) refers to the nymphs as "travelers of the winding roads who delight in caves and grottoes" (trans. Athanassakis 1977: 67). On the relation of the nymphaeum to the grotto, see Neuerburg (1965: 31–9). On the architectural form of the nymphaeum, see Meschini (1958). On "künstliche Grotten" used as nymphaea, see Letzner (1999: 126–9, 183–5). On the "Fassadennymphäen," see Quatember (2011: 87–99). Hülsen (1919: 85) writes,

> Sehr verbreitet war ein vereinfachtes Fassadenschema, das man nach der Form des lunaren Sigma σιγματοειδές nannte. Es zeigt eine völlig dominierende Mittelnische, die dann ihrerseits wieder kleine Bildnischen aufnimmt; so deren sieben in Gerasa, während zu beiden Seiten der Hauptnische nur Platz für je ein Statuentabernakel bleibt. ... Zu dem Sigma-Typus wird man auch den vermutlich nur zweistöckigen Wasserbau bei Porta Maggiore in Rom rechnen (Maaß, Tagesgötter S. 65, Durn, Hdb. D. röm. Arch. S. 474 nach Piranesi), dessen gleichzeitige Bedeutung als Siegesmonument Maaß näher dargelegt hat.

[88] For examples of aqueducts feeding nymphaea, see Aicher (1995: 39, 59–61, 66–7, 164).
[89] Contra van Aken (1951: 272–3). See Ginouvès (1962: 265–82); Settis (1973: 683–740); Muthmann (1975: 77–112).
[90] Shaw's (1991) discussion of the "luxury" status of facilities that drew water directly from the aqueducts is a necessary correction to earlier thinking about the role of aqueducts, but it suffers by ignoring the religious dimension of water consumption. Richard (2012: 17) writes,

> Latin literature keeps the record of a similar terminology associated with the cult of the Nymphs and the different kinds of installations where it was practiced. These are the same as those referred to as nymphaeum in the other written sources, but their name offers a better insight in their religious function. Cicero mentions in the *Pro Milone* an *aedes nympharum*,

And what were the rituals in the community's religious regimen that made use of the nymphaeum's water? The main ritual was one we met in our discussion of Numenius: as part of a bride's prenuptial preparations, she bathed in the water of a pool frequented by nymphs. It did not matter if the nearest nymphaeum was fed by an aqueduct.[91] It did not even matter if she bathed on the spot or had water drawn from the pool and brought to her.[92] The important thing was that she bathed in the water, so that its *life-giving properties* would ensure a fertile union for the bride and her groom. Patrick Marchetti (1995: 243) refers to this as the nymphaeum's "horizon matrimonial."

In light of the nymphaeum's religious function, I suggest that the presence of the word θεόπνους in such a context should be explained along the same lines as Numenius' use of the word—that is, as a reference to the water's *life-giving* (viz. fecundating) effect. Such an explanation, I suggest, represents a more natural line of interpretation than that adopted by Robert. There is, after all, no reason to expect a nymphaeum to preserve a reference to a prophecy from the Clarian Apollo. A reference to the fecundating effect of the nymphaeum's waters, on the other hand, is precisely what we might expect. That is, we should assume that θεόπνους was used in the Laodicean nymphaeum similarly to how it was used in other nymphological associations.

If we are surprised by Robert's quickness to assign an inspirationist meaning to θεόπνους, we must bear in mind that, with the exception of a few isolated instances, the vivificationist understanding of θεόπνευστος/θεόπνους is largely being established here for the first time. We can hardly expect Robert to have entertained any other meaning than the one furnished by the lexicons. He surely had no reason to suspect that that meaning owes its career to Origen. As for the quickness with which Robert invoked a supposed connection with Claros, we must recognize that the Clarian oracle was dear to his heart: he was in charge of excavations at Claros from 1950 to 1961, and he spent a large portion of his subsequent career aggrandizing the network of inscriptional references (and *nonreferences*) to Claros.[93] I am not the first to accuse him of finding references to Claros where they don't exist (e.g., see Busine 2005: 33, 45–7).

Virgil a *nympharum domus* and Martial a *templum*, clearly showing that the primitive religious functions in these late Republican structures were maintained.

[91] Ginouvès (1969: 165–6) writes,

> Certes, la fontaine est devenue "une fantaisie architecturale autour d'une captation ou d'une distribution d'eau, un motif-décor pour l'urbaniste, buffet d'eau, théâtre d'eau, musée de plein air," mais il paraît difficile d'admettre qu'elle a ainsi perdu toute signification, sinon pour la religion, du moins pour la religiosité romaine: les expressions qui désignent certains nymphées, "sanctuaire des Nymphes," "temple des Nymphes," les statues de divinités qui les ornaient et les consacraient, certaines dédicaces de fontaines aux Nymphes et à Aphrodite, ou à Déméter, l'existence de fêtes religieuses en l'honneur de sources, invitent au moins à supposer que le Nymphée n'était pas seulement un bâtiment public comme les autres,—dans la mesure où, jusqu'aux derniers temps de l'Antiquité, s'est conservée, à des niveaux et avec des qualités différentes, une réelle vénération pour les eaux et pour les grottes d'où elles jaillissent: *nullus enim fons non sacer*.

[92] On nuptial rites at nymphaea, see Ginouvès (1962: 265–82); Settis (1973: 685–8).
[93] On Robert's association with Claros, see Robert and Robert (1989).

4

Excursus on Θεόπνευστος in the *Physiologus* and the *Cyranides*

Chapter 1 presented a series of charts (Tables 1.1 through 1.3)—each improving on the ones preceding it—showing which occurrences of θεόπνευστος/θεόπνους are relevant to an investigation of the word's pre-Origenist career. The *Physiologus* and the *Cyranides* failed to make the final chart, as their uses of θεόπνευστος/θεόπνους are dated too late, but I pointed out that the case for excluding these two works required more space than was immediately available. I therefore held off making my case for their exclusion until the present chapter.

In any attempt to map the development of θεόπνευστος/θεόπνους, the *Physiologus* and the *Cyranides* should be discussed together, in that one was probably known to (and influenced) the author or editor of the other. The two works are similar in genre. Patricia Cox (1983: 437) refers to them as the two "most complete extant members of the *Phūsika*"—that is, of paradoxographical treatments of sympathies within the natural world (see Wellmann 1934: 10). The precise relationship between these works, however, is a matter of dispute. Scholars do not even agree on which is the earlier of the two. Max Wellmann (1934: 24) argued that the *Physiologus* took some of its material from the *Cyranides*, but Klaus Alpers (1984: 36) argued that the *Physiologus* is some two hundred years older than the *Cyranides*.[1] Disagreement sometimes gives way to confusion: B. E. Perry (1937: 492) notes that one modern critical edition of the *Physiologus* "reckons [the *Cyranides*] usually among the imitations of the *Physiologus*, but occasionally also among its sources" (!).

The fact that the *Physiologus* and the *Cyranides* are in some way interrelated calls for their joint treatment—at least for the purpose of dating the material—but their respective uses of θεόπνευστος/θεόπνους are almost certainly *not* interrelated. This might seem obvious by the divergence in spelling, with the *Physiologus* using the typically Jewish/Christian spelling θεόπνευστος, and the *Cyranides* using the typically pagan spelling θεόπνους.[2] Their mutual independence in the use of θεόπνευστος/θεόπνους is inferred

---

[1] On the relation of the *Cyranides* to the *Physiologus*, see Ganszyniec (1920): esp. 2.56–65; Festugière (1950: 210); Alpers (1984); Gippert (1997: 171).

[2] See Tannery's (1904: 344) response to Ruelle's reading (in de Mély 1898: 23) of Christian/ Christological references into the *Cyranides*.

on text-critical grounds and not on their use of different spelling conventions. It is unlikely, in fact, that the *opportunity* for borrowing this term even existed at the point of one work's influence on the other. As we will see below, the word we are investigating appears to have crept into both works at late points in their textual histories.

1 The *Physiologus*

The *Physiologus* is a collection of theological and moral lessons based on fanciful details about a wide assortment of animals (real and mythological) or (less often) about stones and plants. The chapters follow a simple pattern—object lessons based on the behaviors or abilities of these animals, with running references to what the "physiologus" (= naturalist) says about these matters.[3] Although it probably has pagan writings or traditions among its sources (e.g., the *Cyranides*),[4] the *Physiologus* is a Christian composition through and through, and its lessons point to the truths of Christian theology and morality. The chapters usually begin with an OT passage that mentions the animal or stone about to be visited, and end with a quotation from the New Testament.[5] Against an earlier view that posited an originally pagan work, subsequently Christianized through the addition of biblical prooftexts, Alpers recognizes that both the nature myths and their biblical tie-ins come from the same hand.[6] The text gives indications that it was written in Egypt—including its use of Egyptian place names, myths, and calendar (see Brunner-Traut 1968; Treu 1998: 428; Alpers 1996: 599; 2007: 227; Schneider 2002: 153).[7] It was originally composed in Greek and later translated into Arabic, Syriac, Armenian, and Ethiopian.

The word θεόπνευστος appears in that stream of the *Physiologus*'s textual tradition represented by mss. ΑΙΕΠΔφr. These manuscripts refer to τῇ θεοπνεύστῳ γραφῇ— in a way that implies an inspirationist meaning for θεόπνευστος (see Sbordone 1936: 57; Kaimakis 1974: 3a–4a).[8] There the chapter on the hedgehog[9] ends by tying

---

[3] See the survey of the *Physiologus*'s chapters in Grant (1999: 52–72).

[4] On the sources of the *Physiologus*'s lore, see Peters (1898: 1–14). Curley (1980: 4) writes,

> Under the influence of neo-platonic currents during the first two centuries A.D., Christian writers conceived of a more systematic φυσιολογία with a mystical dimension nowhere to be found among the ancients. Clement of Alexandria, for example, in Book 4 of his *Stromata* speaks of a γνωστικὴ φυσιολογία by which he appears to mean an initiation into the knowledge of the heavenly mysteries by way of their earthly correspondences (τὰ μικρὰ πρὸ τῶν μεγάλων μυηθέντες μυστηρίων).

[5] Eden (1972: 2) suggests that the *Physiologus* was perhaps written in fulfillment of Job 12:7–9: "But ask now the beasts, and they shall teach thee."

[6] The *Urphysiologus* hypothesis is closely associated with Ahrens (1892). Wellmann (1934: 14) also posited an original pagan version of the *Physiologus*, dated to ca. 200 CE. Laufer (1914: 111 n. 2) argued against a fully literary *Urphysiologus* but claimed that "a primeval *Physiologus*" existed in the first century as "an assemblage of verbal stories current in Alexandria." Cf. Alpers (2000: 599; 2007: 227).

[7] On the use of Egyptian month names in the *Physiologus*, see Gippert (1997: 168–70).

[8] Cf. the Greek text in Pitra (1855: 350–1).

[9] This is chap. 14 in the majority tradition but chap. 17 in Codex Π and in the Armenio-Georgian tradition. On the hedgehog chapter, see Cox (1983: 434–5).

the physiologus's zoological expertise to "the *theopneustic* writing/Scripture": Δικαίως οὖν ὁ Φυσιολόγος ἐφ' ἡμῖν ἥρμωσε τὰς φύσεις τῶν ζῴων τῇ θεοπνεύστῳ γραφῇ ("Thus the physiologus correctly related for us the nature of the animals mentioned in theopneustic scripture"). Given this inspirationist use of θεόπνευστος, it becomes especially important to try to determine the date of the *Physiologus*'s composition.

1.1 The Date of the *Physiologus*

The *Physiologus* has usually been dated to the second century CE, on the supposition that several second-century writings are dependent upon it. To my mind, however, a second-century date for the work is quite impossible. The evidence against such a view is manifold and in some points obvious.[10]

A number of scholars, including Friedrich Lauchert (1889: 65), Emil Peters (1898: 13–14), and Ursula Treu (1966), have argued that the *Physiologus* was written prior even to the works of Barnabas and Justin Martyr, which (they think) are dependent on the *Physiologus* (see Alpers 1984: 14; Pitra 1855: l [on Clement], lxiii [on Tatian]). Thus, Treu (1993: 198) argues, "If the Letter of Barnabas (ch. 10) and also Clement of Rome (that means Ps.-Clement) in his *Recognitiones* (VII 25, p. 231) have both exactly the same text as the *Physiologus* has, then you may be sure that they have used the Physiologus."[11] Alpers (1996: 598) similarly argues for a second-century date, but he places the writing between 150 and 200 CE. He insists on a later date than given by Treu, on the basis of Rudolf Riedinger's recognition of an echo of *Infancy Gospel of James* in ms. G and in the Latin and Ethiopic traditions (see Riedinger 1977: 111–12).[12]

Alan Scott has seen, more clearly than most, the difficulties with dating the *Physiologus* so early. According to him, "all arguments that place it in the second century can be shown to lack any real force" (Scott 1998: 430).[13] Scott (1998: 433) both weakens the supposition that second-century writings draw from the *Physiologus* and turns it around, arguing that either the supposed contacts (e.g., with Justin Martyr) are too trifling to count for much or the direction of dependence (as in the case of

[10] The article on "Physiologus" in the third edition of *Die Religion in Geschichte und Gegenwart* describes a wide range of dates held by scholars (Dinkler-von Schubert 1961), while the article in the fourth edition of that work (and in *RPP* [quoted here]) claims a staunch resolution to the question: "The anonymous text … is now unanimously dated between 150 and 200 CE" (Imorde 2011: 104).

[11] In the 1890s, Lüders (1897: 115 n. 3) and Müller (1896: 531) took exception to Lauchert's (1889: 24) claim that the *Physiologus* was dependent on a lost source used in the early-third-century CE writings of Aelian, disputing the need to posit a connection between the *Physiologus* and Aelian. See Laufer (1914: 111 nn. 2–3). Against Lauchert's suggestion that the unicorn chapter depends on the Virgin Mary's connection to the incarnation of the Word, Müller (1896: 532) posits "eine Reminiscenz aus der Buddha-Legende" (see Lauchert 1889: 48 n. 255).

[12] Scott (1998: 437) cites Alpers's argument approvingly on the *Physiologus*'s relation to Barnabas: Alpers detects (1) that the *Physiologus* derives its versions of Lev. 10:1, 4; 11:12–19 and Deut. 14:10–18 from the *Epistle of Barnabas*, (2) that *Physiologus* chap. 24 echoes *Epist. Barn.* 10.7, and (3) that the typological connection between the crucifixion and Moses stretching out his arms likely comes from *Epist. Barn.* 12.2.

[13] Scott argues that the *Physiologus* cites the Fourth Gospel as Scripture, although "John is not treated as scripture until Tatian and Heracleon in the 150's and 60's" (437). In support of this later dating, see also Wellmann (1930: 10–11); Peterson (1954).

Barnabas) more likely runs in the other direction.[14] The weakness of the link claimed with Justin Martyr, Scott (1998: 433) tells us, is typical for the *Physiologus's* supposed second-century contacts: "most of the alleged parallels between the *Physiologus* and early Christian literature are very general in character."

When do reliable witnesses first appear? According to Scott (1998: 433),

> the first hard evidence of the *Physiologus'* use is in the second half of the fourth century, and here there is a solid phalanx of witnesses. It is apparent, as van den Broek notes, that Epiphanius has used the *Physiologus* in his *Panarion* (written by 377), because in Epiphanius's version of the phoenix story, the worm reborn in the ashes becomes a mature bird *on the third day*, a detail otherwise only known in the *Physiologus*; the same may again be true in the detail that the phoenix shows itself to the priests who had served it.[15]

Scott also finds echoes of the *Physiologus* in Epiphanius' *De Gemmis* (1998: 434; cf. Ahrens 1885: 7) and notes that a particularly impressive echo ("some ninety words" in Latin version b) appears in Ambrose's *Hexaemeron* (written 386–390 CE), with details of the matter suggesting a gap of at least a few decades (Scott 1998: 434–5).[16] Additional support for Scott's *terminus ad quem* is found in Rufinus' use of the *Physiologus* in 407–408 CE (Scott 1998: 435) and in Henry Chadwick's (1976: 93) argument that Priscillian of Avila opposed certain views of the *Physiologus*.

Scott (1998: 436) responds to Treu's and Alpers's arguments for Clement of Alexandria's reliance on the *Physiologus* by noting that their position depends on a reconstruction of the *Hypotyposeis* that Clement scholars have generally dismissed.[17] He also claims that the supposed connection between the *Physiologus* and the world of the Gnostics has been overblown and notes that the appearance of such language, in any event, would not preclude a third-century date, as some of our extant Gnostic treatises (e.g., the *Testimony of Truth*) come from the third century (Scott 1998: 436).[18] Scott (1998: 438–9) also points out that the *Physiologus* everywhere presupposes a view of the biblical canon usually associated with fourth-century developments. In addition, he adduces a couple of objections to an early date registered by earlier scholars: Erik Peterson had pointed to the lateness of the sense that the *Physiologus* assigns to the word πολιτευτής, while Emma Brunner-Traut saw in *Physiologus* chap. 45 evidence of a situation in which the numbers of pagans and Christians within the population were about equal—which holds true for some regions in the fourth century, but for *nowhere* in the second century (Scott 1998: 438, citing Peterson

---

[14] On the *Physiologus's* use of *Barnabas*, see Schneider (2002: 160).

[15] Ponce de Leon's 1587 edition of the *Physiologus* attributed it to Epiphanius.

[16] Latin b is not the oldest Latin version—therefore, "we need to allow time for the *Physiologus* to be translated into Latin, and then for another Latin translation to be made, which in turn was used by Ambrose" (Scott 1998: 435, cf. 441).

[17] In response to Riedinger's reconstruction, Scott (1998: 436) cites a lack of "convincing parallels" between the *Physiologus* and Clement's writings: every purported parallel is a commonplace "with ample examples in other ancient texts." See Riedinger (1973).

[18] The claim that the *Physiologus* includes "Gnostic elements" is found in Treu (1993: 200).

1954, and Brunner-Traut 1984). (Peterson [1954: 70–1] also found evidence of the *Physiologus*'s knowledge of the *Ascension of Isaiah* and the *Acts of Paul and Thecla*—both second-century writings.)

Scott pays particular attention to the relation of the *Physiologus* to Origen—a matter of special interest to the present study. Here, Scott (1998: 440) notes, a literary connection between the two is "more assured," as the parallels are more than zoological: "there is also an unmistakable allegorical parallel" (see Scott 2002). He finds it difficult to believe that Origen was influenced in his allegorical renderings by the *Physiologus* and concludes that the influence ran in the opposite direction. He judges the suggestion that Origen's exegesis was guided by the *Physiologus* "far-fetched" (Scott 1998: 441 [contra, e.g., Treu 1959: 113–17]): "Origen frequently refers to pagan zoological/paradoxographical material, and in doing so he normally relies on pagan sources, not on Christian sources, and certainly not on a primitive work like the *Physiologus*" (Scott 1998: 440). Scott (1998: 441 n. 61) also notes that the *Physiologus* emphatically states that Jesus was crucified only once (chap. 33), which looks like an answer to the charge that Origen held to a repeating act of redemption, for those who do not repent in this life.

As with the *Cyranides*, the question of the *Physiologus*'s date of composition has only an indirect bearing on the philological profile of θεόπνευστος/θεόπνους. The text-critical stream in which θεόπνευστος appears (mss. ΑΙΕΠΔφr) is rather late and cannot be brought near the second-century date so widely attributed to the *Physiologus*. Sbordone (1936: 57) sets these words within square brackets, denoting their absence from mss. MΣasWO.[19] These words are also missing from ms. G, which was unknown to Sbordone but is considered by many to be the earliest extant manuscript of the *Physiologus* (see Perry 1937: 492).[20]

2 The *Cyranides*

The *Cyranides* is comprised of four books, created from material of differing dates, and with different justifications for its title.[21] According to Alpers's (1984: 17) reconstruction, the first book combines the work of a certain Harpocration of Alexandria, addressed to his daughter "Cyranis," with material from the first volume of a three-volume work claiming to have been written by another "Cyranos" (Κυρανίς), purportedly a Persian

---

[19] See also Sbordone's discussion of *Physiologus* manuscripts (xiii–xxv). The chapter on the hedgehog is listed in Sbordone (54) as present in "M – Σ a (λ) s – W O – A E I Π Δ (v) r (j) – Ω o – Eust." See Kaimakis (1974: 2b–3b). The classifications of the manuscript tradition are shown most clearly in Kaimakis's edition, which prints separate texts for ms. groups Σas, WO, and ΑΙΕΠΔφr (46a–47a). Sbordone had divided these manuscripts into three separate redactions, dubbed "primitive, Byzantine, and pseudo-Basil." See Carmody (1941: 96); Declerck (1981: 149).

[20] Cf. the text presented in Offermanns (1966: 62).

[21] Bain (1990: 295) says that it might well be "the most important non-philosophical document in the Hermetic tradition." On the Hermetic aspect of the *Cyranides*, see Wellmann (1934); Festugière (1950: 1.201–16). Kaimakis's (1976) critical edition of the text has been widely criticized. See Meschini (1983: 145–7); Alpers (1984: 61 n. 54); Bain (1990: 298–9; 1993: 427–9).

monarch (see Festugière 1950: 1.203; Bain 2006: 225–6).[22] Book 1 is clearly a patchwork, as shown by the passages of iambic and dactylic verse found within its prose framework (see Ganszyniec 1920: 364; Jordan 2005), and the competing derivations of the work's title illustrate the jumbled nature of its contents. Books 2 and 3 also stem from the work attributed to Cyranos, while book 4 derives from another source.[23] And yet there is a unity to books 2 through 4, so that these three sometimes pass (more confusingly still) by the name "Coiranides" (see Festugière 1950: 201–2 n. 2; Bain 2006: 225). Book 1 contains twenty-four alphabetically arranged chapters, each discussing the respective medical properties of a plant, a bird, a stone, and a fish—the names of which begin with the chapter's head-letter.[24] Books 2 through 4 comprise a bestiary, with book 2 covering land creatures, book 3 covering birds, and book 4 covering fish and other aquatic creatures (see Waegeman 1987: 7–8).

The *TLG* lists the *Cyranides* among the pre-third-century witnesses to the use of θεόπνους. Unlike the Numenius fragment and the *Poimandres*, however, the *Cyranides* apparently uses θεόπνους to describe the god-breathed or god-breathing quality of a certain kind of plant root—a description offered as a text-critical alternative to θεογόνου. A lot turns on our understanding of the words θεογόνου ῥίζης, (ἐν ἄλλῳ γράφει θεόπνου) οὐγ. δ'.[25] The larger passage is as follows:

Cyran. 2.3.22
The preparation of the beverage is as follows: taking three cotylai of rainwater in which a mole has drowned, bring to a boil until a waxy consistency obtains; after this, put water in a bronze vessel and boil it. Then prepare this way: root of verbena, (ἐν ἄλλῳ γράφει θεόπνου) four ounces; single-stem armoise, four ounces; styrax resin (= benzoin), myrrh of Ethiopia, bdellium, four ounces of each; male incense in tears, eight ounces. Having crossed, having mixed, having crushed, add a cotyle of premium honey, and make it boil until it reaches the consistency of honey. Remove [from boiling] and deposit in a vessel of glass and use as indicated beforehand. (Author's translation)

The questions before us are twofold: (1) whether θεόπνους, in this instance, means "inspired" or "life-giving" and (2) whether the *TLG*'s dating of the *Cyranides* is correct. The first question has never been discussed in print, while the second is hotly disputed.

The reader is faced with four possible understandings of a particular kind of plant root—two attaching to θεογόνου (the default description) and two attaching to θεόπνου (the alternate description). Θεογόνος might signify a particular species of

---

[22] Bain (1996: 153) writes, "It is clear that Κυρανίς by late antiquity had become a catch-all title for works of popular medicine and magic." On the derivation of the name "Cyranides," see Zielinski (1905–6: 52 n. 1).

[23] Kaimakis included a fifth and sixth book in the *Cyranides*, but these additional books cannot be identified as truly Cyranidean. See Bain (1996) (echoing Halleux and Schamp 1985: xxviii n. 1).

[24] The listing of stones, birds, plants, and fishes according to their alphabetic placement indicates an interest in litteromancy—combining parts of, or designs of, stones, birds, plants, and fishes into single objects (e.g., a ring) to form a talisman. See de Mély (1898: 1–50).

[25] Author's translation. The reference is given according to Kaimakis (1976).

plant (most likely verbena),[26] or it might mean "divine" more generally. Θεόπνους, on the other hand, might refer to the "inspired" (or "inspiring"?) nature of the root, or it might refer to its *life-giving* (i.e., magico-medicinal) quality. I tend to think that the *Cyranides* redactor's description of a root as theopneustic more likely refers to its life-giving aspect. (Such a use would be similar to the medical use of θεόπνευστος in Pseudo-Plutarch.) After all, what would it mean to describe a root as "inspired"?

The *TLG* places our passage squarely within the second century, but there are two significant problems with this: (1) the *TLG*'s dating of the *Cyranides* is no longer representative of scholarship, and (2) the phrase in which the *Cyranides* employs θεόπνους is missing from the best manuscripts, so we appear to be dealing with a textual gloss inserted by a copyist. Even if the *Cyranides* should turn out to be a second-century writing—a position that still has a respectable following—the passage in question is almost certainly of a later date. Θεόπνους may have entered the text centuries later than the original writing.

The *TLG* took its second-century date for the *Cyranides* from Dimitris Kaimakis's (1976) edition of the text. Throughout the 1980s, most scholars followed Kaimakis's dating, but this view began to lose its hold in the 1990s. Although some recent works continue to follow Kaimakis (e.g., Fowden 1986: 87–8 n. 57 [see below]; Panayiotou 1990; Jori 2004: 1),[27] significant arguments for a fourth-century date have appeared during the past three decades. These began in 1982, with M. L. West's (1982) discovery of acrostic signatures in the part of book 1 that stemmed from "Harpocration"— two that spell ΜΑΓΝΟΥ and two that spell ΜΑΓΝΟΣΜΑΡΚΕΛΛΙΝΩ—apparently identifying the core of Harpocration's source with two figures that West locates in the fourth century.[28] (West and others identify this Harpocration with a fourth-century iatrosophist.)[29] Shortly after West's discovery, a detailed treatment from Alpers (1984) strengthened the identification of the acrostic signatures with fourth-century figures. According to the West–Alpers interpretation of the evidence, "Magnus" most likely refers to Magnus of Nisibis (a fourth-century physician, better known for his literary

---

[26] Pedanius Dioscorides discusses "verbena" (περιστέριον [*lycopus europaeus*]) in *De materia medica* 4.59, "holy vervain" (ἱερὰ βοτάνη [*verbena officinalis*]) in 4.60, and "vervain mallow" (ἀλκαία [*malope malacoides*]) in 3.147. For the use of verbena in magic, *s.v.* "verveine" in the index in Delatte (1938). It is worth noting that a different term (κιναίδιος) might be used for verbena in *Cyran.* 1.10.1–22. See Panayiotou (1990: 318). A parenthetical question mark in Ruelle's (1902: 73) translation may register a doubt about translating θεογόνου ῥίζης as "root of verveine." Alternatively, it might denote Ruelle's failure to include ἐν ἄλλῳ γράφει θεόπνου in his translated material. Note that Thessalos' *De virtutibus herbarum* lists the "plant of Taurus" as "vervain" (*peristereōn orthos* = *verbena officinalis*), and the "plant of Gemini" as "holy vervain" (*peristereōn huptios* = *verbena supina*) (as shown in Moyer 2011: 291).

[27] Cf. Baldwin's (1992: 103) trenchant criticisms of Panayiotou's dating.

[28] Bowersock (1990: 247) called West's discovery "a stunning piece of detection." See Matthews (1994: 260–2). After West's discovery, other scholars claimed to find more acrostic signatures in the text—Führer (1985) found another ΜΑΓΝΟΥ acrostic, while Jordan (2005) speculatively posited yet another ΜΑΓΝΟΥ acrostic in a reconstructed source behind Kaimakis's text, in a reordering of lines now strewn from α.140–2 to α.161–7. Signature acrostics were not uncommon in late antiquity— see, e.g., Nicander, *Theriaca* 345–53 (cf. Lobel 1928); epigram "Proscynème de Maximus" (no. 169 in Bernand 1969: 610–13; see Wagner 1993). See Vogt (1967); Courtney (1990: 8–13).

[29] Baldwin (1992: 103 n. 4) writes, "The Harpocration in question would appear to be the medical writer from Alexandria, possibly to be conflated with the homonymous poet and rhetorician attested at Constantinople in the years 358–63." See Festugière (1950: 1.204). On Harpocration, see Jones, Martindale, and Morris (1971: 408).

activity [see Jones, Martindale, and Morris 1971: 534]),[30] and "Marcellinus" (it was suggested) might be identified with the historian Ammianus Marcellinus.[31] One way in which these two figures might be brought into the same circle is as (supposed) correspondents of Libanius (see West 1982: 481; Bain 2006: 226–7). (Ammianus' own religious and divinatory interests have been duly appreciated in recent decades, so it is not a stretch to imagine his having a hand in a composition that wound up as part of the *Cyranides*.)[32] The text's references to an emperor have Julian the Apostate in

---

[30] Bain (2003: 194 n. 12) writes,

> The poems containing acrostics which feature in Book One are written by one Magnus who in two of them, as David Jordan has pointed out to me, seems to lay claim to the prose work as well as the verses (*Cyr.* 1.7.45ff. and 1.8.11f.) by saying that he is moving from verse to prose (ἀρκείσθω ὅσα προεῖπον. Πεζῷ δὲ λόγῳ καταλέξω καὶ δείξω, "let what I have said [in the preceding verse] suffice. I shall [now] record in prose …," and τοῦτο ὕστερον αὖ μετέπειτα πεζῷ λόγῳ καταλέξω, "I shall record this later in prose").

     See Alpers (1984: 21).

[31] Wilkinson (2009; 2010) has recently challenged the traditional chronology for the career of the epigrammatist Palladas—threatening the traditional dating of Magnus' career, which is in part dated by Palladas' epigram for him. (See Plastira-Valkanou 2003: 188.) If Wilkinson is correct in redating Palladas' career some sixty years earlier than traditionally thought, Magnus will have been an old man (at best) when Ammianus was still in his youth. It would appear, however, that Wilkinson has overstated his case. His dismissal of marginal notes in the *Anth. Pal.* as "nothing more than guesswork" (Wilkinson 2009: 37) is hasty—they might be guesswork or they might be based on a historical source. Wilkinson challenges the assumption that Palladas' words εὐτυχῆ … ὃν θεὸς φιλεί (*Anth. Pal.* 10.90 and 91) refer to Theophilus, patriarch of Alexandria from 385 to 412 CE. This assumption had been strengthened by Bowra's (1960) proposal that the "friend of God" (θεῷ φίλε) to whom Palladas appeals in *Anth. Pal.* 9.175 is this same Theophilus and proposes a date for Palladas' appeal in the early 390s. (The identification of Theophilus as a friend of God would have been strictly the outworking of a pun, as the pagan Palladas would not have agreed with Theophilus' reprisals against non-Christians.) With the support and refinement that Cameron (1965b: 21–2, 26; cf. 1964: 56–7; 1965a: 219–20) gave to Bowra's thesis, and the co-option of this thesis by Jones, Martindale, and Morris (1971), the years 319–400 CE came to represent the standard view for Palladas' life. Wilkinson suggests, in place of this traditional reading of θεῷ φίλε, that the sobriquet referred to the emperor—as we know that it began to be so used beginning with Constantine (Wilkinson [2009]: 44–5] quotes examples). The weakest link in Wilkinson's argument is its assumption that Constantine himself best answers to the description of the "friend of God." Why not any other emperor *after* Constantine? For that matter, why not use θεῷ φίλε to refer to *Julian*, as if to say (as a pagan might) that Julian was most deserving of that sobriquet? In fact, Rhomiopoulou (1981: 304–5) publishes an inscription honoring Julian, in which the word θεοφιλεστάτου appears (in lines 1–2) as the first honorific in description of the emperor—on which, see Bowersock (1983: 83).
      As Matthews (1994: 254) notes, "Marcellinus" is that name "by which the historian would normally be known if only one name were used"—"The only direct later allusion to Ammianus' work, by the sixth-century Latin grammarian Priscian, so refers to him."

[32] That Ammianus should play a role in the appearance of the *Cyranides* fits with his religious and political allegiances. Although he faulted Julian for his "superstition" (*Res Gestae* 25.4.17), he supported the emperor in his Neoplatonism and his religious reforms in general. Matthews (2007: 125) notes how much Ammianus' defense shows about the historian's own theological acumen: "[Ammianus'] digression on divination is neither more nor less than a learned digression, employing technical language in a manner calculated not to offer his own views, but to inform his audience at a certain level of erudition" (430). On Ammianus' view of pagan divination, see Szidat (1981: 71–84); den Boeft (1999; 2008: 78). On Neoplatonism in the *Res Gestae*, see Szidat (1982). A work like the *Cyranides* almost certainly would have appealed to Julian—he not only surrounded himself (during his Persian campaign) with "philosophers" expert in technical divination (viz. reading omens), he also made his own thorough study of Neoplatonist theurgy. See Kaldellis (2005); Stöcklin-Kaldewey (2014: 155–6).

view—which makes a great deal of sense in light of Julian's intense interest in divinatory matters, not to mention his devotion to Hermes.[33]

The acceptance of a fourth-century date among recent students of the *Cyranides* represents a return to the view common (albeit not universal) among pre-Kaimakis readers of the text.[34] It cannot be said, however, that Kaimakis's view has been universally eclipsed. Garth Fowden, for one, is not convinced by West's argument. He notes that "Harpocration" need not refer to West's fourth-century figure, since Tertullian's *De Corona Militis* (written *ca.* 210 CE) alludes to a writing by someone of that name (*De cor.* 7.5).[35] By extension, the acrostic signatures ΜΑΓΝΟΥ and ΜΑΓΝΟΣΜΑΡΚΕΛΛΙΝΩ need not answer to fourth-century figures either. Who then, in Fowden's view, are "Magnus" and "Marcellinus"? He offers the following suggestion (Fowden 1993: 88 n. 57):

> It is worth considering the claim of the two doctors whose portraits twice occur together in Bologna University Library MS. 3632 (saec. xv), fol. 17–26 (where they are entitled μάγνος – μαρκελήνος), 213 (ὁ μάγνος σωφηστής – ὁ μαρκεληνος): Olivieri and Festa, *S.I.F.C.* 3 (1895) 454. These must be Magnus of Ephesus (Kroll, *R.E.* 14.494, no. 28; Kudlien, *R.E.* Supp. 11.1098) and the Marcellinus who shared with him an interest in the pulse (Kroll, *R.E.* 14.1488–9, no. 51). Both were members of the Pneumatist school, and seem to have lived *c.* A.D. 100.[36]

This represents a formidable challenge to placing Harpocration in the fourth century.[37] Fowden's view is supported by Charles Fornara's (1992: 336–7 n. 1) argument against identifying the recipient of Libanius' letter with Ammianus.[38] It might also be noted that Valerius Harpocration (probably a second-century figure [cf. Julius Capitolinus,

---

Rike (1987: 1) challenged readings of Ammianus that marginalize his own religious piety: "Scholars, to be frank, are bored by the personal religion of Ammianus after they have learned their catechism from Julian: the emperor's paganism strikes out from his own writings with the speed and immediacy of an electric impulse; the historian, though, seems to black himself out in whispering moderation." Rike argues that Ammianus' own religious scruples are on display in the *Res Gestae*. But cf. the critique of Rike in Wittchow (2001: 178–203). Kulikowski (2012: 92) faults Rike for failing to discern when elements of the divine and the supernatural serve merely as narrative devices.

[33] Julian credited Hermes as his guide to others among the pantheon. See Athanassiadi (1992: 168); Limberis (2000: 382); Smith (2005: 125–6, 132–5).

[34] De Mély (1898: lxxi) argued for a date between 227 and 400 CE. He was followed by others (e.g., Laufer 1914: 110). See also Festugière (1950: 1.204). See also Sathas's (1888: lxiii) argument for dating the *Cyranides* to the time of Marcus Aurelius. Cf. Ruelle (1898: viii–ix).

[35] "Harpocration industria ederatum argumentatur, quod ederae naturae sit cerebrum ab heluco defensare" (Fontaine 1966: 98). See Wellmann (1934: 12–13).

[36] Fowden is followed in this early dating by Faraone (1999: 11). According to Harris (1973: 190), the physician Marcellinus "probably lived in the second half of the first century some time between Archigenes and Galen (for he quotes the former but does not mention the latter)."

[37] Bain (1990: 296 n. 4) refers to Tertullian's reference as "obscure" and suggests that the "juxtaposed portraits of doctors named Magnus and Marcellinus [in ms. Bologna 3632, fols. 17–26] may be nothing more than a tantalizing coincidence."

[38] Matthews (1994: 260) similarly writes, "The case for connecting the physician Magnus of Nisibis with the historian Ammianus Marcellinus lapses for lack of positive reasons to support it." See Bowersock (1990: 247–8).

Life of Verus 2]) was known to arrange topics alphabetically (cf. his *Lexicon of the Ten Orators*), similarly to the first book of the *Cyranides* (see Graux 1878: 65–7).

I should mention at least two more factors in the struggle to date the *Cyranides*, both of which push the date later than the second century. First, little has been made of the fact that the text provides a manifestly false account of where this Harpocration obtained his material. The text itself argues that Harpocration found these mystical secrets written somewhere in the Persian language, so that what he relates in Greek is supposedly a translation from Persian. The problem with this story is that the language of the text shows no signs of being a translation of any sort. And if "Harpocration" gives a false prehistory of the text, should that not, in itself, create doubts about the claim that the text really goes back to a historical Harpocration? In other words, if the Harpocration the text has in mind is a second-century figure, the earliest parts of the *Cyranides* still might be from a later period. Second, the *Cyranides* is classified as a Hermetic writing on the basis of explicit references to Hermes within the text, but the earliest writings in the *Hermetic Corpus* do *not*, in fact, mention Hermes. This leads to a presumption that those parts of the *Cyranides* that mention Hermes stem from the third century or later.[39]

2.1 The Date of the Phrase in Question (Text-Critical Matters)

The foregoing discussion is about dating that portion of the *Cyranides* that derives from Harpocration. The arguments discussed there do not bear upon the date of the rest of the *Cyranides*, including book 2, which is where θεόπνους appears. In the end, the date we must assign to this particular use of θεόπνους reduces to a text-critical matter.

The second reason Kaimakis's dating might be inapplicable to the *Cyranides*'s use of θεόπνους is more secure than our attempt to date the work as a whole: The phrase in question appears to be a later gloss. The larger passage in which the phrase appears is given as follows in Kaimakis's (1976: 118 [lines 20–23]) edition:

εἶτα διυλίσας τὸ ὕδωρ ἔψε ἐν χαλκῷ ἀγγείῳ ἐπιβαλὼν εἴδη / ταῦτα. εἶτα σκεύαζε οὕτως· θεογόνου ῥίζης, (ἐν ἄλλῳ γράφει θεό- / πνου) οὐγ. δ᾽, ἀρτεμισίας μονοκλώνου οὐγ, [sic] δ᾽, στύρακος καλαμίτου / οὐγ. δ᾽, σμύρνης τρωγλοδυτικῆς οὐγ. δ᾽, βδελλίου οὐγ. δ᾽, σφαιρίου οὐγ.

The parenthesis in this passage notes the witness of "other writings." In the apparatus, Kaimakis notes that seven of the fourteen manuscripts containing this section of the

---

[39] Wellmann (1934: 4) writes,

> Nun ist uns in der Sammlung der sogenannten "Kyraniden" Buch 2–4 nach der von einer Wiener (W, cod. med. gr. 23 der Wiener Hofbibliothek) und einer Pariser Hds. (Paris. gr. 2502, vgl. Mély S. 275f.: M) vertretenen Redaktion eine hermetische Schrift erhalten, die nach der Einleitung Lehren des Hermes an seinen Schüler Asklepios über die Heilwirkungen der Tiere enthält und die im 4. bzw. 5. Jahrh. unter diesem Titel ins Syrische übersetzt worden ist.

text omit both the parenthesis and the phrase that frames the parenthesis—θεογόνου ῥίζης, (ἐν ἄλλῳ γράφει θεόπνου) οὐγ. δ'. Mss. AGHFIOR (from ms. group "1"), DNBP (from group "2"), and WKS (from group "3") contain this section of the text, but the last two manuscript groupings are missing the phrase in question (Kaimakis 1976: 117–18).[40] The Latin translation of 1169 is also missing this phrase (see Delatte 1942: 141). Our attempt to determine whether the work as a whole should be dated to the second century ended in a judgment of *non liquet*, but we can be reasonably certain, on the basis of the foregoing, that the word entered the *Cyranides*'s textual tradition sometime later than the second century.[41]

---

[40] As Kaimakis notes (6), Wellmann and Festugière place MS D closest to Harpocration's text.

[41] On the prominence of lapidary material in the fourth century CE, see Wellmann (1934: 4).

5

Inspirationism and the New Testament

As the preceding chapters have shown, the philological case for attributing a vivificationist meaning to θεόπνευστος in the second century CE is strong. Yet that meaning would fail to inform our understanding of 2 Tim. 3:16 if it did not fit the argument of the letter. As Benjamin Warfield (1900: 128) himself wrote, "The final test of the sense assigned to any word is, of course, derived from its fitness to the context in which it is found." We therefore must look at how θεόπνευστος functions within its NT context:

> 2 Tim. 3:14–17
> 14 But as for you, remain in what you have learned and believed, knowing from whom you have learned,
> 15 and how from the time you were a baby you have known the sacred writings that are able to instruct you unto salvation through faith in Christ Jesus.
> 16 All scripture is theopneustic and useful for teaching, for reproof, for correction, for training in righteousness,
> 17 so that the one who is of God may be complete, equipped for every good work.
> (Author's translation)

The traditional interpretation of this passage understands θεόπνευστος to explain why Scripture is so "useful": it is *inspired*, and nothing is more useful for teaching than a guarantee that one's material is true. But is that really how 2 Timothy sets out its argument? The context suggests that the argument there pursues a different point altogether.

1 Rereading 2 Timothy through a Vivificationist Rendering of θεόπνευστος

A vivificationist reading of θεόπνευστος in v. 16 pays obvious dividends—Scripture is theopneustic for the reasons outlined in the preceding verse: It is "able to instruct you unto salvation through faith in Christ Jesus."[1] It is a commonplace in NT scholarship

---

[1] On v. 15, see Spicq (1969: 786).

that the early church viewed the Old Testament as looking forward to God's saving activity in Jesus Christ and that it saw the New Testament as explicating this activity in more open terms. Understood in light of this commonplace, and in light of the preceding chapters' philological investigation, it appears that when "Paul" admonishes Timothy to look upon "all scripture" as θεόπνευστος, he means to tell him that every part of Scripture testifies to the life-giving Gospel.[2]

1.1 Salvation as Vivification in 2 Tim. 3:14–17

To set matters in proper perspective, we must include vv. 14–15 and 17 in our purview. Verses 14–15 comprise an important part of the thought expressed in v. 16, while v. 17 completes the thought.[3] The most important clues for understanding v. 16 are found in v. 15, which refers to "sacred writings (ἱερὰ γράμματα) that are able to instruct you unto salvation through faith in Christ Jesus."[4] According to the interpretation advanced here—which sees in θεόπνευστος a reference to the life-giving quality of the Gospel found within "all scripture"—these words parallel the idea expressed in the first half of v. 16, as shown in the adjusted rendering below:

> v. 15b: "... sacred writings that are able to instruct you unto salvation through faith in Christ Jesus."
> v. 16a: "All scripture is life-giving [= salvific] and is useful for instruction."

---

[2] Admittedly, the church continued to hold that Scripture was focused on those things "useful for salvation," but it unfortunately nested this focus within an inspirationist view of Scripture. Cf., e.g., Aquinas, *De Veritate* q. 12, a. 2:

> In all things which are ordained to an end, the material object is determined according to the exigency of the end, as is clear in the *Physics* [Bk. II]. But the gift of prophecy is given for the use of the Church, as is clear from I Corinthians [12:7], "And the manifestation of the Spirit is given to every man unto profit ..." Therefore, all those things the knowledge of which can be useful for salvation are the matter of prophecy, whether they are past, future, or eternal, or necessary, or contingent. But those things which cannot pertain to salvation are outside the matter of prophecy. Hence, Augustine writes [*De Genesi ad litteram*, II, 9], "Although our sacred authors knew what shape heaven is, [the Spirit] wants to speak through them only what is useful for salvation." And to the Gospel of St. John [16:13], "But when he, the Spirit of Truth, is come, he will teach you all truth," the *Gloss* adds, "necessary for salvation." Moreover I say necessary for salvation, whether they are necessary for instruction in the faith or for the formation of morals. (Translation from Synave and Benoit 1961: 20–1)

[3] Collins (2002: 262) argues that 2 Tim. 3:14–17 forms a chiasm: vv. 14 and 17 "speak of learning and formation," while vv. 15a and 16 "speak of the Scriptures." His remark that "the center of the chiasm is the achievement of wisdom through faith in Jesus Christ" is wide of the mark, however, in that wisdom, in these verses, is what moves one *to* faith.

[4] The term ἱερὰ γράμματα appears also in Philo, *Vit. Mos.* 2.290, 292; *Leg. Gai.* 195; *Rer. Div. Her.* 106, 159; *Abr.* 61; *Congr.* 34, 90; *Dec.* 8, 37; Josephus, *Ant.* 1.13; 5.61; 10.210. Brox (1969: 261) writes, regarding 2 Tim. 3:15, "Die alttestamentlichen Schriften belehren nämlich über das 'Heil durch den Glauben in Christus Jesus'. Es ist die Überzeugung der frühen Kirche von Anfang an, daß das Alte Testament von Jesus Christus spricht und darin sein eigentlicher Sinn liegt. Dieser Sinn wird allerdings erst im Christusglauben erkannt, wie umgekehrt dann die Schrift in diesem Glauben unterweist." On Jesus as "savior" in 2 Timothy, see Brox (1969: 232–3); Dibelius and Conzelmann (1972: 100–3). See Klöpper (1904: 59).

Verse 16a effectively repeats the thought of v. 15b, but in an abbreviated way, as the point of v. 16 is to expound on the several ways in which this salvific scripture is "useful" (ὠφέλιμος)—that is, "for teaching, for reproof, for correction, and for training in righteousness." The idea of scripture being theopneustic is not the intruding thought that the traditional rendering takes it to be but rather a restatement of the previous verse's point.[5] As such, a vivificationist understanding of θεόπνευστος fits more snugly within the passage than the traditional rendering does.

By viewing salvation in terms of *life*, the understanding argued here invokes a soteriological conceptuality more characteristic of the Pastoral Epistles than of any other portion of the New Testament, except perhaps the Fourth Gospel.[6] Scholars often refer to salvation as a key theme in the Pastorals, and they typically characterize that salvation as the giving of life. I. Howard Marshall, for example, writes that "life is the content of salvation" in 2 Timothy,[7] while George Wieland refers to the letter's soteriology as "the promise of life."[8] This vivificationist soteriology comes to clearest expression in 2 Tim. 1:10, where grace is said to have been "revealed through the appearing of our Savior Christ Jesus, who abolished death and brought life and immortality to light through the gospel" (see Dibelius and Conzelmann 1972: 102).[9] 1 Tim. 1:16 speaks of those who will gain "eternal life" (ζωὴν αἰώνιον), and 4:10 similarly speaks of the "promise of life" (ἐπαγγελία ζωῆς). Tit. 3:7 speaks of the Spirit's power to make us heirs of "eternal life" (ζωῆς αἰωνίου).

The Pastorals clearly should be read (in some sense) as a trilogy,[10] and a vivificationist interpretation of θεόπνευστος allows us to see more clearly that 2 Tim. 3:16 not only restates the main point of the preceding verse (by interweaving ethical instruction, the Gospel, and salvation) but revisits the themes that open 1 Timothy. Charles Thomas Brown (2000: 69–70) writes, in connection with 1 Tim. 1:9–11, that "the gospel sets the boundaries of correct teaching." This is essentially the thought of 2 Tim. 3:15–16 as well, except that now "sacred writings"/"all scripture" is introduced as a source for this Gospel instruction. (In view of the parallelism of expression between vv. 15 and 16, it is probably misguided to explain the distinction between ἱερὰ γράμματα in v. 15 and

---

[5] Contra Miller's (1997: 120–1) contention that vv. 15 and 16 originally belonged to separate "preformed pieces."

[6] On "life" as a soteriological category in the Fourth Gospel, see Filson (1962); McHugh (1992); Vogel (2009: 29–30). See Bultmann (1964: 870–2). On salvific "life" in the New Testament, see Lindblom (1914: 213–43); Clavier (1976: 123–32); Wieland (2006: 36–7); Lehtipuu (2007: 291–2). On the vivificationist aspect of early Christian soteriology more generally, see Léon-Dufour (1986).

[7] According to Marshall (1996: 450), "In relation to their size the Pastoral Epistles contain a greater proportion of salvation words than any other part of the New Testament." See Klöpper (1904: 76); Barrett (1963: 21–4); Towner (1989: 75–119); van Neste (2004: 214–16); Malherbe (2005). Wilson (1979: 20–35) compares the soteriology of the Pastorals with that of Luke-Acts.

[8] Wieland (2006: 107) characterizes it thus in the title of part 3 of his book. (Wolter's [1988: 64–9] discussion of soteriology in the Pastoral Epistles inexplicably omits a discussion of "life.") On the importance of "life" as an eschatological promise, see Léon-Dufour (1986: 162–8, 213–19); Philonenko (2003). On the relation of 1–2 Timothy's understanding of the Gospel to that of Paul's authentic letters, see Strecker (1975): 533–5.

[9] On "the promise of life in Christ Jesus" in 2 Tim. 1:1, see Richards (2002: 108–9).

[10] Contra Richards (2002). This is not to imply that all the Pastorals address the same problems. See Downs (2012: 146 n. 8). Ehrman (2013: 195 [cf. 214–15]) argues that 1 Timothy and Titus are aimed at a different group of opponents than 2 Timothy.

γραφή in v. 16 as more than a rhetorical need to vary one's choice of terms [see Siegert 2004: 206 n. 1].)

2 Tim. 3:14–17's understanding of the connection between Scripture and salvation is a matter of debate. Some readers take that connection to be the kerygmatic/baptismal rehearsal of the Christ event in its soteriological moment, with Scripture figuring as a witness to this event. Others, however, understand the connection more in terms of the development of the moral virtues consequent to coming to faith in Christ, with Scripture serving as a guide to those virtues. Victor Hasler (1978: 75), for example, sees the Old Testament as a handbook to the practice of the virtues. Wieland (2006: 163) takes issue with Hasler's view, as it breaks with the particularistic grounds of the salvation described in v. 15. He brings in Ignatius' soteriologizing of wisdom for comparison:

> We might compare Ignatius's use of σοφίζω in *Smyrn.* 1.1: Δοξάζω'Ιησοῦν Χριστὸν τὸν θεὸν τὸν οὕτως ὑμᾶς σοθίσαντα. Here the outcome is to be established in faith, which has christological content. To be "made wise" is therefore to have become persuaded of certain items of belief with reference to Christ, from his Davidic descent (1.1) to his resurrection (1.2). There is no mention of the role of the OT in this passage from Ignatius, but the pertinent point is that the force of the verb σοφίζω is cognitive rather than behavioural.[11]

The challenge facing the cultivation-of-virtue model is to explain how such a view can give the proper moment to the "christological specificity" of saving faith. Those who adopt such a model typically see a strong correspondence between 2 Timothy and Philo, and explain this through the former's reliance on the latter (see Hanson 1968: 42). Jerome Quinn (1990: 315), for example, describes the Pastorals' soteriology in terms of an "internal, ethical deliverance" of the sort "identified in the Jewish tradition represented by Philo." And Adam Kamesar (2009: 80) sees in 2 Timothy's emphasis on "*all* scripture" a call to allegorize the mundane details one might find there, on the order of Philo's approach: "The assumptions that underlie [Philo's hermeneutical] directives are well expressed in 2 Timothy 3:16." According to Kamesar (2009: 84), both Philo and the Pastor are motivated by a "pan-scriptural didacticism."[12]

---

[11] See Schoedel (1985: 220). Wieland (2006: 163 n. 17) faults Spicq's association of σοφίζω with Jewish *paideia* traditions as "underestimat[ing] the [term's] cognitive aspect in the present context." See Spicq (1969: 786).

[12] Kamesar (2009: 81) writes,

> The passage from 2 Timothy reveals that the Judeo-Hellenistic view of the Bible was not simply didacticist but pan-didacticist, and that this may be attributed to a belief in a more pervasive form of inspiration: "*All Scripture (pasa graphē)* is inspired by God and is beneficial for teaching (*didaskalia*)." This notion was pressed to extremes, and it was believed that every detail of the biblical text conveyed some sort of meaningful lesson. As Philo himself puts it, Moses "does not employ any superfluous word" (*Fug.* 54; cf. *Leg.* 3.147).

See Siegert (2004). Hanson (1968: 45) writes, "We can say with confidence that though Philo does not use it, [θεόπνευστος] exactly expresses Philo's idea of the relation of scripture to the authors of scripture." But cf. Herzer (2004: 230), who sees a difference between Philo's and 2 Timothy's views of Scripture.

I noted in my opening chapter that Irenaeus seems to allude to the claims made in 2 Tim. 3:15–16. In a famous passage that takes its departure from 1 Tim. 3:15's use of "pillars," he refers to Matthew, Mark, Luke, and John as "four pillars, breathing incorruption from every side, and giving life to humans" (τέσσαρας … στύλους, πανταχόθεν πνέοντας τὴν ἀφθαρσίαν, καὶ ἀναζωπυροῦντας τοὺς ἀνθρώπους [*Adv. haer.* 3.11.8]). Although Irenaeus goes back and forth between using "gospel" as a reference to the saving preachment of the apostles and as a "bookish" term, his use of the latter remains very much in touch with the former—which allows for the (implied) interface with the "gospel" of 2 Tim. 3:15. If this reading has anything to commend it, it is worth noting that Irenaeus' implied appeal to 2 Tim. 3:15–16 does not construe salvation according to the cultivation-of-virtue model.

Both construals of 2 Tim. 3:15's reference to "salvation" underscore the importance of teaching, and it might be said that both see the connection between teaching and salvation similarly. The fact that v. 15 awards Scripture an *ability* to save its lifelong disciples may suggest that the cultivation-of-virtue model is at least partially correct (see Meade 1986: 136), but the main lines of 2 Timothy's argument appear to lie in a more traditional understanding of salvation as the giving of life in a more *ontological* sense. The parallelism of thought here with Rom. 15:4 is particularly instructive: "For whatever was written in former days was written for our instruction, so that by steadfastness and by the encouragement of the scriptures we might have hope."

The interpretation adopted here also helps make sense of v. 16's text-critical profile. The majority reading includes a καί between θεόπνευστος and ὠφελεία, but a number of witnesses omit the καί—including the Itala, the Clementine Vulgate, the Syriac Peshitta, the Bohairic, and several patristic witnesses (Origen[lat], Hilary of Poitiers, Ambrosiaster, Primasius). Omitting the καί effectively turns the list of Scripture's useful applications (3:16b) into a direct outworking of its theopneustic nature. The question before us is whether the shorter reading represents a correct grasp of what the text originally tried to say. Bruce Metzger (1994: 580) evidently assumes that it does: καί, he writes, came to be omitted because it "seems to disturb the construction." It is worth noting, however, that the understanding of 2 Tim. 3:15–16 suggested above provides a way of viewing *both* readings as optimal constructions for their respective understandings of θεόπνευστος. To wit: a vivificationist interpretation of θεόπνευστος would appear to call for the inclusion of καί, in that it regards the useful applications of Scripture in v. 16b as a catalogue of additional benefits rather than an outworking of Scripture's theopneustic nature. On the other hand, the onset of Clement's and Origen's regular references to "theopneustic scripture" would have promoted a non-predicative reading of θεόπνευστος in 2 Tim. 3:16—a reading which had little use for καί (cf. Marshall 1999: 793). Hence the word's omission at the hands of a later copyist.

The strength of the cultivation-of-virtue understanding of soteriology depends on the relation between Scripture's salvific moment and those things for which Scripture is said to be useful (ὠφελεία): "for teaching, for reproof, for correction, for training in righteousness" (see Wieland 2006: 165 n. 24). Is salvation the goal of these *uses* of Scripture or are these the benefits of going *on* in Scripture beyond one's baptismal acceptance of the Christ event? There is neither room nor much point in the present discussion to answer this. It suffices to point out that ὠφελεία was a semi-technical term in contemporary usage, where it denoted the moral benefits of a writer's discussion (e.g., Epictetus, *Disc.* 3.21.15; cf. van Unnik 1979: 49–50; Malherbe 1987: 23; Sandnes 2009: 42, 55, 58) and also that it is a favorite word of the Pastor.[13]

1.2 Θεόπνευστος and the Setting of 2 Timothy within Early Christian Controversy

It is widely recognized that 2 Timothy was written not by Paul but by someone writing in the apostle's name several decades after his martyrdom.[14] This raises the question of an approximate date for the book's writing, a matter of interest for our philological investigation of θεόπνευστος. We must bear in mind that the pseudepigraphy of these letters requires a date not only after the death of Paul but also after the deaths of his younger colleagues Timothy and Titus, for if Timothy and Titus were still alive when these letters began to circulate, they might easily have denied being the original recipients of the letters (see Merz 2004: 80). On top of that, the fact that the Pastorals presume the existence of Paul's letters as a circulating corpus suggests a date in the late first century at the earliest.[15] We also need to account for the fact that the second "scriptural" saying in 1 Tim. 5:18 appears to be partly a quotation from the gospel of

---

[13] The word ὠφέλιμος appears four times in the Pastorals (1 Tim. 4:8 [bis]; 2 Tim. 3:16; Tit. 3:8), and nowhere else in the New Testament.

[14] I regard the pseudepigraphy of the Pastorals as ironclad—the opposing position appears to me so strained as only to add weight to the consensus. Ehrman's discussion (2013: 192–222) is perhaps the fullest and clearest treatment. Among the external indications of pseudepigraphy is the lateness of any knowledge of the Pastorals: they are missing from the oldest extant corpus of Pauline writings (P[46]) and would not have fit on the estimated fourteen pages missing at the end—and Marcion was apparently unaware of their existence (see Tertullian, *Adv. Marc.* 5.21). (See Verheyden 2003: 522–5; McDonald 2009: 167–8.) As Quinn (1992: 562) notes, the absence of these letters from the earliest Pauline canon is supported by the order of the current canon: as Paul's writings are presented in descending order according to length, we should expect 1–2 Timothy to *precede* 1–2 Thessalonians. The fact that they follow suggests they were added later. The internal evidence for pseudepigraphy is manifold. MacDonald (1983) has argued that several aspects of the Pastorals' stance on matters are best interpreted as a response to the view of Paul found in the apocryphal *Acts of Paul and Thecla*, with the link extending even to proper names, like Onesiphorus and Hermogenes. See Lieu (2010: 6). One major problem with attributing the Pastorals to Paul is that their theology isn't very Pauline. As Donelson (1986: 60) notes, the author "appears to be a Paulinist not in theology but only in name; he is defending men he knows mostly by reputation and legend. He is basically ignorant of Paul's unique version of Christian salvation and thus passes on a handful of catch phrases which sound like Paul but which do not inform the author's thinking in any substantive way." See Schröter (2012: 198). In the words of Richards (2002: 7):

> There is … a world of philosophical and political language in the Pastorals distant from Paul, a world that values εὐσέβεια, σωφρονισμός, and ἔργα ἀγαθά. Such vocabulary signals a world preoccupied as much with one's duty as a πολίτης in the world ἔξωθεν as with one's love as an ἅγιος to the ἀδελφοί. Both God and Christ are no longer so much Paul's πατήρ and υἱός, respectively, as, each in their turn the Saviour, σωτήρ.

See Harrison (1921); Enslin (1938: 299–307); Dibelius and Conzelmann (1972: 1–5); Bassler (1989: 17–24); Collins (2002: 7, 73); Tsuji (2010); Ramelli (2011c: 566–7); Lips (2011: 221–2); Chester (2013: 139). Bauckham (2008: 123–49) seems only grudgingly to admit the pseudepigraphy of the Pastorals.

[15] As Meade (1986: 130) notes, "the Pastorals represent an advanced 'canon-consciousness' in regard to Pauline tradition, so that even the literary form and its attendant *personalia* become part of the pseudepigraphic framework."

Luke (cf. Lk. 10:7; see Meier 1999: 77), a writing which more and more scholars are assigning to the early second century (see now Landry 2015). Some scholars also think the author of the Pastorals was dependent on Paul's Miletus speech, from Luke's second volume (Acts 20:18b–35; see Schröter 2012: 214). Richard Pervo writes (1994: 38),

> [The Pastoral Epistles (= PE)] exude distance and rely upon authority that has the patina, indeed the halo, of antiquity. In these texts Paul is one of the leading figures of salvation history, not an apostle battling for recognition. Every reading of the PE has to account for their sense of distance, and there is little doubt that the most difficult readings are those which place the recipients within the life of Paul. Historical distance actualizes the text. Readers quite readily take up the PE in terms of what Paul is saying to me/us now rather than what he said to Titus and Timothy then.

What can we say about the *terminus ante quem*? Here the apparent reception of the Pastorals in the writings of Polycarp and Ignatius—a widely but not universally accepted view—requires a date most likely before 130 CE.[16] All things considered, therefore, we may say that the Pastorals probably were written contemporaneously with the Fourth Gospel—that is, in the second or third decade of the second century.

How might we make sense of 2 Tim. 3:16 within an early second-century setting? One *entrée* into this question is to ask why the author of 2 Timothy refers to "all scripture." What was there, in the way of the letter's (real or fictive) occasion, that made a discussion of Scripture's salvific role timely for the author and his original readers? The usual explanations can be sorted into two general approaches. The first posits that the letter aimed to ward off the teachings of a group with Marcionite tendencies—a group that discounted the value of the Old Testament and based its teachings only on the entirely new elements introduced by Christian preaching. This approach often invokes the reference to a "gnosis falsely so-called" in 1 Tim. 6:20 (see Holtzmann 1880: 161; cf. Haufe 1973: 329). One advantage of this approach is that it fits hand-in-glove not only with the threat of Marcion but also with the apparent antiscriptural piety of the circle behind the *Gospel of Thomas*.[17] (It might also fit with a concern about Ebionites, a group that apparently discounted the Prophets and parts of the Pentateuch [cf. Epiphanius, *Pan.* 30.18.4–9; Ps.-Clement, *Hom.* 2.38–39].) According to this way of reading, the author of 2 Timothy was rescuing Scripture from possible neglect and seeking to maintain the salvation–historical nexus between the Gospel and the Old Testament.[18] The second approach posits that the letter's opponents did *not* share

---

[16] See the chart of "probable" and "possible" echoes of the Pastorals in Polycarp, in Berding (1999: 353–5). Berding asks, "How early are we able to make a clear connection between the Pastorals and the church's understanding that they were written by Paul?" (350). This is an odd question, as it seems to suppose that the ruse of pseudepigraphy requires a time lag. (Ehrman [2013: 193] points out that the ruse could take root in twenty years, but I fail to see why it could not take root immediately.) On the Apostolic Fathers' use of the Pastorals, see Merz (2004: 71–3) (on Ignatius), 114–40 (on Polycarp). On Ignatius' use of the Pastorals, cf. also Committee of the Oxford Society of Historical Theology (1905: 71–3).

[17] On *Thomas*'s antiscriptural view, see Baarda (2003); Goodacre (2012: 188–9), with n. 38.

[18] Allusions to the Old Testament are found in 1 Tim. 1:3, 7; 4:13; 5:18; 2 Tim. 3:8, 14–17; Tit. 1:14–15; 3:9. On the use of Genesis in 2 Tim. 2:13–15, see Aageson (2012: 118–19).

the antiscriptural outlook of the Marcionite and Thomasine communities. After all, the Pastorals make it clear that the opponents were in some fashion teachers of the Law (1 Tim. 1:7; Tit. 3:9; cf. 1:14) rather than *abandoners* of the Law (e.g., see Wilson 1979: 90–1).[19] This approach exists in several variations, all of them seeking to explain in what way the teachers of the Law were misguided in their theology.[20]

My own attempt to explain 2 Tim. 3:14–17's defense of Scripture's salvific role belongs to the second approach: the opponents indeed saw great value in the Old Testament. The key to the problem lies in understanding how these verses formulate the connection between Scripture and the gift of life: Scripture is life-giving because it discloses the Gospel to those who read it faithfully.[21] 2 Timothy's opponents, however, have an alternative understanding of how Scripture and salvation are interrelated: they view the connection either as (1) *non*-epistemological or as (2) mediated by Scripture's halakhic prescriptions. That is, they view Scripture as life-giving by virtue of a divine power inherent within it—independent of the conveyance of any sort of Gospel message—or as showing the way to walk faithfully according to the Law. Scripture, on this account, *saves* the reader (however we should understand that)—either independently of his or her putting its prescriptions into practice (as in [1]) or by means of adumbrating one's halakhic burden (as in [2]).

I have already noted the common ground shared by the Pastorals and the Fourth Gospel with regard to their vivificationist construal of salvation. That ground extends to their respective understandings of the actions that lead to life—as Wieland (2006: 37) writes, "The link in 1 Tim 1:16 between ζωὴ αἰώνιος and believing in Christ fits the Johannine picture, as does Christ's coming εἰς τὸν κόσμον (v. 15)." I noted above that the Pastorals were probably written about the same time as the Fourth Gospel. They may, in fact, be indebted to the Fourth Gospel, although that is hardly necessary for my thesis.[22] Whatever the situation, the opponents that the Pastorals imagine bear a striking resemblance to the opponents that lurk behind portions of the Fourth Gospel.[23]

The clearest indication of this sort of opponent in the Fourth Gospel is found in John 5. There, in vv. 39–40, Jesus accuses "the Jews" (cf. 5:18) of altogether missing the Christological mechanism by which Scripture gives life to its readers: "You search the scriptures because (ὅτι) you think (δοκεῖτε) that in them you have eternal life; and it is they that testify on my behalf. Yet you refuse to come to me to have life." Thus the Johannine Jesus collides with the idea that the study (and undoubtedly also the

---

[19] Hanson (1968: 44) thinks that the opponents cannot really be associated with a genuine "incipient Marcionism," given that Marcion rejected the entire Old Testament, while the opponents in the Pastorals are characterized as teachers of the Law.

[20] It has sometimes been suggested that 2 Timothy's attack on those who believe the resurrection "has already taken place" (2:18) is a response to the theology of Colossians and Ephesians (see Col. 2:12; Eph. 2:6; 5:14). See Alkier (2013: 72); Ehrman (2013: 217).

[21] Wieland (2006: 100) writes, "The object of believing is Christ Jesus, who himself saves, and the outcome is eternal life ([1 Tim.] 1:15–16). The salvific efficacy of the teaching ministry is readily understood within this framework."

[22] Trebilco (2004: 598–601) argues for the Pastorals' dependence on the Fourth Gospel, on the basis of shared phraseology and vocabulary. See Stettler (1998: 326). The Fourth Gospel and the Pastorals also share the conspicuous notion that God dwells in a community rather than a building—see Hanson (1983: 135).

[23] See the excursus on "Die Gegner" in Roloff (1988: 228–30).

performance) of Scripture is *inherently* salvific. As Martin Asiedu-Peprah (2001: 108) notes, "the use of ὅτι and δοκεῖτε suggests to the reader that 'The Jews' are mistaken in their belief that their study of the Scriptures constitutes an end in itself." The Jews are mistaken because they fail to discern that Jesus is the life-source to which the Scriptures point (see von Wahlde 2004: 409).[24]

The idea that the Torah gives life to those who embrace it was common in Jewish circles. It had its basis in Scripture itself (see Deut. 30:15–20; Ps. 119; Sir. 17:11; 45:5). According to *m. Abot* 6.7, the Law "gives life to them that practice it both in this world and in the world to come." David Flusser (2009: 203–4) finds the "Law → life" sequence within the earliest form of the blessing recited after the reading of the Torah. He also traces the connection between *doing* Torah (viz., keeping the commandments) and receiving eternal life to Jesus's words to the rich young ruler (Mt. 19:16–17 // Mk 10:17–19 // Lk. 18:18–20) and to *Ps. Sol.* 14.1–5 (Flusser 2009: 205). Konrad Schmid (2012: 301) sees in this understanding of Torah piety a usurping of the life-giving effect of the Temple cult—a development he associates with the presumed "postcultic situation of Psalm 1." A connection between the pursuit of virtue and a reward of "true life" appears in Philo's writings (see Downs 2013: 256–7).[25]

2 Other Purported Scriptural Claims to Inspiration

Some readers might insist that the loss of a presumption about a single word in 2 Timothy would not completely overturn an inspirationist understanding of Scripture's authority. After all, they might say, there are other NT passages that spell out or imply the inspiration of Scripture. It therefore might pay to visit a couple of other passages regularly cited in support of the traditional view.

To say that Scripture nowhere claims to be inspired, of course, runs very much counter to received opinion. Indeed, Warfield (1894: 630) referred to an "avalanche of texts" that threatened to cover any attempt to deny that Scripture teaches its own inspiration: "There are scores, hundreds, of them; and they come bursting upon us in one solid mass. Explain them away? We should have to explain away the whole New Testament." But is it really the case that Scripture *repeatedly* claims or implies its own inspiration? Seeking a more down-to-earth view of the matter, William Abraham (1981: 93) dismissed Warfield's "avalanche" as a "ridiculous and gross exaggeration":

> There is no such avalanche at all. There are in fact three general groups of texts. There are the classical texts of 2 Tim. 3:16 and 2 Peter 1:21. There are those texts that reveal the attitude of Jesus to the Old Testament. Finally there are those texts where little distinction is made between what God says and what Scripture says.

---

[24] A variant of the saying in Jn 5:39 also appears in the *Egerton Gospel*. See Haenchen (1984: 264). Watson (2013: 303) recently voiced the strange supposition that the Johannine Jesus was challenging the Jews to find the term "eternal life" in Scripture—where it does not appear. See the section on "Wisdom, Law, and Life in the Hebrew Bible," in Burkes (1999: 254–7).

[25] On Philo's view of the "death of the soul" as the "decay of virtue" (*Leg.* 1.105), see Zeller (1995: 21, 41–2). See Bultmann (1964: 832–43).

If we are talking about texts typically *adduced* as evidence of Scripture's self-claim to inspiration, then Abraham's threefold classification is helpful. But even these three groups cannot be considered true supports for an inspirationist view of Scripture. In every case, readers have redirected the passage in question to support a claim it does not make.

The remainder of this chapter will look at the two passages most frequently cited in support of the divine inspiration of Scripture: 2 Pet. 1:21 (the other "classical" text in Abraham's first group) and Jn 10:35 (the most prominent representative of the second group).

2.1 2 Pet. 1:19–21

After 2 Tim. 3:16, the most widely cited verse in the case for the inspiration of Scripture is 2 Pet. 1:19–21:

> 19 So we have the prophetic message more fully confirmed. You will do well to be attentive to this as to a lamp shining in a dark place, until the day dawns and the morning star rises in your hearts.
> 20 First of all you must understand this, that no prophecy of scripture is a matter of one's own interpretation,
> 21 because no prophecy ever came by human will, but men and women moved by the Holy Spirit spoke from God.

As we saw in Chapter 1, the Latin Vulgate form of this verse shares with 2 Tim. 3:16 the use of *inspir-*, and both verses use that word in a comment having to do with Scripture (*sed spiritu sancto inspirati*). And so the assumption arose, probably shortly after the Vulgate came to prominence, that 2 Tim. 3:16 and 2 Pet. 1:21 make comparable claims. This assumption has remained in place until the present day.[26]

The problem with taking 2 Pet. 1:21 as a support for the inspiration of Scripture should be obvious for anyone who reads it slowly and deliberately: It does not refer to the inspiration of Scripture per se but rather to the inspiration of prophecies *within* Scripture (v. 20).[27] Nothing in the verse implies that epistolary and narrative writings found within Scripture are also inspired.[28] The discussion leading up to 2 Pet. 1:21 has to do with the assuredness of the Lord's word, as delivered in a prophetic mode. Nothing in this verse can reasonably be construed as a statement about the nature of Scripture itself.[29]

---

[26] E.g., Artola (1999: 67) writes, "Clarificada la actividad del soplo divino en 2 Tim 3,16 será útil completar la investigación examinando el pasaje conceptualmente paralelo de 2 Pe 1,21."

[27] While there were those like Philo (*Rer. Div. Her.* 259–66; *Vit. Mos.* 2.188; 2.246–292; *Dec.* 175; *Quaest. In Exod.* 1.49) who considered all the biblical writers "prophets," 2 Peter's phrase "prophecy of scripture" does not suggest this position.

[28] Sanday (1911: 89) writes that "the judgment in question [in 2 Pet. 1:20–21] certainly covers the prophetic writings, and perhaps others not strictly prophetic into which a prophetic element enters; but it would hardly go beyond these."

[29] Thus Briggs (2007: 268) scolds Webster for "bluntly misread[ing 2 Pet. 1:19] as being about Scripture in general when it is not." See Webster (2003: 36–7).

A few commentators recognize the plain sense of 2 Pet. 1:21 but insist that the category of "prophecy" nevertheless stands duty for the whole of Scripture. James W. Scott (2009a: 142 n. 56), for example, insists that, when the preceding verse mentions "prophecy of scripture," "in view would appear to be the entire content of Scripture." He infers this because "these verses refer to what v. 19 calls 'the prophetic word, to which you will do well to pay attention,' which can hardly refer only to selected portions of Scripture, as that would suggest that the other portions can be ignored." Scott's reasoning is somewhat forced, and it would take a very willing reader to agree with it. An injunction to believe and respect the prophecies preserved in Scripture manifestly would *not* imply what Scott suggests: None of 2 Peter's original readers would have taken an exaltation of Scripture's (formally) prophetic passages as a diminution of its legal or wisdom portions, and so on. It is more likely that "prophecy of scripture" means what it appears to mean, and that v. 21 tells us *only* that these prophecies are inspired. The point of the verse is essentially that the prophecies preserved in Scripture are *real* prophecies.[30]

2.2 Jn 10:35

Jn 10:35 is also frequently cited in support of an inspirationist view of Scripture. Those who cite this verse seem to think it makes their point somewhat forcefully, as it allegedly preserves the words of Jesus himself. It is, in fact, the most prominent example from the second of Abraham's "three general groups of text," purported to "reveal the attitude of Jesus to the Old Testament."

Jesus here makes a statement about Scripture, in the course of an exchange with "the Jews":

Jn 10:31–36

31 The Jews took up stones again to stone him.

32 Jesus answered, "I have shown you many good works from the Father. For which of these works will you stone me?"

33 The Jews answered him, "For good works we do not stone you but for blasphemy and because you, a human being, make yourself as God."

34 Jesus answered them, "Is it not written in your law, 'I said, you are gods'?

35 If those to whom the word of God came were called 'gods'—and the scripture cannot be set aside (καὶ οὐ δύναται λυθῆναι ἡ γραφή)—

36 can you say that the one whom the Father sanctified and sent into the world blasphemes, because I said, 'I am the son of God'?" (Author's translation)

---

[30] Stewart (2003: 222) writes about the "tortuous lengths" to which Louis Gaussen went to justify calling all of Scripture an "oracle":

> Beyond the obviously prophetic role played by Moses and the OT prophets, he must grasp at straws to contend that Wisdom writings and historical books also qualify as prophetic in character. For the New Testament writings, he must not only argue that the apostles functioned as prophets, but that non-apostolic writers (such as Mark, Luke, James and the author of Hebrews) did also.

Evangelicals often equate the claim that Scripture "cannot be set aside" (NEB for οὐ δύναται λυθῆναι)³¹ with the claim that its *meaning* cannot possibly be wrong. Such a view, it is widely supposed, implies that Scripture is *inspired* and *inerrant*.

Those who oppose reading inspirationist implications into Jesus's retort often claim that Jesus is arguing on the Pharisees' terms and that we cannot assume he affirms those terms. By claiming that "scripture cannot be set aside," Jesus is trapping the Pharisees on the terms of their own unbending hermeneutic, so as to cut off the branch on which they are sitting (e.g., see Loader 1997: 472). It is *they* (the Pharisees) who claim, as warrant for their elevation of the Sabbath laws above all exceptions, that "scripture cannot be set aside." Honesty should keep us, however, from going down this route. While there certainly is an element here of Jesus beating the Pharisees at their own game (cf. Jn 3:6–12; 5:31–46), it appears more likely that he agrees with them at the level of presupposition.³²

There is still, however, an obvious problem with the typical Evangelical reading of Jn 10:35, in that it fails to recognize that Jesus is speaking about Scripture's *legal* inviolability, rather than about its factual integrity. The inviolability of the scriptural commandments is connected with their foundational role for halakhic matters, rather than with the text's supposed divinity or inspired status. A legal body obviously can treat certain laws as inviolable, without in any way suggesting that the text in which those laws are imbedded is divinely inspired! (Cf. Jn 5:18 [λύειν τὸ Σάββατον (!)]; 7:23.) Douglas Farrow (1987: 105) writes,

> λυθῆναι as it occurs in this verse is often translated 'to be broken', but this has frequently proved misleading. Arndt and Gingrich classify this occurrence under a heading based on these meanings: *destroy, bring to an end, abolish, do away with*; and with respect to commandments, laws, and statements—*repeal, annul, abolish*. While many want to see in John 10:35 an affirmation that "every statement of Scripture stands immutably, indestructible in its verity, unaffected by denial, human ignorance or criticism, charges of errancy or other subjective attack," that is not quite the point of saying that Scripture is οὐ δύναται λυθῆναι. Christ was not concerned here with the factual verity or accuracy of Scripture, but with the authority of its voice and the binding nature of its testimony.³³

To point to the inviolability of the Jewish Law, therefore, is to make a *legal* remark, rather than a bibliological remark. That this is so is shown by the fact that Jesus uses

---

³¹ Farrow (1987: 105–6) commends the NEB rendering at this point.
³² So, rightly, Whitacre (1982: 37): "Here we find the author using the tradition that he holds in common with his opponents to support Jesus' claim and thereby counter their accusation." Farrow (1987: 105) writes, "While this verse may well include an element of mockery, Warfield is doubtless correct in dismissing any attempt to suggest that Christ was merely hanging the Jews with their own rope and not actually approving the statement about Scripture." See Warfield (1915: 1475–6).
³³ Nightingale (1993: 290) writes, "The lawcode … is conceived of as a written text whose language is sacrosanct. Its pronouncements on legal and extra-legal issues serve to control the citizens' words as well as their deeds." See Cairns (1942); Hansen (1978: 317); Weltin (1987: 114); Yunis (1988); Nightingale (1993); Woozley (2010); Fraistat (2015).

the expression "your law" to refer to a passage from Psalm 82.[34] If his point had been bibliological, we might have expected a reference to "David" rather than to "your law," as the latter is usually used only for the Pentateuch.[35]

It is worth noting that the inviolability of written laws was a bigger deal in the ancient world than it is today. Laws theoretically could be repealed—the repeal of the Oppian Law in 195 BCE is a parade example[36]—but it was a more grievous process than today. James Hanges (1998: 292) notes,

> In the Greek context we find numerous examples of "laws against abrogation of the (written) laws." According to Plato, Socrates believed that to break the law of the state is to act unjustly; Plato personifies the laws of Athens, which then begin to speak to Socrates as if they could suffer damage from his disobedience. One of the reasons the personified Athenian Law gives for Socrates obedience is the existence of a specific law that declares court decisions to be binding; and since Socrates had agreed to obey this particular law, he is thereby obligated to abide even by an unfavorable verdict.[37]

3 Conclusion

The New Testament nowhere claims to be inspired. At most, it claims that the (formally) *prophetic* parts are inspired. Those who recognize the New Testament's claim over the believer must theorize its authority in some other way. It should be noted, however, that this state of affairs is not as off-putting as it might seem: by stepping into the shoes (sandals) of the earliest believers, we can begin to understand that it was the *apostles* as witnesses of the kerygmatic narrative that gave the kerygma its epistemic warrant and that the New Testament functions for latecomers like ourselves as an extension of the apostolic witness. As Grant (1965: 106) notes, "The question of 'scripture' was not as important as the question of 'the word of truth' set forth either orally or in writing." This was the New Testament's view, and it is the view that reigned throughout the second century, although inklings of its demise were present already before the end of the century.

---

[34] "The Law" also refers to a Psalms passage in Jn 15:25 (cf. Pss. 35:19; 69:4). On the Law in the Fourth Gospel, see Jn 1:45, 7:19, 23, 49–51; 8:5, 17; 10:34; 12:34; 15:25; 18:31; 19:7.

[35] In the Fourth Gospel, "Law" is often preceded by a personal pronoun, which seems to indicate that the Law belongs to the Jews and *not* to Jesus. Cf. Jn 8:17 ("your own Law"), 10:34 ("your Law"), 15:25 ("their Law"). See Pancaro (1975: 519). Fernando (2001: 12) faults William Loader for failing to distinguish between the Law and Scripture in the Fourth Gospel.

[36] On the repeal of the Oppian Law, see Culham (1982); Moscovich (1990); Agati Madeira (2004: 92–7).

[37] Hanges quotes Eberhard Ruschenbusch and notes (in a footnote) his two examples: Dio Chrysostom 80.6 and Gellius, *Noetes Atticae* 2.12.1.

6

The Screw Turns: Θεόπνευστος in Irenaeus, Clement of Alexandria, Tertullian, the *De Universo* (of Hippolytus?), and Origen

The foregoing chapters aimed to show that θεόπνευστος/θεόπνοος means "life-giving" every time it appears in second- and early third-century Jewish and pagan sources. Obviously, I would leave too much undone if I didn't try to identify *when* θεόπνευστος began to be read in the manner found throughout the history of Bible translation. Who is the first writer to attribute an inspirationist meaning to θεόπνευστος, and what caused that writer to understand the word differently from his forebears? To find the answer, we need to consider early *Christian* sources outside 2 Timothy. These are the only pre-Origen uses of θεόπνευστος remaining to be discussed.

Which Christian writers, up to and including Origen, give evidence of engaging 2 Tim. 3:16, and how did they understand θεόπνευστος? In what follows, I consider five writers: Irenaeus, Clement of Alexandria, Tertullian, the author of *De Universo* (a work often attributed to Hippolytus), and Origen. Only three of the five actually use the Greek word we are pursuing (Clement, *De Universo*, and Origen), but Irenaeus appears to paraphrase 2 Tim. 3:16, and Tertullian offers a loose Latin rendering of the passage. I will discuss these writers in the order listed above, not just because it is (arguably) chronological but also because I divide the lot between Irenaeus, Tertullian, and Clement, on the one hand, and *De Universo* and Origen, on the other hand. The first three appear to understand θεόπνευστος in vivificationist terms, *De Universo* uses the word in a neutral way, and Origen was the first person in history to understand it in inspirationist terms.

Before looking at these post-NT uses of θεόπνευστος, I should call attention to the "neutral" use of the word, attributed to *De Universo*. Once 2 Tim. 3:16 introduced θεόπνευστος into the church's vocabulary, it was inevitable that the word would, at times, be used as a scriptural index rather than as an actively operative term. In other words, θεόπνευστος was sometimes used merely to denote that Scripture was being discussed on the terms of 2 Timothy or that the "writing" (γραφὴ) being discussed was indeed the *special* writing (= Scripture) mentioned there. In these uses of the word, the question of whether the word's meaning is vivificationist or inspirationist is secondary at best.

1 Θεόπνευστος in Irenaeus

A study of θεόπνευστος normally would not feature Irenaeus, as the word appears nowhere in the Greek remains of his writings, nor is it presumed to underlie those parts surviving only in Latin.[1] In what follows, however, I argue that one of the best known passages in *Adversus haereses* contains a probable allusion to 2 Tim. 3:16 and that it implicitly unpacks a meaning for θεόπνευστος consistent with the philological conclusions of the preceding chapters. (There is admittedly some circularity in my argument, but it is not vicious.)

Adv. haer. 3.11.8 contains Irenaeus' famous justification of the fourfold aspect of the NT gospels.[2] By comparing the four gospels with the fourfold aspect of certain natural and celestial phenomena, Irenaeus shows the inclusion of four gospels in the New Testament to be both fitting and inevitable—as over against those (viz., Marcionites and Gnostics [see Painchaud 1996]) who base their theologizing on a single gospel:

> There can be neither more nor fewer gospels than there are. As there are four regions of the world in which we live, and four principal winds, and as the church is spread over all the land, and has for a column and support the Gospel and the Spirit of life; consequently it has four pillars, breathing incorruption from every side and giving life to humans. From this it is manifest that the Logos is the artificer of all, who sits above the cherubim, and encompasses everything, when manifest to men gave us the fourfold Gospel, encompassed by one Spirit. As David asks, regarding his advent: "You who sit above the cherubim, appear." For the cherubim are four-faced, and their faces are the images of the dispositions of the Son of God. "For the first living creature," it says, "is like a lion," signifying his efficacy, primacy, and royalty. "The second is like a young bull," signifying his sacrificial and priestly station. "The third has the face of a human," recalling his appearance as a man. "The fourth is like a flying eagle," depicting the gift of the Spirit flying upon the church. (Author's translation)

It is difficult to gauge how persuasive this line of argument was in the ancient world.[3] Presumably it was more persuasive than it is now. Martin Hengel (2000: 216) notes that, for the Valentinians, "the 'fourness' (τετράς, τετρακτύς, *quaternatio*) was a

---

[1] The (near) complete text of *Adversus haereses* survives only in Latin (in a version known already to Augustine), Many important passages also survive in Greek fragments.

[2] On *Adv. haer.* 3.11.8, see Gutjahr (1904: 8–11); Hoh (1919: 18–21); Campenhausen (1972: 197–200); Metzger (1987: 154–5); Bruce (1988: 175–6). Cf. Blanchard (1993: 161–3); Bingham (1998: 77–88); Reed (2002: 38); Briggman (2012: 38).

[3] Cf. Cullmann's (1956: 51–2) discussion of "The False Reasons for the Fourfold Gospel propounded by Irenaeus." Hengel (2000: 11) responds that Cullmann "misses the point":

> A modern theological-historical understanding, namely that the evangelists could not exhaust the wealth of the revelation of the incarnate Christ and "therefore … had to bring together all the depictions of the life of Jesus that were available from the apostolic period," would have played straight into the hands of their Gnostic opponents, who claimed that in their writings they were handing on such a diversity, including the secret revelations of the Risen Christ.

fundamental ontological entity, as already with the Pythagoreans, against which [Irenaeus] constantly writes polemic."[4]

Adv. haer. 3.11.8 is extant in Greek, and most commentators recognize Irenaeus' reference to a "pillar and ground" as an allusion to 1 Tim. 3:15, which refers to "the church of the living god" as "the pillar and ground of the truth."[5] This allusion represents a resumption of Irenaeus' original framing of the problematic in the preface to book 3 (cf. there θεμέλιον καὶ στῦλον).[6] But there might also be an additional scriptural allusion in this passage, one that goes consistently unrecognized, in the description of what the four pillars (= gospels) *do*: "breathing incorruption from every side, and giving life to humans" (πανταχόθεν πνέοντας τὴν ἀφθαρσίαν, καὶ ἀναζωπυροῦντας τοὺς ἀνθρώπους).[7] The similarity of this imagery to our revisionist understanding of 2 Tim. 3:15–16 is striking. Once we learn to read 2 Timothy according to a vivificationist understanding of θεόπνευστος, the possibility that Irenaeus echoes this passage becomes clear. The combination of 1 Tim. 3:15 with 2 Tim. 3:15–16, along with the association of quadriformity with universality, allows Irenaeus to refer to the vivifying effect of the Gospel as reaching "on every side."[8] (Irenaeus transfers the Gospel's vivifying effect to the gospels as documents.)[9] The failure of an allusion to 2 Timothy to register with most readers, of course, is simply fallout from the resignification of θεόπνευστος in the early third century. Second-century readers, equipped with a

---

  Bird (2014: 324) calls Irenaeus' argument at this point "not rationalistic but aesthetic." Cf. Campenhausen (1972: 199). Stanton (2004: 66) writes of "the evocative nature of the number four in Irenaeus' day." See Watson (2006: 102–9).

[4] See the discussion of four regions and four winds in Wanke (2000: 346–53).

[5] Irenaeus calls the Gospel the "ground and pillar of our faith" in *Adv. haer.* 3.1.1 and refers to the Gospel and the Spirit as the "pillar and ground" in 3.11.8. Some scholars associate the phrase in 3.1.1 with "the Scriptures" (e.g., Behr 2000: 31 n. 27; Briggman 2012: 51), but the parsing of the passage turns on the question of how to divide the text. Most scholars appear to follow Rousseau's parsing, which associates *the Gospel* with "ground and pillar" (e.g., Reed 2002: 38 n. 70). See Bingham (1998: 78). On 1 Tim. 3:15, see Hanson (1983: 135–6). See Hoh (1919: 8, 102).

[6] Minns (2010: 8) reads the preface to book 3 as making it appear that the contents of books 1–2 correspond to the two-part operation named in the work's full title: *The Detection and Overthrow of Knowledge Falsely So-Called*. See Werner (1889: 39).

[7] It is possible that Irenaeus' use of the "living creatures" (ζῷα) in his argument for the quadriformity of the gospels invokes not only the fact that the creatures are four in number but also the fact that they are called ζῷα. As things described as "living" are often presumed to be life-giving as well (e.g., "living water"), a comparison of the gospels with ζῷα might be intended to suggest the life-giving quality of the former. (Such a reading would imply that the comparisons with the ζῷα do not represent a preexisting complex of material, as argued in Skeat [1992]. Hengel [2000: 215 n. 37] finds Skeat's argument "convincing," but, as Bingham [1998: 90] argues, it underappreciates the Irenaean marks in this material. Watson [2006: 105 n. 17] writes, in response to Skeat, that Irenaeus was perhaps "influenced by Ezek. 1 but has failed to mention it.") Cf. Bultmann (1964: 873). If my reading is correct, Irenaeus' argument can be compared to the likening of the gospels to the four life-giving streams of Paradise, a tradition found in Hippolytus, Cyprian, and Victorinus of Pettau. See Stanton (2004: 90–1).

[8] Hengel (2000: 10) writes, "For Irenaeus the collection forms a unity and therefore he can still call it the 'Gospel.'"

[9] Nevertheless, Stanton (2004: 67) writes, "For Irenaeus, 'the Gospel' and in particular the words of Jesus have a higher authority than the individual writings of the evangelists, even though the gospels are referred to occasionally as 'Scriptures.'" On Irenaeus' use of "gospel," see Blanchard (1993: 151–64).

vivificationist understanding of θεόπνευστος, were in a better position to see an allusion to 2 Tim. 3:16.

Lexical support for hearing an echo of 2 Tim. 3:15–16 in Irenaeus can be found in the wording that Vettius Valens used to unpack θεόπνευστος in his *Anthologies*. For Valens, the existence in us all of "something divine and theopneustic" stands as an assurance that "not everything humans attain is wholly corruptible and wretched" (φθαρτὰ … καὶ μοχθηρὰ). In Valens' reasoning, the quality of being theopneustic stands over against corruptibility. This word-association-by-negation corroborates the suggestion that Irenaeus paraphrased 2 Timothy's use of θεόπνευστος by means of referring to the Gospel message as "breathing incorruption." Having said this, however, it should be noted that it takes a *combination* of the concepts "breathing" and "incorruption" to provide sufficient grounds for hearing an echo of 2 Tim. 3:16. "Incorruption," by itself, cannot provide those grounds, not least because it happens to be one of Irenaeus' favorite terms and a core ingredient in his soteriology.[10] Nor should any of this be taken as an attempt to displace the pneumatological dimension of Irenaeus' formulation. As Anthony Briggman (2012: 52) notes, it is (for Irenaeus) the "connection with the Spirit" that allows/causes the gospels to "breath[e] out incorruptibility" and "vivif[y] human beings."[11] It is of little consequence that 2 Timothy does not share this pneumatological dimension.[12]

The likelihood that Irenaeus intends an echo of 2 Tim. 3:15–16 is bolstered by Benjamin White's (2011: 128) argument for seeing a "programmatic, intertextual relationship between *Adversus haereses* and the Pastoral Epistles."[13] According to White (2011: 146, 132), the language of the Pastoral Epistles "bubbles to the surface of all five books" of *Adversus haereses*, "pop[ping] up explicitly at times, implicitly and allusively at others."[14] The fact that Irenaeus signals his dependence on the Pastorals in the title of his work (cf. 1 Tim. 6:20 [also cited in *Adv. haer.* 2.14.7]) sets up the Pastorals' (collective) suit against "falsely so-called gnosis" as a key for the reader (see White 2011: 126–7).[15] White repeats Johannes Werner's (1889: 12–13) notice that *Adversus haereses* has six explicit uses of the Pastorals introduced by "the Apostle says" or "Paul says" (etc.)—two from each of the Pastorals (*Adv. haer.* 1.praef.1 [1 Tim. 1:4]; 1.16.3 [Tit. 3:10]; 2.14.7 [1 Tim. 6:20]; 3.3.3 [2 Tim. 4:21]; 3.3.4 [Tit. 3:10–11]; 3.14.1 [2 Tim. 4:9–11])—and he tabulates previous scholars' counts of the work's references

---

[10] De Andia (1986: 17) presents the statistics for the appearances of *incorruptela* (and cognates) as follows: *Adversus haereses* contains *incorruptela* fifty-seven times (of which fourteen correspond to extant appearances of ἀφθαρσία in the Greek fragments), *incorruptibilitas* ten times (two corresponding to ἀφθαρσία), *incorruptio* five times (two corresponding to ἀφθαρσία), *incorruptibilis* sixteen times (two corresponding to ἀφθαρσία), and *incorruptus* twice (one corresponding to ἀφθάρτος). See Joppich (1965: 114–445).

[11] Incorruptibility as a soteriological notion appears also in the *Odes of Solomon* (8.23; 11.12; 15.8; 22.10–11; 40.6)—cf. Bultmann (1964: 843).

[12] This is not to deny a pneumatology to 2 Timothy.

[13] According to White, Irenaeus makes "widespread, variegated, and programmatic use of the Pastoral Epistles in *Adversus haereses*" (130).

[14] White notes that scholars once regularly recognized the key role the Pastorals played for Irenaeus, but began downplaying their significance in opposition to the view that it was the Pastorals that made "Paul" useful in the fight against the heresies (127–8).

[15] 1 Tim. 1:4 is cited at the beginning of the preface to the first book. Cf. Looks (1999: 335).

or allusions to the Pastorals (ranging from nineteen to thirty). White's (2011: 132) own count of "probable" uses—"divided quite evenly throughout *Adversus haereses*"—comes to thirty-seven.[16] (Yves-Marie Blanchard counts *thirty-eight* uses of the Pastoral Epistles in *Adversus haereses*, but he doesn't list them.)[17] White also notes that other writers roughly contemporary with Irenaeus (viz., Tertullian and the author of the Muratorian Canon) used the three Pastoral Epistles as a united front.[18] White's appeal to central, controlling scriptural texts in Irenaeus is backed up by Philippe Bacq's (1978: 19, 52) discussion of supporting allusions to "citations clés."

Readers who resist the suggestion that Irenaeus alludes to 2 Tim. 3:15–16 might be drawn to my admission (above) that "incorruption" is a ubiquitous concept in Irenaeus' theologizing. Such an admission, they might say, lessens the need to explain Irenaeus' reference to "breathing incorruption" as an intertextual trope. This objection is not without force. I will only say that, if my intertextual reading is misdirected, Irenaeus' use of the image of "breathing incorruption" still would serve to corroborate my vivificationist reading of 2 Tim. 3:15–16. It would then do so indirectly, by elucidating the sort of vivificationist soteriology that I see in the Pastorals and by showing that a later writer found there the same soteriology (and claimed it as his own).[19] Moreover, we can extend the similarities between Irenaeus' theological system in general and my reading of 2 Tim. 3:15–16 by expounding Irenaeus' understanding of the Gospel as an explicitating "recapitulation" (ἀνακεφαλαίωσις) of the OT message, as the very notion of recapitulation recalls the means by which Scripture, for 2 Timothy, is said to be salvific (see Grant 1997: 50; Skarsaune 1996: 424; Behr 2000: 30; 2013: 127, 139–40). If Irenaeus is *not* echoing 2 Tim. 3:15–16 in *Adv. haer.* 3.11.8, the least we can say is that 2 Timothy anticipates Irenaeus' theology in a rather remarkable way.[20]

2 Θεόπνευστος as Translated by Tertullian

Tertullian is an important witness for the use of θεόπνευστος in pre-Origen Christian circles. He also is unique among the writers included in this study, in that he wrote in Latin rather than Greek (see Harnack 1914: 303).[21] This fact might be thought to

---

[16] As Resch (2009: 74) notes, Irenaeus is much concerned "to display the 'harmony' (*consonantia*) and 'fittingness' of the Scriptures and, *mutatis mutandis*, the Christian faith itself."

[17] Blanchard (1993: 254).

[18] White (2011: 142) writes, "In both Tertullian (*Marc.* 5.21) and the Muratorian Canon (*ll.* 60–3) these letters are grouped together not only because they were written to individuals, but also for their emphasis on 'ecclesiastical discipline' (Muratorian Canon: *ecclesiasticae disciplinae*; Tertullian: *ecclesiastico statu*). ... They present a unified picture of Paul as heresy-fighter."

[19] On Irenaeus' soteriology, see de Andia (1986: 148–81); Holsinger-Friesen (2009: 145–217). Holsinger-Friesen writes, "Just as Irenaeus describes human fallenness in terms of Genesis 1.26 (the 'loss' of the image of God), in parallel fashion ... he uses Genesis 2.7 to describe it as the 'loss' of the breath of life" (172). See *Adv. haer.* 5.12.2–3.

[20] Contra Behr (2000: 28–9), who sees the unity of Scripture assumed by Irenaeus as something new, complicit in the awarding of a new status to the apostolic writings. Behr does not recognize that the unity Irenaeus sees is identical in type and rationale with that of 2 Timothy.

[21] See the chronological table in Gerlo et al. (1954: 1627). See Becker (1954: 346–55). Tertullian wrote a few works in Greek, but Barnes (1985: 253) argues that they were intended for local consumption in Carthage.

afford an avenue of approach not open with the other writers, as it allows us to base our judgment of his view partly on how he renders our word for non-Greek readers. In the end, however, it is the logic of Tertullian's argument that reveals his understanding of the word.

Near the beginning of *De cultu feminarum*, Tertullian makes three attempts, in close succession, to rehabilitate the book of "Enoch"[22] for the sake of his larger argument:

(1.3.1) I know that the writing of Enoch, which gives the role [of marrying women] to the angels, cannot be accepted by some people, because it has not been admitted to the Jewish canon. I think they hold that it could not have come from before the deluge, as it could not have been saved from a catastrophe that destroyed the whole world. If that is their reason, let them recall that Noah was the great-grandson of Enoch and a survivor of the cataclysm, that he had the family name and heard the inherited tradition, and he would have recalled the grace and the predictive powers that his forefathers enjoyed before God, when Enoch mandated to his son Methuselah that he should pass on knowledge to their posterity. Thus Noah undoubtedly could have succeeded in his task of proclaiming, as he would not have kept silent about the providence of God that preserved him, or the glory of his house.

(2) Now, if he could not have had this knowledge directly, there is still a reason for asserting [the antiquity] of this book: he would have been able, in the spirit, to reconstruct the book after it had been destroyed by the violence of the flood, just as, when Jerusalem was destroyed at the hands of Babylonia, every volume of Jewish literature was restored unaltered by Ezra.

(3) But since Enoch gives predictions about our Lord in the same writing, it is not for us to reject anything that pertains to us. And do we not read that every scripture suitable for edification is *divinitus inspirari*?[23] As you know, it was rejected by the Jews, as with the others that speak of Christ. Nor is it astonishing if they do not accept certain writings that speak of him, as they would not receive him when he spoke to them himself. To this we only add: we possess a testimony to Enoch according to Jude the apostle. (Author's translation)[24]

This passage contains a layering of arguments. Against those who claim that no genuinely Enochic writing could have survived the flood, Tertullian contends

---

[22] What Tertullian called "Enoch" probably corresponds to the first thirty-six chapters of our *1 Enoch*.

[23] Tertullian's Latin paraphrase reads: *et legimus omnem scripturam aedificationi habilem divinitus inspirari*. Cf. the Vulgate of 2 Tim. 3:16: *omnis scriptura divinitus inspirata et utilis ad docendum ad arguendum ad corrigendum ad erudiendum in iustitia*.

[24] Latin parenthesis added from Turcan (1971: 60). See Bruce (1988: 182). Whether this is the argument of the whole of *De cultu feminarum* or only of book 1 depends on whether Tertullian wrote books 1 and 2 as parts of a single work. The *Corpus Cluniacense* gives the title *De cultu feminarum* to book 2 only, calling book 1 *De habitu muliebri*. The following see books 1 and 2 as originally distinct: Hauck (1877: 33); Knaake (1903: 633); Harnack (1904: 269–70); Quasten (1950: 294); Säflund (1955: 106–21). The following argue for a unity between the books: Galdi (1927: 543–6); Valgiglio (1974); Isetta (1983). See the discussion in Braun (1966); Turcan (1971: 19–29); Isetta (1986: 21–8); Calef (1996: 113–20).

that we should expect Noah to have preserved his great-grandfather's writing from destruction (1.3.1). Next he argues that, if Enoch's writing *did* disappear in the flood, the book bearing his name might still be authentic, as the Spirit could have equipped Noah to reconstruct that writing after the flood, in the manner of Ezra's reconstruction of every Jewish writing (1.3.2). Finally, he argues on the basis of Enoch's "edifying" content that, on the terms of his loose paraphrase of 2 Tim. 3:16, it either qualifies as Scripture or counts to the same usefulness.[25] It is here, in connection with this final argument, that we gain insight into Tertullian's understanding of θεόπνευστος.

The fact that Tertullian uses a form of *inspir-* does not, in itself, imply that he reads the verse in an inspirationist sense, as the root *inspir-* could simply mean "in-spire" (= insufflate) more generally (rather than "inspire" in the usual, modern sense of the word).[26] (The vivificationist and inspirationist senses of Latin *inspir-* obtain [alternatively] throughout the term's career, and both are found in Tertullian.)[27] Tertullian's use of *divinitus inspirari* makes it seem that he understands the *theopneustia* image in terms of an inspirationist view of Scripture (cf. Harnack 1914: 311). *Inspirari* is normally rendered with a passive voice.

Given that an inspirationist understanding of θεόπνευστος usually goes hand in hand with a passive rendering, the use of the passive voice here might suggest that Tertullian attributed an inspirationist sense to the word. The preponderance of evidence, however, is on the side of a vivificationist reading of this passage.[28] Tertullian's rendering of 2 Tim. 3:16 is paraphrastic and in fact reverses the flow of the verse's inferential scheme. Marie Turcan (1971: 60) is scandalized by the

---

[25] This is the only place Tertullian quotes 2 Tim. 3:16. Rankin (1984: 18) notes, however, that there are at least 100 quotations of, or allusions to, the Pastoral Epistles in Tertullian. See Frisius (2011: 9). I do not understand why Frisius claims that Tertullian fails to provide a ground for assuming Enoch's scriptural status, "save for its origination with Enoch and attestation by Jude" (52). What about Tertullian's argument from 2 Tim. 3:16? It is worth noting that Tertullian elsewhere introduces a quotation of *1 Enoch* with the words "habes scriptum" (*In carn. res.* 32.1). On the use of *1 Enoch* in the early church, see Sundberg (1964: 163–9).

[26] I explained the distinction between "in-spire" and "inspire" in the opening chapter.

[27] See *Thesaurus Linguae Latinae* (1954: 1958). In Tertullian, *inspir-* has, e.g., a clearly inspirationist meaning in *Ad nat.* 1.20.7, *Apol.* 27.4, *De spec.* 10.12, and *De bapt.* 5.4, but it appears to have a vivificationist meaning in *De cor.* 8.16.5. (*S.v.* "inspiratio," "inspiro," "spiro," in Claesson 1974–5.) On the relation between divine breath and the human soul in Tertullian, see Thraede (1986: 729–30). A *vivificationist* understanding of *inspir-* can be found in a work falsely attributed to Tertullian in some manuscripts: *De Iona* retells the story of Jonah and uses *inspirata* in the sense of a life-giving effect to explain how Jonah survived in the belly of the fish—in Thelwall (1885: 132) (vv. 140–44): "Jonah the seer / The while is voyaging, in other craft / Embarked, and cleaving 'neath the lowest waves / A wave: his sails the intestines of the fish, / Inspired with breath ferine (*anima inspirata ferina*); himself, shut in." Manuscripts usually attribute the work to Tertullian or Cyprian. Peiper (1881: 295–6) and Manitius (1891: 241 [see 51–4]) have shown convincingly that *De Iona* is a continuation of *De Sodoma*, with which it always was paired in manuscripts (see Müller 1867). Dando (1965) argues that *De Iona* is the work of the fifth- to sixth-century writer Alcimus Avitus. For an edition of *De Iona*, see Peiper (1881: 221–6).

[28] In the ancient world, to label something (viz., water, a creature) as "life-given" (or "living") often implied that it was also "life-giving." Thus a passive rendering of θεόπνευστος might fit with the vivificationist understanding that we uncovered in the preceding chapters. In other words, the fact that *inspirari* is passive in form would not, by itself, decide whether the word should be taken in an inspirationist or a vivificationist sense.

suggestion that Tertullian would twist this verse so wildly and argues that the text of 2 Timothy with which he worked lacked a crucial καί: "Il est douteux que Tertullien, si respectueux des Écritures, ait consciemment 'travesti' le texte (M.-J. Lagrange, *Histoire anc. du canon du N.T.*, Paris, 1933, p. 54). L'erreur peut venir d'un texte grec qui aurait omis le καί (πᾶσα γραφὴ θεόπνευστος καὶ ὠφέλιμος πρὸς διδασκαλίαν)." Scholars have long noted the freedom with which Tertullian rearranges 2 Tim. 3:16. Adhémar d'Alès (1905: 226 n. 1) describes Tertullian's rendering as "trés libre," and Edmon Gallagher (2012: 21) notes that Tertullian's "rather loose" paraphrase of 2 Tim. 3:16 "seem[s] specially designed for his argument here."[29] But *how* does Tertullian's rendering serve his purpose? And how can he take his reversal of the implicative moment to count as a legitimate reading? The answer appears to lie in a vivificationist understanding of *divinitus inspirari*. On the terms of such a reading, *divinitus inspirari* (or θεόπνευστος) is functionally synonymous with "edification," and it is this synonymity that allows Tertullian to reverse the relationship between the verse's phrases.

When we turn to Tertullian's argument regarding the scriptural status of "Enoch," we see that the role played by 2 Tim. 3:16 remains faithful to how the verse envisions Scripture as a direct support for the Gospel. Tertullian (like the author of 2 Timothy and like Irenaeus) supposes that Scripture is theopneustic because it speaks of Christ.[30] (As F. F. Bruce [1988: 182 n. 14] notes, "['Enoch's'] clear proclamation of Christ is probably its announcement of the coming of the Lord with his holy myriads (1 Enoch 1:9), as quoted and interpreted in Jude 14f.") After conceding (for the sake of argument) that the original writing of Enoch might not be extant after all (*contra* his argument in 1.3.1–2), Tertullian argues for regarding "Enoch" as Scripture on the basis of the book's contents: "this same book tells us of our Lord" (1.3.3). It appears to be *this*—the fact that the book is a witness to salvation in *Christ*—that makes the book theopneustic in Tertullian's eyes. (Indeed, he holds that the Jews removed the book from their canon for this very reason [see Sundberg 1964: 164–5].)[31] Admittedly, this sets up the meaning of the *theopneustia* image somewhat equivocally, as the inclusion of a prophetic viewpoint might be called theopneustic on inspirationist grounds (viz., because it is *prophetically inspired*) or it might be called theopneustic on vivificationist grounds (viz., because it presents the content of the Gospel). It is at this point that

[29] Gallagher notes that Tertullian's rendering is unique among Latin writers.
   There has been much debate over whether Tertullian translated the New Testament into Latin (for his readers' sake) or relied on an earlier Latin translation. Latin translations apparently existed in his day—the proceedings of the trial of the Scillitan Martyrs (Carthage, July 17, 180) refer to certain "books and letters of Paul, a righteous man," and the usual assumption has been that these books and letters were in Latin. (See de Labriolle 1914; Harnack 1914: 306–7; O'Malley 1967: 62; Speigl 1996: 164–5; Houghton 2016: 3–12. See the account in Musurillo 1972: 86–9.) See Dunn (2004: 20–1).
[30] Tertullian elsewhere writes appreciatively of Irenaeus' discussion of doctrine—see *Adversus Valentinianos*, 5. Spence (1897: 564) understood Tertullian's rendering of γραφὴ θεόπνευστος to imply that "any writing which, in so far as it set forth truth, was, to that extent, an emanation from God, the sole source of truth." For Tertullian, the four gospels are "instruments" of the Gospel.
[31] On Tertullian and the *regula fidei*'s relation to Scripture, see Ring (1975: 67–8); Waszink (1979: 24–6); Countryman (1982); Dunn (2006: 147 n. 37).

Tertullian paraphrases 2 Tim. 3:16, *emphasizing Scripture's usefulness for edification* as a criterion for its theopneustic status. This focus on *edification* tips the scale in favor of a vivificationist understanding of θεόπνευστος, as it is difficult to understand how an edifying writing is ipso facto inspired, but it is easy to understand how it might be called "life-giving"—particularly if the quality of being "edifying" is connected with the Gospel in a technical way.

3 Θεόπνευστος in Clement of Alexandria

As far as we know, Clement of Alexandria is the first Christian after the author of 2 Timothy actually to use the word θεόπνευστος. The word appears four times in his extant writings: in *Protr.* 9.87.2; *Strom.* 1.21.124; 7.16.101, 103. It might be, in fact, that Clement's four uses of θεόπνευστος struck a chord with Origen and made it one of his favorite words. At any rate, Benjamin Warfield (1900: 111) was right to note that, with the advent of Clement, the word became "one of the most common technical designations of Scripture."

We will briefly visit each of Clement's uses of θεόπνευστος to see whether there might be an indication of how he understood it. As every one of his uses is an explicit appeal to the wording of 2 Tim. 3:16, it might be expected that some of these passages reveal little or nothing about what he thought the word meant. As it turns out, two of the passages use θεόπνευστος simply to make it clear (by invoking 2 Timothy's language) that Clement has the Old Testament in view:

Strom. 1.21.124

(1) At this time Zorobabel overcame his antagonists through wisdom and obtained from Darius the restoration of Jerusalem for his service, and returned with Ezra to his homeland. (2) Through him came the redemption of the people, and the recognition and restoration of the theopneustic writings (θεοπνεύστων ... λογίων), and he introduced the Passover of salvation, and dissolved marriages with foreigners. (3) And Cyrus proclaimed the reestablishment of the Hebrews, a promise that was fulfilled by Darius, and the Feast of Consecration was observed, as well as that of Tabernacles. (Author's translation)

Strom. 7.16.103

For there are careless readers, who are able to bring out the proper literal sense of the divine scriptures, but who decide, for their own pleasure, to bring out an indirect meaning. They long to interpret symbolically those matters attaching to the theopneustic writings (τοῖς θεοπνεύστοις λόγοις) given by the blessed apostles and teachers, willfully teaching along the lines of other interpretations. (Author's translation)

The word θεόπνευστος functions, in these two passages, only to recall 2 Tim. 3:16, in order to identify "scripture" with the body of writings accepted as scripture by the apostles.[32] (I call this a "neutral" or "noncommittal" use of the word.)

The other two passages, however, use θεόπνευστος in a vivificationist sense. The first is *Protr.* 9.86.2–87.2:

> Now when godliness makes a human resemble God as far as it is able, it claims God as a suitable teacher for he alone is worthy to have the power to make a human as a god. This teaching the apostle recognizes as divine: "But you, O Timothy," he says, "from the time you were a baby you have known the sacred writings, that are able to instruct you unto salvation thought faith in Christ." For truly those [writings] which make us sacred and divine are themselves sacred, and the collected writings, put together [from these], are consequently called "theopneustic" by the same apostle, "useful for teaching, for reproof, for correction, for training in righteousness, so that the one who is of God may be complete, equipped for every good work." No one could be more affectingly moved by the exhortations of other holy men than by those of the Lord, the lover of humans; for this, and nothing else, is his only work: that people should be saved. He cries out, urging people to salvation: "The kingdom of heaven is at hand." He converts people when they draw near [to him] through fear. In this the apostle of the Lord becomes an interpreter of the divine voice in his call to the Macedonians: "The Lord draws near," he says, "be careful lest we be found empty." (Author's translation)

This passage shows that Clement's interpretation of 2 Tim. 3:15–16 is in all essentials identical to my own interpretation. Clement recognizes that the theopneustic aspect of Scripture, affirmed in 2 Tim. 3:16, consists of the role Scripture played in Timothy's salvation (cf. 2 Tim. 3:15) and in the role it plays in teaching, reproof, correction, and instruction in righteousness (2 Tim. 3:16b).

The final passage in which Clement uses θεόπνευστος is *Strom.* 7.16.101:

> Just as Ischomachus makes those who attend to him farmers, and Lampis sea-captains, and Charidemus commanders, and Simon equestrians, and Perdix hucksters, and Crobylus cooks, and Archelaus dancers, and Homer poets, and Pyrrho arguers, and Demosthenes rhetors, and Chrysippus masters of dialectic, and Aristotle scientists, and Plato philosophers, so also the one persuaded by the Lord and who follows the prophecy given through him is finally perfected according to the image of his teacher, and becomes a god moving about in the flesh. Now it is from this height that they fall who do not follow God wherever he may lead, and he leads by means of *the theopneustic writings* (θεοπνεύστους γραφάς). (Author's translation)

---

[32] Kalin (1967: 171) notes that "there is no direct indication that the New Testament is meant" in any of Clement's four passages.

Although this passage appears in a different work from the preceding passage, setting the two in juxtaposition helps us to see the implication of Clement's use of θεόπνευστος in the second passage. Admittedly, some might see this passage's use of θεόπνευστος as merely ornamental, or the reference to prophecy "given through him" might lead some to see an inspirationist use of θεόπνευστος. The role Scripture plays in leading the one who follows God, however, recalls the line of reasoning found in the *Protrepticus*.

Admittedly, this last passage will seem ambiguous to some, or it might appear (in spite of my argument) to support an inspirationist understanding of θεόπνευστος. In my view, it is the clear way in which Clement gives θεόπνευστος a vivificationist sense in *Protr.* 9.86.2–87.2 that makes the difference. If, however, the reader is still convinced that *Strom.* 7.16.101 uses θεόπνευστος with an inspirationist sense, the effect of that reading on my overall thesis would simply amount to moving the inspirationist resignification of θεόπνευστος forward in time some twenty or so years—to place the blame, that is, on Clement rather than on Origen.

The question before us is not whether Clement believed Scripture to be inspired. Other passages make it clear that he did. The question is whether Clement believed that 2 Timothy used θεόπνευστος to indicate that Scripture is inspired. Of the four passages in which he uses the word, two appear to use the word in a neutral sense and two appear to use it in a vivificationist sense. There is nothing to indicate that Clement understood θεόπνευστος in an inspirationist sense.

4 Θεόπνευστος in *De Universo* (Attributed to Hippolytus)

Our next appearance of θεόπνευστος is in *De Universo*, a work often attributed to Hippolytus. Whether he is actually the author is a matter of debate. A work by the title Πρὸς Ἕλληνας καὶ Πλάτωνα ἢ καὶ περὶ τοῦ παντός is found listed with ten others on the back of the third-century statue discovered by Pirro Ligorio in Rome in 1551—works once widely presumed to have been written by Hippolytus.[33] While some scholars continue to think the entire Hippolytan corpus (consisting of the eleven aforementioned works, along with others listed by Eusebius [*Hist. eccl.* 6.22] and Jerome [*De vir. ill.* 61])[34] was written by one man (see Scholten 1991: 501–4),[35] many scholars

---

[33] See the discussion of the Ligorio statue in Cerrato (2002: 91–3); Smith (2009: 493–511). See the reconstruction of the list of works found on the back of the statue, in Morin (1900). That the Ligorio statue goes back to the early third century is proved by the astronomical inaccuracy of the paschal calendar found on one side of the statue's chair, which would have become glaringly obvious by the mid-third century (see Salmon 1873: 84). The statue's reclining figure was reconstructed by Ligorio in the sixteenth century as a male bishop (cf. Lightfoot 1890: 2.440), but Margherita Guarducci (1977; 1989) has shown that the original drawing of the find suggests a female figure (see Frickel 1988: 65–70; Brent 1995: 48–9). According to Brent, recognition of the figure as female (= Sophia?) invites doubts on associating the works listed on the back of the statue with a single figure. (Brent associates the statue with a house-church.) He suggests, instead, that the list is a catalogue of the Roman church's library (cf. also Simonetti 1989), and he bolsters this view by exposing chronological inconsistencies between some of the writings (Brent 1995: 273–4). As Ulrich Volp (2009: 524 n. 17) objects, however, one would expect a library catalogue to include authors' names.

[34] See Smith (2009: 485–92). On the Hippolytan corpus, see d'Alès (1906: xliii–lii, 3–11).

[35] Frickel (1988: 123–210) doubts Hippolytus wrote *Contra Noetum*, but attributes all the other works to him. Cerrato (2002: 107) notes that the idea of a Roman Hippolytus "relies heavily" on

today divide these titles between those written by the real Hippolytus (presumably of Rome) and those written by someone in the East (see Loi 1977; Cerrato 2002: 80–1; Shelton 2008: 13–14). It is now widely supposed that there is an intercanonical seam between the block of works represented by the *Refutatio* and another block represented by *Contra Noetum*.[36] J. A. Cerrato (2002: 69 [cf. 69–71]) argues that the *Chronicon*, *De Universo*, and the *Refutatio* comprise an authorially distinct subset and that no manuscript of these three works names Hippolytus as its author (cf. Scholten 2005; Smith 2009: 14–110). Others claim the evidence leads in the direction of a Western author, or a pair of Western authors (Brent 1995; cf. Stewart-Sykes 2001; 2004). Keying on an attribution in a recension of Pseudo-John Damascene's *Sacra Parallela*, Pierre Nautin (1947: 63–88) argued that a Western figure named "Josippus" wrote the *Refutatio* (= *Elenchus*), the *Chronicon*, and *De Universo*.[37] (This was the figure [he argued] represented on the statue.) As Smith (2009: 20) notes, however, "The Paschal tables on the statue match Eusebius's description of the Paschal table he attributed to Hippolytus." Smith also challenges Cerrato's supposition that commentary writing was strictly an Eastern tradition at the time.[38] Hippolytus' influence on Origen has usually been explained through Origen's visit to Rome (see Eusebius, *Hist. eccl.* 6.14.10; cf. Jerome, *De vir. ill.* 61; Cadiou 1944: 49–51, 77–80),[39] but an Eastern Hippolytus does not fit that explanation. These suppositions can be reconciled if we relocate Origen's meeting with Hippolytus to an Eastern location. Cerrato (2007: 526) suggests a meeting in Antioch, when Origen was made to appear before the empress Julia (post-222), but others suggest a meeting in Alexandria (see Volp 2009: 522).

The work that concerns us went by different names during its early circulation (as noted in Photius, *Bibliotheca* 48) but nowadays is usually called *De Universo*.[40] Neither Eusebius nor Jerome attributes the work to Hippolytus, and no manuscript of the work names Hippolytus as its author. It has been preserved as part of the above-mentioned *Sacra Parallela* (2.801), where different recensions attribute it to different authors—that is, to Josephus, Irenaeus, or Meletius of Antioch. The author of the *Refutatio* (usually attributed to Hippolytus) claims to have written an earlier work entitled Περὶ τῆς τοῦ παντὸς οὐσίας, sometimes thought to be *De Universo*.[41] On the strength of this witness,

---

a pre-Guarducci interpretation of the Ligorio statue. (See below.) Döllinger (1876: 5) was the first to suggest that Hippolytus was an antipope, but Cerrato rightly denounces that thesis as "remote" (103). Lightfoot (1890: 2.412) described Hippolytus as being "at daggers drawn with the heads of the Roman Church."

[36] See Nautin's (1947: 48–53) argument against common authorship of the *Refutatio* and *Contra Noetum*. Frickel (1988: 123) refers to the *Refutatio* and *Contra Noetum* as "Kronzeugen" for the question of single or double authorship of the Hippolytan corpus.

[37] See the response in Botte (1968: 14–17).

[38] Jerome claims that Origen first decided to write commentaries after hearing Hippolytus preach (*Vir. ill.* 61), and Origen's commentary on the Song of Songs has been viewed as "ow[ing] a great deal to Hippolytus" (Boersma 2017: 198 [cf. 201]). Smith (2009: 31 [cf. 33–44]) writes, "The idea that Greek speaking Christians did not write commentaries in the West is simply unsustainable."

[39] Some scholars date this visit to around the year 212 (e.g., Bruce 1988: 178 n. 50) and others to around 215 (Boersma 2017: 198 n. 46).

[40] The ancient witnesses to its original title are a confused mess. See Malley (1965: 23–4); Castelli (2011: 52–60). Cf. Brent (1995: 261–2).

[41] On the authorship of Περὶ τῆς τοῦ παντὸς οὐσίας, see Brent (1995: 261–70). See Nautin (1947: 78–9).

and the Ligorio statue's listing, some hold it to have been penned by a Hippolytus of Rome. John Philoponus' *Opificio Mundi* (sixth century CE) attributes a work entitled Περὶ τῆς τοῦ παντὸς αἰτίας συγγράμματι βούλεται to "Josephus the Hebrew," but it is impossible to accept such a claim.[42] Whatever the origins of the Ἰώσηπος/Ἰώσιππος attribution, it represents a widespread tradition in antiquity, and it opened a door for William Malley (1965) to identify four fragments of a similarly attributed writing called *Contra Graecos* (from *Ms. Parisinus Coislinianus* 305) as originally part of *De Universo*. Finally, mention should be made of Photius (ninth century CE), who writes that *De Universo* was attributed, in the margin of a copy he had used, to Gaius of Rome, but that it was more usually attributed to Josephus the Jew, Justin, or Irenaeus (*Bibliotheca* 48; see Henry 1959: 1.33–35).

Charles Hill (1989a: 114; 1989b) holds that *De Universo's* eschatology differs considerably from what we find in Hippolytus' work (cf. his *Comm. Dan.* 1.21.4; 2.37.3; 3.31.2–3; *De Antichristo* 59).[43] He is equally convinced that Origen could not have written the treatise, as its view of the afterlife is "quite foreign" to what we find in the Alexandrian. Hill considers the best candidate for authorship to be Tertullian (*De Anima* 55.58; *Adv. Marc.* 4.34) or someone influenced by him.[44] Pierre Petitmengin (1990: 346) argues, in response, that the eschatological ideas found in *De Universo* were more widespread than Hill allows. Alice Whealey (1996: 249) similarly writes that it would be "quite remarkable" for one of Tertullian's Greek writings to have survived—she finds it more likely that Tertullian and the author of *De Universo* relied on sources steeped in the same ideas. She notes that Tertullian had read Miltiades (*Adv. Valentinianos* 5) and that the latter had written a work entitled *On the Greeks* (Eusebius, *Hist. eccl.* 5.17.5 [cf. the title on the Ligorio statue and that of Malley's four fragments]).[45] Is it possible, she asks, that the "Meletius" named in one recension of the *Sacra Parallela* is really Miltiades?

The most direct contribution these debates could make to our study involves the question of chronology: Does *De Universo* represent a pre-Origen or a post-Origen witness to the meaning of θεόπνευστος? As we will shortly see, *De Universo* appears to use θεόπνευστος in a *neutral* way—not revealing a true understanding of the word, but using it instead as a semantically unactivated label, to designate "the prophets" as the writers of Scripture.

The word θεόπνευστος appears in line 130 of *De Universo*, where it is used to describe the Old Testament writings. The line in question has been preserved in two different readings. Here is the reading given by Karl Holl (1901: 143)—along with its larger context—followed by my own translation:

---

[42] Williams's (1992: 151–200) stylometric analysis allows only an "infinitesimal" chance that Josephus wrote *De Universo*. See Castelli (2008; 2011).

[43] The difference between the eschatology of *De Universo* and that of other works attributed to Hippolytus is also discussed in Prinzivalli (1979). See Simonetti (1989). See the discussion of "Hades and πρὸς Ἕλληνας καὶ πρὸς Πλάτωνα" in Brent (1995: 266–7). On *De Universo's* eschatology, see Schmidt (1919: 507–12).

[44] On the Tertullianist bent of *De Universo's* eschatology, see d'Alès (1906: 200–2).

[45] According to Whealey (1996: 250), Tertullian probably used *On the Greeks* in writing his *Apologeticus*.

τούτοις ἐὰν πεισθέντες Ἕλληνες καταλείψετε τὴν ματαιότητα τῆς ἐπιγείου καὶ
χρηματεμπόρου σοφίας καὶ μὴ περὶ λέξεις ῥημάτων ἀσχολούμενοι τὸν νοῦν εἰς
πλάνην συνώσητε, ἀλλὰ τοῖς θεοπνεύστοις προφήταις καὶ θεολόγοις ἐξηγηταῖς
ἐγχειρήσαντες τὰς ἀκοὰς θεῷ πιστεύσητε, ἔσεσθε καὶ τούτων κοινωνοὶ καὶ
τῶν μελλόντων τεύξεσθε ἀγαθῶν ἀμέτρου τε οὐρανοῦ ἀνάβασιν καὶ τὴν ἐκεῖ
βασιλείαν ὄψεσθε. φανερώσει γὰρ θεός. ἃ νῦν σεσιώπηται, ἃ οὔτε ὀφθαλμὸς
εἶδεν οὔτε οὖς ἤκουσεν οὔτε ἐπὶ καρδίαν ἀνθρώπου ἀνέβη ὅσα ἡτοίμασεν ὁ θεὸς
ἀγαπῶσιν αὐτόν.

If you Greeks believe in this, you will abandon the vanity of earthly and timebound
wisdom—not pushing your mind towards error by taking stock in the eloquence
of the words. But if you listen to the theopneustic prophets and you believe the
theologians who expound the message of God, you will also share in this: you will
partake in the good things to come, you will see the ascension to the boundless
heaven and the kingdom therein, for God will show what you are now. Neither
the eye has seen, nor the ear heard, nor the human heart received, what God has
prepared for those who love him.

It is not clear whether θεοπνεύστοις in this passage modifies only τοῖς προφήταις, or
whether it also modifies θεολόγοις ἐξηγηταῖς, but contextual considerations favor the
former. Christoph Markschies (2015: 14) prefers the latter view and sees in θεολόγοις
a reference to the Psalms: "Hippolytus places the 'divinely inspired prophets and
theologians' together and evidently means by this the prophets and psalmists of the
old covenant."[46] He allows the pagan use of θεολόγος as a reference to hymn writers
or reciters to govern the author's use of θεολόγοις, but it is not clear what one should
then do with ἐξηγηταῖς. (On Markschies's reading, ἐξηγηταῖς could mean something
like "explanatory," but that seems an unnatural modifier for "psalmist.") Markschies's
reading makes the words προφήταις and θεολόγοις function together as a single
reference to Scripture, but it seems more likely that Hippolytus follows here the standard
heresiological expedient of referring to two groups of authorities: the writers of Scripture
and the faithful tradents of Scripture's correct interpretation. Nautin (1947: 78) translates
the passage along these lines, dividing between "les prophètes divinement inspirés et les
exégètes des paroles divines." The most likely use of θεόπνευστος on this rendering
would see in it nothing more than a delimiting marker for Scripture.

An alternative reading is found in Thomas Hearne's (1720: 288) text, published in
1720 from the Baroccian manuscripts, which reads ἀλλὰ τοῖς θεοπνεύστοις προφήταις
καὶ θεοῦ καὶ λόγου ἐξηγηταῖς. (Paul de Lagarde [1858: 72] preserves the same text as
Hearne, but inserts a comma after προφήταις.)[47] The sense of this reading is perhaps
something like "but the theopneustic prophets and expounders of (the things of) God
and of the Word"—a phrasing that (like Holl's reading) can be taken in two different

---

[46] On the use of θεολόγος as a reference to (pagan) hymn writers or reciters, see Markschies
(2015: 6–9). See the discussion of θεολογεῖν in Malherbe (1970: 216).
[47] The Hearne reading is reproduced by Bonwetsch (1897: 20); Pesch (1906: 4); and (for specific
purposes of studying the variant) in Cherniss (1929: 349).

directions: with θεόπνευστος modifying only "prophets" or with it modifying both "prophets" and "expounders." The former seems more likely. Here, too, we have to do with a "neutral" use of θεόπνευστος.

5 The Resignification of θεόπνευστος in Origen

The *TLG* lists a number of Christian exegetes from the third century CE and later who, upon examination, can be seen to use θεόπνευστος in the sense of *verbally* or *epistemically* "inspired" and who expressly apply that term to their understanding of Scripture's authority.[48] And so, at long last, we encounter a body of authorities who use θεόπνευστος with the meaning now traditionally connected with it. (We may call this θεόπνευστος's "second career.") The watershed in this development appears to be Origen's hermeneutical program—a program that began around 216 CE, at the earliest, and that would leave its mark on the whole of Christian thinking down through the ages.[49] As Origen used θεόπνευστος dozens of times, he was not only the architect of a new meaning for the word but also the main firebrand for the spread of this new meaning.[50] Here I list only those pre-seventh-century figures who used the term twenty times or more, with the number of uses credited by the *TLG*: Gregory of Nyssa (110×), Eusebius (54×), Athanasius (44×), Basil of Caesarea (65×), John Chrysostom (22×), Didymus the Blind (56×), and Cyril of Alexandria (329×). According to the *TLG*, θεόπνευστος also appears numerous times in the NT Catenae (28×), the *Analecta Hymnica Graeca* (86×), and the proceedings of the Ecumenical Councils (134×). The sheer number of references obtaining in the term's second career demonstrates only too clearly that the practice of reading Scripture lost touch with the term's original meaning. It is as though Origen flipped a switch on a powerful machine.[51]

According to Wolfhart Pannenberg (1988: 82–3), Origen's doctrine of the inspiration of Scripture stemmed from his assumption that the Spirit mediates the Son's revelation of the Father, spoken of in Mt. 11:27 (see Origen, *Princ.* 1.3.4):

At the end of the chapter devoted to this issue in his *Principles* (iv.1.7), Origen quoted Rom. 16:25–7, but he understood the grammar of that sentence in a different way from that of modern exegesis, so that he could derive from it his idea that the prophetic Scriptures *mediate* the revelation that occurred in the

---

[48] Of course, we should allow that some uses of θεόπνευστος appear in (uncomprehending) echoes of 2 Timothy.

[49] Most scholars date Origen's first writing to about 222, but Heine dates it to about 216/217. See Heine (2010: 86–9). Hanson (1954: 8) favors a date of 218.

[50] Dively Lauro (2005: 39 n. 12) points out, "Sometimes Origen states that the Holy Spirit inspired the composition of Scripture and at other times that the Holy Spirit composed Scripture." On the date of *De principiis*, see Nautin (1977: 370 n. 20). On Origen's understanding of the nature of Scripture, see Torjesen (1986: 108–18).

[51] Clement's use of θεόπνευστος does not tell us how Origen used the word, but it helps to determine when the word was resignified. On the relationship between Clement and Origen, see van den Hoek (1992: 40). Cf. the chart listing passages in which Origen appears to draw on Clement, in van den Hoek (1992: 47–50).

Son. In his reading the sentence says that the revelation of the divine mystery occurred "through the prophetic writings and the epiphany of our Lord and Saviour Jesus Christ," while the authentic form of the final sentence of Romans distinguishes between the revelation in Jesus Christ and its announcement to all the nations through the prophetic writings. According to Origen, however, the "prophetic writings" are themselves instruments of divine revelation. He was able to derive that idea from 2 Tim. 3:16, but he did so with an interesting comment (iv.1.6): the manifestation of the Son in the incarnation alone demonstrated the divine inspiration of the Old Testament Scriptures, because their divine truth now became evident, with the old prophecies fulfilled.[52]

According to Pannenberg, this is how Origen came to see the New Testament as inspired in the same way as traditionally claimed for the Old Testament. Pannenberg's explanation does not tell the full story, however, as we surely must account for why Origen took θεόπνευστος in a way that departs from how those before him had used the word. This we will attempt at the end of this chapter.

No one had as great an influence as Origen on how the church would come to approach Scripture. Thus it has become customary, in discussing his place in intellectual history, to portray him as a figure towering above all the biblical exegetes who labored through the centuries. Erasmus claimed that Origen's relation to subsequent exegetical tradition is analogous to Homer's relation to subsequent poetic tradition (noted in Scheck 2008: 137). Closer to our own time, Frederic Farrar (1886: 188) compared Origen's influence in church history with that of Socrates in Greek philosophy.[53] Vincent of Lérins marveled at the extent of Origen's output and talent, and asked, "Who in the world ... would not rather adopt that saying, That he would rather be wrong with Origen, than be right with others" (*Commonitory* 17.12 [trans. Heurtley 1886: 144]; see Guarino 2013: 36).[54] The upshot of all this is clear: If anyone was ever

---

[52] Pannenberg (1988: 83 n. 16) writes,

> There is no reason why the same idea could not have been already intended in Rom. 16:25–7, so that it would be unnecessary to read the phrase "prophetic scriptures" in 16:26 as referring to early Christian writings rather than to the Old Testament prophets. Such a reading, which would be unparalleled in early Christian usage and is also contrary to Rom. 3:21, is nevertheless postulated by some modern exegetes because of the function attributed to "the prophetic scriptures" by Rom. 16:26, that they lead "all the nations" to the obedience of faith (cf. Wilckens, op. cit. iii. 150 n. 709), but this has been precisely the function of the fulfilment of prophetic predictions in early Christian theology as it was also assumed in Origen's interpretation of the passage.

[53] Farrar writes that Origen "is the watershed of multitudes of different streams of thought." On Origen's influence, see Bori (1987: 59–72). Melanchthon, with his division of church history into five periods, named the second period after Origen and the third after Augustine. See Scheck (2008: 179–80). The negativity of Melanchthon's judgment on Origen stems from his enthusiasm for Augustine.

[54] As Guarino notes, Vincent's wording may be based on Cicero's praise of Plato. (See Cicero, *Tusculanae disputationes* 1.17.) Cf. Scheck (2008: 162): "[Aldus Manutius] adopted the commonplace assessment of Origen derived from St. Jerome, 'Ubi bene dixit, nemo melius; ubi male, nemo peius,' 'When Origen spoke well, no one has ever said it better, when he spoke badly, no one has ever spoken worse.'"

in the position to effect a change in how the church at large used a given word or how it thought about a given block of doctrine, it was Origen.

5.1 Origen on the Nature and Inspiration of Scripture

Origen's impact on how the church would come to read Scripture can scarcely be overestimated, as it was he, more than anyone, who connected the authority of Scripture with its purportedly inspired status (see esp. *Princ.* 4.1–3; cf. Zöllig 1902; Wiles 1970: 461– 5; Campenhausen 1972: 315).[55] Although a few others spoke of Scripture as inspired, he is the originator of the view that the whole of Scripture is not only inspired per se but, more specifically, that it is *verbally* inspired.[56] His poetics of Scripture stemmed entirely from his view of the text as fundamentally divine. For Origen, Scripture's divine aspect is so full that its meaning lies on multiple levels, all intended by God. On these terms, he laid out the first approach that can truly be called a form of Christian biblicism.[57] He accordingly taught his readers to spurn the sort of general hermeneutic one might use to read a letter or the record of an event (*Princ.* 1.proem.4; 1.3.1; 4.2.7; 4.3.14). Like Philo before him, he saw God as the true author of the biblical text: "Observe each detail which has been written. For, if one knows how to dig into the depth, he will find a treasure in the details, and perhaps also, the precious jewels of the mysteries lie hidden where they are not esteemed" (*Hom. Gen.* 8.1 [trans. Heine 1982: 136]).

As the Bible is not a human text, but divine (*Princ.* 4.1.2–3),[58] it takes a divine key to unlock its riches (see Hällström 1985: 45–6; Vogt 1999: 179). The reader, we are told, needs God's wisdom to recognize the higher mysteries hidden beneath the text's rather plain surface. Origen divided Scripture's readers between ordinary readers and more spiritually attuned readers. Scripture's deeper meanings were over most readers' heads (see *Princ.* 4.1.7; Daley 1998: 12).[59] This understanding of Scripture led to an atomization of its sense units—Scripture does not contain a "single dot" devoid of God's wisdom (*Hom. hier.* 21.2).[60] Origen's understanding also led to a homogenization of Scripture's "useful" nature (ὠφέλιμος, a term derived from 2 Tim. 3:16).[61] He was

---

[55] On Origen's understanding of biblical inspiration, see Fairweather (1901: 65–83); Thraede (1998: 360–1); Simonetti (2000: 424); Hanson (2002: 187–209); Torjesen (1986: 37–8); Sheridan (2007).

[56] Sundberg (1975: 368) writes, "The matter of inspiration … is more intricate in Origen than in any of his predecessors." Kalin (1967: 232; cf. 6) writes, "Origen uses the concept of inspiration with more theological emphasis and force than any other early Christian writer."

[57] As Campenhausen (1972: 319) puts it, "What [Origen] himself likes to emphasise is not the continuity of an actual history but the inner harmony of a self-contained book." Campenhausen writes, "Origen no longer wants to know about 'apostolic' traditions, secret or otherwise; nor does he any longer mention, as Clement had done, any successions of teachers or bearers of the tradition" (309–10).

[58] Origen's terms for Scripture include θεῖοι λόγοι, θεῖα γραφή, θεῖα γράμματα, θεῖα βιβλία, ἱερεῖς βίβλοι, ἱερὰ γράμματα. See Zöllig (1902: 9).

[59] Wood (2015: 60–2) writes, "Scriptural understanding is a participation in the divine, for 'divine doctrines' are themselves incorporeal (i.e. have a distinct metaphysical character)."

[60] On Origen's exegesis, see Campenhausen (1972: 308); Simonetti (2000: 427–9).

[61] On the "usefulness" of Scripture in Origen, see Torjesen (1986: 124–30); Sheridan (2004: 198); King (2005: 98). As Collins (2002: 264) notes, patristic references to 2 Tim. 3:16 "emphasize the usefulness of the Scriptures far more than they do their inspiration." Watson (2013: 534) writes, "For Origen,

also quick to affirm the unity of the two testaments. Scripture should be read as a unity[62]—according to him, the divine nature of the prophets' words and the true ("spiritual") aspect of the Law became manifest in Jesus's mission (*Princ.* 4.1.6; see Daley 1998: 15; Sheridan 2007: 95). This means that reading the Old Testament in light of the Christ event should heighten the reader's sense of the unity of the two Testaments. As Christopher King (2005: 187) notes,

> The words and books of Scripture, [Origen] reasons, are really "one" (λόγος εἷς; ἓν βιβλίον) rather than "many" (πολυλογία; πολλὰ βιβλία), because the meaning of each word and book is "part of the whole Word" (ὧν ἕκαστον θεώρημα μέρος ἐστι τοῦ ὅλου λόγου); they are all intelligibles (θεωρήματα) constitutive of the personal Logos who "was in the beginning with God" (λόγος ὁ ἐν ἀρχῇ πρὸς τὸν θεόν).

Origen is perhaps best known for promoting an allegorical approach to Scripture.[63] He had been preceded in this by Clement, Tertullian, Irenaeus, and others (see Ramelli 2011b: 347), but he went further than them by extending this approach to the *New* Testament. The use of allegory to find hidden meanings in the text was made possible by the supposition that God had written the text, so that the allegorical readings fell within the purview of the divine author's intent.[64] Surface inconcinnities and narrative absurdities are but the text's invitation to dig for "deeper meaning" (viz., for the spiritual sense). These invitations took the form of anthropomorphisms, historical and physical impossibilities (e.g., morning and evening before the sun existed), metaphors, and so on (de Lubac 2007: 129; see Campenhausen 1972: 313–14; Wood 2015: 47–8 n. 54). If the text describes an event that could not possibly have taken place, then the point of the narrative can only be understood allegorically (*Princ.* 4.1.5). If two parallel gospel accounts vary in their details, then one or the other must be offering a deeper lesson (see Watson 2013: 547–50).[65] The same applies to practices and laws that are no longer binding: If they are not directly relevant for the church, then the point of relating them must be derivable through allegory (see Digeser 2012: 60). Origen could not countenance the thought of a passage whose relevance was passé. He applied the

---

the idea of interpreting a passage 'for its own sake' would be barely comprehensible: what would it mean for a passage to benefit from being interpreted?"

[62] On Origen's notion of the unity of Scripture, see de Lubac (2007: 190–204); King (2005: 96–7); Crawford (2013: 145–6). See Simonetti (2000: 425–7). Origen was the first to spread the use of the term "New Testament"—see Heine (2010: 77).

[63] For Origen's use of allegory, see Boersma (2017: 105–30).

[64] See the list of works discussing allegory in an Origenist context, in Ramelli (2011a: 569–70). See also Ramelli (2011b); Dörrie (1974).

[65] Watson (2013: 550) writes,

> From the standpoint Origen … attains, the assumption that difference threatens the gospel itself—a view shared by harmonizers (Tatian, Augustine) and their critics (Reimarus, Lessing)—can only be regarded as perverse. The gospel is *constituted* by difference. The difference that problematizes empirical correspondence does so in order to open up the spiritual sense that makes the gospel gospel: good news bringing joy to the hearer on account of the ultimate well-being it promises.

same reasoning to laws that (he claimed) are absurd (see Sheridan 2007: 96–7; Ramelli 2011b: 357).

The foregoing represent the triggers for allegorical exegesis, but what drives the *theory*? I have shown only that it is provided by the supposition that the text is inspired, but, in Origen, there is more to the notion of inspiration than the usual accounts provide. As Henri de Lubac (2007: 343–4) explains, that Scripture is said to be inspired signifies something different from saying that its *writers* were inspired:

> It does not signify merely that its origin is supernatural, in the sense that its human authors did not write without a special grace χωρὶς χαρίσματος but received from the Spirit of God an impulse or assistance for the purpose of its writing and that one can consequently say it is the work of this Spirit. It signifies besides that and especially … that this Spirit dwells in it. So it is, properly speaking, the Temple of God, and the wealth of meaning of which it is full is like the gold that covers the inner walls of our physical temples.[66]

In keeping with his penchant for allegory, Origen famously taught that Scripture had three levels of meaning, corresponding to the anthropological components of body, soul, and spirit (*Princ.* 4.2.4–6; see esp. Dively Lauro 2005).[67] He also pioneered the familiar notion that the revelatory aspect of Scripture is properly an element of God's plan of salvation: "we speak of the needs of souls, who cannot otherwise reach perfection except through the rich and wise truth about God" (*Princ.* 4.2.7 [*SC* 268.328]; see King 2005: 97). Thus he is the spiritual forefather of the Reformation notion of according the Gospel both a "formal principle" and a "material principle" and (subsidiarily) of the British evangelical couplet "revelation and redemption."

Origen's insistence on the *usefulness* of Scripture also entails a belief in God's accommodation of Scripture's meaning to human levels of understanding (see Koch 1932: 58 n. 1). This is one reason Scripture can be divine yet literarily inferior to other writings. Another reason is that the divine aspect of Scripture was in some way a supervening design upon the merely human contribution of its earthly writers (see Zöllig 1902: 72–3). Thus the text, though divine, continues to exist in the mode of both "spirit" and "letter" (see King 2005: 49–50).

5.2 Origen's Understanding of θεόπνευστος

The evidence discussed in this book suggests that, prior to Origen, θεόπνευστος always conveyed the notion of vivification. Beginning with Origen, the term began to be used in a new way—as conveying the notion of verbal or epistemic inspiration.[68] The following pages attempt to establish that Origen read θεόπνευστος through an

---

[66] See Ramelli (2011a: 572); Boyarin (2010: 40–6).
[67] Wood (2015) argues that this threefold scheme was intended as an argument against the literalism of competing schools, especially the Marcionites. See Daley (1998: 16). Hanson (2002: 235–58); de Lubac (2007: 159–71).
[68] On Origen and 2 Tim. 3:16, see Heither (1996: 143–4).

inspirationist lens. The final pages of the chapter will offer a suggestion as to what caused him to misinterpret the word.

Searching the *TLG* for appearances of θεόπνευστος in Origen's writings generates a list of some forty-eight items:[69]

1. *Princ.* 4.1.title.1	25. *Phil.* 5.1n.2.
2. *Princ.* 4.1.6.3	26. *Phil.* 11.ln.1.
3. *Princ.* 4.1.6.8	27. *Phil.* 12.2.10.
4. *Princ.* 4.2.1.1.	28. *Phil.* 12.2.12.
5. *Comm. Joh.* 1.3.16.2.	29. *Phil.* 12.2.14.
6. *Comm. Joh.* 2.22.142.1.	30. *Phil.* 27.4.11 (chaps. 1–27 edition)
7. *Comm. Joh.* 5.title.1.2.	31. *Phil.* 27.4.11 (chaps. 23, 25–27 edition)
8. *Comm. Joh.* 6.48.248.2.	32. *In Jesu Nave hom. xxvi* p. 419.22.
9. *Comm. Joh.* 10.39.266.3.	33. *In Jesu Nave hom. xxvi* p. 419.24.
10. *Fragmenta in ev. Joh.* Frag. 12.16.	34. *In Jesu Nave hom. xxvi* p. 419.25.
11. *Phil.* p.1b.33.	35. *Scholia in Apocalypsem* 25.1
12. *Phil.* p.1b.70.	36. *Fragmenta in Ps.* Ps. 1 v. 3.7.
13. *Phil.* p.c.1.	37. *Fragmenta in Ps.* Ps. 39 v. 8.5.
14. *Phil.* p.c.5.	38. *Fragmenta ex comm. Exod.* vol. 12, 269.33.
15. *Phil.* p.c.8.	39. *Sel. Deut.* vol. 12 page 812.15.
16. *Phil.* p.c.19.	40. *Sel. Ps.* vol. 12 page 1080.15.
17. *Phil.* 1.ln.1.	41. *Sel. Ps.* vol. 12 page 1080.29.
18. *Phil.* 1.6.3.	42. *Sel. Ps.* vol. 12 page 1081.5.
19. *Phil.* 1.6.10.	43. *Sel. Ps.* vol. 12 page 1084.15.
20. *Phil.* 1.8.2.	44. *Sel. Ps.* vol. 12 page 1140.10.
21. *Phil.* 2.3.4.	45. *Sel. Ps.* vol. 12 page 1600.5.
22. *Phil.* 2.4.6.	46. *Sel. Ezek.* vol. 13 page 809.1.
23. *Phil.* 3.ln.1.	47. *Excerpta in Ps.* vol. 17 p. 120.31.
24. *Phil.* 3.1.13.	48. *Hom. in Job* (frag. in catenis, typus I+II) p. 387.24.

---

[69] Working without the benefit of the *TLG*, Kalin (1967: 44–5) counted only thirteen appearances of θεόπνευστος in Origen.

We also need to supplement the *TLG*'s list with an item "49"—unknown to the *TLG*—in the form of the word's appearance in the recently discovered *Homilies on Psalms*.[70]

This might seem like a lengthy list, but it should be noted that item nos. 11 and 12 belong to the proem of the *Philocalia* and do not represent Origen's hand, while nos. 13 through 16 are found in the *Philocalia*'s table of contents. (These last four *might* duplicate Origen's wording, but that wording is also counted at a later location in the *Philocalia* [in nos. 17, 23, 25, and 26].) There are also some duplications among the remaining items. For one thing, item nos. 30 and 31 represent the same passage, which shows up as two separate entries due to the overlapping of two printed editions of the *Philocalia*. Most of the inflation found in the *TLG* list, however, is due to the overlapping of the *Philocalia* and the works from which it excerpts: the *TLG* treats the *Philocalia* as if it represented additional material, when in fact it reproduces parts of the Origenist corpus—and indeed is the basis for modern reconstructions of parts of that corpus. To wit:

Item no. 17 reproduces no. 1,
no. 18 reproduces no. 2,
no. 19 reproduces no. 3,
no. 20 reproduces no. 4,
no. 21 reproduces no. 41,
no. 22 reproduces no. 42,
no. 24 reproduces no. 43,
no. 25 reproduces no. 7,
no. 27 reproduces no. 32,
no. 28 reproduces no. 33,
no. 29 reproduces no. 34,
nos. 30 and 31 reproduce no. 38.

And so we are left with twenty-eight distinct Origenist passages: items nos. 1–10 and 32–49.

A number of these passages use θεόπνευστος in a non-load-bearing ("neutral") way, so that they give no clear indication of whether Origen understood the word in a vivificationist or an inspirationist sense. By my reckoning, the use of θεόπνευστος in the following passages is *neutral*: *TLG* nos. 1, 6, 17, 21 (par. 41), 23, 25–6, 32 (par. 27), 33 (par. 28), 34 (par. 29), 36–7, 38 (pars. 30–1), 39, 41 (par. 21), 43–4, 46, and 49.[71] In these passages, θεόπνευστος does not do any work, other than to designate "scripture" as a specific subset of all writings. (The word is used in these instances almost as a brand name.) In passages like these, it is difficult to gain a real sense of what Origen

---

[70] The Greek text of this work was discovered in April 2012, in the Tura Papyri, and its discovery allowed the further identification of pieces of a number of homilies known earlier from *Codex Monacensis Graecus* 314. See Perrone (2013; 2016). Θεόπνευστος appears in the text at "Homilia IV in Psalmum LXXVII" §1 (Perrone 2015: 390).

[71] No. 1 is the *title* given to book 4 in *De principiis*, which probably does not go back to Origen. See Bardy (1923: 40–1).

thought the word meant, as his point in using the word was not to activate its meaning but to create an association.

Fortunately, there is still a useful rump of passages from which we might gain an insight into Origen's understanding of θεόπνευστος: *TLG* nos. 2, 3 (par. 19), 4 (par. 20), 5, 7 (par. 15), 8–9. In the next section, I give a brief argument for construing θεόπνευστος in an inspirationist sense in each of these seven passages.

5.3 Select Appearances of θεόπνευστος in Origen

It's no surprise that Origen's most explicitly inspirationist uses of θεόπνευστος appear in either *De principiis* or in his commentary on the Fourth Gospel.[72]

Θεόπνευστος appears twice in *Princ.* 4.1.6 (see Procopé 1996: 477). The first of these is less explicitly inspirationist than the second, but there is probably enough here to determine its meaning:

> *Princ.* 4.1.6 (*TLG* no. 2)
> Now when we thus demonstrate in brief the divine nature of Jesus and appeal to the prophetic words regarding him, we also demonstrate that the writings that prophesy about him are theopneustic (συναποδείκνυμεν θεοπνεύστους εἶναι τὰς προφητευούσας περὶ ἀυτοῦ γραφας), and that the words that announce his sojourning and his teaching were spoken with all power and authority and therefore have held sway over the elect from among the nations. (Author's translation)

At first, it appears that the reference to "the writings which prophesy about him" might be considered *theopneustic* for the same reason 2 Timothy considers them theopneustic. The fact that these words "were spoken with all power and authority," however, tips the scale in favor of an inspirationist meaning, and the use of this quality as an explanation for the perduring power of these words tips it perhaps even more. The second appearance of θεόπνευστος in *Princ.* 4.1.6 is more clearly inspirationist:

> *Princ.* 4.1.6 (second) (*TLG* no. 3)
> And we must add that the inspiration (ἔνθεον) of the prophetic words and the spiritual nature of the law of Moses came to light after the sojourning of Jesus. For in principle it was not possible to demonstrate the *theopneustia* of the old writings (περὶ τοῦ θεοπνεύστου ... τὰς παλαιὰς γραφὰς) before the sojourning of Christ. But the sojourning of Jesus led those who might have suspected that the law and the prophets were not divine to the clear conviction that they were written through heavenly grace. (Author's translation)

---

[72] Four of these seven passages are also found in the *Philocalia*: *Phil.* p.c.8 (*TLG* no. 15) reproduces *Comm. Joh.* 5.title.1.2 (*TLG* no. 7), *Phil.* 1.6.3 (*TLG* no. 18) reproduces *Princ.* 4.1.6.3 (*TLG* no. 2), *Phil.* 1.6.10 (*TLG* no. 19) reproduces *Princ.* 4.1.6.8 (*TLG* no. 3), and *Phil.* 1.8.2 (*TLG* no. 20) reproduces *Princ.* 4.2.1.1 (*TLG* no. 4).

This passage is a continuation of *TLG* no. 2. That Origen puts the theopneustic quality in semantic parallelism with "the inspiration (ἔνθεον) of the prophetic words" is now unmistakable. Here the *theopneustia* of "the old scriptures" was something hidden until "the advent of Jesus." That we are dealing with a proof-from-prophecy scheme, rather than the advent of the inspired reader, is shown by the doubts attributed to "those who might have suspected that the law and the prophets were not divine." This is what is meant, in the sequel to this passage, by "there [coming] at once to men's knowledge those 'good things' of which the letter of the law held a 'shadow'" (see Perrone 2004: 232).[73]

Θεόπνευστος also appears at the beginning of the next chapter of *De principiis*:

Princ. 4.2.1 (*TLG* no. 4)
  Now that we have spoken briefly about the *theopneustia* of the divine scriptures (τοῦ θεοπνεύστους ... τὰς θείας γραφάς), it is necessary to hold forth on the manner of their reading and understanding, for many mistakes have been made. For the hard-hearted and the ignorant among the circumcision do not believe in our savior, for they think they are following closely the prophecies concerning him, and they do not see where he did "preach release to captives," nor build what is in literal truth a "city of God," nor "cut off the chariots from Ephraim and the horse from Jerusalem," nor "eat butter and honey, and choose the good before he knew or preferred evil." (Author's translation)

This passage could have been classified among the "neutral" uses of θεόπνευστος, except that Origen implies that the theopneustic aspect of Scripture is something that requires a special, nonliteral approach. Tying the need for nonliteralness to the supposition that Scripture's true meaning was present all along—as shown in the word's second appearance in *Princ.* 4.1.6 (*TLG* no. 3)—one can only surmise that the *theopneustia* of Scripture is related to its supposedly divine origin.

Origen also used θεόπνευστος in a clearly inspirationist way in his commentary on the Fourth Gospel:

Comm. Joh. 1.16 (*TLG* no. 5)
  And accordingly, consider whether Paul includes his own writings when he says, "All scripture is theopneustic and useful." Do not the sayings "I say, and not the Lord," "I ordain in all churches," "Such things as I suffered in Antioch, in Iconium, in Lystra," and similar words sometimes written by him, display the

---

[73] Zöllig (1902: 13–14) writes,

> Und in der Tat finden wir auch in den entscheidenden Schlusssätzen der einzelnen Beweise das θείας und das θεοπνεύστους εἶναι τὰς Γραφάς regelmässig als gleichbedeutend angeführt; trotz der Doppelbedeutung des Wortes θεόπνευστος dürfte sich der diesem Worte von Origenes beigelegte Sinn nicht schwer ermitteln lassen. Nirgends finden wir es in aktivem Sinne gleich θεόπνοος, "den göttlichen Geist hauchen," verwendet, wielmehr zeigt es stets ein Kausalverhältnis Gottes zur Heiligen Schrift an.

authority of an apostle but not the absolute character of the divinely inspired words (τῶν ἐκ θείας ἐπιπνοίας λόγων)? (Author's translation)

The false conundrum Origen sets up in this passage pits the theopneustic nature of Scripture against Paul's use of the first-person perspective, which should (for the sake of Origen's argument) represent an "apostolic authority." As the argument goes, this "apostolic authority" is something less than "the absolute character of divinely inspired words." If "theopneustic" for Origen meant "life-giving," it would be difficult to see how the argument is supposed to work, for surely the (mere) words of an apostle can be "life-giving" (at least in the sense that 2 Timothy uses that notion). Origen's argument here also unmistakably draws a semantic parallelism between θεόπνευστος and τῶν ἐκ θείας ἐπιπνοίας λόγων.

Later in the same commentary, Origen uses θεόπνευστος to describe Scripture as a single book:

> *Comm. Joh.* 5.proem (*TLG* no. 7)
> What is "much speaking," and what are the "many books"? Even the whole theopneustic scripture (ἡ θεόπνευστος γραφὴ) is one book. (Author's translation)

These words are from a proem found in the *Philocalia*, so it is not clear whether they were penned by Origen. If they *are* Origen's words, they would seem to support his use of θεόπνευστος as an inspirationist term. Their logic seems to be based on the view that all the books of Scripture are written by the same spirit. Having the same author, their continuity of content is all we need to regard them all as one book. This implies that the theopneustic aspect of these books has to do with their inspired nature.[74]

Origen again uses θεόπνευστος with a clearly inspirationist sense in the next book of his commentary:

> *Comm. Joh.* 6.248 (*TLG* no. 8)
> But that the foregoing word by the Spirit that speaks in the theopneustic scriptures (ἐν ταῖς θεοπνεύστοις γραφαῖς λαλοῦντι) is not about sense-perceptible rivers is seen from that which was prophesied in Ezekiel, regarding Pharaoh, king of Egypt. (Author's translation)

Origen says that the Spirit "speaks in the theopneustic Scriptures" and seems to imply that this Spirit-speaking fills Scripture in such a way that it determines the text's meaning wherever one looks for it. Origen does not refer to the Spirit who speaks only in the prophetic portions of Scripture, but rather takes the Spirit-speaking exemplified in Ezekiel as paradigmatic for the "theopneustic Scriptures" in general.

---

[74] For Origen, it is more correct to speak in terms of the "inspired nature" of Scripture than of the "inspired status" of the writings that make up Scripture. This is because the inspiration of these writings was not something that gave them a special *status* vis-à-vis other Christian writings. See Kalin (1967).

Our final example of Origen's inspirationist use of θεόπνευστος comes from book 10 of the same commentary:

Comm. Joh. 10.265 (*TLG* no. 9)
We are persuaded, however, that the distinctiveness of theopneustic scripture (τῆς θεοπνεύστου γραφῆς) is made manifest in such a way, in fact, by being more than human—*viz.* by being according to the wisdom of God—a wisdom hidden in a mystery, which none of the princes of this world know. (Author's translation)

Origen makes it clear here that theopneustic Scripture is inspired: Scripture has a "distinctive character" that "is made manifest ... in a special way." Only an *inspired* Scripture could be said to be "beyond human nature" and to exemplify a divine wisdom out of reach of this world's wisest rulers.

These seven passages represent only a fraction of Origen's total uses of θεόπνευστος, but they firmly establish that our investigation has moved from a period in which θεόπνευστος meant "life-giving" to a period in which it (primarily) meant "divinely inspired." It is θεόπνευστος's second career—its designation of an *inspired status*—that would remain operative throughout the next two millennia and impress itself on most investigators as the only meaning the word ever had.[75]

5.4 A Suggested Source for Origen's Error

If we now can say that Origen was the first person in history to ascribe an inspirationist sense to the word θεόπνευστος, the question remains as to how he came to his misunderstanding. Was he simply unfamiliar with the term, and therefore left to his own devices—the devices, that is, pertaining to a Philonic understanding of Scripture? Or could it be that his understanding of θεόπνευστος was shaped by a misunderstanding of how others employed this term? In what follows, I argue the latter. There is, in fact, a not unlikely scenario that can explain Origen's muddlement.

One of the pre-Origenist uses of θεόπνευστος/θεόπνους we examined in this book is that of Numenius, who used θεόπνους to describe the fecundating power of the water in Homer's cave of the nymphs. Although the evidence that Numenius used the word in a vivificationist sense is clear, it is easy to imagine a reader misunderstanding the nature of the water rites conducted in the cave. They might have viewed the waters as possessing an *oracular* power—the power they possessed, for example, in the well-known use of water from underground streams in the mythology of the sibyl's inspiration. If Origen interpreted Numenius' description of the cave of the nymphs along the lines of the technology of inspiration connected with apolline oracles and

---

[75] That θεόπνευστος took on an inspirationist meaning during Origen's lifetime is also shown by the fact that his contemporary, Dionysius of Alexandria, used the term to refer to a *person* as an inspired author (viz., the author of Revelation) (in Eusebius, *Hist. eccl.* 7.2.5.7). See Kalin (1967: 127–8). By the fourth century, θεόπνευστος began to be applied with some regularity to persons—e.g., the preface to the *Philocalia* refers to Basil and Gregory of Nazianzus as "theopneustic preachers." See the discussion of individuals and councils described as θεόπνευστοι during this period, in Congar (1967: 125–30).

sibyls, it is not unlikely that he interpreted Numenius' use of θεόπνους as a reference to the water's *prophetically* "inspired" nature. All that remains is to imagine Origen adopting this as the general sense of θεόπνευστος, especially as that term applied to Scripture.

This scenario is admittedly speculative, but it is not as fanciful as it appears. For one thing, we know that Origen was closely familiar with Numenius' writings. Róbert Somos (2000: 52, 56) argues convincingly, in fact, that "Numenius was the most important philosopher for Origen" and that "there is no other philosopher whose works Origen was more familiar with than Numenius."[76] Moreover, there is a strong indication that Origen was familiar *with the very passage* in which Numenius used the word θεόπνους, in that he was particularly taken with the fact that Numenius recognized the allegorical nature of Scripture (*C. Cels.* 4.51; see Cook 2008: 16). Although scholars regularly interpret this as a claim that Numenius' works are filled with allegories (see Dillon 1996: 364–5), it is better to see here an allusion to the words of Numenius preserved in Porphyry's *On the Cave of the Nymphs*. Somos (2000: 68) notes that the Numenian perspective adopted by Porphyry also appears elsewhere in Origen:

> In connection with apocatastasis, Origen … writes about the celestial travel of the soul, and although he refers to former Christian texts as sources, he uses such motives in *De principiis* II, 3, 1–5 whose original source is the closing myth of Plato's *Republic* the vision of the Pamphylean "Er," which Numenius discussed in detail and Porphyrius relied on when writing his *On the Cave of the Nymphs*.

Thus it would appear that Origen knew the Numenian passage that Porphyry quotes in *On the Cave of the Nymphs*. I reproduce that passage here for convenience's sake:

> For they ["the ancients"] held that souls settled upon the water which was theopneustic, as Numenius says, and therefore the prophet said "The Spirit of God was moving upon the face of the waters," and therefore the Egyptians depicted all their daimons standing not on dry land but all on a boat—the sun and the rest— and these are construed as the souls descending into genesis and hovering over the water. (*De antr.* 10 [Author's translation])

That θεόπνευστος is used here in a vivificationist sense is made clear by the ritual function of the waters. But what if an early reader of Numenius mistakenly thought of a different sort of ritual—that of consuming or breathing the vapors of the waters

---

[76] Somos (2000: 57–9) goes on to show that Origen and Numenius share a significant amount of terminology, which they use almost identically. In Somos's view, Origen's praise of Numenius represents a "significant exception" to his policy of not praising philosophers (56). On Numenius' influence on Origen, see Berchman (1984: 109–12); Lamberton (1986: 78–82); Kenney (1992: 227–8); Ziebritzki (1994: 27–8); Ramelli (2011b: 344 n. 19). Cf. Jerome, *Ep.* 70.4. See the discussion of Numenius in Sterling (1993: 108–10). Origen might not be the first Christian writer to interact with Numenius, as a number of scholars see the philosopher's views lying behind certain remarks by Justin Martyr—e.g., see Gaston (2009: 575–6). Some later Christian writers also used Numenius—e.g., on Eusebius' use of Numenius, see Ziebritzki (1994: 22); Carriker (1996). See Weber (1962).

for their *oracular* effect? The famous oracle of Apollo at Claros, for example, relied on draughts from a spring on the temple grounds (Tacitus, *Ann.* 2.54; Pliny, *Hist. nat.* 2.232). (See Parke 1985: 137–8; Lane Fox 1987: 172–5; Levin 1989: 1630; Robert and Robert 1992: 287; Stoneman 2011: 92–5. Cf. Connor 1988: 184; Dietrich 1990: 169–70.) The Cumaean sibyl received her inspiration by bathing in a cistern (cf. Justin Martyr, *Cohort.* 37; see Thompson 1952: 123; Clark 1996: 231–3).[77] (Springs were also associated with poetic inspiration [see Dunn 1989: 102–3].)[78] As Robin Lane Fox (1987: 206–7) notes, "Wherever there was water, … there was a possible source of prophecy." Strictly speaking, that θεόπνους means "life-giving" can be affirmed only on the basis of familiarity with the prenuptial rites associated with the cult of the nymphs. If Origen was less familiar with that cult than others were—or if his mind simply leaped to the wrong context—then he easily could have mistaken θεόπνους for a reference to *prophetically inspired* waters. Although there are other details in Numenius' text that should have set him straight, the possibility of misreading the word this way would have been funded by the use made by nymph-haunted waters for divinatory purposes elsewhere.[79] Jennifer Larson (2001: 11) notes that "divinatory powers" were often attributed to nymphs or "to those inspired by them" and that "the nymphs' fundamental association with water, the vector of prophecy and inspiration," was one of the "salient factors" in this attribution. No means of prophetic aid was more cross-culturally available than that of drinking from, or inhaling the vapors from, a sacred spring.[80] A familiarity with the nympological associations of divination in certain locales could easily have led Origen to assume that θεόπνευστος means "inspired."

The position outlined here depends on the actual wording of Origen and not on Porphyry's testimony (*apud* Eusebius) about Origen's background and schooling.[81] Porphyry's description of Origen's reading habits gives a prominent place to Numenius (see Eusebius, *Hist. eccl.* 6.19.5–8; see Ramelli 2009: 227–8), but Origen's close familiarity with Numenius' views can be gleaned from his own writings (see Koch 1932: 228 n. 1).

[77] On the Cumaean Sibyl, see Polara (2007).
[78] See the section on "The Poet's Draught: Water and Inspiration in Rome," in Jones (2005: 56–9); Ziolkowski (1990: 16); Depew (2007).
[79] On the nymphs' role in divination, see Speyer (2015: 9); Neutsch (1957: 17); Connor (1988: 161–2); Larson (2001: 11–20); Ondine Pache (2011: 44). See the discussion of "Prophetic powers of the Nymphs and their mythology," in Ustinova (2009: 58–60)—although Ustinova writes there primarily of the nymphs' use of *honey* (rather than water) as a prophetic aid.
[80] On the use of water from grottoes for prophetic inspiration, see Elderkin (1941). See Clement of Alexandria, *Protr.* 2.10–11; Iamblichus, *De myst.* 3.11.124. Examples of the divinatory use of water in the ancient world can be found in Bouché-Leclercq (1879–82: 1.186, 191, 339; 2.149, 358; 3.257, 268, 312–13, 411; 4.155). See the chapter on "Divination at Sacred Springs," in Halliday (1913: 116–44). See Parke (1985: 94–5).
[81] In a fragment preserved by Eusebius, Porphyry refers to a man he met in his youth, "greatly celebrated" for his writings (*Hist. eccl.* 6.19.5). That man, he tells us, was Origen, an auditor of Ammonius, who worked with the writings of Numenius and Cronius, Apollophanes, Longinus, Moderatus, Nicomachus, and the better known Pythagoreans. (See Eusebius, *Hist. eccl.* 6.19.5–8.) Eusebius accepts that Porphyry is referring to *our* Origen, but rejects the claim that Origen was brought up a heathen (*Hist. eccl.* 6.19.9–10).

7

Post-Origenist Traces of a Vivificationist Understanding of Θεόπνευστος in Nonnus of Panopolis

The preceding chapters sought to establish that θεόπνευστος/θεόπνους, in its *every* pre-Origenist appearance, denotes the *life-giving* quality of the thing(s) it describes. The present chapter adds further support for this view, by showing an outstanding instance in which the original understanding of the word survived into the fifth century. Although Origen's designs on the word gave rise to the now prevalent understanding of θεόπνευστος as "God-inspired," those designs did not root out the vivificationist understanding immediately. In the following pages, we will look at how θεόπνευστος is used in Nonnus of Panopolis's *Paraphrase of the Gospel of John* (= *Paraphrase*), a work setting out the Fourth Gospel in an expanded, hexametric form, following a convention of Christian writers from the fourth through sixth centuries.[1] θεόπνευστος appears in the *Paraphrase* four times.

1 Θεόπνευστος in Nonnus of Panopolis

Nonnus of Panopolis—the "Egyptian Homer," as Tycho Mommsen called him[2]—is known for two writings: the *Dionysiaca* (an epic poem on the god Dionysus) and the *Paraphrase*. Although θεόπνευστος appears only in the latter, our investigation will deal with aspects of both works, so a few words on their characteristics and mutual relationship are in order.

It was once commonly argued that these works have different authors or that they represent different points in a career separated by a religious conversion (e.g., see Collart 1930: 272–3; Keydell 1936: 905; Quasten 1950: 3.114–15).[3] Recent scholarship, however, has removed the impediments to understanding how religiously diverse works might be

---

[1] There are two English translations of the *Paraphrase*: Sherry (1991); Prost (2003).
[2] Mommsen (1895: 237) called Nonnus "der Aegyptische Homeros." On the Egyptian setting of the *Paraphrase*, see Agosti (2003: 95–102). On the Christian context of fifth-century Egypt, see Medina 448.
[3] A more recent defense of non-Nonnian authorship for the *Paraphrase* appears in Sherry (1991).

written by a single hand.[4] Alan Cameron (2000: 175) lists two facts "put[ting] common authorship beyond reasonable doubt": (1) there are allusions to the Dionysiac religion within the *Paraphrase*'s telling of the wedding at Cana, and (2) Adrian Hollis (1976; 1994: 58–9) has shown that both Nonnian works contain echoes or reminiscences of the same hellenistic poems, "in one case each to a different part of the same line of Callimachus's *Hecale*" (see Vian 1997). If this religious double-mindedness makes Nonnus puzzling to us, it also renders him no less an impressive figure. As Glen Bowersock (2000: 95–6) notes, "a writer who can dilate on Dionysus for 48 books and also paraphrase one of the Christian Gospels in verse is obviously someone to be taken seriously as a man of his age and not to be divided into a schizophrenic with pagan and Christian sides—or a pagan past and a Christian present, or the opposite."[5] (Domenico Accorinti [2016: 37] calls Nonnus a "Janus bifrons" [cf. Chuvin 1991: 273].)

Scholars disagree on which work Nonnus wrote first.[6] Earlier scholars, positing a conversion experience, typically saw the *Paraphrase* as the later work. Ever since Albert Wifstrand (1922) showed the metrical irregularities in the *Paraphrase*, however, scholars have tended to see it as the earlier of the two.[7] The presumption is that the greater consistency of the *Dionysiaca*'s metrical scheme is a mark of experience. Cameron (2000: 178–9) allows that some metrical irregularities might be blamed on the use of biblical proper names in the *Paraphrase*, but he notes that that would not account for all the irregularities (cf. Sherry 1991: 88). There is also the intriguing suggestion that the two poems were written concurrently, a view that Robert Shorrock (2011: 51) says "has much to recommend it":

> It would readily explain why at times the *Dionysiaca* appears to have been written in the light of the *Paraphrase*, while at other times the *Paraphrase* appears to have

---

[4] Shorrock (2011: 136 n. 29) writes, "There is no logical reason to suggest that a poet who switches masks is any less committed a Christian than a poet who maintains an exclusively Christian *persona*." See Chuvin (1986). The fourth century is especially noted for Christians' widening appreciation of pagan classics. See Bogner (1934: 328–33); Geffcken (1978: 189). On Christian interaction with pagan classics in the fourth century, see Ševčenko (1980); Kaster (1988: 70–95); Harris (1991: 84). On the date and chronology of Nonnus, see Lind (1934). Liebeschuetz (1996: 77) writes, "The way Dionysus is presented makes it difficult to take the religion of the poem at face value." Cameron (2000: 181) compares the openness of fifth-century Christians toward pagan culture to that of Christians in the Victorian age.

  Some scholars continue to argue that the Dionysiaca and the Paraphrase had different authors. E.g., the editors of the Thesaurus Pseudo-Nonni Quondam Panopolitani (Coulie, Sherry, and CETEDOC 1995: viii) see a gulf between the abilities displayed in metrical composition: "In the Dionysiaca [Nonnus] makes only one mistake of quantity. ... In the Paraphrase there are at least nine Greek words with mistakes (not counting foreign proper names)." (See Sherry's [1991: 106–8] list of the nine "misscanned Greek words that are not personal names.") See the response in Shorrock (2011: 51).

[5] It has sometimes been argued that the poet Nonnus should be identified with Bishop Nonnus of Edessa (see Livrea 1987).

[6] The editors of the *Thesaurus Pseudo-Nonni Quondam Panopolitani* (Coulie, Sherry, and CETEDOC 1995: vii) claim that "the *Paraphrase* is 'centoized' from the *Dionysiaca*" and that the latter "can be firmly dated to 430–450 AD." Others contend that Nonnus' use of θεητόκος also points to a date after 431 (Quasten 1950: 3.116; Golega 1930: 107–8). Cf. Preller (1918: 6–7); Sieber (2017: 158–9).

[7] Shorrock (2001: 9 n. 6) writes, "On metrical grounds alone ... the *Paraphrase* is more likely to have preceded the *Dionysiaca*." See the discussion of Nonnian metrics in Golega (1930: 8–28); Sherry (1991: 79–111).

been written in the light of the *Dionysiaca*. Even [Francis] Vian, who has cautiously defended the priority of the *Paraphrase*, has not been wholly convinced by his own arguments. For example, in his analysis of the Tylus episode in *Dionysiaca* 25, he suggested that an intertextual link with the Lazarus episode in *Paraphrase* 13 would work better if the *Dionysiaca* were the earlier of the two texts.[8]

In fact, the date range that some scholars give for the writing of both works is so compact as to amount to contemporaneity. (Enrico Livrea [2000: 56] writes that both works were published in the period from 445 until 451 [see Tissoni 2008: 78–9].) According to Mary Whitby (2007: 200–1), "the scale and erudition of both works and the limited time-frame available for their composition" makes "the view that they were written contemporaneously … attractive." Konstantinos Spanoudakis (2016: 622) notes,

> What has not been observed is that the two poems seem to be bound together inextricably, in a manner so far uncodified yet extant. … The question of chronological priority aside, the two poems would thus acquire some kind of communality. The *Paraphrasis*, in particular, gains the appearance of a 'historical' continuation and prospective consummation of the longer poem.

Yet there is more on which to base a chronology than asking which work lies downstream from the other.[9] For one thing, there are indications that Nonnus knew Cyril of Alexandria's commentary on the Fourth Gospel (written 425–428 CE; see Cameron 2000: 176; Spanoudakis 2007: 72), as well as the writings of Gregory of Nazianzus.[10] Accorinti (2016: 29) also suggests that Nonnus imitated an epigram by Cyrus of Panopolis dating to 441–442 CE. For a *terminus ante quem*, Accorinti (2016: 30) notes other poets who were influenced by Nonnus as early as *ca.* 471 CE.

Scholars have long recognized allusions to Dionysiac religion in the *Paraphrase* (see Golega 1930: 62–88).[11] The clearest of these appears in the account of the wedding at Cana and in Jesus's claim to be the "true vine" (see Golega 1930: 75–7; Shorrock 2011: 57).[12] (Roberta Franchi [2016: 252] calls the allusion to Dionysus in the latter "obvious for any reader of that time.") A few scholars have dug deeper and found Dionysiac allusions throughout the *Paraphrase* (see Linnemann 1974; Hengel

---

[8] On the "Tylus episode," see Hernández de la Fuente (2013: 479–80). The supposed link with the Lazarus story is resisted in Dijkstra (2016: 87).

[9] See the review of arguments regarding the dates of Nonnus' works, in Miguélez Cavero (2008: 17–18). Cf. Whitby (2007: 200–1). On the dates of Nonnus' life and works, see Accorinti (2016: 28–31). Cf. Cataudella (1974: 443–65).

[10] On Nonnos' relation to Gregory of Nazianzus, see Accorinti (1990); D'Ippolito (1994); Medina (2006: 458–9); Simelidis (2016: 298–307).

[11] Franchi (2016: 247–8) argues that the ease of hiding/finding allusions to Dionysus in the Fourth Gospel determined Nonnus' choice of that gospel as the basis of his poem. Cf. Bacon (1915: 115–17).

[12] Shorrock writes, "In the *Paraphrase*, the wine-stewards return from their attempt to draw wine with 'unwetted (ἀβρέκτοις, 2.16) hands'. It is noteworthy that the only use of the adjective ἀβρέκτος in the *Dionysiaca* with specific reference to wine relates to the transformation of the water of Lake Astacis into wine in Book 17" (64). See Broer (1999); Spanoudakis (2007: 38). See the comparison between *Dion.* 12.110–13 and the triumphal entry in the NT gospels, in Accorinti (2008: 33–6).

1995: 307–8, 315, 326–7; Wick 2004; Eisele 2009; Hernández de la Fuente 2013: 468; Doroszewski 2014; cf. Shorrock 2014).[13] This interchange of Christic and Dionysiac imagery was not something developed de novo by Nonnus but represents a literarizing of several long-thematized contacts between the Christian and the Dionysian figures (see Bacon 1915: 115–17; Smith 1974; Accorinti 1995: 24–5; Hengel 1995: 329–31; Shorrock 2011: 55; Hernández de la Fuente 2013; Friesen 2014; Massa 2014; cf. Kirkpatrick 2013).[14]

The time of the *Paraphrase*'s composition was characterized, among Christians, by an increased openness toward hellenistic culture. While a fourth-century figure like Jerome could have nightmares of being punished for enjoying pagan literature (*Ep.* 22.30), fifth- and sixth-century Christian writers embraced the Greek myths as topics for literary expression (see Lepelley 2010; Shorrock 2011: 20; cf. Athanassiadi 1992: 19).[15] In some cases, this new openness toward Greco-Roman mythology manifested in an appropriation of those myths as ciphers for the truths of the Christian faith (see Keith 2009: 81–3). If philosophers "saved" myths (*apud* Luc Brisson), so also did Christian poets (cf. Lamberton 2006: 165).

Θεόπνευστος appears four times in the *Paraphrase* (see de Stefani 2002: 172–3). Nonnus uses the word three times in an overtly vivificationist sense, while the remaining use (the second of the four) is unclear, but likely vivificationist as well. In spite of the *Paraphrase*'s length, the frequency with which θεόπνευστος appears can hardly be explained simply through Nonnus' daily vocabulary. He never uses the word in the *Dionysiaca*, which is three times longer than the *Paraphrase*. In fact, Nonnus uses θεόπνευστος so often in the *Paraphrase* as to seem gratuitous in choosing it— as if intending to fill his work with scriptural echoes.[16] Thus the *Paraphrase* testifies to a distinct Christianizing of the term, in that it presents a connection between θεόπνευστος and the Gospel's life-giving qualities (see below). In so doing, it restores to the term a meaning that had been largely evacuated from it by Origen's influence.

1.1 *Paraphrase* 1.99 (*ad* Jn 1:27)

The first appearance of θεόπνευστος (*Para.* 1.99) has attracted the most attention, as it is, in several ways, the most interesting of the four. It appears in Nonnus' rewriting of John the Baptist's words about the greater one who is expected (cf. Jn 1:27):

> *Paraphrase* 1.96–99
> "but one is coming after me.

---

[13] Hernández de la Fuente (2013: 481) lists fourteen allusions to Dionysus in the *Paraphrase*. Cf. Spanoudakis (2007); Massa (2014: 210–13).

[14] On Dionysus in poetry prior to Nonnus, see Senmartí (1973). See Pollmann (2017: 140–57). The appearance of both Christ and Dionysus (along with Mary and Ariadne) on textiles from a fourth-century Christian burial (now held at the Abegg Foundation in Switzerland) is often mentioned as representing the (literal) shared space of mythologies we otherwise might expect to be mutually exclusive. See Willers (1992); Bowersock (2000: 112); Schmitz (2009: 175); Hernández de la Fuente (2013: 471–2); Shorrock (2014: 331). Cf. also Willers (1993).

[15] Dijkstra (2016: 83) writes, "we should not fall into the trap of equating Hellenism with 'paganism.'"

[16] Miguélez Cavero (2008: 23) writes, "[Nonnus] frequently resorts to a *contaminatio* of New Testament episodes to enrich the text he had as a base."

> He is present in our midst already today,
> and my mortal hand is not worthy to touch his feet.
> to loosen the strap of his theopneustic sandal (θεοπνεύστοιο πεδίλου)."

(Author's translation)[17]

This appearance of θεόπνευστος figured in Benjamin Warfield's argument for the word's passive sense, although the meaning he attributed to it in this context does not immediately reveal that sense. Warfield (1900: 108) claimed that the sandal was theopneustic by dint of its "divinity," but he was careful to construe that property strictly in terms characterizing Jesus's effect on the sandal: "Here surely the meaning is not directly that our Lord's sandal 'radiated divinity,' though certainly that may be one of the implications of the epithet, but more simply that it partook of the divinity of the divine Person whose property it was and in contact with whom it had been." According to Warfield (1900: 113), "though in the application of the word to individual men and to our Lord's sandals there may be an approach to the sense of 'God-imbued,' this sense is attained by a pathway of development from the simple idea of God-given, God-determined, and the like." His basic point is that θεόπνευστος, in this context, has a passive sense, in and under a developed (local) sense of "divine."

A number of competing renderings find other ways to accommodate the word to its context. The 1861 translation by the Count of Marseilles took the word to imply Jesus's divinity: "ne mérite pas même de dénouer le cordon de la chaussure qui enlace un Dieu!" (Le Comte de Marcellus 1861: 6–7). Claudio de Stefani (2002: 93) translates the last three words in 1.99 as "la cinghia del calzare ispirato da Dio." Prost (2003: 48) renders θεόπνευστος as "God-fashioned," while *The Brill Dictionary of Ancient Greek* defines θεόπνευστος in this passage as "blessed" (Montanari, Goh, and Schroeder 2015: 933), and Lee Sherry (1991: 174) renders it as "god-inspired." All these attempts to understand the sense of θεόπνευστος miss a fascinating intertextual echo in this passage and fail to grasp what Nonnus is saying.

As noted in our introductory remarks on Nonnus, scholars have begun to trace the intricate weave of echoes and correspondences between the main protagonists in the two Nonnian poems, so that the Jesus of the *Paraphrase* is now seen to be subtly endued with the marks of divinity given to Dionysus in the *Dionysiaca*. Cross-pollination takes place in both poems, as Dionysus appears to symbolize Christ, while Christ is lauded through echoes of the Dionysian myth. As Claudio Moreschini and Enrico Norelli (2005: 186) note, "the Christianity of Nonnus in his *Dionysiaca* is ... subtly perceptible to readers capable of grasping the allusions to it and the preciosities that express it" (see Shorrock 2016).

Before exploring the intertextual echo at *Para.* 1.99, we should note that Jesus's feet are described in (possibly) analogous terms at four other places in the *Paraphrase* (see de Stefani 2002: 172). Jesus's feet (or soles) are described as "ambrosial" (ποσὶν ἀμβροσίοις) in 4.13, 9.173, 11.6, and 11.113 (all four translated here by the author):[18]

---

[17] A new edition of the *Paraphrase* is being produced by Enrico Livrea and his students, with installments appearing through the past several decades.

[18] Cf. also references to ambrosia in *Para.* 1.59 (voice), 5.93 (life), 6.97 (hand), 11.79 (response [= promise of resurrection]), and 20.96 (mouth).

Para. 4.13–16 (*ad* Jn 4:5)
And hastening south on his ambrosial feet (ποδὸς ἀμβροσίοιο),
He came to the land of the ancient city of the Samaritans;
To high-built Sichar, where Jacob the gardener
had vineyard grounds which he gave to his son Joseph.

Para. 9.170–74 (*ad* Jn 9:37–38)
Jesus replied, "You even saw him with your eyes,
and he is speaking to you now." And he said,
"Lord, I believe." And lowering his head to earth,
and hunching his curved neck to his ambrosial feet (ποσὶν ἀμβροσίοις),
he embraced the luminous soles of his shoes.

Para. 11.3b–6 (*ad* Jn 11:2)
… Mary, she with the beautiful hair,
who was known as "the hostess of God," washed Christ's feet,
and anointed them with fragrant drops of myrrh,
and with her locks wiped clean his ambrosial soles (ἀμβροσίων ἀπὸ ταρσῶν).

Para. 11.109–13 (*ad* Jn 11:32)
Mary, weeping loudly, came near the place
where he remained with unflinching feet.
He noticed her immediately, the one who was buffeted within her troubled mind;
quivering face down, having fallen to the ground,
before his ambrosial feet (ποσὶν ἀμβροσίοις), she beseeched him.

These four references comprise an important thread in Nonnus' intertextual weave and help explain why Nonnus refers to Jesus's sandal as theopneustic.[19]

The reference to the theopneustic quality of Jesus's sandals is part of Nonnus' program of illuminating Christ's identity through Dionysiac allusions. In this case, however, the allusion may not be directly to the figure of Dionysus but rather to the young satyr Ampelus, who mirrors Dionysus in many ways (see Kröll 2014).[20] Ampelus is introduced in *Dionysiaca* 10 as a divine *Wunderkind*, whose footsteps have a strange effect. Just what that effect might be is a matter of dispute. W. H. D. Rouse's *Loeb* translation (1962: 341) reads: "Where his silvery foot stept the meadow blushed with roses" (νισσομένου δὲ ἐκ ποδὸς ἀργυφέοιο ῥόδων ἐρυθαίνετο λειμών [*Dion.* 10.190]). Instead of killing the ground cover by tramping it down, Ampelus' very footsteps are described as *life-giving*.[21] (This interpretation, if correct, obviously would support a

---

[19] Greek parentheses (throughout) from Scheindler (1881).
[20] On the Ampelus cycle in the *Dionysiaca*, see Carvounis (2017)—see also Tissoni, in Del Corno (1997: 304 n. 23). Cf. Ovid, 3.407–14.
[21] The modern reader will perhaps hear in this sentiment similar to what we find in Eleanor Farjeon's "Morning has Broken" (1931): "Praise for the sweetness, / Of the wet garden, / Sprung in completeness / Where His feet pass." Given that Farjeon also had authored such poems as "Pan-Worship" and "Apollo in Pherae," and books like *Ariadne and the Bull*, it is almost certain she had read the *Dionysiaca* at some point.

vivificationist rendering of θεόπνευστος in *Para.* 1.99.) Byron Harries (1994: 72), on the other hand, interprets the "blushing" of the roses under Ampelus' tread, not as a springing into renewed life but as a flashing of color by movement—and, in line with this, as contributing to the sensuousness of Ampelus' frolicking. There is, however, a third possible understanding of *Dion.* 10.190, which neither Rouse nor Harries seems to have considered: the flashing of a rosy hue wherever Ampelus stepped might be an allusion to *ambrosial* footwear.[22] In the *Odyssey*, we appear to be told that ambrosia is a "ruddy nectar" (νέκταρ ἐρυθρόν [*Od.* 5.93]).[23] Perhaps, then, the flashing of red caused by Ampelus' movement is meant as an indication of this divine substance (Murray 1946: 177). (We are given to understand, by Hesiod's first hymn to Demeter, that a daily anointing with ambrosia was something fit for "the offspring of a god" [Hesiod, *Hymn to Demeter* 235–8 (trans. Evelyn-White 1977: 305–7)].) Such an association would point forward (so to speak) to Christ's "ambrosial feet" in *Para.* 4.13, 9.173, 11.6, and 11.113, and *backward* to Homer: "So she spoke, and bound beneath her feet her beautiful sandals, ambrosial, golden (καλὰ πέδιλα, ἀμβρόσια χρύσεια), which were wont to bear her both over the waters of the sea and over the boundless land swift as the blasts of the wind" (*Od.* 1.96–98; Murray 1946: 11).[24]

Another passage in Homer may shed more light on Jesus's ambrosial feet/ theopneustic sandals: in *Il.* 24.340–42 (// *Od.* 1.96–98; 5.44–46), Homer describes "fine sandals, ambrosial and golden" (καλὰ πέδιλα ἀμβρόσια χρύσεια), which allow Hermes to pass "over the sea and over the boundless earth as fast as blasts of wind" (see McPhee 2016: 769). Whether the "ambrosial" aspect of Hermes' sandals is directly responsible for their hoverboard-like abilities is unclear, but the association of ambrosial sandals with such abilities is itself clear and may well be an intended allusion in Nonnus' poem. In that case, Jesus's feet/footwear may be associated with his water-walking in Mark and Matthew.[25]

Obviously, the image we are intended to see depends on the sense in which sandals or feet might be called "ambrosial." Some translators assume that calling something "ambrosial" more or less means to call it "immortal" (so A. T. Murray [1946: 10 n. 1] at *Od.* 1.97) or "deathless" (so Prost [2003: 122, 134] at *Para.* 9.173 and 11.113).[26] (See

---

[22] Nonnus' description of Ampelus' silver sandals participates in a long tradition of silver-shod deities. See de Stefani (2002: 172–3). Cf. Kingsley (1995: 294 n. 17). In late antiquity, there was no shortage of representations of, or references to, divine feet or sandals. See Chicarro (1950); García y Bellido (1960: 135–9) (esp. nos. 3, 4, 5); Speyer (1973); Arena (1983: 100); Canto (1984); Valls, Canicero, and Vaquero (1995: 335); Mitchell (1999: 107); Petridou (2009: 83–4). When Empedocles' bronze sandal survived his leap into Mount Etna, it was taken as a sign that he had become immortal. See Kingsley (1995: 289–316); Joost-Gaugier (2006: 15). The sixth-century *Piacenza Pilgrim* relates that Jesus's footprints left their mark on a square stone, said to be the platform on which he stood before Pilate. Measurements taken from the footprints and worn on the body are said to heal diseases. (See text in Peters 1985: 167.) Even the Apostle Paul's sandals were said to have been preserved in a box, according to the *Apocalypse of Paul*. See Dilley (2010: 594–5).

[23] On the ruddiness of nectar, see Pulleyn (1997).

[24] Nonnus made a great deal of the ability of divine beings to move across water without getting wet— see Newbold (2001: 176–8).

[25] This, in spite of McPhee's (2016: 769) recent dissociation of the hydrofoil footwear of hellenistic gods and Jesus's water-walking in the gospels.

[26] Ambrosia and nectar are used to prevent the decomposition of Patroclus in *Il.* 19.37–39.

Zanni 2008: 392–3.) But what if being "ambrosial" implies a life-giving quality by way of a more visual association—such that the object so described literally dripped life-giving ambrosia? That would certainly explain the flashing of red with Ampelus' every footstep. (Nonnus appears to be working with the earlier [viz., Homeric] view of ambrosia, which did not view it as something over against nectar, but rather saw ambrosia and nectar as one and the same.)[27] Nonnus, as is well known, constructed the *Dionysiaca* largely by redeploying Homeric words and phrases. (Shorrock [2001: 25] writes, "there is hardly a line in the whole poem that does not contain some Homeric reminiscence—in terms of vocabulary or imagery" [see Vian 1991; Bannert and Kröll 2016; cf. Nonnus, *Dion.* 13.51].) It would be in keeping with the character of Nonnus' writing, therefore, to see an allusion to Homer's "ambrosial sandals" in *Dion.* 10.190.[28]

If Jesus' sandals are then said to be life-giving in *Para.* 1.99, it is not unlikely that Nonnus intended this as an allusion to Ampelus. After all, the payoff for cross-referencing Jesus and Ampelus would be generous: the latter, after his death, was "resurrected" by being metamorphosed into the vine signified by his name (see Hernández de la Fuente 2013: 474), while the former gave a discourse on his own identity as the "true vine" (Jn 15:1).[29]

Admittedly, it matters little, in the end, whether describing one's footwear as "ambrosial" implies their life-giving quality by way of a more hardwired synonymity, as adopted by Murray and Prost, or in the more visually involved manner suggested in the preceding paragraph. Either way the vivificationist associations of the footwear

---

[27] Roscher (1883: 39) writes,

> Die Alten sich Nektar und Ambrosia nicht als verschiedene Substanzen, sondern nur als verschiedene Formen derselben Substanz dachten, welche flüssig das berauschende Getränk, in festerer Form aber die Speise der Götter bildete. So kam es, dass die beiden Benennungen Nektar und Ambrosia hie und da mit einander vertauscht werden konnten, so dass ἀμβροσία auch das Getränk, νέκταρ auch die Speise der Götter bezeichnete."

See Homer, *Od.* 9.359. At Homer, *Il.* 19.347, ambrosia is liquid.

[28] The use of θεόπνευστος as a prod for an intertextual reading recalls Whitby's (2007: 206) description: "Beneath the glittering opulence of Nonnus' adjectives lies a carefully contrived and allusive purpose, a witty display of erudition, unobtrusive but responsive to probing, with links both to classical literature and to contemporary theological discussion." Miguélez Cavero (2008: 316) writes,

> The editions of the *Paraphrase* agree that Nonnus' technique of "translation" includes the substitution of κοινή terms with epicisms; pronouns and demonstrative adjectives are replaced with more elaborate forms or nominal expressions; free temporal uses are replaced with a complex set of substitutions (e.g. imperfect instead of aorist in indicative, imperfect and aorist instead of historical present); syntactical rewriting (e.g. he frequently substitutes a relative phrase for a participle).

(Schmitz [2009: 178] notes the pervasiveness of this feature in the *Dionysiaca*.) Harries (1994: 64) even speaks of Nonnus' borrowings as a sort of empire-building. Cf. Liebeschuetz's (1996: 80) list of possible literary echoes in the *Dionysiaca*. On Homer's influence in Christian writings of the period, see Sandnes (2011: 31).

[29] Kröll (2014: 255) writes,

> Clearly it is not Nonnus' main interest to present Ampelus—who is hardly known in traditional mythology—as an independent and autonomous figure within his epic narrative. With this rhetorical technique applied here by the poet we can catch an early glimpse of the goal of both the Ampelus-episode and the whole of the *Dionysiaca*. It is not Ampelus but Dionysus who should be characterized here.

are secure: *Para.* 9.173 and 11.113 describe Jesus's feet as *life-giving*. The same is almost certainly true of 1.99.

1.2 *Paraphrase* 2.89 (*ad* Jn 2:17)

We can deal with the remaining appearances of θεόπνευστος more summarily.

Nonnus' second use of θεόπνευστος is the one listed above as ambiguous. The word appears in *Para.* 2.89 as a designation of Scripture, in connection with the Fourth Gospel's quotation of Ps. 69:9:

> *Para.* 2.88–90
> his disciples recalled
> that it was written in the theopneustic book (θεοπνεύστῳ ... βίβλῳ),
> "My zeal for your sacred house devours me." (Author's translation)[30]

The context would seem to allow for either an inspirationist or a vivificationist understanding of θεόπνευστος. Past renderings of this passage, of course, are all based on the former.[31]

That Scripture should be described here as "inspired" makes sense, of course, in the light of Origen's influential views on the nature of Scripture's authority. That Scripture should be described as "life-giving," however, makes sense in the light of the Fourth Gospel's later reference to the Pharisees "suppos[ing] they have life" in Scripture, and to Jesus' corrective claim that Scripture's life-giving role consisted in its pointing *to him* (Jn 5:39). As Scripture is quoted here (in Jn 2:17) as pointing to Jesus, and as the disciples themselves make that connection, it might be especially appropriate if Nonnus intended an echo of Jn 5:39.[32] That he did so, however, is far from certain. Thus we cannot use this appearance of θεόπνευστος as unequivocal support for our case, but we *can* understand it in light of that case.

1.3 *Paraphrase* 4.2 (*ad* Jn 4:1)

Θεόπνευστος also appears in *Para.* 4.2:

> Nonnus, *Para.* 4.1–6
> And when the Lord found out,

---

[30] See Livrea (2000: 272–3).

[31] Le Comte de Marcellus (1861: 15) translates 2.89 as: "Or les disciples se souvinrent qu'il est écrit dans le livre inspiré de Dieu: Le zèle de ta divine maison me dévore." Livrea (2000: 149) translates as: "I discepoli allora si ricordarono di quanto è vergato nel libro ispirato da Dio: 'Mi divora lo zelo della tua divina casa.'" Sherry (1991: 180) translates as: "The disciples remembered what was engraved in the god-inspired book, 'The zeal of your holy house devours me.'" Prost (2003: 58) translates as: "That it was written in their God-inspired book: / 'My zeal for your sacred house devours me.'"

[32] Prost (2003: 85) translates Nonnus' rendering (5.154–58) of Jn 5:39 as follows: "Ye seek for written rules from God-dictated books; / From them you hope to have, in future time to come, / Eternal life. But see, those very books you prize, / They shout my prophecy in voice oracular / Like deathless trumpets. " Cf. González's (2000: 286) translation of Nonnus' ζωὴν οὐ μινύθουσαν as "non-diminishing life."

that those around the theopneustic baths (θεοπνεύστων … λοετρῶν)—
viz. the heavy-hearted, difficult swarm of zealous Pharisees—
had heard how Jesus, drawing the wandering men to the light,
baptized in water, and had more disciples
than John. (Author's translation)

The Count of Marseilles rendered θεοπνεύστων … λοετρῶν as "purifications inspirée de Dieu" (Le Comte de Marcellus 1861: 24). Mariangela Caprara (2005: 118, 143) rendered it as "battesimo ispirato da Dio" and connected this description with Jesus's reference to baptizing "in Spirito Santo."[33] It seems unlikely, however, that λοετρῶν would be used of spirit baptism, and it makes little exegetical or narrative sense to speak of spirit baptism in this context.

The use of θεόπνευστος in 4.2 appears to possess a vivificationist meaning, as the purpose of the baptismal rite of Jesus (or rather of his disciples) was to bestow life through a gesture of repentance. Caprara (2005: 143) finds in the designation of these baptisms as "theopneustic" a pointed contrast with the baptisms administered by John, described by Nonnus in *Para.* 1.121, as a new birth "not by fire or the spirit" (ἀπύροισι καὶ ἀπνεύστοισι λοετροῖς). It matters little where we locate Nonnus' understanding of the Johannine baptism along the spectrum from Jewish purity ritual and the baptismal rite of the Great Church: a connection with the giving of life is ready to hand in any case.

1.4 *Paraphrase* 10.136 (*ad* Jn 10:38)

Θεόπνευστος also appears in *Para.* 10.131b–38:

If I do not accomplish my life-giving (ζωαρκέος) father's work,
do not believe me. But if through life-giving words (βιοδώτορι μύθῳ)
from my eternal father I perform works of merit—
such that you looked upon as eyewitnesses—
then learn from these theopneustic words (θεοπνεύστῳ … μύθῳ).
As my father works through me, so also I with him
appear yoked together, undivided, with my father. (Author's translation)

Here again, it is clear that θεόπνευστος means "life-giving," and not "inspired."[34] We should note, in particular, the parallelism between θεοπνεύστῳ τινὶ μύθῳ ("theopneustic words") in line 136 and βιοδώτορι μύθῳ ("life-saving words") in line 133. Both expressions are developments of the reference to ζωαρκέος ἔργα τοκῆος ("life-giving father's work") in line 132.

---

[33] Cf. Sherry's (1991: 186) rendering: "And when the lord recognized that the heavy-hearted contentious swarm of extremely jealous Pharisees had heard about the god-inspired lustrations."

[34] Contra Le Comte de Marcellus (1861: 80): "langage inspiré de Dieu." Contra Sherry's (1991: 228) "god-inspired report."

8

In Lieu of a Conclusion: Inspirationism's Waning as a Blessing in Disguise—The Truth of the Gospel vs. the "Truth" of Scripture in Evangelical and Postconservative Hermeneutics

Benjamin Jowett (1860: 344) once warned,

> Errors about words, and the attribution to words themselves of an excessive importance, lie at the root of theological as of other confusions. In theology they are more dangerous than in other sciences, because they cannot so readily be brought to the test of facts.[1]

This book has attempted to demonstrate that the philological profile for θεόπνευστος links the term to two very different semantic fields. One group of witnesses uses the word in the sense of vivification. This use is widespread, but it takes on a narrow technical meaning within a NT context, where it refers to the life-giving quality of the gospel. A second use of θεόπνευστος resignifies the word, giving it the now familiar sense of inspiration. This meaning apparently owes its rise to the influence of Philonic thought upon the Alexandrian Christian tradition, along with (perhaps) a misreading of Porphyry on Origen's part. Although the verbal-inspirationist meaning has ruled in the minds of translators and commentators, the vivificationist meaning represents the thought of 2 Tim. 3:16. Rather than refer to "all scripture" as "inspired," the author of 2 Timothy calls attention to Scripture's "life-giving" quality, a quality it has by virtue of conveying the life-giving gospel.

Where does all this take us? If Christians can be persuaded that Scripture nowhere claims to be inspired, what impact might that have on their understanding of Christian theology in general? For many, such an admission would precipitate a crisis—perhaps even a crisis of *faith*. Since the time of Origen, the Christian understanding of the

---

[1] Teeple (1960: 165) writes, "A … weakness of theological presuppositions is that they resist all change. They tend to become dictators which control men's minds, and men are afraid to change them. As a group, scientists are far more willing to admit that they have been mistaken and more ready to change their presuppositions than are theologians."

nature of Scripture has been so thoroughly ensconced in the notion of Scripture's inspiration that any attempt to break free from that notion will seem like trying to remove the ground floor from an elaborate house of cards.

For those who base Scripture's authority on its (supposed) inspired status, the payoff for that status is a guarantee that the text is *true*. Turning this around, we might say that the degree (or level of detail) to which one holds the text to be true is indexed to one's commitment to the doctrine of inspiration. The *inspiration* of Scripture and the *truth* of Scripture have gone hand in hand. If the inspirationist understanding of Scripture's authority should be called into question, what will become of biblical *truth*? This question represents the sort of fear that motivates many defenses of the inspiration of Scripture.[2]

Most Christians assume, as a matter of basic commitment, that the Bible is "true" in some *thoroughgoing* way—it is not enough merely to affirm the truth of its kerygmatic center. The title of a popular-level article by Luke Timothy Johnson spells this out at the level of presupposition: It asks "How is the Bible true?" rather than "How *much in* the Bible is true?" In his final paragraph, Johnson (2009: 16) places his fundamental assumption on the table, by referring to the Bible's proper readers as "those who ascribe absolute truth to it."[3] But why should Johnson assume that the Bible must be "true" in a thoroughgoing way? One answer is that Christians generally are thought of as "Bible believers," so that "believing the Bible" is something they should do. And to be a "believer" in something, of course, is to assume it to be true.

1 The Evangelical and Postconservative Tracks

There have been two tracks by which the truth of "inspired" Scripture has generally been understood. These tracks have Augustine and Origen for their figureheads. Both men taught that Scripture was thoroughly inspired, but they differed in that Augustine defended the historical accuracy of everything in Scripture, while Origen allowed for Scripture's narrative account to contain historical inaccuracies.

Augustine tied the inspiration of Scripture to the factual accuracy of its narrative. Truth and accuracy, to his way of thinking, are nearly synonymous.[4] Origen could accept—even welcome—material disagreements among the Evangelists, but Augustine ruled out that scenario: the truth of Scripture, for him, is a matter of its historical accuracy. Apparent discrepancies must be responsive to harmonization. Augustine stated his guiding principle as follows: "If I do find anything in those books which seems contrary to truth, I decide that either the text is corrupt, or the translator did not follow what was really said, or that I failed to understand it" (*Ep. 82* [trans. Parsons 1951: 392]). The need to harmonize extends to matters of the gospels' chronologies, so

---

[2] E.g., Murray (1940: 74) writes, "It is obvious ... that our work and purpose are determined by our conception of what the Bible is. And what the Bible is is just the question of its inspiration."

[3] Another popular-level article that builds upon the assumption that the Bible must somehow be true in a thoroughgoing way is Placher (1995).

[4] I do not mean to imply that this way of thinking is wrong. See below.

that reading the Fourth Gospel in parallel with the Synoptics requires us to understand that Jesus cleansed the Temple *twice* (*Cons.* 2.129; see Barker 2015: 5–6).[5] (In the sixteenth century, Andreas Osiander would beat Augustine at this game by claiming that Jesus cleansed the Temple *three* times [see Strickland 2014: 13–14]!)[6] Augustine even wrote a lengthy treatise (*De consensu evangelistarum*) attempting to iron out the disagreements between the gospels.

By contrast, Origen went out of his way, by some accounts, to multiply the inaccuracies in the scriptural narrative, because he held that they serve as an indication, for the reader, that the true meaning of the passage at hand lies at a deeper, "spiritual" level.[7] In his words,

> The Word of God has arranged for certain stumbling-blocks, as it were, and hindrances and impossibilities to be inserted in the midst of the law and the history, in order that we may not be completely drawn away by the sheer attractiveness of the language, and so either reject the true doctrines absolutely, on the ground that we learn from the scriptures nothing worthy of God, or else by never moving away from the letter fail to learn anything of the more divine element. (*Princ.* 4.2.9 [trans. Butterworth 1936: 285])

Thus the Bible, for Origen, is a *true* text, but its truth is often a matter of reading it *in spite of* its inaccuracies. As James Barker (2015: 3) notes, "Origen attempted to defend the inspiration, reliability, and veracity of the gospels by privileging spiritual truth over historical truth."[8] Origen writes,

> I do not condemn, I suppose, the fact that [the four evangelists] have also made some minor changes in what happened so far as history is concerned, with a view to the usefulness of the mystical object of [those matters]. Consequently, they have related what happened in [this] place as though it happened in another, or that happened at this time as though at another time, and they have composed what is reported in this manner with a certain degree of distortion. For their intention was to speak the truth spiritually and materially at the same time where that was possible but, where it was not possible in both ways to prefer the spiritual to the

---

[5] Augustine did, however, allow some lesser chronological disagreements to stand. See Schökel (1965: 115–16).

[6] By contrast, Origen asserts that the Temple cleansing never happened at all (*Comm. Joh.* 10.20–34).

[7] Kalin (1967: 50–1) writes,

> The reader of scripture is alerted to press on to the spiritual meaning by things like trivialities, incongruities, inconsistencies. It is clear that the spiritual meaning itself is what is important and that it does not just function for Origen as an "out" in the face of some offensive passage. For he often creates difficulties where they do not obviously appear, so that he can hasten beyond the letter.

Farrar (1886: 191) writes, "[Origen's] system rose in reality not from reverence for the Scriptures, but from a dislike to their plain sense which had at all costs to be set aside." But cf. Crouzel's pushback (1989: 63) against such an assessment: "Origen's objection to the literal meaning bears only on unimportant details which often represent only manners of speech arising from a certain rhetoric."

[8] Trigg (1988: 164) writes, "truth, for Origen, is not factual information but saving knowledge."

material. The spiritual truth is often preserved in the material falsehood so to speak. (*Comm. Joh.* 10.5.19–20 [trans. Heine 1989: 259])[9]

If the Bible can be shown to be false in some historical particular, then (according to this line of reasoning) the nature of the Bible's truth should be sought in something other than the referential integrity of its surface claims. Modern proponents of an Origenistic spiritual sense typically divide the provisions for that sense between typological readings (in which the surface sense of the text remains true and useful) and allegorical readings (in which the surface sense is *no longer* true or useful).[10] It is not uncommon for those most beholden to Origen's views to dispense with his use of allegory, seeing it as a reading mode that threatens the gospel narrative.[11] Those who do so often align his use of typology with his Jewish inheritance, and his use of allegory with his (non-Jewish) Hellenistic inheritance. As Peter Martens (2008) has shown, however, this division of terminology cannot be easily aligned with Origen's thinking on the matter.[12]

Augustine and Origen have their philosophical and methodological counterparts in today's theological scene. The former is the father of Evangelicalism, while the latter is the father of a bevy of "postconservative" approaches, including postliberalism (loosely associated with "narrative theology"), the canonical approach, and other (Barth-style) "literal sense" approaches. But we should say, at this point, that neither Origen nor Augustine can be blamed for the excesses of their modern progeny. Origen had no inkling of North American narrative theology's attempt to smuggle a text-bound understanding of "meaning" and "truth" into the church's legacy of reading Scripture,

---

[9] See Sparks (2008: 112–13).

[10] O'Keefe (2004: 49) writes that allegory "detaches a text from historical events," while typology "continues to value history by maintaining a connection." Hušek (2016: 103) writes, "Origen's exposition of passages that lack somatic meaning is close to [Paul] Ricœur's understanding of myth. Both authors emphasize the need to go beyond the letter and look for the meaning hidden behind it." See Dolidze (2013).

[11] Martens (2008: 295–6) writes,

> We are told that allegory is not Christian, but rather foreign, be it Platonic, Stoic, rabbinic, and/or Philonic (J. Daniélou, R. P. C. Hanson, W. A. Bienert, R. A. Norris); allegory is concerned with texts and not events (J. Daniélou); it is arbitrary (R. P. C. Hanson, F. Young); it is unhistorical (W. A. Bienert); it destroys narrative sequence (F. Young); it undermines the literal sense (J. D. Dawson). Typology, in contrast, is saved from these failings.

[12] Martens (2008: 307) shows that Origen, in one place (*Comm. in I Cor.* 35), "easily juxtaposes two independent Pauline expressions, one from Galatians and the other from 1 Corinthians, moving effortlessly between describing Abraham's two wives and two sons as an allegorical *and* as a typical (*or* typological) phenomenon. This piece of evidence strikingly indicates how a typological phenomenon for Origen was not opposed to an allegorical one." He writes, "There is no hint that Origen opposes the 'typic' terms in exegetical contexts to 'allegory.' Not only is a τύπος, as a figure of speech, synonymous with an 'allegory,' but the nonliteral interpretation of this τύπος is *itself an allegorical interpretation*. The very task of the allegorical interpretation of a τύπος is to discern its ἀλήθεια." O'Keefe (2004: 49) similarly writes, "Origen and other ancient authors did not … consistently distinguish between typology and allegory." See Crouzel (1989: 64, 80–2). Childs (1993: 35) writes, "Once [Origen's] method of interpretation is correctly understood then it … becomes apparent why the sharp distinction between allegory and typology, which was still defended by Daniélou does not apply." See Clark (1999: 70–103); Mitchell (2009: 185–6); Parsons (2015: 51–2).

and Augustine was careful to warn against the damage inflicted on the Gospel's credibility when believers wield naïve views about scientific matters.

1.1 Evangelicals and Postconservatives on the Presumed "Truth" of Scripture

Evangelicals live by the slogan "The Bible says it—I believe it."[13] For them, the believer's commitment to the truth of Scripture constitutes a readiness to believe in the referential integrity of every passage that (formally) purports to convey a matter of history or cosmology.[14] If Scripture says that Methuselah lived 969 years, then there really was a man named "Methuselah," and he really lived 969 years. If Scripture says that God flooded the earth in the days of Noah and that he charged Noah with saving a remnant of every animal species, many Evangelicals would bet their bottom dollar that it really happened. Such a commitment also implies that there can be no material inconsistencies between parallel accounts in Scripture. Thus James W. Scott (2009a: 150) is being a good Evangelical (but a poor scholar) when he derides Herman Ridderbos's willingness to let Scripture take him where it will: "When Ridderbos appeals to God's freedom to allow one evangelist to 'correct' another one, he has pushed it too far, in effect making God deny himself."[15] This view that the voice of Scripture is *everywhere* the voice of God is, for many, the hallmark of Evangelical identity.

"For many," that is, but not for all: In fairness, I should point out that Evangelicals differ among themselves on Scripture's more difficult claims and that, historically speaking, Ridderbos has as much right to the label "Evangelical" as Scott has (see Harris 2015: 335). While some on the more Fundamentalist side of the aisle are fully capable of believing that the universe is only 6000 years old, others relent of this sort of biblicism when it brings to bear such an enormous intellectual burden. Augustine was savvy enough to prefer good science over the bid to read Scripture as a handbook on cosmology and nature:

> It is a disgraceful and dangerous thing for an infidel to hear a Christian, presumably giving the meaning of Holy Scripture, talking nonsense on these topics; and we should take all means to prevent such an embarrassing situation, in which people show up vast ignorance in a Christian and laugh it to scorn. The shame is not so much that an ignorant individual is derided, but that people outside the

---

[13] Harris (2006: 810) writes, "Their apologetic stance ... is that we must know that the Bible is true before we can go on to say anything else concerning God. Without a reliable Bible, they fear either that they cannot get started in faith, or that their faith must surely collapse." Dodd (1960: 21) writes,

> The most determined "Fundamentalists" do not show any strong desire to force into general acceptance *every* statement of Scripture. They are rather concerned either to maintain the dogma of infallibility for its own sake, because it seems to them a part of Christianity, or to protect certain cherished beliefs which they would not leave at the mercy of an irreligious criticism.

[14] As Noll (1991: 145) writes, "When evangelicals say that the Bible is true, they are usually making a series of interrelated affirmations about the nature of the world, the character of religion, and the structure of epistemology."

[15] On Evangelical resistance to differences between the gospels, see Strickland (2014).

household of faith think our sacred writers held such opinions, and, to the great loss of those for whose salvation we toil, the writers of our Scripture are criticized and rejected as unlearned men. If they find a Christian mistaken in a field which they themselves know well and hear him maintaining his foolish opinions about our books, how are they going to believe those books in matters concerning the resurrection of the dead, the hope of eternal life, and the kingdom of heaven, when they think their pages are full of falsehoods and on facts which they themselves have learnt from experience and the light of reason? (*De Genesi ad litteram* 1.19.39 [trans. Taylor 1982: 42–3])[16]

While Evangelicals have Augustine for their figurehead, not all follow him in the wisdom of these restraints. Not a few have wielded their principles with precisely the sort of recklessness that Augustine deplored and set themselves up as enemies of science. (In so doing, of course, they often say that they are not against science per se, but only against science as actually practiced.)

What about the postconservative view? Given that postconservatives share the presumption that the Bible is true, how should we expect them to handle the notion of "truth" when it becomes clear that the Bible contains factual errors? As the falsity of Scripture, in part or whole, is not admissible on the terms of the reigning presumption, the only way one can admit the existence of factual errors in Scripture is to neutralize those errors by redefining "truth" in non-propositional terms. Anyone even marginally aware of recent Anglo-American theological trends (especially the conglomeration of approaches going under the name "Theological Interpretation of Scripture") will recognize the commonness of this gesture.[17] The last thirty years of theological

---

[16] Cf. Sparks (2008: 12).

[17] Barr (1989: 8) argued that most scholars (even historical-critical scholars) hold to "something with some likeness to allegory" in their reading of Scripture, because they want to make Scripture true in a way that gives their work purpose. Unfortunately, the response to Barr on this score has turned on his idiosyncratic use of "allegory" and has missed his larger point altogether. Barr (1977: 54) elsewhere writes,

> People tended to say, yes, the Bible is of course right, but not in the literal sense in which the fundamentalists take it; that is, people held to the rightness of what the Bible says, but tried to take it in a more indirect sense, to make it apply in a more vague and general way. Sometimes, indeed, this approach may be justified. But at many points the reverse must be said: the text should indeed be understood "literally," in that the literal sense was the one intended by the author, but this must mean that, in passing from the sense of the text to the statement of what happened, or to a statement of the real theological entities involved, one must make a critical reconstruction which does not follow the exact lines of the text: in other words one must take a line that for the fundamentalist means that the text is "wrong." The common criticism of fundamentalism for being "literal" has too often been a plea for a vaguer understanding of scripture, when what was needed was a critical approach to scripture.

It is worth noting that this tactic of safeguarding the "truth" of Scripture by complexifying the notion of truth has been mirrored in recent efforts to safeguard the supposed "unity" of Scripture (a purely Origenist value)—e.g., Hays (2011: 29–30) writes, "If we fail to find unity in Scripture it may be because the unity we are looking for is too simple; our criteria for coherence are too flat and literalistic. ... We may fail to find unity in the Bible because we are looking for it in too narrow a textual field."

writing has been characterized (to the point of banality) by a glib ridiculing of the "Enlightenment" notion of "propositional truth."

Although Origen thought it was the truth of the "spiritual" reading of Scripture that needed safeguarding, his approach does not represent an anticipation of the postconservative bid to redefine truth as the internal coherence of the biblical narrative. In calling Origen a figurehead for postconservativism, therefore, I must admit the fit is less than perfect. That is not because postconservatives have out-origenized Origen or improved on him in any way. Rather, it is because they have fallen for some rather poor thought habits underpinning a number of projects in Continental philosophy. Where Origen sought to *relocate* truth, postconservatives have sought to *redefine* it.

If "truth" is not "propositional," then what (according to postconservatives) is it? What revisionist models are available for the reader who wants Scripture to be "true" in a thoroughgoing way but who is unwilling to adopt the Evangelical strategies of forced harmonization and of exalting Scripture over science? The basic options are two in number: (1) the reader can define "truth" as a text-determined commodity (like the inner coherence of Scripture's narrative) or (2) he/she can define "truth" as agreement with the Bible's reception by the church, so that the reading strategies of the Bible's intended readers define what is true. Both strategies pit themselves against the usual "correspondence" understanding of truth found in the Augustinian approach.[18] The early Hans Frei is a leading example of someone who followed the first approach—that is, who defined "truth" and "meaning" as text-determined commodities.[19] Frei's colleague Brevard Childs (1970: 104) exemplifies the second approach. Childs writes,

> In our opinion, the claim for the inspiration of Scripture is the claim for the uniqueness of the canonical context of the church through which the Holy Spirit works. Although there are innumerable other contexts in which to place the Bible— this is part of the humanity of the witness—divine inspiration is a way of claiming a special prerogative for this one context. The Bible, when understood as the Scriptures of the church, functions as the vehicle for God's special communicating of himself to this church and the world.

There is obviously something very Origenist about extending inspiration in this way. As Albert Sundberg, Jr. (1975: 364) notes, "Origen affirms the identity of the Spirit of truth who revealed the spiritual interpretation to the apostles with the Spirit who reveals the spiritual interpretation to the church" (see Jacobsen 2010: 290).[20]

---

[18] I purposely avoid using the word "theory" (as in "correspondence theory") in this context, as it is a misnomer. The word "truth" is not a nomenclature, in the sense of naming something empirically defined (like a cloud or a pine tree), but is a conceptual term outfitted with alternative definitions. As such, "truth" per se is not something about which one can theorize, and invoking a particular use of the word "truth" is not a form of theorizing.

[19] The development of Frei's views is chronicled in Placher (1993).

[20] See the appreciative discussion of Origen in Childs (1977: 81; 1993: 32–5).

1.2 Escaping the Augustinian and Origenist Rat Races

The recent return of the Origenist paradigm is based partly on perceived problems with the understanding of truth bound up with the Augustinian paradigm, but the fact of the matter is that the neo-Origenist response takes a bad situation and makes it worse. When all is said and done, there is *nothing* wrong (or "modernist") about the understanding of truth underpinning the Evangelical approach to Scripture. The problem with the Evangelical approach lies elsewhere: with its insistence that the Bible is true in a *thoroughgoing* way.

But there is good news, which is that the Christian doesn't have to ground his/her theological musings in the mistaken commitments that characterize Church history or Continental philosophy. The extrication of history's bibliological errors doesn't have to be as systemically threatening as some make it to be. The New Testament itself shows what Christian theology looked like before things became so complicated. If the earliest Christians managed to profess and preach the Gospel without embroiling it in doctrines about Scripture's inspiration, infallibility, and/or inerrancy, shouldn't that be an indication that we can do the same?[21] In point of fact, while Christians have long taken Scripture or the church as the epistemic ground of their faith, the earliest Christian communities took the *Gospel* as that ground. Arranging things the same way as the apostles and the churches they founded, we should look on Scripture as a collection of religiously relevant and helpful writings (portions of which are prophetically inspired), and as the medium in which the Gospel has been passed down through the ages, but *not* as an infallible, all-relevant corpus whose inspired status lends authority to the Gospel. The Gospel's epistemic guarantee (historically and philosophically) precedes the canon. It comes from the apostolic witness. According to Barr (1980: 33–4),

> When people say that Christianity is dependent on historical events, in the sense that but for these events the faith would be vain, the number of events that they have in mind is quite small; and this is the difference between scripture and

---

[21] Barr (1980: 118–19) writes,

> The core of the New Testament faith in its early days was not a written text or a scripture but the preaching of Jesus Christ crucified and risen. There is no indication that the production of a "New Testament" parallel in type or in authority to the Old was envisaged in the beginning. Jesus nowhere commanded that a written account of his deeds or sayings should be put down and nowhere did he sanction, much less command, the production of a New Testament. And, in spite of the full honour and authority ascribed to the Old Testament as the word of God, it does not follow from this that early Christianity was thereby designed or understood to be a scriptural religion in the way in which the Old Testament religion, as seen not from within the early Old Testament situation itself but from within the perspectives of the first century AD, was a scriptural religion. For the undoubted authority of the Old Testament and its undisputed status as word of God did not mean for the men of the New Testament that it was the communicator of salvation, and in particular not the communicator of salvation for the Gentiles. Only the preaching of Jesus Christ as crucified and risen communicated salvation in the Christian sense. The Old Testament might well confirm and support that word of salvation, it might have prophesied it from ancient times, but it no longer was in itself that word.

creeds. The passion and resurrection of Jesus Christ is the main specific historical reference in the creeds. Scripture on the other hand mentions large numbers of historical or apparently historical events, but no one supposes that all of these bear a relation to Christianity analogical to Jesus' crucifixion under Pontius Pilate or his resurrection from the dead.[22]

The New Testament's authority does *not* derive from any sort of inspiration or other guarantee of infallibility. Rather, it comes from the (faith-embraced) fact that the apostles told the truth about what they had witnessed.[23] Since eyewitnesses plainly can tell the truth without being inspired to do so, a doctrine of inspiration is an unnecessary complication, and it does not really answer to the main type of guarantee that the New Testament gives about the truth of the kerygma—which is simply the word of eyewitnesses.[24] When Mark Noll (1991: 143) writes that "the most important conviction of evangelical scholars is that the Bible is true," we can add (in the vein of a history-of-ideas remark) that the most important conviction of *the apostles* was that the *Gospel* is true.[25] The choice before us is whether to throw in with the church or with the apostles.

In this light, we should welcome the sort of bibliology suggested by Richard Longenecker (2004: 53):

> What we have in the NT are (1) *declarations* of the gospel and the ethical principles that derive from the gospel, as principally contained in the early Christian confessions, and (2) *descriptions*—whether in the form of Gospels, letters, accounts of representative exploits, sermons, tractates, or an apocalypse—of how

---

[22] Barr's detractors never tire of painting him as a liberal, but, as Sparks (2008: 199) notes, "his theological destinations can tend toward the conservative end of the spectrum." See Goldingay (1977); Barton (2016: 273–4).

[23] Althaus (1959: 50–1) writes,

> It is not enough to say that because the word is the word of God, it has its authority in itself. This by no means fully expresses the specific authority of the apostolic preaching. In addition to the distinguishing mark of its particular content—to use Luther's expression, "it deals with Christ"—it has this other characteristic, that in it we have to deal with the "first witnesses," with a witness given in historical proximity and immediate relationship to the history of Jesus. The general concept of the word of God does not underline this special content. So it is not enough to say, in relation to the apostolic *kerygma*: "The word, just because it is the word of God, has its authority in itself." For this statement does not do justice to the historical element in the authority. Nor may this historical element be overlooked even in the contemporary preaching of the Church; its authority depends on the fact that the present word of preaching is interpretation of the apostolic witness, whose authority depends on its "authenticity"—that is, on the historical reference, that it goes back to the witnesses of the history of Jesus, including the Resurrection.

[24] Alexander (an avid inerrantist) conceded this point long ago (1838: 222): "A book may be authentic, without having the least claim to inspiration, as are all true narratives of facts, written by men of veracity in the exercise of their unassisted powers."

[25] Barr (1980: 34) writes, "There is a wide gap between the actual narrative form and detailed content of the Bible and the ground that can be covered by any argument from the soteriological function of events."

that gospel proclamation and its inherent principles were contextualized in diverse cultural contexts, circumstances, and situations during the apostolic period.

Others might offer equally deserving assizes of the New Testament—the important thing is that we allow it to be what it *appears* to be. It is time to submit postbiblical dogma to the rule of exegesis and common sense. And it is time for those who have always known that it is the Gospel (rather than Scripture) that gives Christian theology its epistemic ground to come in from the cold. The NT Christian is not a Bible believer but a *Gospel* believer.[26]

---

[26] See the chapter on "Staying Evangelical," in Barr (1984: 156–62). Cf. Nicholson and Barton (2013: xxiii–xxiv): "Introducing a conceptual space between the gospel and the Bible enables one to be more relaxed about biblical interpretation and thus more likely to read what is actually there in Scripture rather than what one would like to find. Distancing the Bible from theology is essential if the Bible is to be properly interpreted."

Bibliography

Aageson, James W., 2012, "Genesis in the Deutero-Pauline Epistles," in Maarten, J. J. Menken and Steve Moyise (eds.), *Genesis in the New Testament*, 117–29, LNTS 466, London: Bloomsbury.

Abraham, William J., 1981, *The Divine Inspiration of Holy Scripture*, Oxford: Oxford University Press.

Abraham, William J., 1998, *Canon and Criterion in Christian Theology: From the Fathers to Feminism*, Oxford: Oxford University Press.

Accorinti, Domenico, 1990, "Sull'autore degli scoli mitologici alle orazioni di Gregorio di Nazianzo," *Byz* 60 (1–2): 5–24.

Accorinti, Domenico, 1995, "Hermes e Cristo in Nonno," *Prometheus* 21: 24–32.

Accorinti, Domenico, 2008, *Nonno di Panopoli, Le Dionisiache. Volume quarto (canti XL–XLVIII)*, 2nd ed., Biblioteca Universale Rizzoli, Milan: Classici Greci e Latini.

Accorinti, Domenico, 2016, "The Poet from Panopolis: An Obscure Biography and a Controversial Figure," in Domenico Accorinti (ed.), *Brill's Companion to Nonnus of Panopolis*, 11–53, BCCS, Leiden: Brill.

Achtemeier, Paul J., 1980, *The Inspiration of Scripture: Problems and Proposals*, Biblical Perspectives on Current Issues, Philadelphia: Westminster.

Agati Madeira, Eliane Maria, 2004, "La *lex Oppia* et la condition juridique de la femme dans la Rome républicaine," *Revue internationale des droits de l'antiquité* 51: 87–99.

Agosti, Gianfranco, 2003, *Nonno di Panopoli, Parafrasi del Vangelo di San Giovanni, Canto Quinto*, Studi e Testi 22, Firenze: Università degli Studi di Firenze.

Agostini, Giulio, 2009, "Buddhist Dreams, Wet Dreams and Herophilus of Alexandria," in Daniela Boccassini (ed.), *Sogni e visioni nel mondo indo-mediterraneo*, 91–105, Quaderni di Studi Indo-Mediterranei 2, Alessandria: Orso.

Ahrens, Karl, 1885, *Zur Geschichte des sogenannten Physiologus*, Ploen: Hirt.

Ahrens, Karl, 1892, *Das "Buch der Naturgegenstände,"* Kiel: Haeseler.

Aicher, Peter J., 1993, "Terminal Display Fountains (*Mostre*) and the Aqueducts of Ancient Rome," *Phoenix* 47 (4): 339–52.

Aicher, Peter J., 1995, *Guide to the Aqueducts of Ancient Rome*, Wauconda, IL: Bolchazy–Carducci.

Alexander, Archibald, 1838, *Evidences of the Authenticity, Inspiration, and Canonical Authority of the Holy Scriptures*, rev. ed., Philadelphia: Presbyterian Board of Publication.

Alexandre, Charles (ed.), 1841, *Oracula Sibyllina*, Paris: Didot.

Alexandre, Charles (ed.), 1869, *Oracula Sibyllina*, 2nd ed., Paris: Didot.

Alkier, Stefan, 2013, *The Reality of the Resurrection: The New Testament Witness*, Waco: Baylor University Press.

Allert, Craig D., 2007, *A High View of Scripture? The Authority of the Bible and the Formation of the New Testament Canon*, Evangelical Ressourcement, Grand Rapids, MI: Baker Academic.

Allison, Dale C., Jr., 2003, *Testament of Abraham*, CEJL, Berlin: de Gruyter.

Alpers, Klaus, 1984, "Untersuchungen zum griechischen Physiologus und den Kyraniden," in Heimo Reinitzer (ed.), *All Geschöpf ist Zung´ und Mund: Beiträge aus dem Grenzbereich von Naturkunde und Theologie*, 13–87, Vestigia Bibliae 6, Hamburg: Wittig.

Alpers, Klaus, 1996, "Physiologus," *TRE* 26: 596–602.

Alpers, Klaus, 2007, "Physiologus," *BNP* 11: 227–8.

Alt, Karin, 1993, *Weltflucht und Weltbejahung: Zur Frage des Dualismus bei Plutarch, Numenios, Plotin*, Akademie der Wissenschaften und der Literatur: Abhandlungen der geistes- und sozialwissenschaftlichen Klasse 8, Mainz: Akademie der Wissenschaften und der Literatur.

Althaus, Paul, 1959, *Fact and Faith in the Kerygma of Today*, Philadelphia: Muhlenberg.

Amandry, Pierre, 1984, "Le Culte des Nymphes et de Pan à l'Antre Corycien," in *L'Antre Corycien, II*, 395–425, BCHSup 9, Paris: Boccard.

Ammann, Hermann, 1956, "Zum griechischen Verbaladjektiv auf –τός," in *ΜΝΗΜΗΣ ΧΑΡΙΝ: Gedenkschrift Paul Kretschmer*, 1.10–23, 2 vols., Wien: Wiener Sprachgesellschaft.

Anderson-Stojanović, Virginia R., 1987, "The Chronology and Function of Ceramic Unguentaria," *AJA* 91 (1): 105–22.

Andò, Valeria, 1996, "*Nymphe*: la sposa e la Ninfe," *QUCC* 52: 47–79.

Arbel, Vita Daphna, 2012, *Forming Feminity in Antiquity: Eve, Gender, and Ideologies in the Greek Life of Adam and Eve*, Oxford: Oxford University Press.

Arena, Renato, 1983, "Per la lettura di due iscrizioni greche arcaiche," *ZPE* 53: 99–102.

Artola, Antonio M., 1999, "El momento de la inspiración en la constitución de la escritura según 2 Tim 3,16," *EstBíb* 57 (1–4): 61–82.

Asiedu-Peprah, Martin, 2001, *Johannine Sabbath Conflicts as Juridical Controversy*, WUNT 2/132, Tübingen: Mohr-Siebeck.

Assmann, Jan, 1997, *Moses the Egyptian: The Memory of Egypt in Western Monotheism*, Cambridge: Harvard University Press.

Assmann, Jan, 1999, *Ägyptische Hymnen und Gebete: Übersetzt, kommentiert und eingeleitet*, 2nd ed., Freiburg: Universitätsverlag.

Atchley, E. G. Cuthbert F., 1909, *A History of the Use of Incense in Divine Worship*, Alcuin Club Collections 13, London: Longmans, Green.

Athanassakis, Apostolos N. (trans.), 1977, *The Orphic Hymns: Text, Translation and Notes*, SBLTT 12, Greco-Roman Religion Series 4, Missoula, MT: Scholars Press.

Athanassiadi, Polymnia, 1992, *Julian: An Intellectual Biography*, London: Routledge.

Auffarth, Christoph, 1992, "Protecting Strangers: Establishing a Fundamental Value in the Religions of the Ancient Near East and Ancient Greece," *Numen* 39 (2): 193–216.

Aune, David E., 1997, *Revelation 1–5*, WBC 52a, Waco: Word.

Aupert, Pierre, 1974, *Le Nymphée de Tipasa et les Nymphées et "Septizonia" Nord-Africains*, Collection de l'École française de Rome 16, Rome: École Française de Rome.

Austin, M. R., 1981, "How Biblical is 'The Inspiration of Scripture'?," *ExpTim* 93 (3): 75–9.

Baarda, Tjitze, 2003, "The Gospel of Thomas and the Old Testament," *Proceedings of the Irish Biblical Association* 26: 1–28.

Bacchielli, Lidiano, 1995, "Apollonio Rodio e il Santuario Cireneo delle *Nymphai Chthoniai*," *QUCC* 51 (3): 133–7.

Bachvarova, Mary R., 2009, "Suppliant Danaids and Argive Nymphs in Aeschylus," *Classical Journal* 104 (4): 289–310.

Bacon, Benjamin W., 1915, "After Six Days: A New Clue for Gospel Critics," *HTR* 8 (1): 94–120.

Bacq, Philippe, 1978, *De l'ancienne à la nouvelle Alliance selon S. Irénée. Unité du livre IV de l'*Adversus Haereses, Le Sycomore, Paris: Lethielleux.

Baert, Barbara, 2016, *Locus Amoenus and the Sleeping Nymph: Ekphrasis, Silence and Genius Loci*, Studies in Iconology 3, Leuven: Peeters.

Bain, David, 1990, "'Treading Birds': An Unnoticed Use of πατέω (Cyranides, 1. 10. 27, 1. 19. 9)," in E. M. Craik (ed.), *Owls to Athens: Essays on Classical Subjects Presented to Sir Kenneth Dover*, 295–304, Oxford: Clarendon.

Bain, David, 1993, "Marcianus Graecus 512 (678) and the Text of the *Cyranides*: Some Preliminary Observations," *Rivista di Filologia e di Istruzione Classica* 121 (4): 427–49.

Bain, David, 1996, "Some Textual and Lexical Notes on *Cyranides* 'Books Five and Six'," *C&M* 47: 151–67.

Bain, David, 1998, "Eight Further Conjectures on the *Cyranides*," *Scholia* 7 (1): 121–5.

Bain, David, 2003, "ΜΕΛΑΝΙΤΙΣ ΓΗ in the *Cyranides* and Related Texts: New Evidence for the Origins and Etymology of Alchemy?," in Todd Klutz (ed.), *Magic in the Biblical World: From the Rod of Aaron to the Ring of Solomon*, 191–218, JSNTSup 245, London: T&T Clark.

Bain, David, 2006, "Koiraniden (Kyraniden)," *RAC* 21.224–32.

Baird, J. Arthur, 2002, *Holy Word: The Paradigm of New Testament Formation*, JSNTSup 224; Classics in Biblical and Theological Studies Supplements 1, Sheffield: Sheffield Academic Press.

Baldwin, Barry, 1992, "*Cyranidea*: Some Improvements," *ICS* 17 (1): 103–7.

Ballentine, Floyd G., 1904, "Some Phases of the Cult of the Nymphs," *HSCP* 15: 77–119.

Baltes, Matthias, 1975, "Numenios von Apamea und der platonische Timaios," *VC* 29 (4): 241–70.

Bannert, Herbert, and Nicole Kröll, 2016, "Nonnus and the Homeric Poems," in Domenico Accorinti (ed.), *Brill's Companion to Nonnus of Panopolis*, 481–506, BCCS, Leiden: Brill.

Barclay, John M. G., 1996, *Jews in the Mediterranean Diaspora: From Alexander to Trajan (323 BCE–117 CE)*, Edinburgh: T&T Clark.

Bardy, Gustave, 1923, *Recherches sur l'histoire du texte et des versions latines du De Principiis d'Origène*, Mémoires et Travaux 25, Paris: Champion.

Barker, James W., 2015, *John's Use of Matthew*, Emerging Scholars, Minneapolis: Fortress.

Barnes, Timothy, 1985, *Tertullian: A Historical and Literary Study*, Oxford: Clarendon.

Barns, J. W. B., and H. Zilliacus, 1960, *The Antinoopolis Papyri*, part 2, Graeco-Roman Memoirs 37, London: Egypt Exploration Society.

Barnstone, Willis, 2003, "Poimandres," in Willis Barnstone and Marvin Meyer (eds.), *The Gnostic Bible: Gnostic Texts of Mystical Wisdom from the Ancient and Medieval Worlds*, 502–11, Boston: New Seeds.

Barnstone, Willis, 2005, "Hermes Trismegistus: Poimandres," in Willis Barnstone (ed.), *The Other Bible: Jewish Pseudepigrapha, Christian Apocrypha, Gnostic Scriptures, Kabbalah, Dead Sea Scrolls*, 567–74, San Francisco: Harper.

Barr, James, 1973, *The Bible in the Modern World*, London: SCM.

Barr, James, 1977, *Fundamentalism*, London: SCM.

Barr, James, 1980, *The Scope and Authority of the Bible*, Explorations in Theology 7, London: SCM.

Barr, James, 1984, *Beyond Fundamentalism: Biblical Foundations for Evangelical Christianity*, Philadelphia: Westminster.

Barr, James, 1989, "The Literal, the Allegorical, and Modern Biblical Scholarship," *JSOT* 14 (44): 3–17.

Barrett, C. K., 1963, *The Pastoral Epistles*, New Clarendon Bible, Oxford: Clarendon.

Barrow, John, and Thomas Young [both uncredited], 1818, "Observations Relating to Some of the Antiquities of Egypt, from the Papers of the Late Mr. Davison. Published in Walpole's Memoirs. 1817," *Quarterly Review* 19 (38): 391–424.

Bárta, Miroslav, 2003, *Sinuhe, the Bible, and the Patriarchs*, Praha: Set Out.

Bartelink, G. J. M., 1993, "Die *Oracula Sibyllina* in den frühchristlichen griechischen Schriften von Justin bis Origenes (150–250 nach Chr.)," in J. den Boeft and A. Hilhorst (eds.), *Early Christian Poetry: A Collection of Essays*, 23–33, VCSup 22, Leiden: Brill.

Barton, John, 2016, "James Barr and the Future of Biblical Theology," *Int* 70 (3): 264–74.

Bartoš, Hynek, 2015, *Philosophy and Dietetics in the Hippocratic On Regimen: A Delicate Balance of Health*, SAM 44, Leiden: Brill.

Bassler, Jouette M., 1989, *1 Timothy, 2 Timothy, Titus*, Abingdon New Testament Commentaries, Nashville: Abingdon.

Bate, H. N., 1918, *The Sibylline Oracles: Books III–V*, Translations of Early Documents, London: SPCK.

Bauckham, Richard, 2008, *The Jewish World around the New Testament: Collected Essays I*, WUNT 233, Tübingen: Mohr-Siebeck.

Bauckham, Richard, 2009, *Jesus and the God of Israel: God Crucified and Other Studies on the New Testament's Christology of Divine Identity*, Grand Rapids, MI: Eerdmans.

Bauer, Johannes B., 1965, "Drei Cruces," *BZ* 9: 84–91.

Bean, George E., 1971, *Turkey Beyond the Maeander: An Archaeological Guide*, London: Benn.

Beatrice, Pier Franco, 2009, "The Oriental Religions and Porphyry's Universal Way for the Soul's Deliverance," in Corinne Bonnet, Vinciane Pirenne-Delforge, and Danny Praet (eds.), *Les Religions Orientales dans le Monde Grec et Romain: Cent Ans après Cumont (1906–2006): Bilan Historique et Historiographique Colloque de Rome, 16–18 Novembre 2006*, 343–68, Institut Historique Belge de Rome Études de Philologie, d'Archéologie et d'Histoire Anciennes 45, Brussels: Belgisch Historisch Instituut te Rome.

Beck, Lily Y. (trans.), 2005, *Pedanius Dioscorides of Anazarbus. De materia medica*, Altertumswissenschaftliche Texte und Studien 38, Hildesheim: Olms–Weidmann.

Beck, Roger, 2014, "The Adventures of Six Men in a Boat: The Astral Determinants of a Maritime Narrative in the *Anthologies* of Vettius Valens," in Marília P. Futre Pinheiro, Gareth Schmeling, and Edmund P. Cueva (eds.), *The Ancient Novel and the Frontiers of Genre*, 61–7, Ancient Narrative Supplementum 18, Eelde: Barkhuis.

Becker, Carl, 1954, *Tertullians Apologeticum: Werden und Leistung*, München: Kösel-Verlag.

Behr, C. A., 1968, *Aelius Aristides and the Sacred Tale*, Amsterdam: Hakkert.

Behr, John, 2000, *Asceticism and Anthropology in Irenaeus and Clement*, OECS, Oxford: Oxford University Press.

Behr, John, 2013, *Irenaeus of Lyons: Identifying Christianity*, Christian Theology in Context, Oxford: Oxford University Press.

Beltrami, Arnaldus, 1908, "Ea quae apud Pseudo-Phocylidem *Veteris et Novi Testamenti* vestigia deprehenduntur," *Rivista di Filologia e di Istruzione Classica* 36 (3): 411–23.

Belzoni, Giovanni, 1822, *Narrative of the Operations and Recent Discoveries within the Pyramids, Temples, Tombs, and Excavations, in Egypt and Nubia; and of a Journey to the Coast of the Red Sea, in Search of the Ancient Berenice; and Another to the Oasis of Jupiter Ammon*, 2 vols., 3rd ed., London: John Murray.

Benci, Tomasso, 1548, *Il Pimandro di Mercurio Trimegisto*, Firenze: Lenzoni.

Bengel, Johann Albrecht, 1742, *Gnomon Novi Testamenti: in quo ex nativa verborum VI simplicitas, profunditas, concinnitas, salubritas sensuum coelestium indicatur*, Tübingen: Schramm.

Benton, Sylvia, 1934–5, "Excavations in Ithaca, III," *ABSA* 35: 45–73.

Berchman, Robert M., 1984, *From Philo to Origen: Middle Platonism in Transition*, BJS 69, Chico, CA: Scholars Press.

Berding, Kenneth, 1999, "Polycarp of Smyrna's View of the Authorship of 1 and 2 Timothy," *VC* 53 (4): 349–60.

Bergk, Theodore, 1882, *Poetae Lyrici Graeci*, 2 vols., Leipzig: Teubner.

Bergson, Leif, 1965, *Der griechische Alexanderroman Rezension β*, Acta Universitatis Stockholmiensis 3, Stockholm: Almqvist & Wiksell.

Berkowitz, Luci, and Karl A. Squitier, 1990, *Thesaurus Linguae Graecae: Canon of Greek Authors and Works*, 3rd ed., New York: Oxford University Press.

Bernand, Étienne, 1969, *Inscriptions métriques de l'Égypte gréco-romaine. Recherches sur la poésie épigrammatique des grecs en Égypte*, Annales littéraires de l'Université de Besançon 98, Paris: Les Belles Lettres.

Bernays, Jacob, 1856, *Ueber das Phokylideische Gedicht: Ein Beitrag zur hellenistischen Litteratur*, Berlin: Hertz.

Bernsdorff, Hans, 1994, "Die Abfahrt der Argonauten im Hylasidyll Theokrits," *RhMP* 137 (1): 66–72.

Berthelot, Katell, 2012, "Philo and the Allegorical Interpretation of Homer in the Platonic Tradition (with an Emphasis on Porphyry's *De Antro Nympharum*)," in Maren R. Niehoff (ed.), *Homer and the Bible in the Eyes of Ancient Interpreters*, 155–74, JSRC 16, Leiden: Brill.

Berthelot, M., 1887–8, *Collection des anciens alchimistes grecs*, 3 vols., Paris: Steinheil.

Bestmann, H. J., 1885, *Geschichte der christlichen Sitte*, pt. 2: *Die katholische Sitte der alten Kirche in ihrer geschichtlichen Entwicklung*, Nördlingen: Beck.

Bingham, D. Jeffrey, 1998, *Irenaeus' Use of Matthew's Gospel in Adversus Haereses*, Traditio Exegetica Graeca, Leuven: Peeters.

Birch, S., 1852–3, "On Excavations by Capt. Caviglia, in 1816, behind, and in the Neighbourhood of, the Great Sphinx," *Museum of Classical Antiquities: A Quarterly Journal of Ancient Art* 2: 27–34.

Bird, Michael F., 2014, *The Gospel of the Lord: How the Early Church Wrote the Story of Jesus*, Grand Rapids, MI: Eerdmans.

Birley, Anthony R., 1999, *Septimius Severus: The African Emperor*, rev. ed., London: Routledge.

Bishop, Charles Edward, 1892, "Verbals in -ΤΟΣ in Sophocles," *AJP* 13 (50): 171–99 (51): 329–42 (52): 449–62.

Blanchard, Yves-Marie, 1993, *Aux sources du canon, le témoignage d'Irénée*, Cogitatio Fidei 175, Paris: Cerf.

Blass, Friedrich, Albert Debrunner, and Robert W. Funk, 1961, *A Greek Grammar of the New Testament and Other Early Christian Literature*, Chicago: University of Chicago Press.

Bloch, René, 2011, *Moses und der Mythos: Die Auseinandersetzung mit der griechischen Mythologie bei jüdisch-hellenistischen Autoren*, JSJSup 145, Leiden: Brill.

Bluhme, Friedrich, 1906, *De Ioannis Laurentii Lydi Libris Περι μηνων, Observationum Capita Duo*, Halle: Wischan and Burkhardt.

Blümel, Carol, 1950, "Drei Weihreliefs an die Nymphen," in Felix Eckstein (ed.), *ΘΕΩΡΙΑ: Festschrift für W.-H. Schuchhardt*, 23–8, Deutsche Beiträge zur Altertumswissenschaft 12–13, Baden: Grimm.

Boda, Mark J., 2011, "Word and Spirit, Scribe and Prophet in Old Testament Hermeneutics," in Kevin L. Spawn and Archie T. Wright (eds.), *Spirit and Scripture: Exploring a Pneumatic Hermeneutic*, 25–45, New York: T&T Clark International.

Boeckh, August (ed.), 1828–77, *Corpus Inscriptionum Graecarum*, 4 vols., Berlin: Officina Academica.

Boersma, Hans, 2017, *Scripture as Real Presence: Sacramental Exegesis in the Early Church*, Grand Rapids, MI: Baker Academic.

Bogner, Hans, 1934, "Die Religion des Nonnos von Panopolis," *Phil* 89 (43): 320–33.

Bonwetsch, G. Nathanael, 1897, *Studien zu den Kommentaren Hippolyts zu Buche Daniel und Hohen Liede*, TU 16/2, Leipzig: Hinrichs.

Borgeaud, Philippe, 1979, *Recherches sur le dieu Pan*, Bibliotheca Helvetica Romana 17, Geneva: Institut Suisse de Rome.

Bori, Pier Cesare, 1987, *L'interpretazione infinita. L'ermeneutica cristiana antica e le sue trasformazioni*, Saggi 326, Bologna: Il Mulino.

Borovilou-Genakou, Aphrodite, 2002, "Baroccianus Gr. 50: ΕΠΙΜΕΡΙΣΜΟΙ ΚΑΤΑ ΣΤΟΙΧΕΙΟΝ ΓΡΑΦΙΚΑ. Terminus ante quem pour le lexique de Théodose le Grammairien (IXᵉ s.)," *Byz* 72 (1): 250–69.

Borthwick, E. K., 1963, "The Oxyrhynchus Musical Monody and Some Ancient Fertility Superstitions," *AJP* 84 (3): 225–43.

Bosworth, C. E., 1974–5, "Henry Salt, Consul in Egypt 1816–1827 and Pioneer Egyptologist," *BJRL* 57 (1): 69–91.

Botte, Bernard, 1968, *Hippolyte de Rome. La Tradition Apostolique*, SC 11, 2nd ed., Paris: Cerf.

Bouché-Leclercq, A., 1879–82, *Histoire de la divination dans l'antiquité*, 4 vols., Paris: Leroux.

Boudon-Millot, Véronique, 2009, "Le *De dignotione ex insomniis* (Kühn VI, 832–835) est-il un traité authentique de Galien?," *REG* 122 (2): 617–34.

Bousset, Wilhelm, 1973, *Hauptprobleme der Gnosis*, FRLANT 10, Göttingen: Vandenhoeck & Ruprecht.

Bowersock, G. W., 1983, Review of Polymnia Athanassiadi-Fowden, *Julian and Hellenism, an Intellectual Biography*, in *ClR* 97 (1): 81–3.

Bowersock, G. W., 1984, "The Miracle of Memnon," *Bulletin of the American Society of Papyrologists* 21 (1–4): 21–32.

Bowersock, G. W., 1990, Review of J. Matthews, *The Roman Empire of Ammianus*, *JRS* 80: 244–50.

Bowersock, G. W., 2000, *Selected Papers on Late Antiquity*, Munera: Studi storici sulla Tarda Antichità 16, Bari: Edipuglia.

Bowra, C. M., 1960, "Palladas and the Converted Olympians," *ByzZ* 53 (1): 1–7.

Box, G. H., 1927, *The Testament of Abraham: Translated from the Greek Text with Introduction and Notes*, London: SPCK.

Boyarin, Daniel, 2010, "Origen as Theorist of Allegory: Alexandrian Context," in Rita Copeland and Peter T. Struck (eds.), *The Cambridge Companion to Allegory*, 38–54, Cambridge: Cambridge University Press.

Braun, François-Marie, 1955, "Hermétisme et Johannisme," *RevThom* 55 (1): 22–42; (2): 259–99.

Braun, R., 1966, "Le probleme des deux livres *De cultu feminarum*," *StPatr* 7: 133–42.

Braund, D., 2007, "Parthenos and the Nymphs at Crimean Chersonesos: Colonial Appropriation and Native Integration," in Alain Bresson, Askold Ivantchik, and Jean-Louis Ferrary (eds.), *Une koinè pontique: cités grecques, sociétés indigènes et empires mondiaux sur le littoral nord de la mer noire (viie s. a.C.–iiie s. p.C.)*, 191–200, Ausonius Éditions, Mémoires 18, Bordeaux: Ausonius.

Breasted, James Henry, 1906, *Ancient Records of Egypt: Historical Documents from the Earliest Times to the Persian Conquest*, Ancient Records, Chicago: University of Chicago Press.

Brent, Allen, 1995, *Hippolytus and the Roman Church in the Third Century: Communities in Tension before the Emergence of a Monarch-Bishop*, VCSup 31, Leiden: Brill.

Briggman, Anthony, 2012, *Irenaeus of Lyons and the Theology of the Holy Spirit*, OECS, Oxford: Oxford University Press.

Briggs, Richard S., 2007, "Perspectives on Scripture: Its Status and Purpose. A Review Article," *HeyJ* 48 (2): 267–74.

Brillante, Carlo, 1990, "L'interpretazione dei sogni nel Sistema di Erofilo," in Marie-Madeleine Mactoux and Evelyne Geny (eds.), *Mélanges Pierre Lévêque*, vol. 4: *Religion*, 79–87, Centre de Recherches d'Histoire Ancienne 96, Annales Littéraires de l'Université de Besancon 413, Paris: Les Belles Lettres.

Brisson, Luc, 1996, *Introduction à la Philosophie du Mythe*, vol. 1: *Sauver les Mythes*, Essais d'Art et de Philosophie, Paris: Vrin.

Brisson, Luc, 2004, *How Philosophers Saved Myths: Allegorical Interpretation and Classical Mythology*, trans. Catherine Tihanyi, Chicago: University of Chicago Press.

Broer, Ingo, 1999, "Das Weinwunder zu Kana (Joh 2,1-11) und die Weinwunder der Antike," in Ulrich Mell and Ulrich B. Müller (eds.), *Das Urchristentum in seiner literarischen Geschichte: Festschrift für Jürgen Becker zum 65. Geburtstag*, 291–308, BZNW 100, Berlin: de Gruyter.

Brown, Charles Thomas, 2000, *The Gospel and Ignatius of Antioch*, StBibLit 12, New York: Lang.

Brown, Truesdell S., 1978, "Aristodicus of Cyme and the Branchidae," *AJP* 99 (1): 64–78.

Browning, Robert, 1963, "An Unpublished Corpus of Byzantine Poems," *Byz* 33 (2): 289–316.

Brox, Norbert, 1969, *Die Pastoralbriefe*, 4th ed., RNT 7/2, Regensburg: Pustet.

Bruce, F. F., 1988, *The Canon of Scripture*, Downers Grove, IL: InterVarsity.

Brunner-Traut, Emma, 1968, "Ägyptische Mythen im Physiologus (zu Kapitel 26, 25 und 11)," in Wolfgang Helck (ed.), *Festschrift für Siegfried Schott zu seinem 70. Geburtstag am 20. August 1967*, 13–44, Wiesbaden: Harrassowitz.

Brunner-Traut, Emma, 1984, "Der ägyptische Ursprung des 45. Kapitels des Physiologus und seine Datierung," in Hartwig Altenmüller and Dietrich Wildung (eds.), *Studien zur altagyptischen Kultur*, 559–68, Hamburg: Buske.

Büchli, Jörg, 1987, *Der Poimandres: Ein paganisiertes Evangelium*, WUNT 2/27, Tübingen: Mohr-Siebeck.

Budé, Guillaume, 1510, *Plutarchi cheronei de Placitis Philosophorum Naturalibus Libri Quinq*, Rome: Mazochium.

Buffière, Félix, 1956, *Les Mythes d'Homère et la Pensée Grecque*, Collection d'Études Anciennes, Paris: Les Belles Lettres.

Bultmann, Rudolf, 1948, "Zur Geschichte der Lichtsymbolik im Altertum," *Phil* 97 (1–4): 1–36.

Bultmann, Rudolf, 1964, "ζάω κτλ.," pt. A: "ζωή in Greek Usage," 832–43, in *TDNT* 2.

Burkes, Shannon, 1999, "Wisdom and Law: Choosing Life in Ben Sira and Baruch," *JSJ* 30 (3): 254–76.

Burkhardt, Helmut, 1988, *Die Inspiration heiliger Schriften bei Philo von Alexandrien*, Monographien und Studienbücher 340, Giessen: Brunnen-Verlag.

Busine, Aude, 2005, *Paroles d'Apollon. Pratiques et traditions oraculaires dans l'Antiquité tardive (IIᵉ–VIᵉ siècles)*, RGRW 156, Leiden: Brill.

Butterworth, G. W. (trans.), 1936, *Origen, On First Principles*, London: SPCK.

Byre, Calvin S., 1994, "On the Description of the Harbor of Phorkys and the Cave of the Nymphs, *Odyssey* 13.96–112," *AJP* 115 (1): 1–13.

Cadiou, René, 1944, *Origen: His Life at Alexandria*, St. Louis: Herder.

Cairns, Huntington, 1942, "Plato's Theory of Law," *Harvard Law Review* 56 (3): 359–87.

Calef, Susan A., 1996, "Rhetorical Strategies in Tertullian's *De cultu feminarum*," Ph.D. dissertation, University of Notre Dame, Notre Dame, IN.

Cameron, Alan, 1964, "Palladas and the Nikai," *JHS* 84: 54–62.

Cameron, Alan, 1965a, "Notes on Palladas," *ClQ* 15 (2): 215–29.

Cameron, Alan, 1965b, "Palladas and Christian Polemic," *JRS* 55 (1–2): 17–30.

Cameron, Alan, 2000, "The Poet, the Bishop, and the Harlot," *GRBS* 41 (2): 175–88.

Campagna, Lorenzo, 2006, "Monumental Fountains at Hierapolis of Phrygia during the Severan Age: The Nymphaeum of the Tritons and the Nymphaeum of the Sanctuary of Apollo," in Gilbert Wiplinger (ed.), *Cura Aquarum in Ephesus: Proceedings of the Twelfth International Congress on the History of Water Management and Hydraulic Engineering in the Mediterranean Region. Ephesus/Selçuk, Turkey, October 2–10, 2004*, 387–95, BabSup 12, Österreichisches Archäologisches Institut 42, 2 vols., Leuven: Peeters.

Campbell, David A., 1984, "Stobaeus and Early Greek Lyric Poetry," in Douglas E. Gerber (ed.), *Greek Poetry and Philosophy: Studies in Honour of Leonard Woodbury*, 51–7, Scholars Press Homage Series, Chico, CA: Scholars Press.

Campbell, Malcolm, 1990, "Theocritus Thirteen," in E. M. Craik (ed.), *"Owls to Athens": Essays on Classical Subjects Presented to Sir Kenneth Dover*, 113–19, Oxford: Clarendon.

Campenhausen, Hans von, 1972, *The Formation of the Christian Bible*, Philadelphia: Fortress.

Camplani, Alberto, 1993, "Riferimenti biblici nella letteratura ermetica," *Annali di storia dell'esegesi* 10 (2): 375–425.

Canart, Paul, 1978, "Le livre grec en Italie méridionale sous les règnes Normand et Souabe: aspects matériels et sociaux," *ScrCiv* 2: 103–62.

Canfora, Luciano, 1995, *Lo spazio letterario della Grecia antica*, vol. 2: *La ricezione e l'attualizzazione del testo*, Rome: Salerno.

Canto, Alicia M., 1984, "Les plaques votives avec plantae pedum d'Italica: un essai d'interpretation," *ZPE* 54: 183–94.

Capart, J., A. H. Gardiner, and B. van de Walle, 1936, "New Light on the Ramesside Tomb-Robberies," *JEA* 22 (2): 169–93.

Caprara, Mariangela, 2005, *Nonno di Panopoli. Parafrasi del Vangelo di San Giovanni. Canto IV*, Pisa: Normale.

Carlini, Antonio, 1985, "Le passeggiate di Erma verso Cuma (su due luoghi controversi del *Pastore*)," in S. F. Bondì, S. Pernigotti, F. Serra, and A. Vivian (eds.), *Studi in onore di Edda Bresciani*, 105–9, Pisa: Giardini.

Carlini, Antonio, 1997, "Appunti sulla Versione Interlineare di Teognide e ps.-focilide nel Par. Suppl. Gr. 388," in Ugo Criscuolo and Riccardo Maisano (eds.), *Synodia. Studia humanitatis Antonio Garzya septuagenario ab amicis atque discipulis dicata*, 121–35, Naples: d'Auria.

Carmody, Francis J., 1941, "Physiologus Latinus Versio Y," *University of California Publications in Classical Philology* 12 (7): 95–134.

Carnoy, Albert, 1956, "Les Nymphes des sources en Grèce," *Le Muséon* 69: 187–95.

Carrez-Maratray, Jean-Yves, 1993, "Une énigme du Sphinx: I. Metr. 130," *ZPE* 95: 149–52.

Carriker, Andrew J., 1996, "Some Uses of Aristocles and Numenius in Eusebius' *Praeparatio Evangelica*," *JTS* 47 (2): 543–9.

Cartlidge, David R., and David L. Dungan, 1980, *Documents for the Study of the Gospels*, Philadelphia: Fortress.

Carvounis, Katerina, 2017, "Dionysus, Ampelus, and Mythological Examples in Nonnus' *Dionysiaca*," in Herbert Bannert and Nicole Kröll (eds.), *Nonnus of Panopolis in Context II: Poetry, Religion, and Society. Proceedings of the International Conference on Nonnus of Panopolis, 26th–29th September 2013, University of Vienna, Austria*, 33–51, MnemSup 408; Leiden: Brill.

Castelli, Emanuele, 2008, "The Author of the Refutatio omnium haeresium and the attribution of the De universo to Flavius Josephus," in Gabriella Aragione and Enrico Norelli (eds.), *Des évêques, des écoles et des hérétiques. Actes du colloque international sur la "Réfutation de toutes les hérésies" Genève, 13–14 juin 2008*, 219–31, Prahins: Zèbre.

Castelli, Emanuele, 2011, *Un falso letterario sotto il nome di Flavio Giuseppe. Ricerche sulla tradizione del ΠΕΡΙ ΤΟΥ ΠΑΝΤΟΣ e sulla produzione letteraria cristiana a Roma nei primi decenni del III secolo*, JACErg 7, Münster: Aschendorff.

Cataudella, Q., 1974, *Utriusque Linguae. Studi e ricerche di letteratura greca e latina*, vol. 1, Messina: d'Anna.

Cavallo, Guglielmo, 1980, "La trasmissione scritta della cultura greca antica in Calabria e in Sicilia tra i secoli X–XV. Consistenza, tipologia, fruizione," *ScrCiv* 4: 157–245.

Caviglia, Giovanni Battista, 1837a, "A Brief Account of the Discoveries Made in Egypt, between the Years 1820 and 1836," *Tait's* 4: 706–8.

Caviglia, Giovanni Battista, 1837b, Letter from Caviglia to Colonel Campbell, in *Tait's* 4: 708–9.

Cerrato, J. A., 2002, *Hippolytus between East and West: The Commentaries and the Provenance of the Corpus*, OTM, Oxford: Oxford University Press.

Cerrato, J. A., 2007, "Hippolytus," in Donald K. McKim (ed.), *Dictionary of Major Biblical Interpreters*, 524–9, Downers Grove, IL: IVP Academic.

Chadwick, Henry, 1976, *Priscillian of Avila*, Oxford: Clarendon.

Chambers, John David, 1882, *The Theological and Philosophical Works of Hermes Trismegistus, Christian Platonist*, Edinburgh: T&T Clark.

Chastel, André, 1975, *Marsile Ficin et l'Art*, 2nd ed., Travaux d'Humanisme et Renaissance 2, Geneva: Librairie Droz.

Chazon, E. Glickler, 1985–6, "Moses' Struggle for his Soul: A Prototype for the *Testament of Abraham*, the *Greek Apocalypse of Ezra*, and the *Apocalypse of Sedrach*," *SecCent* 5 (3): 151–64.

Cherniss, Harold, 1929, "The So-called Fragment of Hippolytus, περὶ ᾅδου," *CP* 24 (4): 346–50.

Chester, Andrew, 2013, "The Relevance of Jewish Inscriptions for New Testament Ethics," in Jan Willem van Henten and Joseph Verheyden (eds.), *Early Christian Ethics in*

Interaction with Jewish and Greco-Roman Contexts, 107–45, Studies in Theology and Religion 17, Leiden: Brill.

Chicarro, C. Fernández, 1950, "Lápidas votivas con huellas de pies y exvotos reproduciendo parejas de pies, del Museo Arqueológico Provincial de Seville," *Revista de Archivos, Bibliotecas y Museos* 56 (3): 617–35.

Childs, Brevard S., 1970, *Biblical Theology in Crisis*, Philadelphia: Westminster.

Childs, Brevard S., 1977, "The Sensus Literalis of Scripture: An Ancient and Modern Problem," in Herbert Donner, Robert Hanhart, and Rudolf Smend (eds.), *Beiträge zur Alttestamentlichen Theologie: Festschrift für Walther Zimmerli zum 70. Geburtstag*, 80–93, Göttingen: Vandenhoeck & Ruprecht.

Childs, Brevard S., 1993, *Biblical Theology of the Old and New Testaments: Theological Reflection on the Christian Bible*, Philadelphia: Fortress.

Chlup, Radek, 2007, "The Ritualization of Language in the *Hermetica*," *Aries* 7 (2): 133–59.

Choufrine, Arkadi, 2002, *Gnosis, Theophany, Theosis: Studies in Clement of Alexandria's Appropriation of His Background*, Patristic Studies 5, New York: Lang.

Chuvin, Pierre, 1986, "Nonnos de Panopolis entre paganisme et christianisme," *Bulletin de l'Association Guillaume Budé* 45 (4): 387–96.

Chuvin, Pierre, 1991, *Mythologie et géographie dionysiaques. Recherches sur l'œuvre de Nonnos de Panopolis*, Vates 2, Clermont–Ferrand: ADOSA.

Claesson, Gösta, 1974–5, *Index Tertullianeus*, 3 vols., Paris: Études Augustiniennes.

Clark, Elizabeth A., 1999, *Reading Renunciation: Asceticism and Scripture in Early Christianity*, Princeton: Princeton University Press.

Clark, Raymond J., 1996, "The Avernian Sibyl's Cave: From Military Tunnel to Mediaeval Spa," *C&M* 47: 217–43.

Clavier, Henri, 1976, *Les variétes de la pensée biblique et le problème de son unité: Esquisse d'une Théologie de la Bible sur les textes originaux et dans leur contexte historique*, NovTSup 43, Leiden: Brill.

Cole, Susan Guettel, 1988, "The Uses of Water in Greek Sanctuaries," in Robin Hägg, Nanno Marinatos, and Gullög C. Nordquist (eds.), *Early Greek Cult Practice: Proceedings of the Fifth International Symposium at the Swedish Institute at Athens, 26–29 June, 1986*, 161–5, Skrifter Utgivna av Svenska Institutet i Athen 4/38, Stockholm: Åstroms.

Collart, Paul, 1930, *Nonnos de Panopolis: Études sur la composition et le texte des Dionysiaques*, Recherches d'Archéologie de Philologie et d'Histoire 1, Cairo: Institut Français d'Archéologie Orientale.

Collins, John J., 1972, *The Sibylline Oracles of Egyptian Judaism*, SBLDS 13, Missoula, MT: Society of Biblical Literature.

Collins, John J., 1974, "The Provenance of the Third Sibylline Oracle," *Bulletin of the Institute of Jewish Studies* 2: 1–18.

Collins, John J., 1983, "Sibylline Oracles," *OTP* 1.317–472.

Collins, John J., 1986, *Between Athens and Jerusalem: Jewish Identity in the Hellenistic Diaspora*, New York: Crossroad.

Collins, John J., 1997, *Jewish Wisdom in the Hellenistic Age*, OTL, Louisville: Westminster John Knox.

Collins, John J., 1998, "The Jewish Transformation of Sibylline Oracles," in Ileana Chirassi Colombo and Tullio Seppilli (eds.), *Sibille e Linguaggi Oracolari: Mito Storia Tradizione. Atti del Convegno - Macerata - Norcia - Settembre 1994*, 369–87, Pisa: Istituti Editoriali e Poligrafici Internazionali.

Collins, John J., 2014, "Sibylline Discourse," in Eibert Tigchelaar (ed.), *Old Testament Pseudepigrapha and the Scriptures*, 195–210, BETL 270, Leuven: Peeters.

Collins, Raymond F., 2002, *I & II Timothy and Titus: A Commentary*, NTL, Louisville: Westminster John Knox.

Combeaud, Bernard (ed.), 2010, *D. M. Ausonii Burdigalensis opuscula Omnia*, Bourdeaux: Mollat.

Committee of the Oxford Society of Historical Theology, 1905, *The New Testament in the Apostolic Fathers*, Oxford: Clarendon.

Congar, Yves M.-J., 1967, *Tradition and Traditions: An Historical and a Theological Essay*, New York: Macmillan.

Connor, W. R., 1988, "Seized by the Nymphs: Nymphology and Symbolic Expression in Classical Greece," *ClA* 7 (2): 155–89.

Constantinou, Eugenia Scarvelis, 2008, "Andrew of Caesarea and the Apocalypse in the Ancient Church of the East: Studies and Translation," Ph.D. dissertation, 2 vols., Université Laval, Quebec.

Cook, John Granger, 2004, *The Interpretation of the Old Testament in Greco-Roman Paganism*, STAC 23, Tübingen: Mohr-Siebeck.

Cook, John Granger, 2008, "Porphyry's Attempted Demolition of Christian Allegory," *International Journal of the Platonic Traditions* 2 (1): 1–27.

Cook, John Granger, 2012, "Porphyry's Critique of the Jewish Scriptures: Three New Fragments," in Siegfried Kreuzer, Martin Meiser, and Marcus Sigismund (eds.), *Die Septuaginta – Entstehung, Sprache, Geschichte*, 561–81, WUNT 1/286, Tübingen: Mohr-Siebeck.

Copenhaver, Brian P., 1992, *Hermetica: The Greek* Corpus Hermeticum *and the Latin* Asclepius *in a New English Translation with Notes and Introduction*, Cambridge: Cambridge University Press.

Corpus inscriptionum Latinarum 6, 1862–, Berlin: Reimer.

Corsten, Thomas, 1997, *Die Inschriften von Laodikeia am Lykos*, pt. 1: *Die Inschriften*, Inschriften griechischer Städte aus Kleinasien 49, Bonn: Habelt.

Costabile, Felice, 1991, "Gli *anathemata* delle Ninfe e le erme fittili a tre teste," in *eadem*, *I Ninfei di Locri Epizefiri: Architettura – culti erotici – sacralità delle acque*, 95–101, Soveria Mannelli: Rubbettino.

Coulie, Bernard, Lee Francis Sherry, and CETEDOC (eds.), 1995, *Thesaurus Pseudo-Nonni Quondam Panopolitani*, Corpus Christianorum Thesaurus Patrum Graecorum, Turnhout: Brepols.

Countryman, L. Wm., 1982, "Tertullian and the Regula Fidei," *SecCent* 2 (4): 208–27.

Courtney, Edward, 1990, "Greek and Latin Acrostichs," *Phil* 134 (1–2): 3–13.

Cox (Miller), Patricia, 1983, "The *Physiologus*: A *Poiēsis* of Nature," *CH* 52 (4): 433–43.

Cox (Miller), Patricia, 1994, *Dreams in Late Antiquity: Studies in the Imagination of a Culture*, Princeton: Princeton University Press.

Cox, Ronald, 2007, *By the Same Word: Creation and Salvation in Hellenistic Judaism and Early Christianity*, BZNW 145, Berlin: de Gruyter.

Craigie, W. A., 1896, "The Testament of Abraham," in Allan Menzies (ed.), *The Ante-Nicene Fathers*, vol. 9, 183–201, Buffalo: Christian Literature.

Cramer, Frederick H., 1954, *Astrology in Roman Law and Politics*, Philadelphia: American Philosophical Society.

Crawford, Matthew R., 2013, "Scripture as 'One Book': Origen, Jerome, and Cyril of Alexandria on Isaiah 29:11," *JTS* 64 (1): 137–53.

Cremer, Hermann, 1866, *Biblisch-theologisches Wörterbuch der Neutestamentlichen Gräcität*, Gotha: Perthes.

Cremer, Hermann, 1872, *Biblisch-theologisches Wörterbuch der Neutestamentlichen Gräcität*, 2nd ed., Gotha: Perthes.

Cremer, Hermann, 1880, "Inspiration," *RE* 6.746–64.

Cribiore, Raffaella, 1995, "A Hymn to the Nile," *ZPE* 106: 97–106.

Critchley, Steven George, 2005, "Pagan Taylor: The Emergence of a Public Character 1785–1804. An Enquiry into the Life and Selected Works of Thomas Taylor the Platonist (1758–1835)," Ph.D. dissertation, University of York, York.

Crouzel, Henri, 1989, *Origen: The Life and Thought of the First Great Theologian*, San Francisco: Harper & Row.

Culham, Phyllis, 1982, "The *Lex Oppia*," *Latomus* 41 (4): 786–93.

Culianu, Ioan P., 1981, "Ordine e disordine delle sfere: Macrob. *In S. Scip.*, I 12, 13–14, P. 50, 11–24 Willis," *Aevum* 55 (1): 96–110.

Cullmann, Oscar, 1956, *The Early Church: Studies in Early Christian History and Theology*, Philadelphia: Westminster.

Cumont, Franz, 1912, *Astrology and Religion among the Greeks and Romans*, American Lectures on the History of Religions, New York: Putnam.

Cumont, Franz, 1942, *Recherches sur le symbolisme funéraire des romains*, Paris: Geuthner.

Cumont, Franz, and Eugène Cumont, 1906, *Studia Pontica*, vol. 2: *Voyage d'Exploration archéologique dans le Pont et la Petite Armenie*, Bruxelles: Lamertin.

Cunningham, William, 1878, *Theological Lectures on Subjects Connected with Natural Theology, Evidences of Christianity, the Canon and Inspiration of Scripture*, New York: Carter.

Curley, Michael J., 1980, "'Physiologus,' Φυσιολογία and the Rise of Christian Nature Symbolism," *Viator* 11: 1–10.

d'Alès, Adhémar, 1905, *La théologie de Tertullien*, BTH, Paris: Beauchesne.

d'Alès, Adhémar, 1906, *La théologie de Saint Hippolyte*, BTH, Paris: Beauchesne.

d'Ippolito, Gennaro, 1994, "Nonno e Gregorio di Nazianzo," in Francesco Del Franco (ed.), *Storia poesia e pensiero nel mondo antico: Studi in onore di Marcello Gigante*, 197–208, Saggi Bibliopolis 46, Naples: Bibliopolis.

Daley, Brian E., 1998, "Origen's *De Principiis*: A Guide to the Principles of Christian Scriptural Interpretation," in John Petruccione (ed.), *Nova et Vetera: Patristic Studies in Honor of Thomas Patrick Halton*, 3–21, Washington, DC: Catholic University of America Press.

Dana, Madalina, 2011, "Les relations des cites du Pont-Euxin ouest et nord avec les centres cultuels du monde grec," *ACSS* 17 (1): 47–70.

Dando, Marcel, 1965, "Alcimus Avitus (*c.* 450–*c.* 518) as the Author of the *De Resurrectione Mortuorum*, *De Pascha* (*De Cruce*), *De Sodoma* and *De Iona*, Formerly Attributed to Tertullian and Cyprian," *C&M* 26: 258–75.

Daumas, François, 1982, "Le fonds égyptien de l'hermétisme," in Julien Ries, Yvonne Janssens, and Jean-Marie Sevrin (eds.), *Gnosticisme et Monde Hellénistique: Actes du Colloque de Louvain-la-Neuve (11–14 mars 1980)*, 3–25, Publications de l'Institut Orientaliste de Louvain 27, Louvain-la-Neuve: Université Catholique de Louvain.

Davila, James, 2005, *The Provenance of the Pseudepigrapha: Jewish, Christian, or Other?*, JSJSup 105, Leiden: Brill.

de Andia, Ysabel, 1986, *Homo Vivens: Incorruptibilité et divinisation de l'homme selon Irénée de Lyon*, Paris: Études Augustiniennes.

de Bruyne, Donatien, 1929, "Étude sur le texte latin de la Sagesse," *RBén* 41: 101–33.

de Foix Candalle, Francois, 1574, *Mercurii Trismegisti Pimandras Utraque Lingua Restitutus*, Bourdeaux: Millanges.

de Foix Candalle, Francois, 1579, *Le Pimandre de Mercure Trismegiste de la Philosophie Chrestienne Cognoissance du Verb Divin, et de l'Excellence des Œuvres de Dieu*, Bourdeaux: Millanges.

de Labriolle, P., 1914, "Tertullien a-t-il connu une version latine de la Bible?," *Bulletin d'ancienne littérature et d'archéologie chrétiennes* 4: 210–13.

de Lagarde, Paul Anthony, 1858, *Hippolyti Romani, Quae Feruntur Omnia Graece*, Leipzig: Teubner.

de Lubac, Henri, 2007, *History and Spirit: The Understanding of Scripture According to Origen*, San Francisco: Ignatius.

de Mély, F., 1898, *Les lapidaires de l'antiquité et du moyen âge*, vol. 2: *Les lapidaires grecs*, HistSci, Paris: Leroux.

de Stefani, Claudio, 2002, *Nonno di Panopoli. Parafrasi del Vangelo di S. Giovanni. Canto I*, Eikasmos 6, Bologna: Pàtron.

de Vos, Mariette, 1997, *Dionysus, Hylas e Isis sui monti di Roma. Tre monumenti con decorazione parietale in Roma antica (Palatino, Quirinale, Oppio)*, Soprintendenza Archeologica di Roma Università degli Studi di Trento, Roma: Istituto Poligrafico e Zeca dello Stato.

Dean-Otting, Mary, 1984, *Heavenly Journeys: A Study of the Motif in Hellenistic Jewish Literature*, Judentum und Umwelt 8, Frankfurt: Lang.

Declerck, J. H., 1981, "Remarques sur la tradition du *Physiologus* grec," *Byz* 51 (1): 148–58.

DeConick, April D., 1996, *Seek to See Him: Ascent and Vision Mysticism in the Gospel of Thomas*, VCSup 33, Leiden: Brill.

Del Corno, Dario (ed.), 1997, *Nonno di Panopoli, Le Dionisiache I (Canti 1–12)*, Milan: Adephi.

Delatte, A., 1938, *Herbarius: Recherches sur le cérémonial usité chez les anciens pour la cueillette des simples et des plantes magiques*, BFPLUL 81, Liége: Faculté de Philosophie et Lettres.

Delatte, Louis, 1942, *Textes Latins et Vieux Français relatifs aux Cyranides*, BFPLUL 93, Liége: Faculté de Philosophie et Lettres.

Delcor, Mathias, 1973, *Le Testament d'Abraham: Introduction, Traduction du Texte Grec et Commentaire de la Recension Grecque Longue*, SVTP 2, Leiden: Brill.

Demougeot, Émilienne, 1952, "Saint Jérôme, les oracles sibyllins et stilicon," *Revue des Études Anciennes* 54 (1–2): 83–92.

den Boeft, Jan, 1999, "Pure Rites: Ammianus on the Magi," in Jan Willem Drijvers and E. David Hunt (eds.), *The Late Roman World and Its Historian: Interpreting Ammianus Marcellinus*, 207–15, London: Routledge.

den Boeft, Jan, 2008, "Ammianus Marcellinus' Judgement of Julian's Piety," in Alberdina Houtman, Albert de Jong, and Magda Misset-van de Weg (eds.), Empsychoi Logoi—*Religious Innovations in Antiquity: Studies in Honour of Pieter Willem van der Horst*, 65–79, AJEC 73, Leiden: Brill.

Denis, Albert-Marie, 1970, *Introduction aux pseudépigraphes grecs d'Ancien Testament*, SVTP 1, Leiden: Brill.

Denzey Lewis, Nicola, 2013, *Cosmology and Fate in Gnosticism and Graeco-Roman Antiquity: Under Pitiless Skies*, NHMS 81, Leiden: Brill.

Depew, Mary, 2007, "Springs, Nymphs, and Rivers. Models of Origination in Third-Century Alexandrian Poetry," in Anton Bierl, Rebecca Lämmle, and Katharina

Wesselmann (eds.), *Literatur und religion 2: Wege zu einer mythisch-rituellen Poetik bei den Griechen*, 141–69, MythosEikonPoiesis 1/2, Berlin: de Gruyter.

Derchain, Ph., 1962, "L'authenticité de l'inspiration égyptienne dans le 'Corpus Hermeticum," *RHR* 161 (2): 175–98.

Derron, Pascale, 1980, "Inventaire des Manuscrits du Pseudo-Phocylide," *Revue d'histoire des textes* 10: 237–47.

Derron, Pascale, 1986, *Pseudo-Phocylides, Sentences*, Budé, Paris: Les Belles Lettres.

des Places, Édouard, 1973, *Numénius, Fragments*, Budé, Paris: Les Belles Lettres.

Dibelius, Martin, and Hans Conzelmann, 1972, *The Pastoral Epistles*, Hermeneia, Philadelphia: Fortress.

Diehl, Ernest, 1950, *Anthologia Lyrica Graeca*, fasc. 2: *Theognis, Ps.-Pythagoras, Ps.-Phocylides, Chares, Anonymi Aulodia*, Leipzig: Teubner.

Diekamp, Franz, 1938, *Analecta Patristica: Texte und Abhandlungen zur griechischen Patristik*, Orientalia Christiana Analecta 117, Rome: Pontificium Institutum Orientalium Studiorum.

Diels, Hermann, 1879, *Doxographi Graeci*, Berlin: Reimer.

Dieterich, A., 1893, *Nekyia. Beiträge zur Erklärung der neuentdeckten Petrusapokalypse*, Leipzig: Teubner.

Dietrich, Bernard C., 1990, "Oracles and Divine Inspiration," *Kernos* 3: 157–74.

Digeser, Elizabeth DePalma, 2012, *A Threat to Public Piety: Christians, Platonists, and the Great Persecution*, Ithaca, NY: Cornell University Press.

Dijkstra, Jitse H. F., 2016, "The Religious Background of Nonnus," in Domenico Accorinti (ed.), *Brill's Companion to Nonnus of Panopolis*, 75–88, BCCS, Leiden: Brill.

Dilley, Paul C., 2010, "The Invention of Christian Tradition: 'Apocrypha,' Imperial Policy, and Anti-Jewish Propaganda," *GRBS* 50 (4): 586–615.

Dillon, John, 1996, *The Middle Platonists: 80 B.C. to A.D. 220*, rev. ed., Ithaca, NY: Cornell University Press.

Dinkler-von Schubert, Erika, 1961. "Physiologus," in Kurt Galling (ed.), *Religion in Geschichte und Gegenwart*, 3rd ed., vol. 5: *P–Se*, 364–5, Tübingen: Mohr-Siebeck.

Dively Lauro, Elizabeth Ann, 2005, *The Soul and Spirit of Scripture within Origen's Exegesis*, Bible in Ancient Christianity 3, Boston: Brill.

Dobson, J. F., 1925, "Herophilus of Alexandria," *Proceedings of the Royal Society of Medicine* 18 (Section of the History of Medicine): 19–32.

Dodd, C. H., 1935, *The Bible and the Greeks*, London: Hodder & Stoughton.

Dodd, C. H., 1960, *The Authority of the Bible*, rev. ed., London: Fontana Books.

Dodds, E. R., 1951, *The Greeks and the Irrational*, Berkeley: University of California Press.

Dodds, E. R., 1960, "Numenius and Ammonius," in *Les Sources de Plotin*, 1–61, EntAntCl 5, Geneva: Fondation Hardt.

Dolidze, Tina, 2013, "Equivocality of Biblical Language in Origen," *StPatr* 56: 65–72.

Döllinger, John J. Ign. von, 1876, *Hippolytus and Callistus; or, the Church of Rome in the First Half of the Third Century*, Edinburgh: T&T Clark.

Donelson, Lewis R., 1986, *Pseudepigraphy and Ethical Argument in the Pastoral Epistles*, Hermeneutische Untersuchungen zur Theologie 22, Tübingen: Mohr-Siebeck.

Doran, Robert, 1986, "Narrative Literature," in Robert A. Kraft and George W. E. Nickelsburg (eds.), *Early Judaism and Its Modern Interpreters*, 287–310, The Bible and Its Modern Interpreters 2, Atlanta: Scholars Press.

Dorandi, Tiziano, 1989, "Aétios (Aétius)," in Richard Goulet (ed.), *Dictionnaire des Philosophes Antiques*, 58–9, Paris: Éditions du Centre National de la Recherche Scientifique.

Dorl-Klingenschmid, Claudia, 2006, "Brunnenbauten als Medium des interkommunalen Wettbewerbs," in Gilbert Wiplinger (ed.), *Cura Aquarum in Ephesus: Proceedings of the Twelfth International Congress on the History of Water Management and Hydraulic Engineering in the Mediterranean Region. Ephesus/Selçuk, Turkey, October 2–10, 2004*, 381–6, BabSup 12, Österreichisches Archäologisches Institut 42, 2 vols., Leuven: Peeters.

Doroszewski, Filip, 2014, "Judaic Orgies and Christ's Bacchic Deeds: Dionysiac Terminology in Nonnus' *Paraphrase of St. John's Gospel*," in Konstantinos Spanoudakis (ed.), *Nonnus of Panopolis in Context: Poetry and Cultural Milieu in Late Antiquity*, 287–301, TCSup 24, Berlin: de Gruyter.

Dörrie, Heinrich, 1974, "Zur Methodik antiker Exegese," *ZNW* 65 (1–2): 121–38.

Dowden, Ken, 1989, *Death and the Maiden: Girls' Initiation Rites in Greek Mythology*, London: Routledge.

Dowel, John (trans.), 1909, "Of those Sentiments Concerning Nature with which Philosophers Were Delighted," in William W. Goodwin (ed.), *Plutarch's Essays and Miscellanies*, 3: 104–93, 5 vols., Plutarch's Lives and Writings 8, Boston: Little, Brown.

Downs, David J., 2012, "Faith(fulness) in Christ Jesus in 2 Timothy 3:15," *JBL* 131 (1): 143–60.

Downs, David J., 2013, "The God Who Gives Life That Is Truly Life: Meritorious Almsgiving and the Divine Economy in 1 Timothy 6," in David Downs and Matthew L. Skinner (eds.), *The Unrelenting God: God's Action in Scripture. Essays in Honor of Beverly Roberts Gaventa*, 242–60, Grand Rapids, MI: Eerdmans.

Drabkin, I. E. (trans.), 1950, *Caelius Aurelianus, on Acute Diseases and on Chronic Diseases*, Chicago: University of Chicago Press.

Dronke, Peter, 1990, *Hermes and the Sibyls: Continuations and Creations*, Cambridge: Cambridge University Press.

du Preau, Gabriel, 1557, *Deux Livres de Mercure Trismegiste Hermés tres ancien Theologien, et excellant Philosophe*, Paris: Groulleau.

Duffy, John M., Philip F. Sheridan, Leendert G. Westerink, and Jeffrey A. White (= Seminar Classics 609, State University of New York at Buffalo), 1969, *Porphyry: The Cave of the Nymphs in the Odyssey*, Arethusa Monographs 1, Buffalo: State University of New York at Buffalo Press.

Dunn, Francis M., 1989, "Horace's Sacred Spring (*Ode*, I.1)," *Latomus* 48 (1): 97–109.

Dunn, Geoffrey D., 2004, *Tertullian*, ECF, London: Routledge.

Dunn, Geoffrey D., 2006, "Tertullian's Scriptural Exegesis in *de prasescriptione haereticorum*," *JECS* 14 (2): 141–55.

Dyck, Andrew R., 1993, "Aelius Herodian: Recent Studies and Prospects for Future Research," *ANRW* II.34.1: 772–94.

Ebeling, Florian, 2007, *The Secret History of Hermes Trismegistus: Hermeticism from Ancient to Modern Times*, Ithaca, NY: Cornell University Press.

Eckart, Karl-Gottfried, 1999, *Das Corpus Hermeticum einschließlich der Fragmente des Stobaeus*, Münsteraner Judaistische Studien 3, Münster: LIT.

Eden, P. T., 1972, *Theobaldi "Physiologus"*, Mittellateinische Studien und Texte 6, Leiden: Brill.

Edwards, M. J., 1990, "Atticizing Moses? Numenius, the Fathers and the Jews," *VC* 44 (1): 64–75.

Edwards, M. J., 1992, "The Vessel of Zosimus the Alchemist," *ZPE* 90: 55–64.

Edwards, M. J., 1994, "Gnostics, Greeks, and Origen: The Interpretation of Interpretation," *JTS* 44 (1): 70–89.

Edwards, M. J., 1996, "Porphyry's 'Cave of the Nymphs' and the Gnostic Controversy,"
   Hermes 124 (1): 88–100.
Edwards, M. J., 2010, "Numenius of Apamea," in Lloyd P. Gerson (ed.), *The Cambridge
   History of Philosophy in Late Antiquity*, 2 vols., 1: 115–25, Cambridge: Cambridge
   University Press.
Effe, Bernd, 1992, "Die Hylas-Geschichte bei Theokrit und Apollonios
   Rhodios: Bemerkungen zur Prioritätsfrage," *Hermes* 120 (3): 299–309.
Ehrman, Bart D., 1993, *The Orthodox Corruption of Scripture: The Effect of Early
   Christological Controversies on the Text of the New Testament*, New York: Oxford
   University Press.
Ehrman, Bart D., 2013, *Forgery and Counterforgery: The Use of Literary Deceit in Early
   Christian Polemics*, Oxford: Oxford University Press.
Eidinow, Esther, 2007, *Oracles, Curses, and Risk among the Ancient Greeks*, Oxford: Oxford
   University Press.
Eisele, Wilfried, 2009, "Jesus und Dionysos. Göttliche Konkurrenz bei der Hochzeit zu
   Kana (Joh 2,1-11)," *ZNW* 100 (1): 1–28.
Elderkin, G. W., 1940, "The Homeric Cave on Ithaca," *CP* 35 (1): 52–4.
Elderkin, G. W., 1941, "The Natural and the Artificial Grotto," *Hesperia* 10 (2): 125–37.
Engelmann, Helmut, 1976, *Die Inschriften von Kyme*, Inschriften griechischer Stäte aus
   Kleinasien 5, Bonn: Habelt.
Enslin, Morton Scott, 1938, *Christian Beginnings*, New York: Harper.
Erho, Ted M., 2009, "The Ahistorical Nature of *1 Enoch* 56:5–8 and Its Ramifications upon
   the *Opinio Communis* on the Dating of the *Similitudes of Enoch*," *JSJ* 40 (1): 23–54.
Ervin, Miriam, 1959, "Geraistai Nymphai Genethliai and the Hill of the Nymphs: A
   Problem of Athenian Mythology and Topography," *Platon* 11 (21): 146–59.
Evans, Craig A., 1993, *Word and Glory: On the Exegetical and Theological Background of
   John's Prologue*, JSNTSup 89, Sheffield: Sheffield Academic Press.
Evelyn-White, Hugh G. (trans.), 1977, *Hesiod, the Homeric Hymns and Homerica*, LCL 57,
   Cambridge: Harvard University Press.
Everard, John, 1650, *The Divine Pymander of Hermes Mercurius Trismegistus in XVII
   Books*, London: Three Bibles in the Poultrey.
Ewald, Heinrich, 1855, *Jahrbücher der Biblischen wissenschaft, Siebentes Jahrbuch: 1854–
   1855*, Göttingen: Dieterich.
Ewald, Heinrich, 1858, *Jahrbücher der Biblischen wissenschaft, Neuntes Jahrbuch: 1857–
   1858*, Göttingen: Dieterich.
Eyre, Chris, 1976, "Fate, Crocodiles and the Judgement of the Dead: Some Mythological
   Allusions in Egyptian Literature," *Studien zur altägyptischen Kultur* 4: 103–14.
Fairweather, William, 1901, *Origen and Greek Patristic Theology*, The World's Epoch-
   Makers, New York: Scribner.
Faivre, Antoine, 1995, *The Eternal Hermes: From Greek God to Alchemical Magus*, Grand
   Rapids, MI: Phanes.
Falconer, William Armistead (trans.), 1923, *Cicero* vol. 20, LCL 154, Cambridge: Harvard
   University Press.
Fantham, Elaine, 2009, *Latin Poets and Italian Gods*, Robson Classical Lectures,
   Toronto: University of Toronto Press.
Faraone, Christopher A., 1999, *Ancient Greek Love Magic*, Cambridge: Harvard
   University Press.
Farina, Antonio, 1962, *Silloge Pseudofocilidea: Introduzione—Testo Critico—Traduzione—
   Commento*, Collana di Studi Greci 37, Naples: Libreria Scientifica Editrice.

Farjeon, Eleanor, 1931, "Morning Has Broken," in Percy Dearmer, Martin Shaw, and Ralph Vaughan Williams (eds.), *Songs of Praise*, 2nd ed., Oxford: Oxford University Press, hymn no. 30.

Farkasfalvy, Denis, 2006, "Biblical Foundations for a Theology of Inspiration," *Nova et Vetera* 4 (4): 719–46.

Farrar, Frederic W., 1886, *History of Interpretation: Eight Lectures*, London: Macmillan.

Farrow, Douglas, 1987, *The Word of Truth and Disputes about Words*, Winona Lake, IN: Carpenter.

Faure, Paul, 1961–2, "La Grotte de Léra (Kydonias) et la Nymphe Akakallis," Κρητικά Χρονικά 15–16: 195–9.

Felder, Stephen, 2002, "What Is *The Fifth Sibylline Oracle*?," *JSJ* 33 (4): 363–85.

Feldman, Louis H., 1993, *Jew and Gentile in the Ancient World: Attitudes and Interactions from Alexander to Justinian*, Princeton: Princeton University Press.

Ferguson, Everett, 2003, *Backgrounds of Early Christianity*, 3rd ed., Grand Rapids, MI: Eerdmans.

Fernando, G. Charles A., 2001, *The Relationship between Law and Love in the Gospel of John*, Ph.D. dissertation, St. Paul University, Ottawa.

Ferrary, Jean-Louis, 2005, "Les mémoriaux de délégations du sanctuaire oraculaire de Claros et leur chronologie," *CRAI* 149 (2): 719–65.

Ferrero, D. de Bernardi, 1987, "Acque e ninfei," in Vincenzo Sanfo (ed.), *Hierapolis di Frigia: 1957–1987*, 64–70, Milano: Fabbri.

Festugière, A. J., 1932, *L'idéal religieux des Grecs et l'Évangile*, Paris: Gabalda.

Festugière, A. J., 1948, *L'Hermétisme*, K. Humanistika Vetenskapssamfundets i Lund Årsberättelse 1947–1948 I, Lund: Gleerup.

Festugière, A. J., 1950, *La Révélation d'Hermès Trismégiste*, EBib, 4 vols., 2nd ed., Paris: Gabalda.

Feuling, J. B., 1879, *Phocylides Poem of Admonition*, trans. H. D. Goodwin, Andover: Draper.

Ficino, Marsilio, 1505, *Pimander, Mercurij Trismegisti liber de sapientia et potestate dei*, Paris: Stephanus.

Filson, Floyd V., 1962, "The Gospel of Life: A Study of the Gospel of John," in William Klassen and Graydon F. Snyder (eds.), *Current Issues in New Testament Interpretation: Essays in Honor of Otto A. Piper*, 111–23, New York: Harper.

Fischer, Bonifatius, Johannes Gribomont, H. F. D. Sparks, and W. Thiele (eds.), 1975, *Biblia Sacra, Iuxta Vulgatam Versionem*, vol. 2, 2nd ed., Stuttgart: Württembergische Bibelanstalt.

Fishburne, Charles W., 1970, "I Corinthians III. 10–15 and the Testament of Abraham," *NTS* 17 (1): 109–15.

Fletcher, Angus, 1964, *Allegory: The Theory of a Symbolic Mode*, Ithaca, NY: Cornell University Press.

Flusser, David, 2009, *Judaism of the Second Temple Period*, vol. 2: *The Jewish Sages and Their Literature*, Grand Rapids, MI: Eerdmans.

Fontaine, Jacques (ed.), 1966, *Q. Septimi Florentis Tertulliani, De Corona*, Érasme, Paris: Presses Universitaires de France.

Fornara, Charles W., 1992, "Studies in Ammianus Marcellinus I," *Historia* 41 (3): 328–44.

Forte, Anthony J., 2011, "The Old Latin Version of Sirach: Editio Critica and Textual Problems," in Jean-Sébastien Rey and Jan Joosten (eds.), *The Texts and Versions of the Book of Ben Sira: Transmission and Interpretation*, 199–214, JSJSup 150, Leiden: Brill.

Fowden, Garth, 1993, *The Egyptian Hermes: A Historical Approach to the Late Pagan Mind*, Mythos, Princeton: Princeton University Press.

Fraistat, Shawn, 2015, "The Authority of Writing in Plato's Laws," *Political Theory* 43 (5): 657–77.

Franchi, Roberta, 2016, "Approaching the 'Spiritual Gospel': Nonnus as Interpreter of John," in Domenico Accorinti (ed.), *Brill's Companion to Nonnus of Panopolis*, 240–66, BCCS, Leiden: Brill.

Fraser, A. D., 1941, "The Ithacan Cave of the *Odyssey*," *CP* 36 (1): 57–60.

Fraser, Kyle A., 2004, "Zosimos of Panopolis and the Book of Enoch: Alchemy as Forbidden Knowledge," *Aries* 4 (2): 125–47.

Frede, Michael, 1987, "Numenius," *ANRW* 2.36.2: 1034–75.

Freistedt, Emil, 1928, *Altchristliche Totengedächtnistage und ihre Beziehung zum Jenseits-Glauben und Totenkultus der Antike*, Liturgiegeschichtliche Quellen und Forschungen 24, Münster: Aschendorff.

Frickel, Josef, 1988, *Das Dunkel um Hippolyt von Rom. Ein Lösungsversuch: Die Schriften Elenchos und Contra Noëtum*, Grazer theologische Studien 13, Graz: Universität Graz.

Friedlieb, J. H., 1852, *Die Sibyllinischen Weissagungen. Vollstaendig gesammelt, nach neuer Handschriften – Vergleichung, mit kritischem Commentare und metrischer deutscher Uebersetzung*, Leipzig: Weigel.

Friedrich, Gerhard, 1964, "εὐαγγελίζομαι," *TDNT* 2.707–37.

Friesen, Courtney J. P., 2014, "Dionysus as Jesus: The Incongruity of a Love Feast in Achilles Tatius's *Leucippe and Clitophon* 2.2," *HTR* 107 (2): 222–40.

Frisius, Mark A., 2011, *Tertullian's Use of the Pastoral Epistles, Hebrews, James, 1 and 2 Peter, and Jude*, Studies in Biblical Literature 143, New York: Lang.

Führer, Rudolf, 1985, "Noch ein Akrostichon in den Kyraniden," *ZPE* 58: 270.

Funk, Francis Xaver, 1887, *Doctrina Duodecim Apostolorum. Canones apostolorum ecclesiastici ac Reliquae doctrinae de duabus viis expositiones veteres*, Tübingen: Laupp.

Funk, Francis Xaver, Wilhelm Schneemelcher, and Karl Bihlmeyer (eds.), 1970, *Die apostolischen Väter*, 3rd ed., Sammlung ausgewählter kirchen- und dogmengeschichtlicher Quellenschriften 2/1.1, Tübingen: Mohr-Siebeck.

Gager, John G., 1972, *Moses in Greco-Roman Paganism*, SBLMS 16, Nashville: Abingdon.

Gager, John G., 1973, "The Dialogue of Paganism with Judaism: Bar Cochba to Julian," *HUCA* 44: 89–118.

Gagné, Renaud, 2006, "What Is the Pride of Halicarnassus?," *ClA* 25 (1): 1–33.

Gaisford, Thomas, 1822, *Joannis Stobæi Florilegium*, vol. 1, Oxford: Clarendon.

Galdi, M., 1927, "De Tertulliani 'de cultu feminarum' et Cypriani 'ad virgines' libellis Commentatio," in *Raccolta di scritti in onore de Felice Ramorino*, 539–67, Pubblicazioni della Università Cattolica del Sacro Cuore, Scienze Filologiche 7, Milano: Società editrice "Vita e Pensiero."

Gallagher, Edmon, 2012, *Hebrew Scripture in Patristic Biblical Theory: Canon, Language, Text*, VCSup 114, Leiden: Brill.

Ganszyniec, R., 1920–21, "Studien zu den Kyraniden," *Byzantinisch-Neugriechische Jahrbücher* 1: 353–67, 2: 56–65, 445–52.

García y Bellido, Antonio, 1960, "Némesis y su culto en España," *Boletin de la Real Academia de la Historia* 147: 119–47.

Gaster, Moses, 1893, "The Apocalypse of Abraham," *Transactions of the Society of Biblical Archæology* 9 (1): 195–226.

Gaston, Thomas E., 2009, "The Influence of Platonism on the Early Apologists," *HeyJ* 50 (4): 573–80.

Gauger, Jörg-Dieter, 1998, *Sibyllinische Weissagungen: Griechisch-deutsch*, Wissenschaftlich Beratung, Düsseldorf: Artemis & Winkler.

Gaussen, Louis, 1841, *Theopneustia: The Plenary Inspiration of the Holy Scriptures*, London: Samuel Bagster and Sons.

Geerard, Maurice (ed.), 1974–87, *Clavis patrum Graecorum*, CChr Series Latina, 5 vols., Turnhout: Brepols.

Geffcken, Johannes, 1902a, *Komposition und Entstehungszeit der Oracula Sibyllina*, TU 23, Leipzig: Hinrichs.

Geffcken, Johannes, 1902b, *Die Oracula Sibyllina*, Die griechischen christlichen Schriftsteller der ersten drei Jahrunderte, Leipzig: Hinrichs.

Geffcken, Johannes, 1978, *The Last Days of Greco-Roman Paganism*, Europe in the Middle Ages, Selected Studies 8, Amsterdam: North-Holland.

Gerlo, A., A. Kroymann, R. Willems, J. H. Waszink, J. G. P. Borleffs, A. Reifferscheid, G. Wissowa, E. Dekkers, J. J. Thierry, E. Evans, and A. Harnack (eds.), 1954, *Quinti Septimi Florentis Tertulliani Opera*, part 2: *Opera Montanistica*, CChr Series Latina 2, Turnholt: Brepols.

Gesner, Conrad, 1543, *Ioannis Stobei Sententiae ex thesauris graecorum delectae*, Tiguri: Froschoverus.

Gesner, Conrad, 1557, *Ioannis Stobei Sententiae ex thesauris graecorum delectae*, 2nd ed., Paris: Perier.

Gesner, Conrad, 1609, *Ioannis Stobei Sententiae ex thesauris graecorum delectae*, 3rd ed., Lyons: Frellon.

Gesner, Conrad, and Rijklof Michaël van Goens, 1765, *Porphyrius, De Antro Nympharum*, Utrecht: van Paddenburg.

Gilbert, Maurice, 1984, "Wisdom Literature," in Michael E. Stone (ed.), *Jewish Writings of the Second Temple Period: Apocrypha, Pseudepigrapha, Qumran Sectarian Writings, Philo, Josephus*, 283–324, CRINT 2/2, Assen: Van Gorcum.

Gilbert, Maurice, 2008, "The Vetus Latina of Ecclesiasticus," in Géza G. Xeravits and József Zsengellér (eds.), *Studies in the Book of Ben Sira: Papers of the Third International Conference on the Deuterocanonical Books, Shime'on Centre, Pápa, Hungary, 18–20 May, 2006*, 1–9, JSJSup 127, Leiden: Brill.

Gile, Jason, 2011, "The Additions to Ben Sira and the Book's Multiform Textual Witness," in Jean-Sébastien Rey and Jan Joosten (eds.), *The Texts and Versions of the Book of Ben Sira: Transmission and Interpretation*, 237–56, JSJSup 150, Leiden: Brill.

Ginouvès, René, 1962, *Balaneutikè: Recherches sur le bain dans l'antiquité grecque*, Bibliothèque des Écoles Françaises d'Athènes et de Rome 200, Paris: Boccard.

Ginouvès, René, 1969, "L'Architecture," in Jean des Gagniers, Pierre Devambez, Lilly Kahil, and René Ginouvès, *Laodicée du Lycos. Le Nymphée, Campagnes 1961–1963*, 13–185, Québec: Les Presses de l'Université Laval.

Gippert, Jost, 1997, "Physiologus. Die Verarbeitung antiker Naturmythen in einem frühchristlichen Text," *Studia Iranica, Mesopotamica et Anatolica* 3: 161–77.

Giuman, Marco, 2008, *Melissa. Archeologia delle api e del miele nella Grecia antica*, Università degli studi di Cagliari, Roma: Bretschneider.

Gnuse, Robert, 1985, *The Authority of the Bible: Theories of Inspiration, Revelation and the Canon of Scripture*, New York: Paulist.

Goldingay, John F., 1977, "James Barr on Fundamentalism," *Churchman* 91 (4): 295–308.

Golega, Joseph, 1930, *Studien über die Evangeliendichtung des Nonnos von Panopolis. Ein Beitrag zur Geschichte der Bibeldichtung im Altertum*, Breslauer Studien zur historischen Theologie 15, Breslau: Müller and Seifert.

González, José M., 2000, "*Musai Hypophetores*: Apollonius of Rhodes on Inspiration and Interpretation," *HSCP* 100: 269–92.

Goodacre, Mark, 2012, *Thomas and the Gospels: The Case for Thomas's Familiarity with the Synoptics*, Grand Rapids, MI: Eerdmans.

Goodman, Martin, 1986, "Jewish Literature Composed in Greek," in Emil Schürer, *The History of the Jewish People in the Age of Jesus Christ (175 B.C.–A.D. 135)*, 3.470–704, rev. ed., ed. Geza Vermes, Fergus Millar, Matthew Black, and Martin Goodman, 3 vols., Edinburgh: T&T Clark.

Goold, G. P. (trans.), 1977, *Manilius. Astronomica*, LCL 469, Cambridge: Harvard University Press.

Goram, Otto, 1859, "De Pseudo-Phocylide," *Phil* 14 (1–4): 91–112.

Gow, A. S. F., and D. L. Page, 1965, *The Greek Anthology: Hellenistic Epigrams*, 2 vols., Cambridge: Cambridge University Press.

Grant, Robert M., 1947, "The Bible of Theophilus of Antioch," *JBL* 66 (2): 173–96.

Grant, Robert M., 1965, *The Formation of the New Testament*, New York: Harper & Row.

Grant, Robert M., 1997, *Irenaeus of Lyons*, ECF, London: Routledge.

Grant, Robert M., 1999, *Early Christians and Animals*, London: Routledge.

Graux, Ch., 1878, "Lettre inédite d'Harpocration a un empereur, publiée d'après un manuscrit de la *Biblioteca nacional* de Madrid," *RevPhil* 2: 65–77.

Greaves, Alan M., 2012, "Divination at Archaic Branchidai-Didyma," *Hesperia* 81 (2): 177–206.

Groff, William, 1897, "L'étude sur la sorcellerie, ou le role que la Bible a joué chez les sorciers," *Bulletin de l'Institut Égyptien* 8: 67–81.

Gruen, Erich S., 1998, *Heritage and Hellenism: The Reinvention of Jewish Tradition*, Hellenistic Culture and Society 30, Berkeley: University of California Press.

Gruen, Erich S., 2002, *Diaspora: Jews amidst Greeks and Romans*, Cambridge: Harvard University Press.

Guarducci, Margherita, 1977, "La statua di 'Sant'Ippolito'," in *Ricerche su Ippolito*, StEphAug 13, 17–30, Rome: Institutum Patristicum Augustinianum.

Guarducci, Margherita, 1989, "La 'Statua di Sant'Ippolito' e la sua provenienza," in *Nuove ricerche su Ippolito*, 61–74, StEphAug 30, Rome: Institutum Patristicum Augustinianum.

Guarino, Thomas G., 2013, *Vincent of Lérins and the Development of Christian Doctrine*, Foundations of Theological Exegesis and Christian Spirituality, Grand Rapids, MI: Baker Academic.

Guidorizzi, Giulio, 1973, "L'Opuscolo di Galeno 'De Dignotione ex Insomniis'," *Bollettino del Comitato per la preparazione dell'edizione nazionale dei classici greci e latini* 21: 81–105.

Guillaumin, Marie-Louise, 1976, "L'Exploitation des 'Oracles Sibyllins' par Lactance et par le 'Discours a l'Assemblée des Saints'," in J. Fontaine and M. Perrin (eds.), *Lactance et son temps: Recherches actuelles. Actes du IVe Colloque d'Études Historiques et Patristiques Chantilly 21–23 septembre 1976*, 185–202, Théologie Historique 48, Paris: Beauchesne.

Gundel, Wilhelm, and Hans Georg Gundel, 1966, *Astrologumena: Die astrologische Literatur in der Antike und ihre Geschichte*, Sudhoffs Archiv 6, Wiesbaden: Steiner.

Guthrie, Kenneth, 1987, *The Neoplatonic Writings of Numenius*, Great Works of Philosophy, Lawrence, KS: Selene.

Gutjahr, F. S., 1904, *Die Glaubwürdigkeit des Irenäischen Zeugnisses über die Abfassung des vierten kanonischen Evangeliums*, Graz: Leuschner & Lubensky.

Haardt, Robert, 1971, *Gnosis: Character and Testimony*, trans. J. F. Hendry, Leiden: Brill.

Hachlili, Rachel, 2005, *Jewish Funerary Customs, Practices and Rites in the Second Temple Period*, JSJSup 94, Leiden: Brill.

Hadas, Moses, 1972, *Hellenistic Culture: Fusion and Diffusion*, New York: Norton.

Haenchen, Ernst, 1965, *Gott und Mensch: Gesammelte Aufsätze*, Tübingen: Mohr-Siebeck.

Haenchen, Ernst, 1984, *John 1: A Commentary on the Gospel of John Chapters 1–6*, Hermeneia, Philadelphia: Fortress.

Hahm, David E., 1990, "The Ethical Doxography of Arius Didymus," *ANRW* 2.36.4: 2935–3055.

Halfmann, Helmut, 1986, *Itinera principum: Geschichte und Typologie der Kaiserreisen im Römischen Reich*, Heidelberger Althistorische Beiträge und Epigraphische Studien 2, Stuttgart: Steiner.

Hall, S. G. (trans.), 1972, "Poimandres," in Werner Foerster, *Gnosis: A Selection of Gnostic Texts*, vol. 1: *Patristic Evidence*, ed. R. McL. Wilson, 326–35, Oxford: Clarendon.

Halleux, Robert, and Jacques Schamp, 1985, *Les lapidaires grecs*, Budé, Paris: Les Belles Lettres.

Halliday, W. R., 1913, *Greek Divination: A Study of Its Methods and Principles*, London: Macmillan.

Hällström, Gunnar af, 1985, *Charismatic Succession: A Study on Origen's Concept of Prophecy*, Publications of the Finnish Exegetical Society 42, Helsinki: Finnish Exegetical Society.

Halm-Tisserant, Monique, and Gérard Siebert, 1997, "Nymphai," in Fondation pour le Lexicon Iconographicum Mythologiae Classicae, *Lexicon Iconographicum Mythologiae Classicae*, 891–902, vol. 8, Zurich: Artemis.

Hanges, James C., 1998, "1 Corinthians 4:6 and the Possibility of Written Bylaws in the Corinthian Church," *JBL* 117 (2): 275–98.

Hani, Jean, 1974, "Les nymphes du Nil," *L'Antiquité Classique* 43 (1): 212–24.

Hansen, Mogens Herman, 1978, "*Nomos* and *Psephisma* in Fourth-Century Athens," *GRBS* 19 (4): 315–30.

Hanson, Anthony Tyrrell, 1968, *Studies in the Pastoral Epistles*, London: SPCK.

Hanson, Anthony Tyrrell, 1983, *The Living Utterances of God: The New Testament Exegesis of the Old*, London: Darton, Longman and Todd.

Hanson, R. P. C., 1954, *Origen's Doctrine of Tradition*, London: SPCK.

Hanson, R. P. C., 2002, *Allegory and Event: A Study of the Sources and Significance of Origen's Interpretation of Scripture*, Louisville: Westminster John Knox.

Harland, Philip A., 2011, "Pausing at the Intersection of Religion and Travel," in Philip A. Harland (ed.), *Travel and Religion in Antiquity*, 1–26, Studies in Christianity and Judaism 21, Waterloo, ON: Wilfrid Laurier University Press.

Harnack, Adolf, 1886, *Lehrbuch der Dogmengeschichte*, vol. 1: *Die Entstehung des kirchlichen Dogmas*, Freiburg: Mohr-Siebeck.

Harnack, Adolf, 1904, *Geschichte der altchristlichen Litteratur bis Eusebius*, vol. 2: *Die Chronologie der altchristlichen Litteratur bis Eusebius*, Leipzig: Hinrichs.

Harnack, Adolf, 1914, "Tertullians Bibliothek christlicher Schriften," *Sitzungsberichte der Königlich Preussischen Akademie der Wissenschaften* 10: 303–34.

Harries, Byron, 1994, "The Pastoral Mode in the *Dionysiaca*," in Neil Hopkinson (ed.), *Studies in the* Dionysiaca *of Nonnus*, 63–85, CPSSup 17, Cambridge: Cambridge Philological Society.

Harrington, Daniel J., 1996, *Wisdom Texts from Qumran*, Literature of the Dead Sea Scrolls, London: Routledge.

Harris, C. R. S., 1973, *The Heart and Vascular System in Ancient Greek Medicine: From Alcmaeon to Galen*, Oxford: Clarendon.

Harris, Harriet A., 2006, "Fundamentalism(s)," in Judith M. Lieu and J. W. Rogerson (eds.), *Oxford Handbook of Biblical Studies*, 810–40, Oxford: Oxford University Press.

Harris, Harriet A., 2008, *Fundamentalism and Evangelicals*, OTM, Oxford: Oxford University Press.

Harris, Harriet A., 2015, "Fundamentalist Readings of the Bible," in John Riches (ed.) *The New Cambridge History of the Bible*, vol. 4: *From 1750 to the Present*, 328–43, Cambridge: Cambridge University Press.

Harris, J. Rendel, 1885, *The Teaching of the Apostles and the Sibylline Books*, Cambridge: Wallis.

Harris, William V., 1991, "Why Did the Codex Supplant the Book-Roll?," in John Monfasani and Ronald G. Musto (eds.), *Renaissance Society and Culture: Essays in Honor of Eugene F. Rice, Jr.*, 71–85, New York: Italica.

Harris, William V., 2009, *Dreams and Experience in Classical Antiquity*, Cambridge: Harvard University Press.

Harrison, P. N., 1921, *The Problem of the Pastoral Epistles*, London: Oxford University Press.

Hasebroek, Johannes, 1921, *Untersuchungen zur Geschichte des Kaisers Septimius Severus*, Heidelberg: Winter.

Hasler, Victor, 1978, *Die Briefe an Timotheus und Titus (Pastoralbriefe)*, Zürcher Bibelkommentare 12, Zurich: Theologischer.

Hassan, Selim, 1953, *Excavations at Giza, 1936-1937*, vol. 8: *The Great Sphinx and Its Secrets: Historical Studies in the Light of Recent Excavations*, Cairo: Government Press.

Hauck, Albert, 1877, *Tertullian's Leben und Schriften*, Erlagen: Deichert.

Haufe, Günter, 1973, "Gnostische Irrlehre und ihre Abwehr in den Pastoralbriefen," in Karl-Wolfgang Tröger (ed.), *Gnosis und Neues Testament: Studien aus Religionswissenschaft und Theologie*, 325–39, Gütersloh: Gerd Mohn.

Hawass, Zahi, 1995, "The Programs of the Royal Funerary Complexes of the Fourth Dynasty," in David O'Connor and David P. Silverman (eds.), *Ancient Egyptian Kingship*, 221-62, PrÄ 9, Leiden: Brill.

Hawass, Zahi, 1998, *The Secret of the Sphinx: Restoration Past and Present*, Cairo: American University in Cairo Press.

Hays, Richard B., 2011, "The Future of Scripture," *Wesleyan Theological Journal* 46 (1): 24–38.

Hearne, Thomas, 1720, *A Collection of Curious Discourses*, Oxford: The Theater.

Hedrick, Charles W., Jr., 2000, *History and Silence: Purge and Rehabilitation of Memory in Late Antiquity*, Austin: University of Texas Press.

Heerink, Mark A. J., 2007, "Going a Step Further: Valerius Flaccus' Metapoetical Reading of Propertius' Hylas," *ClQ* 57 (2): 606–20.

Heide, Martin, 2012, *Das Testament Abrahams. Edition und Übersetzung der arabischen und äthiopischen Versionen*, Aethiopistische Forschungen 76, Wiesbaden: Harrassowitz.

Heine, Ronald E. (trans.), 1982, *Origen, Homilies on Genesis and Exodus*, FC, Washington, DC: Catholic University of America Press.

Heine, Ronald E. (trans.), 1989, *Origen, Commentary on the Gospel According to John, Books 1-10*, FC 80, Washington, DC: Catholic University of America Press.

Heine, Ronald E., 2010, *Origen: Scholarship in the Service of the Church*, Christian Theology in Context, Oxford: Oxford University Press.

Heinen, Heinz, 2007, "Ägypten im Römischen Reich. Beobachtungen zum Thema Akkulturation und Identität," in Stefan Pfeiffer (ed.), *Ägypten under fremden Herrschern zwischen persischer Satrapie und römischer Provinz*, 186–207, Oikumene Studien zur antiken Weltgeschichte 3, Frankfurt am Main: Antike.

Heither, Theresia, 1996, "Origenes als Exeget. Ein Forschungsüberblick," in Georg Schöllgen and Clemens Scholten (eds.), *Stimuli: Exegese und ihre Hermeneutik in Antike und Christentum. Festschrift für Ernst Dassmann*, 141–53, JACErg 23, Münster: Aschendorff.

Hengel, Martin, 1995, *Studies in Early Christology*, Edinburgh: T&T Clark.

Hengel, Martin, 2000, *The Four Gospels and the One Gospel of Jesus Christ*, London: SCM.

Henry, René (ed.), 1959, *Photius. Bibliothèque*, 7 vols., Budé, Paris: Les Belles Lettres.

Hense, Otto, 1894, *Ioannis Stobaei Anthologii, Libri Duo Priores*, vol. 3: *Anthologii Librum Tertium*, Berlin: Weidmann.

Hercher, Rudolf, 1858, *Aeliani, De natura animalium, varia historia, epistolae et fragmenta. Porphyrii philosophi, De abstinentia et De antro nympharum. Philonis Byzantii: De septem orbis spectaculis*, Paris: Didot.

Herkenne, Henr., 1899, *De Veteris Latinae Ecclesiastici capitibus i–xliii, una cum notis ex eiusdem libri translationibus aethiopica, armeniaca, copticis, latina altera, syro-hexaplari depromptis*, Leipzig: Hinrichs.

Hernández, Juan, Jr., 2011, "The Relevance of Andrew of Caesarea for New Testament Textual Criticism," *JBL* 130 (1): 183–96.

Hernández de la Fuente, David, 2013, "Parallels between Dionysos and Christ in Late Antiquity: Miraculous Healings in Nonnus' *Dionysiaca*," in Alberto Bernabé, Miguel Herrero de Jáuregui, Ana Isabel Jiménez San Cristóbal, and Raquel Martín Hernández (eds.), *Redefining Dionysos*, 464–87, MythosEikonPoiesis 5, Berlin: de Gruyter.

Herzer, Jens, 2004, "'Von Gottes Geist durchweht': Die Inspiration der Schrift nach 2Tim 3,16 und bei Philo von Alexandrien," in Roland Deines and Karl-Wilhelm Niebuhr (eds.), *Philo und das Neue Testament: Wechselseitige Wahrnehmungen: 1. Internationales Symposium zum Corpus Judaeo-Hellenisticum 1.–4. Mai 2003, Eisenach/Jena*, 223–40, WUNT 1/172, Tübingen: Mohr-Siebeck.

Heslam, Peter S., 2000, "The Meeting of the Wellsprings: Kuyper and Warfield at Princeton," in Luis E. Luco (ed.), *Religion, Pluralism, and Public Life: Abraham Kuyper's Legacy for the Twenty-First Century*, 22–44, Grand Rapids, MI: Eerdmans.

Heurtley, C. A. (trans.), 1886, "The Commonitory of Vincent of Lérins," *NPNF* (2nd series) 11.127–59.

Heurtley, W. A., 1939–40, "Excavations in Ithaca, 1930–35," *ABSA* 40: 1–13.

Hill, Charles E., 1989a, "Hades of Hippolytus or Tartarus of Tertullian? The Authorship of the Fragment *De Universo*," *VC* 43 (2): 105–26.

Hill, Charles E., 1989b, "Hippolytus and Hades: The Authorship of the Fragment *De Universo*," *StPatr* 21: 254–9.

Hill, Douglas, 1967, "On the Third Day," *ExpTim* 78 (9): 266–7.

Himmelfarb, Martha, 2009, "Abrahamic Writings," *RPP* 1.16–17.

Himmelmann-Wildschütz, Nikolaus, 1957, *ΘΕΟΛΗΠΤΟΣ*, Marburg-Lahn: Archäologisches Seminar Marburg.

Hoffmann, Gustav, 1903, "Zwei Hymnen der Thomasakten," *ZNW* 4: 273–309.

Hoh, J., 1919, *Die Lehre des Hl. Irenäus über das Neue Testament*, Neutestamentliche Abhandlungen 7/4–5, Münster: Aschendorff.

Holl, Karl (ed.), 1901, *Fragmente vornicänischer Kirchenväter aus den Sacra Parallela*, TU 20/2, Leipzig: Hinrichs.

Hollis, Adrian, 1976, "Some Allusions to Earlier Hellenistic Poetry in Nonnus," *ClQ* 26 (1): 142–50.

Hollis, Adrian, 1994, "Nonnus and Hellenistic Poetry," in Neil Hopkinson (ed.), *Studies in the* Dionysiaca *of Nonnus*, 43–62, CPSSup 17, Cambridge: Cambridge Philological Society.

Holowchak, M. Andrew, 2002, *Ancient Science and Dreams: Oneirology in Greco-Roman Antiquity*, Lanham, MD: University Press of America.

Holsinger-Friesen, Thomas, 2009, *Irenaeus and Genesis: A Study of Competition in Early Christian Hermeneutics*, Journal of Theological Interpretation Supplement 1, Winona Lake, IN: Eisenbrauns.

Holtzmann, Heinrich Julius, 1880, *Die Pastoralbriefe, kritisch und exegetisch behandelt*, Leipzig: Engelmann.

Holzhausen, Jens, 1994, *Der "Mythos vom Menschen" im hellenistischen Ägypten: Eine Studie zum "Poimandres" (= CH I), zu Valentin und dem gnostischen Mythos*, Theophaneia 33, Bodenheim: Athenäum–Hain–Hanstein.

Holzhausen, Jens, 1997, "Hermes Trismegistos: Poimandres," in Carsten Colpe and Jens Holzhausen, *Das Corpus Hermeticum Deutsch: Übersetzung, Darstellung und Kommentierung in drei Teilen*, 1.10–22, Clavis Pansophiae, 3 vols., Stuttgart–Bad Cannstatt: Frommann–Holzboog.

Hooker, Mischa André, 2007, "The Use of Sibyls and Sibylline Oracles in Early Christian Writers," Ph.D. dissertation, University of Cincinnati, Cincinnati.

Horton, George, 1929, *Home of Nymphs and Vampires: The Isles of Greece*, Indianapolis: Bobbs–Merrill.

Hošek, Radislav, 1974, "Kyme (A Historical Survey)," in Jan Bouzek (ed.), *Anatolian Collection of Charles University (Kyme I)*, 179–206, Praha: Universita Karlova.

Houghton, H. A. G., 2016, *The Latin New Testament: A Guide to its Early History, Texts, and Manuscripts*, Oxford: Oxford University Press.

Hülsen, Julius, 1919, *Milet. Ergebnisse der Ausgrabungen und Untersuchungen seit dem Jahre 1899*, vol. 1/5: *Das Nymphaeum*, Berlin: de Gruyter.

Hulskamp, Maithe, 2016, "*On Regimen* and the Question of Medical Dreams in the Hippocratic Corpus," in Lesley Dean-Jones and Ralph M. Rosen (eds.), *Ancient Concepts of the Hippocratic: Papers Presented at the XIIIth International Hippocrates Colloquium Austin, Texas, August 2008*, 258–70, SAM 46, Leiden: Brill.

Hušek, Vit, 2016, "Origen, Paul Ricœur and the Role of Literal Meaning," in Anders-Christian Jacobsen (ed.), *Origeniana Undecima: Origen and Origenism in the History of Western Thought. Papers of the 11th International Origen Congress, Aarhus University, 26–31 August 2013*, 95–103, BETL 279, Leuven: Peeters.

Huttner, Ulrich, 1997, "Wolf und Eber: die Flüsse von Laodikeia in Phrygien," in Johannes Nollé, Bernhard Overbeck, and Peter Weiss (eds.), *Internationales Kolloquium zur kaiserzeitlichen Münzprägung Kleinasiens, 27.-30. April 1994 in der Staatlichen Münzsammlung, München*, 93–109, Nomismata 1, Milano: Ennerre.

Huttner, Ulrich, 2013, *Early Christianity in the Lycus Valley*, trans. David Green, AJEC 85, Early Christianity in Asia Minor 1, Leiden: Brill.

Huxley, G. L., 1989, "Thracian Hylas," *JHS* 109: 185–6.

Ilan, Tal, 2016, "The Jewish Community in Egypt before and after 117 CE in Light of Old and New Papyri," in Yair Furstenberg (ed.), *Jewish and Christian Communal Identities in the Roman World*, 203–24, AJEC 94, Leiden: Brill.

Imorde, Joseph, 2011, "Physiologus," *RPP* 10.104–5.

Inscriptiones graecae 14, 1873, Berlin: de Gruyter.

Irigoin, Jean, 1969, "L'Italie méridionale et la tradition des textes antiques," *Jahrbuch der Österreichischen Byzantinischen Gesellschaft* 18: 37–55.

Irigoin, Jean, 1975, "La culture grecque dans l'Occident latin du VIIe au XIe siècle," in *La cultura antica nell'Occidente latino dal VII all'XI secolo*, 435–6, Settimane di studio del Centro Italiano di studi sull'alto Medioevo 22, Spoleto: Presso la sede del Centro.

Irigoin, Jean, 2000, "Deux servantes maitresses en alternance: paléographie et philologie," in Giancarlo Prato (ed.), *I manoscritti greci tra riflessione e dibattito: Atti del V Colloquio Internazionale di Paleografia Greca (Cremona, 4–10 ottobre 1998)*, 589–600, 2 vols., Papyrologica Florentina 31, Florence: Edizioni Gonnelli.

Isager, Signe, 1998, "The Pride of Halikarnassos: Editio princeps of an inscription from Salmakis," *ZPE* 123: 1–23.

Isetta, Sandra, 1983, "La struttura unitaria del 'De cultu feminarum' di Tertulliano," *Civiltà Classica e Cristiana* 4 (1): 43–68.

Isetta, Sandra, 1986, *L'Eleganza delle donne*, Biblioteca Patristica, Firenze: Nardini.

Israeli, Shlomit, 1998, "*ṯ3w n ʿnḫ* ('breath of life') in the Medinet Habu War Texts," in Irene Shirun-Grumach (ed.), *Jerusalem Studies in Egyptology*, 271–83, Ägypten und Altes Testament 40, Wiesbaden: Harassowitz.

Jackson, Howard M., 1999, "A New Proposal for the Origin of the Hermetic God Poimandres," *ZPE* 128: 95–106.

Jacobsen, Anders-Christian, 2010, "Allegorical Interpretation of Geography in Origen's Homilies on the Book of Joshua," *Religion and Theology* 17 (3–4): 289–301.

Jaeger, Werner, 1961, *Paideia: The Ideals of Greek Culture*, vol. 3: *The Conflict of Cultural Ideals in the Age of Plato*, Oxford: Blackwell.

James, Montague Rhodes, 1892, *The Testament of Abraham: The Greek Text Now First Edited with an Introduction and Notes*, Texts and Studies 11/2, Cambridge: Cambridge University Press.

Jansen, Enno, 1980, *Testament Abrahams*, JSHRZ 3/2, Gütersloh: Gütersloher Verlagshaus.

Jansen, H. Ludin, 1977, "Die Frage nach Tendenz und Verfasserschaft im Poimandres," in Geo Widengren (ed.), *Proceedings of the International Colloquium on Gnosticism, Stockholm August 20–25, 1973*, 157–63, Filologisk-filosofiska 17, Kungliga Vitterhets historie och antikvitets akademiens handlingar, Stockholm: Almqvist & Wiksell International.

Jenson, Robin M., 2011, *Living Water: Images, Symbols, and Settings of Early Christian Baptism*, VCSup 105, Leiden: Brill.

Johnson, Aaron P., 2006, *Ethnicity and Argument in Eusebius' Praeparatio Evangelica*, OECS, Oxford: Oxford University Press.

Johnson, Aaron P., 2013, *Religion and Identity in Porphyry of Tyre: The Limits of Hellenism in Late Antiquity*, Greek Culture in the Roman World, Cambridge: Cambridge University Press.

Johnson, Luke Timothy, 2009, "How is the Bible True? Let Me Count the Ways," *Commonweal* 136 (10): 12–16.

Jones, A. H. M., J. R. Martindale, and J. Morris, 1971, *The Prosopography of the Later Roman Empire*, vol. 1: *A. D. 260–395*, Cambridge: Cambridge University Press.

Jones, Prudence J., 2005, *Reading Rivers in Roman Literature and Culture*, Roman Studies: Interdisciplinary Approaches, Lanham, MD: Lexington Books.

Jones, W. H. S. (trans.), 1979, *Hippocrates*, vol. 4, LCL 150, Cambridge: Harvard University Press.

Joost-Gaugier, Christiane L., 2006, *Measuring Heaven: Pythagoras and His Influence on Thought and Art in Antiquity and the Middle Ages*, Ithaca, NY: Cornell University Press.

Joppich, Godehard, 1965, *Salus Carnis: Eine Untersuchung in der Theologie des hl. Irenäus von Lyon*, Münsterschwarzacher Studien 1, Münsterschwarzach: Vier-Türme-Verlag.

Jordan, David, 2005, "Notes on Verses in *Cyranides*, Book I," *ZPE* 154: 117–24.

Jordan, Paul, 1998, *Riddles of the Sphinx*, Washington Square: New York University Press.

Jori, Alberto, 2004, "Cyranides," *BNP* 4.1–2.

Jowett, Benjamin, 1860, "On the Interpretation of Scripture," in *Essays and Reviews*, 330–433, London: Longman, Green, Longman, and Roberts.

Kaibel, George (ed.), 1878, *Epigrammata Graeca ex Lapidibus Conlecta*, Berlin: Reimer.

Kaimakis, Dimitris (ed.), 1974, *Der Physiologus nach der ersten Redaktion*, BKP 63, Meisenheim am Glan: Hain.

Kaimakis, Dimitris, 1976, *Die Kyraniden*, BKP 76, Meisenheim am Glan: Hain.

Kaldellis, Anthony, 2005, "Julian, the Hierophant of Eleusis, and the Abolition of Constantius' Tyranny," *ClQ* 55 (2): 652–5.

Kaletsch, Hans, 2003, "Cyme," *BNP* 3.1048–50.

Kalin, Everett Roy, 1967, "Argument from Inspiration in the Canonization of the New Testament," Th.D. dissertation, Harvard University, Cambridge.

Kamesar, Adam, 1993, *Jerome, Greek Scholarship, and the Hebrew Bible: A Study of the Quaestiones Hebraicae in Genesim*, OCM, Oxford: Clarendon.

Kamesar, Adam, 2009, "Biblical Interpretation in Philo," in Adam Kamesar (ed.), *The Cambridge Companion to Philo*, 65–91, Cambridge: Cambridge University Press.

Karivieri, Arja, 2010, "Magic and Syncretic Religious Culture in the East," in David M. Gwynn and Susanne Bangert (eds.), *Religious Diversity in Late Antiquity*, 401–34, Late Antique Archaeology 6, Leiden: Brill.

Kaster, Robert A., 1988, *Guardians of Language: The Grammarian and Society in Late Antiquity*, TCH 11, Berkeley: University of California Press.

Kay, N. M. (ed.), 2001, *Ausonius Epigrams*, London: Duckworth.

Kearns, Conleth, 2011, *The Expanded Text of Ecclesiasticus: Its Teaching on the Future Life as a Clue to Its Origin*, ed. Pancratius C. Beentjes, DCLS 11, Berlin: de Gruyter.

Keith, Chris, 2009, *The Pericope Adulterae, the Gospel of John, and the Literacy of John*, NTTSD 38, Leiden: Brill.

Kelsey, David H., 1975, *The Uses of Scripture in Recent Theology*, Philadelphia: Fortress.

Kenney, John Peter, 1992, "*Proschresis* Revisited: An Essay in Numenian Theology," in Robert J. Daly (ed.), *Origeniana Quinta: Historica – Text and Method – Biblica – Philosophica – Theologica – Origenism and Later Developments. Papers of the 5th International Origen Congress, Boston College, 14–18 August 1989*, 217–30, BETL 105, Leuven: Leuven University Press.

Kerkeslager, Allen, 2006, "The Jews in Egypt and Cyrenaica, 66–c. 235 CE," in Allen Kerkeslager, Claudia Setzer, Paul Trebilco, and David Goodblatt, "The Diaspora from 66 to c. 235 CE," 53–68, in Stephen T. Katz (ed.), *Cambridge History of Judaism*, 53–92, vol. 4: *The Late Roman-Rabbinic Period*, Cambridge: Cambridge University Press.

Kessels, A. H. M., 1969, "Ancient Systems of Dream-Classification," *Mnemosyne* 22 (4): 389–424.

Kessels, A. H. M., 1978, *Studies on the Dream in Greek Literature*, Utrecht: HES.

Keydell, Rudolf, 1936, "Nonnos. 15," *PW* 17.904–20.

King, David A., 2004, "A Hellenistic Astrological Table Deemed Worthy of Being Penned in Gold Ink: The Arabic Tradition of Vettius Valens' Auxiliary Function for Finding the Length of Life," in Charles Burnett, Jan P. Hogendijk, Kim Plofker, and Michio Yano (eds.), *Studies in the History of the Exact Sciences in Honour of David Pingree*, 666–714, Islamic Philosophy, Theology and Science Texts and Studies 54, Leiden: Brill.

King, J. Christopher, 2005, *Origen on the Song of Songs as the Spirit of Scripture: The Bridegroom's Perfect Marriage-Song*, OTM, Oxford: Oxford University Press.

Kingsley, Peter, 1993, "Poimandres: The Etymology of the Name and the Origins of the Hermetics," *Journal of the Warburg and Courtauld Institutes* 56: 1–24.

Kingsley, Peter, 1995, *Ancient Philosophy, Mystery, and Magic: Empedocles and Pythagorean Tradition*, Oxford: Clarendon.

Kirk, Alan, 2016, *Q in Matthew: Ancient Media, Memory, and Early Scribal Transmission of the Jesus Tradition*, LNTS 564, London: Bloomsbury.

Kirkpatrick, Jonathan, 2013, "The Jews and their God of Wine," *ARG* 15 (1): 167–85.

Kitchen, Kenneth A., 1970–90, *Ramesside Inscriptions: Historical and Biographical*, Monumenta Hannah Sheen dedicata 5, 8 vols., Oxford: Blackwell.

Klauck, Hans-Josef, 2003, *The Religious Context of Early Christianity: A Guide to Graeco-Roman Religions*, Minneapolis: Fortress.

Klawans, Jonathan, 2017, "The Pseudo-Jewishness of Pseudo-Phocylides," *JSP* 26 (3): 201–33.

Klein, Franz-Norbert, 1962, *Die Lichtterminologie bei Philon von Alexandrien und in den hermetischen Schriften: Untersuchungen zur Struktur der religiösen Sprache der hellenistischen Mystik*, Leiden: Brill.

Klöpper, A., 1904, "Zur Soteriologie der Pastoralbriefe (Tit. 3, 4–7; 2. Tim. 1, 9–11; Tit. 2, 11–14)," *ZWT* 47 (1): 57–88.

Knaake, I. A., 1903, "Die Predigten des Tertullian und Cyprian," *TSK* 76 (4): 606–39.

Knohl, Israel, 2008, " 'By Three Days, Live': Messiahs, Resurrection, and Ascent to Heaven in *Hazon Gabriel*," *JR* 88 (2): 147–58.

Koch, Hal, 1932, *Pronoia und Paideusis: Studien über Origenes und sein Verhaltnis zum Platonismus*, Arbeiten zur Kirchengeschichte 22, Berlin: de Gruyter.

Kocsis, E., 1962, "Ost–West Gegensatz in den jüdischen Sibyllinen," *NovT* 5 (2–3): 105–10.

Koester, Helmut, 1995, "What Is—and Is Not—Inspired," *BRev* 11 (5): 18–19.

Kohler, K., 1895, "The Pre-Talmudic Haggada. II. C. The Apocalypse of Abraham and Its Kindred," *JQR* 7 (4): 581–606.

Köhnken, Adolf, 1996, "Paradoxien in Theokrits Hylasgedicht," *Hermes* 124 (4): 442–62.

Komorowska, Joanna, 2004, *Vettius Valens of Antioch: An Intellectual Monography*, Kraków: Księgarnia Akademicka.

Kraemer, David, 2000, *The Meanings of Death in Rabbinic Judaism*, London: Routledge.

Kraft, Robert A., 1976, "Reassessing the 'Recensional Problem' in Testament of Abraham," in George W. E. Nickelsburg Jr. (ed.), *Studies on the Testament of Abraham*, 121–37, SBLSCS 6, Missoula: Scholars Press.

Krauss, S., 1906, "Pseudo-Phocylides," *JewEnc* 10.255–6.

Kroll, Guilelmus, 1906, *Codicum Romanorum*, Catalogus Codium Astrologorum Graecorum 5/2, Bruxelles: Polleunis & Ceuterick.

Kroll, Guilelmus, 1908, *Vettii Valentis: Anthologiarum Libri*, Berlin: Weidmann.

Kroll, Josef, 1928, *Die Lehren des Hermes Trismegistos*, Beiträge zur Geschichte der Philosophie des Mittelalters Texte und Untersuchungen 12/2–4, Münster: Aschendorff.

Kröll, Nicole, 2014, "Rhetorical Elements in the Ampelus-episode: Dionysus' Speech to Ampelus (Nonn. *Dion.* 10.196–216)," in Konstantinos Spanoudakis (ed.), *Nonnus of Panopolis in Context: Poetry and Cultural Milieu in Late Antiquity with a Section on Nonnus and the Modern World*, 251–63, TCSup 24, Berlin: de Gruyter.

Krüpe, Florian, 2011, *Die Damnatio memoriae: Über die Vernichtung von Erinnerung. Eine Fallstudie zu Publius Septimius Geta (198–211 n. Chr.)*, Gutenberg: Computus.

Kühn, Karl Gottlob, 1823, *Medicorum Graecorum Opera quae Exstant*, vol. 6: *Claudii Galeni t. VI*, Leipzig: Knobloch.

Kühn, Karl Gottlob, 1830, *Medicorum Graecorum Opera quae Exstant*, vol. 19: *Claudii Galeni t. XIX*, Leipzig: Knobloch.

Kulikowski, Michael, 2012, "Coded Polemic in Ammianus Book 31 and the Date and Place of its Composition," *JRS* 102: 79–102.

Kurtz, Donna C., and John Boardman, 1971, *Greek Burial Customs*, Ithaca, NY: Cornell University Press.

Lacroix, Léon, 1953, "Fleuves et nymphes eponyms sur les monnaies grecques," *Revue Belge de Numismatique* 99: 5–21.

Lagona, Sebastiana, 1993a, "Kyme Eolica," in Fede Berti, Daria De Bernardi Ferrero, Marcella Frangipane, and Sebastiana Lagona (eds.), *Arslantepe, Hierapolis, Iasos, Kyme: Scavi archeologici italiani in Turchia*, 249–301, Venezia: Marsilio.

Lagona, Sebastiana, 1993b, "Kyme eolica: fonti, storia, topografia," in Giovanni Rizza (ed.), *Studi su Kyme Eolica: Atti della Giornata di Studio della Scuola di Specializzazione in Archeologia dell'Università di Catania, Catania, 16 maggio 1990*, 19–33, Cronache di Archeologia 32, Catania: Scuola di Specializzazione in Archeologia.

Lagrange, M.-J., 1924, "L'Hermétisme," *RB* 33 (4): 481–97.

Lahe, Jaan, 2011, *Gnosis und Judentum: Alttestamentliche und jüdische Motive in der gnostischen Literatur und das Ursprungsproblem der Gnosis*, NHMS 75, Leiden: Brill.

Lamberton, Robert D. (trans.), 1983, *Porphyry: On the Cave of the Nymphs*, Barrytown, NY: Station Hill.

Lamberton, Robert D., 1986, *Homer the Theologian: Neoplatonist Allegorical Reading and the Growth of the Epic Tradition*, TCH 9, Berkeley: University of California Press.

Lamberton, Robert D., 2006, Review of Luc Brisson, *How Philosophers Saved Myths: Allegorical Interpretation and Classical Mythology*, *CP* 101 (2): 161–5.

Lanchester, H. C. O., 1913, "The Sibylline Oracles," *APOT* 2.368–406.

Landry, David, 2015, "Reconsidering the Date of Luke in Light of the Farrer Hypothesis," in John C. Poirier and Jeffrey Peterson (eds.), *Marcan Priority without Q: Explorations in the Farrer Hypothesis*, 160–90, LNTS 455, London: Bloomsbury.

Lane Fox, Robin, 1987, *Pagans and Christians*, New York: Knopf.

Lardreau, Guy, 1989, *Porphyre: L'Antre des Nymphes dans l'Odyssée*, Lagrasse: Verdier.

Larson, Jennifer, 2001, *Greek Nymphs: Myth, Cult, Lore*, Oxford: Oxford University Press.

LaRue, Rodrigue, Gilles Vincent, and Bruno St.-Onge (eds.), 1985, *Clavis scriptorum Graecorum et Latinorum*, 4 vols., Trois-Rivières: Université du Québec à Trois-Rivières, Service de la Bibliothèque.

Lauchert, Friedrich, 1889, *Geschichte des Physiologus*, Strassburg: Trübner.

Laufer, Berthold, 1914, *Chinese Clay Figures*, pt. 1: *Prolegomena on the History of Defensive Armor*, Field Museum of Natural History 177, Anthropological Series 13/2, Chicago: Field Museum of Natural History.

Lawall, Gilbert, 1967, *Theocritus' Coan Pastorals: A Poetry Book*, Washington, DC: Center for Hellenic Studies.

Layton, Bentley, 1987, *The Gnostic Scriptures*, Garden City, NY: Doubleday.

Le Clerc, Jean, 1690, *Five Letters Concerning the Inspiration of the Holy Scriptures*, London: n.p.

Le Comte de Marcellus (Marie Louis Jean Andre Charles Demartin du Tyrac), 1861, *Paraphrase de l'Évangile selon Saint Jean par Nonnos de Panopolis*, Paris: Didot.

Leclant, Jean, 1994, "Avant-propos: L'eau vivifiante dans l'Égypte ancienne," in René Ginouvès, Anne-Marie Guimier-Sorbets, Jacques Jouanna, and Laurence Villard (eds.), *L'Eau, la Santé et la Maladie dans le Monde Grec: Actes du colloque organisé à Paris (CNRS et Fondation Singer-Polignac) du 25 au 27 novembre 1992 par le Centre de recherché "Archéologie et système d'information" et par l'URA 1255 "Médecine grecque"*, 7–12, BCHSup 28, Athènes: École Française d'Athènes.

Lee, Yongbom, 2012, *The Son of Man as the Last Adam: The Early Church Tradition as a Source of Paul's Adam Christology*, Eugene, OR: Pickwick.

Leemans, E.-A., 1937, *Studie over den wijsgeer Numenius van Apamea: met uitgave der fragmenten*, Mémoires de la Classe des lettres 2/37/2, Bruxelles: Palais des Académies.

Lefkowitz, Mary R., 2002, "'Predatory' Goddesses," *Hesperia* 71 (4): 325–44.

Legrand, Thierry, 2011, "La Version latine de Ben Sira: État de la question, essai de classement thématique des 'additions,'" in Jean-Sébastien Rey and Jan Joosten (eds.), *The Texts and Versions of the Book of Ben Sira: Transmission and Interpretation*, 215–34, JSJSup 150, Leiden: Brill.

Lehner, Mark Edward, 1991, "Archaeology of an Image: The Great Sphinx of Giza," Ph.D. dissertation, 3 vols., Yale University, New Haven.

Lehner, Mark Edward, 2002, "Unfinished Business: The Great Sphinx. Why It Is Most Probable That Khafre Created the Sphinx," *Aeragram: Newsletter of Ancient Egypt Research Associates* 5 (2): 10–14.

Lehtipuu, Outi, 2007, *The Afterlife Imagery in Luke's Story of the Rich Man and Lazarus*, NovTSup 123, Leiden: Brill.

Leicht, Reimund, 2011, "The Planets, the Jews and the Beginnings of 'Jewish Astrology,'" in Gideon Bohak, Yuval Harari, and Shaul Shaked (eds.), *Continuity and Innovation in the Magical Tradition*, 271–88, JSRC 15, Leiden: Brill.

Lennig, Arthur, 1969, *Traum und Sinnestäuschung bei Aischylos, Sophokles, Euripides*, Berlin: Omnia-Organisation.

Lentz, Augustus (ed.), 1867, *Herodiani Technici Reliquiae*, Grammatici Graeci 3, Leipzig: Teubner.

Léon-Dufour, Xavier, 1986, *Life and Death in the New Testament: The Teaching of Jesus and Paul*, San Francisco: Harper & Row.

Lepelley, Claude, 2010, "The Use of Secularised Latin Pagan Culture by Christians," in David M. Gwynn and Susanne Bangert (eds.), *Religious Diversity in Late Antiquity*, 477–92, Late Antique Archaeology 6, Leiden: Brill.

Lepsius, R., 1849, *Denkmäler aus Ägypten und Äthiopien nach den Zeichnungen der von seiner Majestät dem Könige von Preussen Friedrich Wilhelm IV nach diesen Ländern Gesendeten und in den Jahren 1842–1845, ausgeführten wissenschaftlichen Expedition auf Befehl seiner Majestät*, Berlin: Nicolaische.

Letronne, Antoine-Jean, 1842–8, *Recueil des inscriptions grecques et latines de l'Égypte*, 3 vols., Paris: Imprimerie Royale.

Letzner, Wolfram, 1999, *Römische Brunnen und Nymphaea in der westlichen Reichshälfte*, 2nd ed., Charybdis 2, Münster: LIT.

Levi, Doro, 1923–4, "L'antro delle ninfe e di Pan a Farsalo in Tessaglia," *Annuario della R. Scuola Archeologica di Ateno e delle Missioni Italiane in Oriente* 6–7: 27–42.

Levin, Saul, 1989, "The Old Greek Oracles in Decline," 1599–1649, ANRW 2.18.2.

Liddell, Henry George, and Robert Scott, 1940, *A Greek-English Lexicon*, 9th ed., revised by Henry Stuart Jones, Oxford: Clarendon.

Liebeschuetz, Wolfgang, 1996, "The Use of Pagan Mythology in the Christian Empire with Particular Reference to the *Dionysiaca* of Nonnus," in Pauline Allen and Elizabeth Jeffreys (eds.) *The Sixth Century: End or Beginning?*, 75–91, Byzantina Australiensia 10, Brisbane: Australian Association for Byzantine Studies.

Lieu, Judith M., 2010, "The Battle for Paul in the Second Century," *ITQ* 75 (1): 3–14.

Lightfoot, J. B., 1890, *The Apostolic Fathers*, pt. 1: *S. Clement of Rome*, New York: Macmillan.

Lightfoot, J. B., 1898, *The Apostolic Fathers*, ed. J. R. Harmer, rev. ed., London: Macmillan.

Lightfoot, J. L., 2007, *The Sibylline Oracles: With Introduction, Translation, and Commentary on the First and Second Books*, Oxford: Oxford University Press.

Limberis, Vasiliki, 2000, " 'Religion' as the Cipher for Identity: The Cases of Emperor Julian, Libanius, and Gregory Nazianzus," *HTR* 93 (4): 373–400.

Lincke, Karl F. A., 1903, *Samaria und seine Propheten: Ein religionsgeschichtlicher Versuch mit einer Textbeilage: Die Weisheitslehre des Phokylides, griechisch und deutsch*, Tübingen: Mohr-Siebeck.

Lind, L. Robert, 1934, "The Date of Nonnos of Panopolis," *CP* 29 (1): 69–73.

Lindblom, Johannes, 1914, *Das ewige Leben: Eine Studie über die Entstehung der religiösen Lebensidee im Neuen Testament*, Uppsala: Almquist and Wiksell.

Lindsell, Harold, 1976, *The Battle for the Bible*, Grand Rapids, MI: Zondervan.

Linnemann, Eta, 1974, "Die Hochzeit zu Kana und Dionysos: Oder das Unzureichende der Kategorien Übertragung und Identifikation zur Erfassung der religionsgeschichtlichen Beziehungen," *NTS* 20 (4): 408–18.

Lips, Hermann von, 2011, "Die Timotheus- und Titusakten und die Leidensthematik in den Pastoralbriefen. Aspekte zur Entstehungszeit und Intention der Pastoralbriefe," *Early Christianity* 2 (2): 219–41.

Livrea, Enrico, 1987, "Il poeta ed il vescovo: la questione nonniana e la storia," *Prometheus* 13 (2): 97–123.

Livrea, Enrico, 2000, *Nonno di Panopoli, Parafrasi del Vangelo di San Giovanni. Canto B*, Biblioteca Patristica, Bologna: Dehoniane.

Lloyd, G. E. R., 2003, *In the Grip of Disease: Studies in the Greek Imagination*, Oxford: Oxford University Press.

Lloyd, G. E. R., 2018, "Astral Science in Greek and Latin," in David Brown (ed.), *The Interactions of Ancient Astral Science*, 192–323, Bremen: Hempen.

Lloyd-Jones, Hugh, 1999, "The Pride of Halicarnassus," *ZPE* 124: 1–14.

Loader, William, 1997, *Jesus' Attitude towards the Law: A Study of the Gospels*, WUNT 2/97, Tübingen: Mohr-Siebeck.

Lobel, Edgar, 1928, "Nicander's Signature," *ClQ* 22 (2): 114–15.

Loewenstamm, Samuel E., 1976, "The Testament of Abraham and the Texts Concerning the Death of Moses," in George W. E. Nickelsburg Jr. (ed.), *Studies on the Testament of Abraham*, 219–25, SBLSCS 6, Missoula: Scholars Press.

Loi, Vincenzo, 1977, "La problematica storico-letteraria su Ippolito di Roma," in *Ricerche su Ippolito*, 9–16, StEphAug 13, Rome: Institutum Patristicum Augustinianum.

Loisy, Alfred, 1921, *Le quatrième évangile – Les épitres dites de Jean*, 2nd ed., Paris: Nourry.

Longenecker, Richard N., 2004, "Major Tasks of an Evangelical Hermeneutic: Some Observations on Commonalities, Interrelations, and Differences," *Bulletin for Biblical Research* 14 (1): 45–58.

Looks, Carsten, 1999, *Das Anvertraute bewahren: Die Rezeption der Pastoralbriefe im 2. Jahrhundert*, Münchner Theologische Beiträge, München: Utz.

Lorton, David, 1974, *The Juridical Terminology of International Relations in Egyptian Texts through Dyn. XVIII*, Johns Hopkins Near Eastern Studies, Baltimore: Johns Hopkins University Press.

Lüders, Heinrich, 1897, "Die Sage von Ṛṣyaśṛṅga," in *Nachrichten von der Königl. Gesellschaft der Wissenschaften zu Göttingen. Philologisch-historische Klasse aus dem Jahre 1897*, 87–135, Göttingen: Horstmann.

Ludlow, Jared W., 2002a, *Abraham Meets Death: Narrative Humor in the* Testament of Abraham, JSPSup 41, London: Sheffield Academic Press.

Ludlow, Jared W., 2002b, "The *Testament of Abraham*: Which Came First—Recension A or Recension B?," *JSP* 13 (1): 3–15.

Ludlow, Jared W., 2005, "Humor and Paradox in the Characterization of Abraham in the *Testament of Abraham*," in Jo-Ann A. Brant, Charles W. Hedrick, and Chris Shea (eds.), *Ancient Fiction: The Matrix of Early Christian and Jewish Narrative*, 199–214, SBL Symposium 32, Atlanta: Society of Biblical Literature, 2005.

Luria, S., 1929, "Entstellungen des Klassikertextes bei Stobaios," *RhMP* 78 (1): 81–104.

Lyman, Rebecca, 2003. "Hellenism and Heresy," *JECS* 11 (2): 209–22.

Mack, Burton L., and Roland E. Murphy, 1986, "Wisdom Literature," in Robert A. Kraft and George W. E. Nickelsburg (eds.), *Early Judaism and Its Modern Interpreters*, 371–410, The Bible and Its Modern Interpreters 2, Atlanta: Scholars Press.

MacLachlan, Bonnie, 2009, "Women and Nymphs at the Grotta Caruso," in Giovanni Casadio and Patricia A. Johnston (eds.), *Mystic Cults in Magna Graecia*, 204–16, Austin: University of Texas Press.

MacMullen, Ramsay, 1971, "Social History in Astrology," *Ancient Society* 2: 105–16.

MacMullen, Ramsay, 1981, *Paganism in the Roman Empire*, New Haven: Yale University Press.

MacRae, George, 1976, "The Judgment Scene in the Coptic Apocalypse of Paul," in George W. E. Nickelsburg Jr. (ed.), *Studies on the Testament of Abraham*, 285–8, SBLSCS 6, Missoula: Scholars Press.

Macurdy, G. H., 1942, "Platonic Orphism in the Testament of Abraham," *JBL* 61 (4): 213–26.

Mahé, Jean-Pierre, 1978, *Hermès en Haute-Égypte: Les texts hermétiques de Nag Hammadi et leurs parallèles grecs et latins*, vol. 1, Bibliothèque copte de Nag Hammadi: Textes 3, Quebec: Les Presses de l'Université Laval.

Mahé, Jean-Pierre, 1987, "Hermes Trismegistos," in Mircea Eliade (ed.), *The Encyclopedia of Religion*, 6.287–93, New York: Macmillan.

Makarov, Igor A., and Sergeï V. Ushakov, 2009, "A Red-figure Kylix with an Inscription from Tauric Chersonesos," *ACSS* 15 (3–4): 243–59.

Malherbe, Abraham J., 1970, "Athenagoras on the Poets and Philosophers," in Patrick Granfield and Josef A. Jungmann (eds.), *KYPIAKON: Festschrift Johannes Quasten*, 214–25, 2 vols., Münster: Aschendorff.

Malherbe, Abraham J., 1987, *Paul and the Thessalonians: The Philosophic Tradition of Pastoral Care*, Philadelphia: Fortress.

Malherbe, Abraham J., 2005, " 'Christ Jesus Came into the World to Save Sinners': Soteriology in the Pastoral Epistles," in Jan G. van der Watt (ed.), *Salvation in the New Testament: Perspectives on Soteriology*, 331–58, NovTSup 121, Leiden: Brill.

Malkin, Irad, 2001, "The *Odyssey* and the Nymphs," *Gaia* 5: 11–27.

Malley, William J., 1965, "Four Unedited Fragments of the *De Universo* of the Pseudo-Josephus Found in the *Chronicon* of George Hamartolus (Coislin 305)," *JTS* 16 (1): 13–25.

Manitius, M., 1891, *Geschichte der christlich-lateinischen Poesie bis zur Mitte des 8. Jahrhunderts*, Stuttgart: Cotta.

Mansfeld, J., and D. T. Runia, 1997, *Aëtiana: The Method and Intellectual Context of a Doxographer*, vol. 1: *The Sources*, PhA 73, Leiden: Brill.

Marböck, Johannes, 1971, *Weisheit im Wandel. Untersuchungen zur Weisheitstheologie bei Ben Sira*, BBB 37, Bonn: Hanstein.

Marböck, Johannes, 1976, "Gesetz und Weisheit. Zum Verständnis des Gesetzes bei Jesus ben Sira," *BZ* 20: 1–21.

Marchetti, Patrick, 1995, "Le nymphée et l'agora d'Argos," in Patrick Marchetti and Kostas Kolokotsas, *Le nymphée de l'agora d'Argos. Fouille, étude architecturale et historique*, 187–290, École Française d'Athènes, Études Péloponnésiennes 11, Paris: Boccard.

Marcus, Ralph, 1949, "The Name *Poimandrēs*," *JNES* 8 (1): 40–3.

Mark, Samuel, 2005, *Homeric Seafaring*, College Station: Texas A & M University Press.

Markschies, Christoph, 2015, *Christian Theology and Its Institutions in the Early Roman Empire: Prolegomena to a History of Early Christian Theology*, Baylor–Mohr Siebeck Studies in Early Christianity, Waco: Baylor University Press.

Marshall, I. Howard, 1996, "Salvation in the Pastoral Epistles," in Hubert Cancik, Hermann Lichtenberger, and Peter Schäfer (eds.), *Geschichte – Tradition – Reflexion: Festschrift für Martin Hengel zum 70. Geburtstag*, vol. 3: *Frühes Christentum*, 449–69, ed. Hermann Lichtenberger, Tübingen: Mohr-Siebeck.

Marshall, I. Howard, 1999, *A Critical and Exegetical Commentary on the Pastoral Epistles*, ICC, Edinburgh: T&T Clark.

Martens, Peter W., 2008, "Revisiting the Allegory/Typology Distinction: The Case of Origen," *JECS* 16 (3): 283–317.

Martin, Troy W., 1999, "The TestAbr and the Background of 1Pet 3,6," *ZNW* 90 (1–2): 139–46.

Maspero, G., 1867, *L'Inscription dédicatoire du Temple d'Abydos. Texte, traduction & notes, suivi d'un essai sur la jeunesse de Sésostris*, Paris: Librairie Franck.

Maspero, G., 1893, *Études de Mythologie et d'Archéologie*, Bibliothèque Égyptologique comprenant les Œuvres des Égyptologues Français 1, Paris: Leroux.

Massa, Francesco, 2014, *Tra la vigna e la croce. Dioniso nei discorsi letterari e figurativi cristiani (II–IV secolo)*, Potsdamer Altertumswissenschaftliche Beiträge 47, Stuttgart: Steiner.

Mastonarde, Donald J., 1968, "Theocritus' Idyll 13: Love and the Hero," *TAPA* 99: 273–90.

Matthews, John F., 1994, "The Origin of Ammianus," *ClQ* 44 (1): 252–69.

Matthews, John F., 2007, *The Roman Empire of Ammianus*, rev. ed., Ann Arbor: Michigan Classical Papers.

Mattila, Sharon Lea, 2000, "Ben Sira and the Stoics: A Reexamination of the Evidence," *JBL* 119 (3): 473–501.

Mauerhofer, Kenneth, 2004, *Der Hylas-Mythos in der antiken Literatur*, BAlt 208, München: Saur.

McCane, Byron R., 2003, *Roll Back the Stone: Death and Burial in the World of Jesus*, Harrisburg: Trinity Press International.

MacDonald, Dennis Ronald, 1983, *The Legend and the Apostle: The Battle for Paul in Story and Canon*, Philadelphia: Westminster.

McDonald, Lee Martin, 2009, *Forgotten Scriptures: The Selection and Rejection of Early Religious Writings*, Louisville: Westminster John Knox.

McGuire, Anne, 1986, "Conversion and Gnosis in the *Gospel of Truth*," *NovT* 28 (4): 338–55.

McHugh, John, 1992, " 'In Him was Life'," in James D. G. Dunn (ed.), *Jews and Christians: The Parting of the Ways A.D. 70 to 135. The Second Durham–Tübingen*

Research Symposium on Earliest Christianity and Judaism (Durham, September, 1989), 123–58, WUNT 66, Tübingen: Mohr-Siebeck.

McPhee, Brian D., 2016, "Walk, Don't Run: Jesus's Water Walking Is Unparalleled in Greco-Roman Mythology," *JBL* 135 (4): 763–77.

Mead, G. R. S., 1906, *Thrice-Greatest Hermes: Studies in Hellenistic Theosophy and Gnosis*, 3 vols., London: Theosophical Publishing Society.

Meade, David G., 1986, *Pseudonymity and Canon: An Investigation into the Relationship of Authorship and Authority in Jewish and Earliest Christian Tradition*, WUNT 1/39, Tübingen: Mohr-Siebeck.

Medina, Antonio Villarrubia, 2006, "La *Paráfrasis a Juan* de Nono de Panópolis: Cuestiones Previas y Notas Generales," *Habis* 37: 445–61.

Meier, John P., 1999, "The Inspiration of Scripture: But What Counts as Scripture?," *Mid-Stream* 38 (1–2): 71–8.

Meinardus, Otto F. A., 1974, *St. John of Patmos and the Seven Churches of the Apocalypse*, Athens: Lycabettus.

Meineke, August, 1855, *Ioannis Stobaei Florilegium*, vol. 1, Leipzig: Teubner.

Melville, Ronald (trans.), 1997, *Lucretius, On the Nature of the Universe*, Oxford: Clarendon.

Ménard, Louis, 1866, *Hermès Trismégiste: Traduction complète précédée d'une étude sur l'origine des livres hermétiques*, Paris: Librairie Académique.

Meredith, A., 1985, "Allegory in Porphyry and Gregory of Nyssa," *StPatr* 16: 423–7.

Merlan, P., 1970, "Greek Philosophy from Plato to Plotinus," in A. H. Armstrong (ed.), *The Cambridge History of Later Greek and Early Medieval Philosophy*, 14–132, rev. ed., Cambridge: Cambridge University Press.

Mertens, Michèle, 2002, "Alchemy, Hermetism and Gnosticism at Panopolis c. 300 A.D.: The Evidence of Zosimus," in A. Egberts, B. P. Muhs, and J. van der Vliet (eds.), *Perspectives on Panopolis: An Egyptian Town from Alexander the Great in the Arab Conquest. Acts from an International Symposium held in Leiden on 16, 17 and 18 December 1998*, 165–75, Papyrologica Lugduno–Batava 31, Leiden: Brill.

Merz, Annette, 2004, *Die fiktive Selbstauslegung des Paulus: Intertextuelle Studien zur Intention und Rezeption der Pastoralbriefen*, NTOA 52, Göttingen: Vandenhoeck & Ruprecht.

Meschini, Anna, 1983, "Le Ciranidi nel Marc. Gr. 512," *Atti della Accademia Pontaniana* 31: 145–77.

Meschini, S., 1958, "Ninfei e Fontane," in *Enciclopedia dell'Arte Antica Classica e Orientale*, 508–12, Roma: Istituto della Enciclopedia Italiana.

Metzger, Bruce M., 1987, *The Canon of the New Testament: Its Origin, Development, and Significance*, Oxford: Clarendon.

Metzger, Bruce M., 1994, *A Textual Commentary on the Greek New Testament*, 2nd ed., Stuttgart: Deutsche Bibelgesellschaft.

Michaeli, Talila, 2009, *Visual Representations of the Afterlife: Six Roman and Early Byzantine Painted Tombs in Israel*, Leiden: Alexandros.

Migoubert, Yann, 2003, "Le *ms*. Baroccianus 50 et la tradition manuscrite de la *Batrachomyomachie*," *Gaía* 7: 405–9.

Miguélez Cavero, Laura, 2008, *Poems in Context: Greek Poetry in the Egyptian Thebaid 200–600 AD*, Sozomena: Studies in the Recovery of Ancient Texts 2, Berlin: de Gruyter.

Mihai, Adrian, 2010, "Soul's Aitherial Abode according to the Poteidaia Epitaph and the Presocratic Philosophers," *Numen* 57 (5): 553–82.

Miller, James D., 1997, *The Pastoral Letters as Composite Documents*, SNTSMS 93, Cambridge: Cambridge University Press.

Miller, Maria Magdalena, 2009, *Die Hermetischen Schriften – Corpus Hermeticum*, Hildesheim: Olms.

Mills, Barriss (trans.), 1963, *The Idylls of Theokritos*, West Lafayette, IN: Purdue University Press.

Minns, Denis, 2010, *Irenaeus: An Introduction*, London: T&T Clark International.

Mirguet, Françoise, 2010, "Attachment to the Body in the Greek *Testament of Abraham*: A Reappraisal of the Short Recension," *JSP* 19 (4): 251–75.

Mirguet, Françoise, 2014, "Beyond Authority: The Construction of Scriptures in the *Testament of Abraham*," in Eibert Tigchelaar (ed.), *Old Testament Pseudepigrapha and the Scriptures*, 211–29, BETL 270, Leuven: Peeters.

Mitchell, Margaret M., 2009, "Christian Martyrdom and the 'Dialect of the Holy Scriptures': The Literal, the Allegorical, the Martyrological," *BibInt* 17 (1–2): 177–206.

Mitchell, Stephen, 1999, "The Cult of Theos Hypsistos between Pagans, Jews, and Christians," in Polymnia Athanassiadi and Michael Frede (eds.), *Pagan Monotheism in Late Antiquity*, 81–148, Oxford: Clarendon.

Mitford, Terence B., 1980, *The Nymphaeum of Kafizin: The Inscribed Pottery*, Kadmos Supplement 2, Berlin: de Gruyter.

Momigliano, Arnaldo, 1992, *Nono contributo alla storia degli studi classici e del mondo antico*, ed. Riccardo di Donato, Storia e Letteratura 180, Roma: Edizioni di Storia e Letteratura.

Mommsen, Tycho, 1895, *Beiträge zu der Lehre von den griechischen Präpositionen*, Berlin: Weidmann.

Monaca, Mariangela, 2008, *Oracoli Sibillini*, Collana di Testi Patristici, Roma: Città Nuova.

Montanari, Franco, Madeleine Goh, and Chad Matthew Schroeder, 2015, *The Brill Dictionary of Ancient Greek*, Leiden: Brill.

Moreschini, Claudio, 2006, "Soteria ermetica e soteria cristiana: affinità generiche e punti di contatto," in Istituto patristico Augustinianum (ed.), *Pagani e cristiani alla ricerca della salvezza (secoli I–III): XXXIV Incontro di studiosi dell'antichità Cristiana. Roma, 5–7 maggio 2005*, 261–74, StEphAug 96, Roma: Institutum Patristicum Augustinianum.

Moreschini, Claudio, and Enrico Norelli, 2005, *Early Christian Greek and Latin Literature: A Literary History*, vol. 2: *From the Council of Nicea to the Beginning of the Medieval Period*, Peabody, MA: Hendrickson.

Morgan, Kathryn A., 2000, *Myth and Philosophy from the Presocratics to Plato*, Cambridge: Cambridge University Press.

Morin, D. G., 1900, "L'origine des canons d'Hippolyte. Note lue au Congrès archéologique de rome, le 23 avril 1900," *RBén* 17 (1–4): 241–51.

Moscovich, M. James, 1990, "Dio Cassius and the Repeal of the Lex Oppia," *Ancient History Bulletin* 4: 10–16.

Most, Glenn W. (trans.), 2007, *Hesiod, The Shield, Catalogue of Women, Other Fragments*, LCL 503, Cambridge: Harvard University Press.

Moulton, James Hope, and George Milligan, 1929, *The Vocabulary of the Greek Testament: Illustrated from the Papyri and Other Non-literary Sources*, London: Hodder & Stoughton.

Mounce, William D., 1982, *Pastoral Epistles*, WBC 46, Nashville: Nelson.

Moyer, Ian S., 2011, *Egypt and the Limits of Hellenism*, Cambridge: Cambridge University Press.

Müller, F. W. K., 1896, "Ikkaku sennin: Eine mittelalterliche japanische Oper," 513–37, In *Festschrift für Adolf Bastian zu seinem 70. Geburtstag, 26. Juni 1896*, Berlin: Reimer.

Müller, Lucian, 1867, "Zu Tertullians Gedichten *de Sodoma* und *de Iona*," *RhMP* 22: 329–44.

Munoa, Phillip B., III, 1998. *Four Powers in Heaven: The Interpretation of Daniel 7 in the Testament of Abraham*, JSJSup 28, Sheffield: Sheffield Academic Press.

Murgatroyd, P., 1992, "Setting in Six Versions of the Hylas Myth," in Carl Deroux (ed.), *Studies in Latin Literature and Roman History* 6, 84–93, Collection Latomus 217, Bruxelles: Latomus.

Murphy, Roland E., 1996, *The Tree of Life: An Exploration of Biblical Wisdom Literature*, 2nd ed., Grand Rapids, MI: Eerdmans.

Murphy-O'Connor, Jerome, 1968, "Truth: Paul and Qumran," in Jerome Murphy-O'Connor (ed.), *Paul and Qumran: Studies in New Testament Exegesis*, 179–230, London: Chapman.

Murray, A. T. (ed.), 1946, *Homer, The Odyssey*, vol. 1, LCL 104, Cambridge: Harvard University Press.

Murray, Gilbert, 1951, *Five Stages of Greek Religion*, Boston: Beacon.

Murray, John, 1940, "The Inspiration of the Scripture," *WTJ* 2 (2): 73–104.

Murray, Oswyn, 1970, "Hecataeus of Abdera and Pharaonic Kingship," *JEA* 56: 141–71.

Musurillo, Herbert (trans.), 1972, *The Acts of the Christian Martyrs*, Oxford: Oxford University Press.

Muth, Susanne, 1998, *Erleben von Raum – Leben im Raum: Zur Funktion mythologischer Mosaikbilder in der römisch-kaiserzeitlichen Wohnarchitektur*, Archäologie und Geschichte 10, Heidelberg: Verlag Archäologie und Geschichte.

Muthmann, Friedrich, 1975, *Mutter und Quelle: Studien zur Quellenverehrung im Altertum und im Mittelalter*, Basel: Archäologischer Verlag.

Nauck, Augustus, 1886, *Porphyrii, Philosophi Platonici: Opuscula Selecta*, Leipzig: Teubner.

Nautin, Pierre, 1947, *Hippolyte et Josipe. Contribution a l'histoire de la littérature chrétienne du troisième siècle*, Études et Textes pour l'Histoire du Dogme de la Trinité 1, Paris: Cerf.

Nautin, Pierre, 1977, *Origène. Sa vie et son œuvre*, Christianisme Antique 1, Paris: Beauchesne.

Nebot, Xavier Renau, 1999, *Textos Herméticos*, Biblioteca Clásica Gredos 268, Madrid: Gredos.

Neuerburg, Norman, 1965, *L'Architettura delle fontane e dei ninfei nell'Italia antica*, Memorie dell'Accademia di Archeologia Lettere e Belle Arti di Napoli 5, Napoli: Macchiaroli.

Neugebauer, O., 1954, "The Chronology of Vettius Valens' Anthologiae," *HTR* 47 (1): 65–7.

Neugebauer, O., and H. B. van Hoesen, 1959, *Greek Horoscopes*, Memoirs of the American Philosophical Society 48, Philadelphia: American Philosophical Society.

Neutsch, Bernhard, 1957, *ΤΑΣ ΝΥΝΦΑΣ ΕΜΙ ΗΙΑΡΟΝ: Zum unterirdischen Heiligtum von Paestum*, Abhandlungen der Heidelberger Akademie der Wissenschaften: Philosophisch-historische Klasse 1957/2, Heidelberg: Winter.

Newbold, R., 2001, "The Character and Content of Water in Nonnus and Claudian," *Ramus* 30 (2): 169–89.

Newbold, William R., 1940, "Thrice Greatest Hermes," in Gordon H. Clark, *Selections from Hellenistic Philosophy*, 192–218, New York: Appleton–Century–Crofts.

Nicholson, Ernest, and John Barton, 2013, "James Barr Remembered," in John Barton (ed.), *Bible and Interpretation: The Collected Essays of James Barr*, vol. 1: *Interpretation and Theology*, xii–xxxiv, Oxford: Oxford University Press.

Nickel, Joseph, 1833, *Das Mahngedicht des Phokylides in metrischer Uebersetzung, mit beigefügtem Urtexte und erläuternden Anmerkungen: Ein Geschenk für die studirende Jugend*, Mainz: Ruach.

Nickelsburg, George W. E., Jr., 1976a, "Eschatology in the Testament of Abraham: A Study of the Judgment Scene in the Two Recensions," in George W. E. Nickelsburg Jr. (ed.), *Studies on the Testament of Abraham*, 23–64, SBLSCS 6, Missoula: Scholars Press.

Nickelsburg, George W. E., Jr., 1976b, "Structure and Message in the Testament of Abraham," in George W. E. Nickelsburg Jr. (ed.), *Studies on the Testament of Abraham*, 85–93, SBLSCS 6, Missoula: Scholars Press.

Niebuhr, Karl-Wilhelm, 2008, "Life and Death in *Pseudo-Phocylides*," in Alberdina Houtman, Albert de Jong, and Magda Misset-van de Weg (eds.), Empsychoi Logoi— *Religious Innovations in Antiquity: Studies in Honour of Pieter Willem van der Horst*, 469–83, AJEC 73, Leiden: Brill.

Niehoff, Maren R., 2011, *Jewish Exegesis and Homeric Scholarship in Alexandria*, Cambridge: Cambridge University Press.

Nightingale, Andrea, 1993, "Writing/Reading a Sacred Text: A Literary Interpretation of Plato's *Laws*," *CP* 88 (4): 279–300.

Nikiprowetzky, Valentin, 1987, "Oracles Sibyllins," in André Dupont-Sommer and Marc Philonenko (eds.), *La Bible. Écrits intertestamentaires*, 1035–140, Bibliothèque de la Pléiade, Gallimard.

Nir, Rivka, 2004, "The Aromatic Fragrances of Paradise in the *Greek Life of Adam and Eve* and the Christian Origin of the Composition," *NovT* 46 (1): 20–45.

Nock, Arthur Darby, 1961, "Nymphs and Nereids," *MUSJ* 37: 297–308.

Nock, A. D., and A.-J. Festugiére, 1945, *Corpus Hermeticum*, 2 vols., Budé, Paris: Les Belles Lettres.

Noll, Mark A., 1991, *Between Faith and Criticism: Evangelicals, Scholarship, and the Bible in America*, 2nd ed., Society of Biblical Literature Confessional Perspectives, Grand Rapids, MI: Baker.

Nolland, John, 1989, *Luke 1–9:20*, WBC 35a, Waco: Word.

Nordheim, Eckhard von, 1980, *Die Lehre der Alten, I*, ALGHJ 13, Leiden: Brill.

O'Brien, D. P., 1997, "The Cumaean Sibyl as the Revelation-bearer in the *Shepherd of Hermas*," *JECS* 5 (4): 473–96.

O'Keefe, John J., 2004, "Allegory," in John Anthony McGuckin (ed.), *The Westminster Handbook to Origen*, 49–50, Louisville: Westminster John Knox.

O'Malley, Thomas P., 1967, *Tertullian and the Bible: Language – Imagery – Exegesis*, Latinitas Christianorum Primaeva 21, Utrecht: Dekker & Van De Vegt N.V. Nijmegen.

O'Meara, Dominic J., 1989, *Pythagoras Revived: Mathematics and Philosophy in Late Antiquity*, Oxford: Clarendon.

Oakley, John H., 1990, "Hylas," in Fondation pour le Lexicon Iconographicum Mythologiae Classicae, *Lexicon Iconographicum Mythologiae Classicae*, 574–9, vol. 5/1, Zurich: Artemis.

Oakley, John H., and Rebecca H. Sinos, 1993, *The Wedding in Ancient Athens*, Wisconsin Studies in Classics, Madison: University of Wisconsin Press.

Oberhelman, Steven M., 1983, "Galen, *On Diagnosis from Dreams*," *Journal of the History of Medicine and Allied Sciences* 38 (1): 36–47.

Oberhelman, Steven M., 1993, "Dreams in Graeco-Roman Medicine," *ANRW* 2.37.1: 121–56.

Offermanns, Dieter, 1966, *Der Physiologus nach den Handschriften G und M*, BKP 22, Meisenheim am Glan.

Ogilvie, R. M., 1962, "The Song of Thyrsis," *JHS* 82: 106–10.

Ogilvie, R. M., 1978, *The Library of Lactantius*, Oxford: Clarendon.

Ondine Pache, Corinne, 2011, *A Moment's Ornament: The Poetics of Nympholepsy in Ancient Greece*, Oxford: Oxford University Press.

The Oxford English Dictionary, 1989, 19 vols., 2nd ed., Oxford: Clarendon.

Paget, James Carleton, 2007, "Egypt," in Markus Bockmuehl and James Carleton Paget (eds.), *Redemption and Resistance: The Messianic Hopes of Jews and Christians in Antiquity*, 183–97, London: T&T Clark.

Pahl, Michael, 2009, *Discerning the "Word of the Lord": The "Word of the Lord" in 1 Thessalonians 4:15*, LNTS 389, London: T&T Clark.

Painchaud, Louis, 1996, "The Use of Scripture in Gnostic Literature," *JECS* 4 (2): 129–47.

Palm, Adolf, 1933, *Studien zur Hippokratischen Schrift ΠΕΡΙ ΔΙΑΙΤΗΣ*, Tübingen: Tübinger Chronik.

Panayiotou, George, 1990, "Paralipomena Lexicographica Cyranidea," *ICS* 15 (2): 295–338.

Pancaro, Severino, 1975, *The Law in the Fourth Gospel: The Torah and the Gospel, Moses and Jesus, Judaism and Christianity According to John*, NovTSup 42, Leiden: Brill.

Pannenberg, Wolfhart, 1988, "Revelation in Early Christianity," in G. R. Evans (ed.), *Christian Authority: Essays in Honour of Henry Chadwick*, 76–85, Oxford: Clarendon.

Parke, H. W., 1985, *The Oracles of Apollo in Asia Minor*, London: Helm.

Parker, Robert, 1985, "Greek States and Greek Oracles," in P. A. Cartledge and F. D. Harvey (eds.), *Crux: Essays Presented to G.E.M. de Ste. Croix on His 75th Birthday*, 298–326, History of Political Thought 6/1–2, Exeter: Academic.

Parker, Robert, 2011, *On Greek Religion*, Townsend Lectures/Cornell Studies in Classical Philology 60, Ithaca, NY: Cornell University Press.

Parsons, Stuart E., 2015, *Ancient Apologetic Exegesis: Introducing and Recovering Theophilus's World*, Eugene, OR: Pickwick.

Parsons, Wilfrid, 1951, *Saint Augustine, Letters*, vol. 1, FC 12, New York: Fathers of the Church.

Parthey, Gustavus, 1854, *Hermetis trismegisti: Poemander. Ad fidem codicum manu scriptorum*, Berlin: Nicolai.

Paton, W. R., 1970, *The Greek Anthology*, vol. 2, LCL 68, Cambridge: Harvard University Press.

Pearson, Birger, 1981, "Jewish Elements in *Corpus Hermeticum* I (Poimandres)," in Roelof van den Broek and Maarten J. Vermaseren (eds.), *Studies in Gnosticism and Hellenistic Religions presented to Gilles Quispel on the Occasion of His 65th Birthday*, 336–48, EPRO 91, Leiden: Brill.

Pease, Arthur Stanley, 1923, *M. Tulli Ciceronis De Divinatione Liber Secundus*, University of Illinois Studies in Language and Literature 8/2, Urbana: University of Illinois Press.

Peek, Werner, 1972, "Zu drei Epigrammen aus Kleinasien," *Phil* 116 (1–2): 254–60.

Peiper, Rudolf, 1881, *Cypriani Galli Poetae, Heptateuchos*, CSEL 23, Vienna: Tempsky.

Pennington, Jonathan T., 2007, *Heaven and Earth in the Gospel of Matthew*, Grand Rapids, MI: Baker Academic.

Pépin, Jean, 1966, "Porphyre, exegete d'Homère," in *Porphyre*, 229–72, EntAntCl 12, Geneva: Fondation Hardt.

Perrin, Bernadotte (trans.), 1914, *Plutarch, Lives*. LCL 46, Cambridge: Harvard University Press.

Perrone, Lorenzo, 2004, "Ἴχνος ἐνθουσιασμοῦ: Origene, Platone e le scritture ispirate," in Angela Maria Mazzanti and Francesca Calabi (eds.), *La rivelazione in Filone di Alessandria: Natura, legge, storia: Atti de VII Convegno di Studi del Gruppo Italiano di Ricerca su Origene e la Tradizione Alessandrina*, 231–48, Biblioteca di Adamantius 2, Villa Verucchio: Pazzini.

Perrone, Lorenzo, 2013, "Rediscovering Origen Today: First Impressions of the New Collection of Homilies on the *Psalms* in the *Codex monacensis Graecus 314*," *StPatr* 56: 103–22.

Perrone, Lorenzo (ed.), 2015, *Die neuen Psalmenhomilien: Eine kritische Edition des Codex Monacensis Graecus 314*, Die Griechischen Christlichen Schriftsteller der ersten Jahrhunderte 19, Berlin: de Gruyter.

Perrone, Lorenzo, 2016, "The Find of the Munich Codex: A Collection of 29 Homilies of Origen on the Psalms," in Anders-Christian Jacobsen (ed.), *Origeniana Undecima: Origen and Origenism in the History of Western Thought. Papers of the 11th International Origen Congress, Aarhus University, 26–31 August 2013*, 201–33, BETL 279, Leuven: Peeters.

Perry, B. E., 1937, Review of Francesco Sbordone, *Physiologus*, *AJP* 58 (4): 488–96.

Pervo, Richard I., 1994, "Romancing an Oft-Neglected Stone: The Pastoral Epistles and the Epistolary Novel," *Journal of Higher Criticism* 1: 25–47.

Pesch, Christiano, 1906, *De Inspiratione Sacrae Scripturae*, Freiburg: Herder.

Peters, Emil, 1898, *Der griechische Physiologus und seine orientalischen Übersetzungen*, Festschriften der Gesellschaft für deutsche Philologie 15, Berlin: Calvary.

Peters, F. E., 1985, *Jerusalem: The Holy City in the Eyes of Chroniclers, Visitors, Pilgrims, and Prophets from the Days of Abraham to the Beginning of Modern Times*, Princeton: Princeton University Press.

Peterson, Erik, 1954, "Die Spiritualität des griechischen Physiologos," *ByzZ* 47 (1): 60–72.

Petitmengin, Pierre, 1990, entry 51, in René Braun *et al*, "Chronica Tertullianea et Cyprianea 1989," *Revue des Études Augustiniennes* 36 (2): 328–54.

Petrain, David, 2000, "Hylas and *Silva*: Etymological Wordplay in Propertius 1.20," *HSCP* 100: 409–21.

Petridou, Georgia, 2009, "*Artemidi to ichnos*: Divine Feet and Hereditary Priesthood in Pisidian Pogla," *Anatolian Studies* 59: 81–93.

Pfister, Fr., 1959, "Ekstase," *RAC* 4.944–87.

Phillips, John, 2002, "Plato's *Psychogonia* in Later Platonism," *ClQ* 52 (1): 231–47.

Philonenko, Marc, 1975, "Le Poimandrès et la liturgie juive," in Françoise Dunand and Pierre Lévêque (eds.), *Les syncrétismes dans les religions de l'antiquité: Colloque de Besançon (22–23 octobre 1973)*, 204–11, EPRO 46, Leiden: Brill.

Philonenko, Marc, 1979, "Une Utilisation du Shema dans le Poimandrès," *RHPR* 59 (3–4): 369–72.

Philonenko, Marc, 2003, "Le Vivificateur: Étude d'eschatologie comparée (de 4Q521 aux *Actes de Thomas*)," *RHPR* 83 (1): 61–9.

Picard, Ch., 1922, *Éphèse et Claros. Recherches sur les sanctuaires et les cultes de l'Ionie du Nord*, Bibliothèque des Écoles Françaises d'Athènes et de Rome 123, Paris: Boccard.

Piñero, Antonio, 1988, "Sobre el Sentido de ΘΕΟΠΝΕΥΣΤΟΣ: 2 Tim 3,16," *FN* 1 (2): 143–53.

Pingree, David (ed.), 1986, *Vettii Valentis Antiocheni, Anthologiarum libri novem*, Bibliotheca Teubneriana, Leipzig: Teubner.

Pingree, David, 2001, "From Alexandria to Baghdād to Byzantium. The Transmission of Astrology," *IJCT* 8 (1): 3–37.

Pitra, Joannes Baptista, 1855, *Spicilegium solesmense complectens sanctorum patrum scriptorumque ecclesiasticorum*, vol. 3, Analecta Sacra 5, Paris: Didot.

Placher, William C., 1993, "Introduction," in Hans W. Frei, *Theology and Narrative: Selected Essays*, 3–25, ed. George Hunsinger and William C. Placher, New York: Oxford University Press.

Placher, William C., 1995, "Is the Bible True?," *Christian Century* 112 (28): 924–8.

Plastira-Valkanou, Maria, 2003, "AP 11.281: A Satirical Epitaph on Magnus of Nisibis," *AC* 72: 187–94.

Platnauer, Maurice, 1918, *The Life and Reign of the Emperor Lucius Septimius Severus*, London: Milford.

Poirier, John C., 2014, "Psalm 16:10 and the Resurrection of Jesus 'on the Third Day' (1 Corinthians 15:4)," *Journal for the Study of Paul and His Letters* 4 (2): 149–68.

Polara, Giovanni, 2007, "Cuma nella poesia latina," in Lucia A. Scatozza Höricht (ed.), *Kyme e l'Eolide da Augusto a Costantino. Atti dell'Incontro Internazionale di studio Missione archeologica italiana, Napoli, 12–13 dicembre 2005*, 45–55, Napoli: Luciano.

Pollmann, Karla, 2017, *The Baptized Muse: Early Christian Poetry as Cultural Authority*, Oxford: Oxford University Press.

Portogalli, Bianca Maria Tordini, 1997, *Ermete Trismegisto: Corpo Ermetico e Asclepio*, Conoscenza Religiosa 6, Milano: Studio Editoriale.

Potter, D. S., 1990, *Prophecy and History in the Crisis of the Roman Empire: A Historical Commentary on the* Thirteenth Sibylline Oracle, OCM, Oxford: Clarendon.

Pouilloux, Jean, 1982, "Le dernier livre de T. B. Mitford," *RevPhil* 56 (108): 99–103.

Praechter, Karl, 1910, "Richtungen und Schulen im Neuplatonismus," in *Genethliakon: Carl Robert zum 8. März 1910*, 103–56, Berlin: Weidmann.

Preller, Antonius Henricus, 1918, *Quaestiones Nonnianae. Desumptae e Paraphrasi Sancti Evangelii Joannei cap. XVIII–XIX*, Nijmegen: N. V. Centrale.

Prinzivalli, Emanuela, 1979, "Due passi escatologici del *Perì pantòs* di Ippolito," *Vetera Christianorum* 16: 63–75.

Procopé, J. F., 1996, "Greek Philosophy, Hermeneutics and Alexandrian Understanding of the Old Testament," in Magne Sæbø (ed.), *Hebrew Bible/Old Testament: The History of Its Interpretation*, 451–77, Göttingen: Vandenhoeck & Ruprecht.

Prost, M. A., 2003, *Nonnos of Panopolis, the Paraphrase of the Gospel of John*, Ventura: Writing Shop Press.

Puech, Henri-Charles, 1934, "Numénius d'Apamée et les theologies orientales au second siècle," in *Mélanges Bidez*, 745–78, Annuaire de l'Institut de Philologie et d'Histoire Orientales 2, Bruxelles: Secrétariat de l'Institut.

Pulci Doria, L. Breglia, 1996, "Eforo: l'ottica cumana di uno storico 'universale'," in P. Carlier (ed.), *Le IVᵉ siècle av. J.-C.: Approches historiographiques: Actes du Colloque International (Nancy, 28–30 septembre 1994)*, 41–55, Nancy: Association pour la diffusion de la recherche sur l'Antiquité – Études anciennes.

Pulleyn, Simon, 1997, "Horace: *Odes* 3.3.12: *Purpureo bibet ore nectar*," *Mnemosyne* 50 (4): 482–4.

Purcell, Nicholas, 2005, "The Ancient Mediterranean: The View from the Customs House," in W. V. Harris (ed.), *Rethinking the Mediterranean*, 200–32, Oxford: Oxford University Press.

Puschmann, Theodor (trans.), 1963, *Alexander von Tralles. Zur Geschichte der Medicin*, 2 vols., Amsterdam: Hakkert.

Quasten, Johannes, 1950, *Patrology*, vol. 2: *The Anti-Nicene Literature after Irenaeus*, Utrecht: Spectrum.

Quatember, Ursula, 2011, *Das Nymphaeum Traiani in Ephesos*, Forschungen in Ephesos 11/2, Wien: Österreichischen Akademie der Wissenschaften.

Quinn, Jerome D., 1990, *The Letter to Titus*, AB 35, New York: Doubleday.

Quinn, Jerome D., 1992, "Timothy and Titus, Epistles to," *ABD* 6.560–71.

Quispel, Gilles, 1992, "Hermes Trismegistus and the Origins of Gnosticism," *VC* 46 (1): 1–19.

Rackham, H. (trans.), 1940, *Pliny, Natural History*, vol. 3, LCL 353, Cambridge: Harvard University Press.

Ragone, Giuseppe, 2006, *APXAIOΛOΓIAI: Tra Ionia ed Eolide*, Naples: Luciano.

Rahmani, L. Y., 1994, *A Catalogue of Jewish Ossuaries in the Collection of the State of Israel*, Jerusalem: Israel Antiquities Authority.

Raine, Kathleen, and George Mills Harper, 1969, *Thomas Taylor the Platonist: Selected Writings*, Bollingen 88, Princeton: Princeton University Press.

Ramelli, Ilaria L. E. (ed.), 2006, *Corpus Hermeticum: Edizione e commento di A. D. Nock e A.-J. Festugière—edizione dei testi ermetici copti e comment di I. Ramelli: Testo greco, latino e copto*, Bompiani il pensiero occidentale, Milano: Bompiani.

Ramelli, Ilaria L. E., 2009, "Origen, Patristic Philosophy, and Christian Platonism: Re-Thinking the Christianisation of Hellenism," *VC* 63 (3): 217–63.

Ramelli, Ilaria L. E., 2011a, "Ancient Allegory and Its Reception through the Ages," *IJCT* 18 (4): 569–78.

Ramelli, Ilaria L. E., 2011b, "The Philosophical Stance of Allegory in Stoicism and its Reception in Platonism, Pagan and Christian: Origen in Dialogue with the Stoics and Plato," *IJCT* 18 (3): 335–71.

Ramelli, Ilaria L. E., 2011c, "The Pastoral Epistles and Hellenistic Philosophy: 1 Timothy 5:1–2, Hierocles, and the 'Contraction of Circles,'" *CBQ* 73 (3): 562–81.

Ramsay, William Mitchell, 1895–97, *The Cities and Bishoprics of Phrygia, Being an Essay of the Local History of Phrygia from the Earliest Times to the Turkish Conquest*, 2 vols., Oxford: Clarendon.

Rankin, David, 1984, "Tertullian's Use of the Pastoral Epistles in His Doctrine of Ministry," *AusBR* 32: 18–37.

Ransome, Hilda M., 1937, *The Sacred Bee in Ancient Times and Folklore*, London: George Allen & Unwin.

Redfield, James M., 2003, *The Locrian Maidens: Love and Death in Greek Italy*, Princeton: Princeton University Press.

Reed, Annette Yoshiko, 2002, "ΕΥΑΓΓΕΛΙΟΝ: Orality, Textuality, and the Christian Truth in Irenaeus' *Adversus Haereses*," *VC* 56 (1): 11–46.

Reed, Annette Yoshiko, 2009, "The Construction and Subversion of Patriarchal Perfection: Abraham and Exemplarity in Philo, Josephus, and the *Testament of Abraham*," *JSJ* 40 (2): 185–212.

Reed, Annette Yoshiko, 2013, "Testament of Abraham," in Louis H. Feldman, James L. Kugel, and Lawrence H. Schiffman (eds.), *Outside the Bible: Ancient Jewish Writings Related to Scripture*, 1671–97, Philadelphia: Jewish Publication Society.

Reiche, Harald A. T., 1993, "Heraclides' Three Soul-Gates: Plato Revised," *TAPA* 123: 161–80.

Reiser, Marius, 1997, *Jesus and Judgment: The Eschatological Proclamation in Its Jewish Context*, Minneapolis: Fortress.

Reiterer, Friedrich Vincenz, 2008, "The Interpretation of the Wisdom Tradition of the Torah within Ben Sira," in Angelo Passaro and Giuseppe Bellia (eds.), *The Wisdom of Ben Sira: Studies on Tradition, Redaction, and Theology*, 209–31, DCLS 1, Berlin: de Gruyter.

Reitzenstein, Richard, 1904, *Poimandres. Studien zur griechischägyptischen und frühchristlichen Literatur*, Leipzig: Teubner.

Renberg, Gil H., 2017, *Where Dreams May Come: Incubation Sanctuaries in the Greco-Roman World*, 2 vols., RGRW 184, Leiden: Brill.

Rennell of Rodd, Lord, 1932–3, "The Ithaca of the Odyssey," *ABSA* 33: 1–21.

Resch, Dustin G., 2009, "The Fittingness and Harmony of Scripture: Toward an Irenaean Hermeneutic," *HeyJ* 50 (2): 74–84.

Rhomiopoulou, Katerina, 1981, "New Inscriptions in the Archaeological Museum, Thessaloniki," in Harry J. Dell (ed.), *Ancient Macedonian Studies in Honor of Charles F. Edson*, 299–305, Thessaloniki: Institute for Balkan Studies.

Richard, Julian, 2012, *Water for the City, Fountains for the People: Monumental Fountains in the Roman East. An Archaeological Study of Water Management*, Studies in Eastern Mediterranean Archaeology 9, Turnhout: Brepols.

Richards, William A., 2002, *Difference and Distance in Post-Pauline Christianity: An Epistolary Analysis of the Pastorals*, StBibLit 44, New York: Lang.

Riedinger, Rudolf, 1973, "Der Physiologos und Klemens von Alexandreia," *ByzZ* 66 (2): 273–307.

Riedinger, Rudolf, 1977, Review of Dimitris Kaimakis, *Der Physiologos nach der ersten Redaktion*, *ByzZ* 70 (1): 109–12.

Rike, R. L., 1987, *Apex Omnium: Religion in the Res Gestae of Ammianus*, TCH 15, Berkeley: University of California Press.

Riley, Mark, 1987, "Theoretical and Practical Astrology: Ptolemy and His Colleagues," *TAPA* 117: 235–56.

Ring, Thomas Gerhard, 1975, *Auctoritas bei Tertullian, Cyprian und Ambrosius*, Cassiciacum 29, Würzburg: Augustinus-Verlag.

Robert, Louis, 1954, *Les Fouilles de Claros. Conférence donnée a l'Université d'Ankara le 26 octobre 1953 sous les auspices de la Société Turque d'Histoire (Türk Tarih Kurumu)*, Limoges: Bontemps.

Robert, Louis, 1969, "Les inscriptions," in Jean des Gagniers, Pierre Devambez, Lilly Kahil, and René Ginouvès, *Laodicée du Lycos. Le Nymphée, Campagnes 1961–1963*, 247–389, Québec: Les Presses de l'Université Laval.

Robert, Louis, and Jeanne Robert, 1989, *Claros*, vol. 1.1, Décrets hellénistiques, Paris: Editions Recherche sur les civilisations.

Robert, Louis, and Jeanne Robert, 1992, "Décret de Colophon pour un Chresmologue de Smyrne appelé à diriger l'Oracle de Claros," *Bulletin de correspondance hellénique* 116 (1): 279–91.

Robertson, A. T., 1934, *A Grammar of the Greek New Testament in the Light of Historical Research*, 4th ed., Nashville: Broadman.

Robinson, Edward, 1836, *A Greek and English Lexicon of the New Testament*, Boston: Crocker and Brewster.

Robinson, Edward, 1872, *A Greek and English Lexicon of the New Testament*, rev. ed., Edinburgh: T&T Clark.

Rogers, Guy MacLean, 2012, *The Mysteries of Artemis of Ephesos: Cult, Polis, and Change in the Graeco-Roman World*, Synkrisis, New Haven: Yale University Press.

Rohde, Erwin, 1925, *Psyche: The Cult of Souls and Belief in Immortality among the Greeks*, International Library of Psychology, Philosophy and Scientific Method, London: Kegan Paul, Trench, Trubner.

Roloff, Jürgen, 1988, *Der erste Brief an Timotheus*, EKKNT 15, Zürich: Benziger.

Romagnoli, Carla Amirante, 2014, *Sibille, Oracoli e libri sibillini*, Palermo: Saladino.

Romano, Allen J., 2009, "The Invention of Marriage: Hermaphroditus and Salmacis at Halicarnassus and in Ovid," *ClQ* 59 (2): 543–61.

Ronconi, Filippo, 2005, "La miscellanea che non divenne mai silloge: il caso del Bodl. Barocci 50," in Rosa Maria Piccione and Matthias Perkams (eds.), *Selecta colligere, II. Beiträge zur Technik des Sammelns und Kompilierens griechischer Texte von der Antike bis zum Humanismus*, 295–353, Hellenica 18, Alessandria: Orso.

Ronconi, Filippo, 2007, *I Manoscritti Greci Miscellanei. Ricerche su esemplari dei secoli IX–XII*, Testi, Studi, Strumenti 21, Spoleto: Fondazione Centro Italiano di Studi sull'Alto Medioevo.

Roscalla, Fabio, 1998, *Presenze simboliche dell'ape nella grecia antica*, Pubblicazioni della Facoltà di Lettere e Filosofia dell'Università di Pavia 86, Firenze: La nuova Italia.

Roscher, Wilhelm Heinr., 1883, *Nektar und Ambrosia*, Leipzig: Teubner.

Rose, H. J., 1956, "Divine Disguisings," *HTR* 49 (1): 63–72.

Rossel, Hannibal, 1585, *Divinus Pymander Hermetis Mercurii Trismegisti*, vol. 1, Cracow: Lazarus.

Rouse, W. H. D. (trans.), 1962, *Nonnos, Dionysiaca*, vol. 1, LCL 344, London: Heinemann.

Rousselle, Aline, 1988, *Porneia: On Desire and the Body in Antiquity*, Family, Sexuality and Social Relations in Past Times, Oxford: Blackwell.

Rowan, Clare, 2012, *Under Divine Auspices: Divine Ideology and the Visualisation of Imperial Power in the Severan Period*, Cambridge: Cambridge University Press.

Ruelle, C.-E., 1898, "Notice bibliographique et paléographique," in F. de Mély, *Les Lapidaires de l'antiquité et du moyen âge*, vol. 2: *Les lapidaires grecs*, vii–xvii, HistSci, Paris: Leroux.

Ruelle, Ch.-Ém., 1902, *Les lapidaires de l'antiquité et du moyen âge*, vol. 3: *Les lapidaires grecs*, HistSci, Paris: Leroux.

Runia, David T., 2008, "Stobaeus," *BNP* 13.846–50.

Russell, Michael, 1831, *View of Ancient and Modern Egypt; with an Outline of Its Natural History*, Harper's Stereotype Edition, New York: Harper.

Rzach, Aloisius, 1891, *Oracula Sibyllina*, Vienna: Tempsky.

Saffrey, Henri Dominique, 1975, "Un lecteur antique des oeuvres de Numénius: Eusèbe de Césarée," in Antonio Maddalena (ed.), *Forma Futuri: Studi in onore del Cardinale Michele Pellegrino*, 145–53, Torino: Bottega d'Erasmo.

Säflund, Gösta, 1955, *De Pallio und die stilistische Entwicklung Tertullians*, Skrifter Utgivna av Svenska Institutet i Rom 8/8, Lund: Gleerup.

Safrai, S., 1987, "Home and Family," in S. Safrai and M. Stern (eds.), *The Jewish People in the First Century*, vol. 2: *Historical Geography, Political History, Social, Cultural and Religious Life and Institutions*, 728–92, CRINT 1/2, Assen: Van Gorcum.

Şahin, Sencer, 1987, "Epigraphica Asiae Minoris neglecta et iacentia," *EpAn* 9: 47–72.

Salaman, Clement, Dorine van Oyen, William D. Wharton, and Jean-Pierre Mahé, 2000, *The Way of Hermes: New Translations of* The Corpus Hermeticum *and* The Definitions of Hermes Trismegistus to Asclepius, Rochester, VT: Inner Traditions.

Salmon, George, 1873, "Some Notes on the Chronology of Hippolytus," *Hermathena* 1 (1): 82–128.

Sanday, W., 1911, *Inspiration: Eight Lectures on the Early History and Origin of the Doctrine of Biblical Inspiration*, 7th ed., London: Longmans, Green.

Sanders, E. P. (trans.), 1983, "Testament of Abraham" (rec. A), *OTP* 1.882–95.

Sandnes, Karl Olav, 2009, *The Challenge of Homer: School, Pagan Poets and Early Christianity*, LNTS 400, London: T&T Clark.

Sandnes, Karl Olav, 2011, *The Gospel "According to Homer and Virgil": Cento and Canon*, NovTSup 138, Leiden: Brill.

Santa Cruz, Julio Gómez, 2007, "La simbologia del agua en la cultura romana," in Julio Mangas and Santiago Martínez Caballero (eds.), *El Agua y Las Ciudades Romanas*, 73–97, Antigüedad 2, Madrid: Móstoles Ediciones.

Sathas, C. N., 1888, *Documents inédits relatifs à l'histoire de la Grèce au Moyen Âge*, vol. 7, Μνημεγα Ελληνικης Ιστοριας, Paris: Maisonneuve.

Sbordone, Francesco, 1936, *Physiologus*, Mediolani: Dante Alighieri-Albrighi.

Scarpi, Paolo, 2009, *La Rivelazione segreta di Ermete Trismegisto*, 2 vols., Rome: Valla.

Scheck, Thomas P., 2008, *Origen and the History of Justification: The Legacy of Origen's Commentary on Romans*, Notre Dame: University of Notre Dame Press.

Scheindler, Augustinus (ed.), 1881, *Nonni Panopolitani. Paraphrasis S. Evangelii Ioannei*, Leipzig: Teubner.

Schlesinger, Eilhard, 1933, *Die griechische Asylie*, Giessen: Töpelmann.

Schleusner, Johann Friedrich, 1819, *Novum Lexicon Graeco-Latinum in Novum Testamentum*, 4th ed., 2 vols., Leipzig: Weidmann.

Schlier, H., 1960, "La notion paulinienne de la parole de Dieu," in Albert Descamps (ed.), *Littérature et Théologie Pauliniennes*, 127–41, RechBib 5, Bruges: Desclée de Brouwer.

Schmid, Konrad, 2012, "The Canon and the Cult: The Emergence of Book Religion in Ancient Israel and the Gradual Sublimation of the Temple Cult," *JBL* 131 (2): 289–305.

Schmidt, Carl, 1919, *Gespräche Jesu mit seinen Jüngern nach der Auferstehung: Ein katholisch-apostolisches Sendschreiben des 2. Jahrhunderts*, TU 43, Leipzig: Hinrichs.

Schmidt, Ernst A., 1968, "Die Leiden des verliebten Daphnis," *Hermes* 96 (4): 539–52.

Schmidt, Francis, 1976, "The Two Recensions of the Testament of Abraham: In Which Direction Did the Transformation Take Place?," in George W. E. Nickelsburg Jr. (ed.), *Studies on the Testament of Abraham*, 78–80, SBLSCS 6, Missoula: Scholars Press.

Schmidt, Francis, 1986, *Le Testament grec d'Abraham: Introduction, édition critique des deux recensions grecques, traduction*, TSAJ 11, Tübingen: Mohr-Siebeck.

Schmitz, Thomas A., 2009, "Nonnus and His Tradition," in Richard B. Hays, Stefan Alkier, and Leroy A. Huizenga (eds.), *Reading the Bible Intertextually*, 171–89, Waco: Baylor University Press.

Schnabel, Eckhard J., 1985, *Law and Wisdom from Ben Sira to Paul: A Tradition Historical Enquiry into the Relation of Law, Wisdom, and Ethics*, WUNT 2/16, Tübingen: Mohr-Siebeck.

Schneider, Horst, 2002, "Das Ibis-Kapitel im *Physiologus*," *VC* 56 (2): 151–64.

Schoedel, William R., 1985, *Ignatius of Antioch*, Hermeneia, Philadelphia: Fortress.

Schökel, Luis Alonso, 1965, *The Inspired Word: Scripture in the Light of Language and Literature*, New York: Herder and Herder.

Scholten, Clemens, 1991, "Hippolytos II (von Rom)," *RAC* 15.492–551.

Scholten, Clemens, 2005, Review of J. A. Cerrato, *Hippolytus between East and West*, *VC* 59 (1): 85–92.

Schrader, Hermann (ed.), 1880, *Porphyrii Quaestionum Homericarum ad Iliadem pertinentium religuias*, Leipzig: Teubner.

Schrijvers, P. H., 1977, "La classification des rêves selon Hérophile," *Mnemosyne* 30 (1): 13–27.

Schröter, Jens, 2012, "Paul the Founder of the Church: Reflections on the Reception of Paul in the Acts of the Apostles and the Pastoral Epistles," in David P. Moessner, Daniel Marguerat, Mikeal C. Parsons, and Michael Wolter (eds.), *Paul and the Heritage of Israel: Paul's Claim upon Israel's Legacy in Luke and Acts in the Light of the Pauline Letters*, 195–219, LNTS 452, London: T&T Clark.

Schultz, Wolfgang, 1910, *Dokumente der Gnosis*, Jena: Diederichs.

Schulze, L., 1896, review of Hermann Cremer, *Biblisch-theologisches Wörterbuch der Neutestamentlichen Gräcität*, 8th ed., *Theologisches Literaturblatt* 17 (21): 250–4.

Schweizer, Eduard, 1964, "θεόπνευστος," 453–5, *TDNT* 6.

Scott, Alan, 1998, "The Date of the *Physiologus*," *VC* 52 (4): 430–41.

Scott, Alan, 2002, "Zoological Marvel and Exegetical Method in Origen and the *Physiologus*," in Charles A. Bobertz and David Brakke (eds.), *Reading in Christian Communities: Essays on Interpretation in the Early Church*, 80–9, CJA 14, Notre Dame: University of Notre Dame Press.

Scott, James W., 2009a, "The Inspiration and Interpretation of God's Word, with Special Reference to Peter Enns," pt. 1: "Inspiration and Its Implications," *WTJ* 71 (1): 129–83.

Scott, James W., 2009b, "Reconsidering Inerrancy: A Response to A. T. B. McGowan's *The Divine Authenticity of Scripture*," *WTJ* 71 (1): 185–209.

Scott, Walter, 1924–36, *Hermetica: The Ancient Greek and Latin Writings Which Contain Religious or Philosophic Teachings Ascribed to Hermes Trismegistus*, 4 vols., Oxford: Clarendon.

Segal, Charles, 1974a, "Death by Water: A Narrative Pattern in Theocritus (Idylls 1, 13, 22, 23)," *Hermes* 102 (1): 20–38.

Segal, Charles, 1974b, "'Since Daphnis Dies': The Meaning of Theocritus' First Idyll," *MH* 31 (1): 1–22.

Segal, M. H., 1934–5, "The Evolution of the Hebrew Text of Ben Sira," *JQR* 25 (2): 91–149.

Segal, Robert A., 1986, *The Poimandres as Myth: Scholarly Theory and Gnostic Meaning*, Religion and Reason 33, Berlin: Mouton de Gruyter.

Senmartí, Antonio González, 1973, "El tema de Dioniso en la poesía prenonniana," *Boletin del Instituto de Estudios Helénicos* 7 (1): 53–9.

Settis, Salvatore, 1973, "'Esedra' e 'ninfeo' nella terminologia architettonica del mondo romano. Dall'età repubblicana alla tarda antichità," *ANRW* 1.4: 661–745.

Ševčenko, Ihor, 1980, "A Shadow Outline of Virtue: The Classical Heritage of Greek Christian Literature (Second to Seventh Century)," in Kurt Weitzmann (ed.), *Age of Spirituality: A Symposium*, 53–73, Princeton: Princeton University Press.

Shaw, Brent D., 1991, "The Noblest Monuments and the Smallest Things: Wells, Walls and Aqueducts in the Making of Roman Africa," in A. Trevor Hodge, *Future Currents in Aqueduct Studies*, 63–91, Collected Classical Papers 2, Leeds: Cairns.

Shelton, W. Brian, 2008, *Martyrdom from Exegesis in Hippolytus: An Early Church Presbyter's Commentary on Daniel*, Milton Keynes: Paternoster.

Sheridan, Mark, 2004, "Scripture," in John Anthony McGuckin (ed.), *The Westminster Handbook to Origen*, 197–201, Westminster Handbooks to Christian Theology, Louisville: Westminster John Knox.

Sheridan, Mark, 2007, "Origen's Concept of Scripture: The Basis of Early Christian Interpretation," *Downside Review* 125 (439): 93–110.

Sherry, Lee Francis, 1991, "The Hexameter Paraphrase of St. John attributed to Nonnus of Panopolis: Prolegomenon and Translation," Ph.D. dissertation, Columbia University, New York.

Shorey, Paul (trans.), 1980, *Plato, The Republic*, LCL 276, Cambridge: Harvard University Press.

Shorrock, Robert, 2001, *The Challenge of Epic: Allusive Engagement in the* Dionysiaca *of Nonnus*, MnemSup 210, Leiden: Brill.

Shorrock, Robert, 2011, *The Myth of Paganism: Nonnus, Dionysus and the World of Late Antiquity*, Classical Literature and Society, London: Bristol Classical Press.

Shorrock, Robert, 2014, "A Classical Myth in a Christian World: Nonnus' Ariadne Episode (*Dion.* 47.265–475)," in Konstantinos Spanoudakis (ed.), *Nonnus of Panopolis in Context: Poetry and Cultural Milieu in Late Antiquity*, 313–32, TCSup 24, Berlin: de Gruyter.

Shorrock, Robert, 2016, "Christian Themes in the *Dionysiaca*," in Domenico Accorinti (ed.), *Brill's Companion to Nonnus of Panopolis*, 577–600, BCCS, Leiden: Brill.

Sieber, Fabian, 2017, "Words and Their Meaning: On the Chronology of the *Paraphrasis of St John's Gospel*," in Herbert Bannert and Nicole Kröll (eds.), *Nonnus of Panopolis in Context II: Poetry, Religion, and Society. Proceedings of the International Conference on Nonnus of Panopolis, 26th–29th September 2013, University of Vienna, Austria*, 156–65, MnemSup 408, Leiden: Brill.

Siegert, Folker, 2004, "Die Inspiration der Heiligen Schriften: Ein philonisches Votum zu 2Tim 3,16," in Roland Deines and Karl-Wilhelm Niebuhr (eds.), *Philo und das Neue Testament: Wechselseitige Wahrnehmungen: I. Internationales Symposium zum Corpus Judaeo-Hellenisticum 1.–4. Mai 2003, Eisenach/Jena*, 205–22, WUNT 1/172, Tübingen: Mohr-Siebeck.

Silverman, David P., 1995, "The Nature of Egyptian Kingship," in David O'Connor and David P. Silverman (eds.), *Ancient Egyptian Kingship*, 49–92, PrÄ 9, Leiden: Brill.

Simelidis, Christos, 2016, "Nonnus and Christian Literature," in Domenico Accorinti (ed.), *Brill's Companion to Nonnus of Panopolis*, 289–307, BCCS, Leiden: Brill.

Simon, Marcel, 1983, "Sur quelques aspects des Oracles Sibyllins juifs," in David Hellholm (ed.), *Apocalypticism in the Mediterranean World and the Near East: Proceedings of the International Colloquium on Apocalypticism, Uppsala, August 12–17, 1979*, 219–33, Tübingen: Mohr-Siebeck.

Simonetti, Manlio, 1989, "Aggiornamento su Ippolito," in *Nuove ricerche su Ippolito*, 75–131, Studia Ephemeridis Augustinianum 30, Roma: Institutum Patristicum Augustinianum.

Simonetti, Manlio, 2000, "Scrittura sacra," in Adele Monaci Castagno (ed.), *Dizionario Origene: La cultura, il pensiero, le opere*, 424–37, Rome: Città Nuova.

Simonini, Laura (ed.), 1986, *Porfirio: L'antro delle ninfe*, Classici 48, Milano: Adelphi.

Şimşek, Celal, 2007, *Laodikeia (Laodikeia ad Lycum)*, Istanbul: Yayinlari.

Skarsaune, Oskar, 1996, "The Development of Scriptural Interpretation in the Second and Third Centuries—Except Clement and Origen," in Magne Sæbø (ed.), *Hebrew Bible / Old Testament: The History of Its Interpretation*, vol. 1: *From the Beginnings to the Middle Ages (Until 1300)*, 373–442, Göttingen: Vandenhoeck & Ruprecht.

Skeat, T. C., 1992, "Irenaeus and the Four-Gospel Canon," *NovT* 34 (2): 194–9.

Smend, Rudolf, 1906, *Die Weisheit des Jesus Sirach*, Berlin: Reimer.

Smith, James Reuel, 1922, *Springs and Wells in Greek and Roman Literature: Their Legends and Locations*, New York: Putnam.

Smith, Morton, 1974, "On the Wine God in Palestine (Gen. 18, Jn. 2, and Achilles Tatius)," in *Salo Wittmayer Baron Jubilee Volume, on the Occasion of His Eightieth Birthday*, 815–29, 2 vols., Jerusalem: American Academy for Jewish Research.

Smith, Rowland, 2005, *Julian's Gods: Religion and Philosophy in the Thought and Action of Julian the Apostate*, London: Routledge.

Smith, Yancy Warren, 2009, "Hippolytus' Commentary on the Song of Songs in Social and Critical Context," Ph.D. dissertation, Brite Divinity School, Fort Worth.

Sommerstein, Alan H. (trans.), 2008, *Aeschylus. Fragments*, LCL 505, Cambridge: Harvard University Press.

Somos, Róbert, 2000, "Origen and Numenius," *Adamantius* 6: 51–69.

Sourvinou-Inwood, Christiane, 2004, "Hermaphroditos and Salmakis: The Voice of Halikarnassos," in Signe Isager and Poul Pedersen (eds.), *The Salmakis Inscription and Hellenistic Halikarnassos*, 59–84, Halicarnassian Studies 4, Odense: University Press of South Denmark.

Sourvinou-Inwood, Christiane, 2005, *Hylas, the Nymphs, Dyonysos and Others: Myth, Ritual, Ethnicity*, Skrifter Utgivna av Svenska Institutet i Athen 19, Stockholm: Åströms.

Spalinger, Anthony, 2009, *The Great Dedicatory Inscription of Ramesses II: A Solar-Osirian Tractate at Abydos*, Culture and History of the Ancient Near East 33, Leiden: Brill.

Spanoudakis, Konstantinos, 2007, "Icarius Jesus Christ? Dionysiac Passion and Biblical Narrative in Nonnus' Icarius Episode (Dion. 47,1-264)," *Wiener Studien* 120: 35–92.

Spanoudakis, Konstantinos, 2016, "Pagan Themes in the *Paraphrase*," in Domenico Accorinti (ed.), *Brill's Companion to Nonnus of Panopolis*, 601–24, BCCS, Leiden: Brill.

Sparks, Kenton L., 2008, *God's Word in Human Words: An Evangelical Appropriation of Critical Biblical Scholarship*, Grand Rapids, MI: Baker Academic.

Speigl, Jakob, 1996, "Tertullian als Exeget," in Georg Schöllgen and Clemens Scholten (eds.), *Stimuli. Exegese und ihre Hermeneutik in Antike und Christentum: Festschrift für Ernst Dassmann*, 161–76, JACErg 23, Münster: Aschendorffsche Verlagsbuchhandlung.

Spence, R. M., 1897, "2 Timothy iii. 15, 16," *ExpTim* 8 (12): 563–5.

Sperti, Luigi, 2000, "Ricognizione archeologica a Laodicea di Frigia: 1993–1998," in Gustavo Traversari (ed.), *Laodicea di Frigia*, 1.29–103, 2 vols., Roma: Bretschneider.

Speyer, Wolfgang, 1973, "Die Segenskraft des 'göttlichen' Fußes: Eine Anschauungsform antiken Volksglaubens und ihre Nachwirkung," in W. den Boer (ed.), *Romanitas et Christianitas; studia Iano Henrico Waszink a. d. VI Kal. Nov. a. MCMLXXIII XIII lustra complenti oblata*, 293–301, Amsterdam: North-Holland.

Speyer, Wolfgang, 2015, "Nymphen," *RAC* 26.1–27.

Spicq, Ceslas, 1969, *Les Épitres Pastorales*, EBib, Paris: Gabalda.

Spielvogel, Jörg, 2006, *Septimius Severus*, Gestalten der Antike, Darmstadt: Wissenschaftliche Buchgesellschaft.

Stadelmann, Rainer, 2001, "Sphinx," in Donald B. Redford (ed.), *The Oxford Encyclopedia of Ancient Egypt*, 3.307–10, New York: Oxford University Press.

Stanton, Graham N., 2004, *Jesus and Gospel*, Cambridge: Cambridge University Press.

Stauber, J., and R. Merkelbach (eds.), 1996, "Die Orakel des Apollon von Klaros," *EpAn* 27: 1–53.

Sterling, Gregory E., 1993, "Platonizing Moses: Philo and Middle Platonism," *SPhiloA* 5: 96–111.

Stern, Menahem, 1980, *Greek and Latin Authors on Jews and Judaism*, vol. 2: *From Tacitus to Simplicius*, Fontes ad Res Judaicas Spectantes, Jerusalem: Israel Academy of Sciences and Humanities.

Stettler, Hanna, 1998, *Die Christologie der Pastoralbriefe*, WUNT 2/105, Tübingen: Mohr-Siebeck.

Stewart, Kenneth J., 2003, "A Bombshell of a Book: Gaussen's *Theopneustia* and its Influence on Subsequent Evangelical Theology," *EvQ* 75 (3): 215–37.

Stewart-Sykes, Alistair (ed.), 2001, *Hippolytus: On the Apostolic Tradition*, Crestwood, NY: St. Vladimir's Seminary Press.

Stewart-Sykes, Alistair, 2004, "*Traditio Apostolica*: The Liturgy of Third-century Rome and the Hippolytean School or Quomodo historia liturgica conscribenda sit," *St. Vladimir's Theological Quarterly* 48: 233–48.

Stöcklin-Kaldewey, Sara, 2014, *Kaiser Julians Gottes verehrung im Kontext der Spätantike*, STAC 86, Tübingen: Mohr-Siebeck.

Stone, Michael E., 1972, *The Testament of Abraham: The Greek Recensions*, Texts and Translations 2, Pseudepigrapha Series 2, Missoula: Society of Biblical Literature.

Stone, Michael E., 2002, *Adam's Contract with Satan: The Legend of the Cheirograph of Adam*, Bloomington: Indiana University Press.

Stoneman, Richard, 2011, *The Ancient Oracles: Making the Gods Speak*, New Haven: Yale University Press.

Stovell, Beth M., 2013, "Rivers, Springs, and Wells of Living Water: Metaphorical Transformation in the Johannine Corpus," in Stanley E. Porter and Andrew W. Pitts (ed.), *Christian Origins and Hellenistic Judaism: Social and Literary Contexts for the New Testament*, Texts and Editions for New Testament Study 10, 461–91, Early Christianity in Its Hellenistic Context 2, Leiden: Brill.

Strecker, Georg, 1975, "Das Evangelium Jesu Christi," in Georg Strecker (ed.), *Jesus Christus in Historie und Theologie: Neutestamentliche Festschrift für Hans Conzelmann zum 60. Geburtstag*, 503–48, Tübingen: Mohr-Siebeck, 1975.

Strickland, Michael, 2014, *The Evangelicals and the Synoptic Problem*, American University Studies 336, New York: Lang.

Sundberg, Albert C., Jr., 1964, *The Old Testament of the Early Church*, Harvard Theological Studies 20, Cambridge: Harvard University Press.

Sundberg, Albert C., Jr., 1975, "The Bible Canon and the Christian Doctrine of Inspiration," *Int* 29 (4): 352–71.

Susemihl, Franz, 1892, *Geschichte der griechischen Litteratur in der Alexandrinerzeit*, 2nd ed., Leipzig: Teubner.

Synave, Paul, and Pierre Benoit, 1961, *Prophecy and Inspiration: A Commentary on the Summa Theologica II–II, Questions 171–178*, New York: Desclée.

Szidat, Joachim, 1981, *Historischer Kommentar zu Ammianus Marcellinus Buch XX–XXI*, pt. 2: *Die Verhandlungsphase*, Historia Einzelschriften 38, Wiesbaden: Steiner.

Szidat, Joachim, 1982, "Der Neuplatonismus und die Gebildeten im Westen des Reiches: Gedanken zu seiner Verbreitung und Kenntnis ausserhalb der Schultradition," *MH* 39 (1): 132–45.

Tabor, James D., 1981, "Resurrection and Immortality: Paul and Poimandres," in Everett Ferguson (ed.), *Christian Teaching: Studies in Honor of LeMoine G. Lewis*, 72–91, Abilene: Abilene Christian University Book Store.

Tannery, Paul, 1904, "Les Cyranides," *REG* 17: 335–49.

Tate, J., 1927, "The Beginnings of Greek Allegory," *ClR* 41 (6): 214–15.

Tate, J., 1934, "On the History of Allegorism," *ClQ* 28 (2): 105–14.

Taylor, J. H. (trans.), 1982, *St. Augustine*, vol. 1: *The Literal Meaning of Genesis*, Ancient Christian Writers, vol. 41, New York: Newman.

Taylor, Thomas, 1789, *The Philosophical and Mathematical Commentaries of Proclus on the First Book of Euclid's Elements*, 2 vols., London: Taylor.

Taylor, Thomas, 1823, *Select Works of Porphyry; Containing His Four Books on Abstinence from Animal Food; His Treatise on the Homeric Cave of the Nymphs; and His Auxiliaries to the Perception of Intelligible Natures*, London: Rodd.

Teeple, Howard M., 1960, "Notes on Theologians' Approach to the Bible," *JBL* 79 (2): 164–6.

Temkin, Owsei, 1991, *Hippocrates in a World of Pagan and Christians*, Baltimore: Johns Hopkins University Press.

ten Berge, Bram, 2013, "Dreams in Cicero's *De Divinatione*," *ARG* 15 (1): 53–66.

Terry, Milton S., 1890, *The Sibylline Oracles: Translated from the Greek into English Blank Verse*, New York: Hunt & Eaton.

Terry, Milton S., 1899, *The Sibylline Oracles: Translated from the Greek into English Blank Verse*, 2nd ed., New York: Eaton & Mains.

Teyssèdre, Bernard, 1990, "Les représentations de la fin des temps dans le chant V des *Oracles Sibyllins*. Les strates de l'imaginaire," *Apocrypha* 1: 147–65.

Thayer, Joseph Henry, 1889, *A Greek-English Lexicon of the New Testament: Being Grimm's Wilke's Clavis Novi Testamenti*, New York: American Book Company.

Thedinga, Johann Friedrich, 1875, *De Numenio Philosopho Platonico: Dissertatio Philologica*, Bonn: Georgi.

Thelwall, S., 1885, *Tertullian, Part Fourth; Minucius Felix; Commodian; Origen, Parts First and Second*, ANF 4, New York: Scribner.

Thesaurus Linguae Latinae, 1954, vol. 7 (1), fasc. 10, Leipzig: Teubner.

Thiele, Walter, 1992, *Vetus Latina: Die Reste der altlateinischen Bibel*, vol. 11 (2): *Sirach (Ecclesiasticus)*, fasc. 4: *Sir 3,31–7,30*, Freiburg: Herder.

Thiele, Walter, 1997, "Die lateinische Sirachtexte als Zeugnis der griechischen Sirachüberlieferung," in J. Ådna, S. J. Hafemann, and Otfried Hofius (eds.), *Evangelium, Schriftauslegung, Kirche: Festschrift für Peter Stuhlmacher zum 65. Geburtstag*, 394–402, Göttingen: Vandenhoeck & Ruprecht.

Thielemann, Ph., 1893, "Die lateinische Übersetzung des Buches Sirach," *Archiv für lateinische Lexicographie und Grammatik* 8: 511–61.

Thielemann, Ph., 1894, "Die europäischen Bestandteile des lateinischen Sirach," *Archiv für lateinische Lexicographie und Grammatik* 9: 247–84.

Thiselton, Anthony C., 1980, *The Two Horizons: New Testament Hermeneutics and Philosophical Description with Special Reference to Heidegger, Bultmann, Gadamer, and Wittgenstein*. Carlisle: Paternoster.

Thomas, Johannes, 1992, *Der jüdische Phokylides: Formgeschichtliche Zugänge zu Pseudo-Phokylides und Vergleich mit der neutestamentlichen Paränese*, NTOA 23, Freiburg: Universitätsverlag.

Thompson, Bard, 1952, "Patristic Use of the Sibylline Oracles," *Review of Religion* 6 (3–4): 115–36.

Thompson, Mark D., 2012, "The Divine Investment in Truth: Toward a Theological Account of Biblical Inerrancy," in James K. Hoffmeier and Dennis R. Magary (ed.), *Do Historical Matters Matter to Faith? A Critical Appraisal of Modern and Postmodern Approaches to Scripture*, 71–97. Wheaton, IL: Crossway.

Thraede, Klaus, 1986, "Hauch," *RAC* 13.714–34.

Thraede, Klaus, 1998, "Inspiration," *RAC* 18.329–65.

Tiedemann, Dieterich, 1781, *Hermes Trismegistis: Poemander oder von der göttlichen Macht und Weisheit*, Berlin: Nicolai.

Tissoni, Francesco, 2008, "Ciro di Panopoli riconsiderato (con alcune ipotesi sulla destinazione delle *Dionisiache*)," in Sergio Audano (ed.), *Nonno e i suoi lettori*, 67–81, Hellenica 27, Alessandria: Edizioni dell'Orso.

Torjesen, Karen Jo, 1986, *Hermeneutical Procedure and Theological Method in Origen's Exegesis*, Patristische Texte und Studien 28, Berlin: de Gruyter.

Towner, Philip H., 1989, *The Goal of Our Instruction: The Structure of Theology and Ethics in the Pastoral Epistles*, JSNTSup 34, Sheffield: JSOT Press.

Towner, Philip H., 2006, *The Letters to Timothy and Titus*, NICNT, Grand Rapids, MI: Eerdmans.

Trebilco, Paul, 2004, *The Early Christians in Ephesus from Paul to Ignatius*, WUNT 1/166, Tübingen: Mohr-Siebeck.

Trembath, Kern Robert, 1987, *Evangelical Theories of Biblical Inspiration: A Review and Proposal*, New York: Oxford University Press.

Treu, Ursula, 1959, "'Otterngezücht': Ein patristischer Beitrag zur Quellenkunde des Physiologus," *ZNW* 50: 113–22.

Treu, Ursula, 1966, "Zur Datierung des Physiologus," *ZNW* 57 (1–2): 101–4.

Treu, Ursula, 1993, "The *Physiologus* and the Early Fathers," *StPatr* 24: 197–200.

Treu, Ursula, 1998, "The Greek Physiologus," in T. W. Hillard, R. A. Kearsley, C. E. V. Nixon, and A. M. Nobbs (eds.), *Ancient History in a Modern University*, vol. 2: *Early Christianity, Late Antiquity and Beyond*, 426–32, Grand Rapids, MI: Eerdmans.

Trigg, Joseph W., 1988, "Divine Deception and the Truthfulness of Scripture," in Charles Kannengiesser and William L. Petersen (eds.), *Origen of Alexandria: His World and His Legacy*, 147–64, CJA 1, Notre Dame, IN: University of Notre Dame Press.

Trincavelli, Victor, 1536, *Ioannis Stobaei, Collectiones Sententiarum*, Venice: Zanetti.

Tröger, Karl-Wolfgang, 1973, "Die hermetische Gnosis," in Karl-Wolfgang Tröger (ed.), *Gnosis und Neues Testament: Studien aus Religionswissenschaft und Theologie*, 97–119, Gütersloh: Mohn.

Tronci, Liana, 2014, "Verbal Adjectives," in *Encyclopedia of Ancient Greek Language and Linguistics*, 476, 3 vols., Leiden: Brill.

Tsuji, Manabu, 2010, "Persönliche Korrespondenz des Paulus: Zur Strategie der Pastoralbriefe als Pseudepigrapha," *NTS* 56 (2): 253–72.

Turcan, Marie, 1971, *Tertullien. La Toilette des Femmes (De cultu feminarum)*, SC 173, Paris: Cerf.

Türk, Gustave, 1895, *De Hyla*, Breslauer Philologische Abhandlungen 7/4, Breslau: Koebner.

Turner, James, 2014, *Philology: The Forgotten Origins of the Modern Humanities*, Princeton: Princeton University Press.

Turner, John D., 2006, "The Gnostic Sethians and Middle Platonism: Interpretations of the *Timaeus* and *Parmenides*," *VC* 60 (1): 9–64.

Turner, Nigel, 1955, "The 'Testament of Abraham': Problems in Biblical Greek," *NTS* 1 (3): 219–23.

Turner, Nigel (trans.), 1984, "The Testament of Abraham," in H. F. D. Sparks (ed.), *The Apocryphal Old Testament*, 393–421, Oxford: Clarendon.

Tusa, Aldina Cutroni, 1993, "La ninfa e la Fontana," in Juliette de La Genière *et al* (eds.), *Studi sulla Sicilia Occidentale in onore di Vincenzo Tusa*, 33–7, Padua: Bottega d'Erasmo.

Usick, Patricia, and Deborah Manley, 2007, *The Sphinx Revealed: A Forgotten Record of Pioneering Excavations*, British Museum Research Publications 164, London: British Museum.

Ustinova, Yulia, 2009, *Caves and the Ancient Greek Mind: Descending Underground in the Search for Ultimate Truth*, Oxford: Oxford University Press.

Uždavinys, Algis, 2009, *The Heart of Plotinus: The Essential Enneads, Including Porphyry's On the Cave of the Nymphs*, Bloomington, IN: World Wisdom.

Valgiglio, Ernesto, 1974, "*Cultus* e problema dell'unità nel *De cultu feminarum* di Tertulliano," *Rivista di studi classici* 22: 15–48.

Valls, R. Martín, M. V. Romero Canicero, and S. Carretero Vaquero, 1995, "Aras Votivas de Petavonium," *Zephyrus* 48: 331–45.

van Aken, A. R. A., 1951, "Some Aspects of Nymphaea in Pompeii, Herculaneum and Ostia," *Mnemosyne* 4 (1): 272–84.

van Bemmelen, Peter Maarten, 1987, *Issues in Biblical Inspiration: Sanday and Warfield*, Andrews University Seminary Doctoral Dissertation Series 13, Berrien Springs, MI: Andrews University Press.

van den Broek, R., and G. Quispel, 1991, *Corpus Hermeticum*, Pimander 2, Amsterdam: Pelikaan.

van den Hoek, Annewies, 1992, "Origen and the Intellectual Heritage of Alexandria: Continuity or Disjunction?," in Robert J. Daly (ed.), *Origeniana Quinta: Historica – Text and Method – Biblica – Philosophica – Theologica – Origenism and Later Developments. Papers of the 5th International Origen Congress, Boston College, 14–18 August 1989*, 40–50, BETL 105, Leuven: Leuven University Press.

van den Kerchove, Anna, 2011, "Les hermétistes et les conceptions traditionnelles des sacrifices," in N. Belayche et J.-D. Dubois (éd.), *L'Oiseau et le poisson. Cohabitations religieuses dans les mondes grec et romain*, 61–80, Religions dans l'histoire, Paris: Presses de l'Université Paris Sorbonne.

van den Kerchove, Anna, 2012, *La voie d'Hermès: Pratiques rituelles et traités hermétiques*, NHMS 77, Leiden: Brill.

van der Horst, Pieter W., 1978, *The Sentences of Pseudo-Phocylides: With Introduction and Commentary*, SVTP 4, Leiden: Brill.

van der Horst, Pieter W., 1985, "Pseudo-Phocylides," *OTP* 2.565–82.

van der Horst, Pieter W., 2010, "Porphyry on Judaism: Some Observations," in Zeev Weiss, Oded Irshai, Jodi Magness, and Seth Schwartz (eds.), *"Follow the Wise": Studies in Jewish History and Culture in Honor of Lee I. Levine*, 71–83, Winona Lake, IN: Eisenbrauns.

van Erp Taalman Kip, A. Maria, 1987, "And Daphnis Went to the Stream: The Meaning of Theocritus 1, 140–141," *Hermes* 115 (2): 249–51.

van Haelst, Joseph, 1976, *Catalogue des papyrus littéraires juifs et chrétiens*, Série papyrologie 1, Paris: Sorbonne.

van Henten, Jan Willem, 2000, "*Nero Redivivus* Demolished: The Coherence of the Nero Traditions in the *Sibylline Oracles*," *JSP* 11 (21): 3–17.

van Neste, Ray, 2004, *Cohesion and Structure in the Pastoral Epistles*, JSNTSup 280, London: T&T Clark.

van Straten, F. T., 1976, "Daikrates' Dream: A Votive Relief from Kos, and Some Other Kat'onar Dedications," *Bulletin Antieke Beschaving* 51: 1–27.

van Unnik, W. C., 1979, "Luke's Second Book and the Rules of Hellenistic Historiography," in J. Kremer (ed.), *Les Actes des Apôtres: Traditions, rédaction, théologie*, 37–60, BETL 48, Leuven: Leuven University Press.

van Winden, J. C. M., 1959, *Calcidius on Matter—His Doctrine and Sources: A Chapter in the History of Platonism*, PhA 9, Leiden: Brill.

Varner, Eric R., 2004, *Mutilation and Transformation:* Damnatio Memoriae *and Roman Imperial Portraiture*, Monumenta Graeca et Romana 10, Leiden: Brill.

Vatri, Giuseppe M., 2009, *Ermete Trismegisto: Corpus Hermeticum (i trattati greci)*, Cosenza: Brenner.

Vawter, Bruce, 1972, *Biblical Inspiration*, Theological Resources, Philadelphia: Westminster.

Verheyden, J., 2003, "The Canon Muratori: A Matter of Dispute," in J.-M. Auwers and H. J. De Jonge (eds.), *The Biblical Canons*, 487–556, BETL 163, Leuven: Peeters.

Vian, Francis (ed.), 1974, *Apollonios de Rhodes. Argonautigues*, vol. 1, *Chants I–II*, Budé, Paris: Les Belles Lettres.

Vian, Francis, 1991, "Nonno ed Omero," Κοινωνια 15: 5–18.

Vian, Francis, 1997, "ΜΑΡΤΥΣ chez Nonnos de Panopolis: Étude de sémantique et de chronologie," *REG* 110 (1): 143–60.

Vigna, Pierre Dalla, and Carlo Tondelli, 2000, *Ermete Trismegisto, scritti teologico-filosofici*, vol. 1: *Corpo ermetico; Asclepio*, Collana mimesis, Milano: Associazione cultural Mimesis.

Vogel, Manuel, 2009, "Einführung in die Schrift," in Eckart Reinmuth (ed.), *Joseph und Aseneth*, 3–31, Scripta Antiquitatis Posterioris ad Ethicam Religionemque pertinentia 15, Tübingen: Mohr-Siebeck.

Vogt, Ernst, 1967, "Das Akrostichon in der griechischen Literatur," *Antike und Abendland* 13 (1): 80–95.

Vogt, Hermann Josef, 1999, *Origenes als Exeget*, Paderborn: Schöningh.

Volp, Ulrich, 2009, "Hippolytus," *ExpTim* 120 (11): 521–9.

von Arnim, Hans (ed.), 1903–24, *Stoicorum veterum fragmenta*, 4 vols., Leipzig: Teubner.

von Bothmer, Dietrich, 1981, "The Death of Sarpedon," in Stephen L. Hyatt (ed.), *The Greek Vase: Papers Based on Lectures Presented to a Symposium Held at Hudson Valley Community College at Troy, New York in April of 1979*, 63–80, Latham, NY: Hudson-Mohawk Association of Colleges & Universities.

von Metternich, Wolf Freiherr (=Alethophilus), 1706, *Hermetis Trismegisti: Erkenntniß der Natur und des darin sich offenbahrenden Grossen Gottes*, Hamburg: Heyls and Liebezeits.

von Rad, Gerhard, 1964, "ζάω κτλ.," *TDNT* 2.832–75.

von Rad, Gerhard, 1972, *Wisdom in Israel*, London: SCM.

von Staden, Heinrich, 1989, *Herophilus: The Art of Medicine in Early Alexandria*, Cambridge: Cambridge University Press.

von Stuckrad, Kocku, 1996, *Frommigkeit und Wissenschaft: Astrologie in Tanach, Qumran, und frührabbinischer Literatur*, Europäische Hochschulschriften 23/572, Frankfurt: Lang.

von Wahlde, Urban C., 2004, "He Has Given to the Son to Have Life in Himself (John 5,26)," *Bib* 85 (3): 409–12.

Vyse, Howard, 1840–2, *Operations Carried on at the Pyramids of Gizeh in 1837*, 3 vols., London: Weale and Nickisson.

Wace, A. J. B., and M. S. Thompson, 1908–9, "A Cave of the Nymphs on Mount Ossa," *ABSA* 15: 243–7.

Waegeman, Maryse, 1987, *Amulet and Alphabet: Magical Amulets in the First Book of Cyranides*, Amsterdam: Gieben.

Wagman, Robert S., 2011, "Building for the Nymphs," *ClQ* 61 (2): 748–51.

Wagner, Guy, 1993, "Le decurion Paccius Maximus, champion de l'acrostiche," *ZPE* 95: 147–8.

Walter, Nikolaus, 1983, "Pseudepigraphische jüdisch-hellenistische Dichtung: Pseudo-Phokylides, Pseudo-Orpheus, Gefälschte Verse auf Namen griechischer Dichter," in Ernst Vogt and Nikolaus Walter, *Poetische Schriften*, 173–278, JSHRZ 4/3, Gütersloh: Gerd Mohn.

Wanke, Daniel, 2000, *Das Kreuz Christi bei Irenäus von Lyon*, BZNW 99, Berlin: de Gruyter.

Ward, Timothy, 2002, *Word and Supplement: Speech Acts, Biblical Texts, and the Sufficiency of Scripture*, Oxford: Oxford University Press.

Warfield, Benjamin B., 1889, "Paul's Doctrine of the Old Testament," *Presbyterian Quarterly* 3 (3): 389–406.

Warfield, Benjamin B., 1893, "The Real Problem of Inspiration," *PRR* 4 (14): 177–221.

Warfield, Benjamin B., 1894, "The Inspiration of the Bible," *BSac* 51 (204): 614–40.

Warfield, Benjamin B., 1900, "God-Inspired Scripture," *PRR* 11 (41): 89–130.

Warfield, Benjamin B., 1915, "Inspiration," *ISBE* 1473–83.

Warning, Wilhelm Westphal, 1909, *De Vettii Valentis sermone*, Anklam: Poettcke.

Waszink, J. H., 1979, "Tertullian's Principles and Methods of Exegesis," in William R. Schoedel and Robert L. Wilken (eds.), *Early Christian Literature and the Classical Intellectual Tradition: In honorem Robert M. Grant*, 17–31, Théologie historique 54, Paris: Beauchesne.

Waterhouse, Helen, 1996, "From Ithaca to the *Odyssey*," *ABSA* 91: 301–17.

Watson, Francis, 2006, "Are There Still Four Gospels? A Study in Theological Hermeneutics," in A. K. M. Adam (ed.), *Reading Scripture with the Church: Toward a Hermeneutic for Theological Interpretation*, 95–116, Grand Rapids, MI: Baker Academic.

Watson, Francis, 2013, *Gospel Writing: A Canonical Perspective*, Grand Rapids, MI: Eerdmans.

Weber, G., 1898, "Die Hochdruck-Wasserleitung von Laodicea ad Lycum," *Jahrbuch des kaiserlich deutschen Archäologischen Instituts* 13: 1–13.

Weber, Karl-Otto, 1962, *Origenes der Neuplatoniker: Versuch einer Interpretation*, Zetemata 27, Munich: Beck.

Webster, John, 2003, *Holy Scripture: A Dogmatic Sketch*, Current Issues in Theology, Cambridge: Cambridge University Press.

Weiland, Hendrik Christoffel, 1935, *Het Oordeel der Kerkvaders over het Orakel*, Amsterdam: Paris.

Weinberg, Florence M., 1987, *The Cave: The Evolution of a Metaphoric Field from Homer to Ariosto*, Studies in the Humanities Literature – Politics – Society 4, New York: Lang.

Wellmann, Max, 1924–5, "Über Träume," *Archiv für Geschichte der Medizin* 16 (1–2): 70–72.

Wellmann, Max, 1930, *Der Physiologus: Eine religionsgeschichtlich-naturwissenschaftliche Untersuchung*, PhilSup 22, Leipzig: Dieterich.

Wellmann, Max, 1934, *Marcellus von Side als Arzt und die Koiraniden des Hermes Trismegistos*, PhilSup 27/2, Leipzig: Dieterich.

Weltin, E. G., 1987, *Athens and Jerusalem: An Interpretative Essay on Christianity and Classical Culture*, AAR Studies in Religion 49, Atlanta: Scholars Press.

Werner, Johannes, 1889, *Der Paulinismus des Irenaeus. Eine kirchen- und dogmengeschichtliche Untersuchung über das Verhältnis des Irenaeus zu der paulinischen Briefsammlung und Theologie*, Leipzig: Hinrichs.

West, M. L., 1982, "Magnus and Marcellinus: Unnoticed Acrostics in the *Cyranides*," *ClQ* 76 (2): 480–1.

Whealey, A., 1996, "Hippolytus' Lost *De Universo* and *De Resurrectione*: Some New Hypotheses," *VC* 50 (3): 244–56.

Whiston, William, 1715, *A Vindication of the Sibylline Oracles, to Which Are Added the Genuine Oracles Themselves; with the Ancient Citations from Them; in Their Originals, and in English: and a Few Brief Notes*, 2 parts, London: Roberts.

Whitacre, Rodney A., 1982, *Johannine Polemic: The Role of Tradition and Theology*, SBLDS 67, Chico, CA: Scholars Press.

Whitby, Mary, 2007, "The Bible Hellenized: Nonnus' *Paraphrase* of St John's Gospel and 'Eudocia's' Homeric Centos," in J. H. D. Scourfield (ed.), *Texts and Culture in Late Antiquity: Inheritance, Authority, and Change*, 200–1, Swansea: Classical Press of Wales.

White, Alfred Canon, and Mariana Monteiro, 1905, *"As David and the Sibyls Say": A Sketch of the Sibyls and the Sibylline Oracles*, Edinburgh: Sands.

White, Benjamin L., 2011, "How to Read a Book: Irenaeus and the Pastoral Epistles Reconsidered," *VC* 65 (2): 125–49.

White, Heather, 1977, "A Case of *Arte Allusiva* in Theocritus," *AC* 46 (2): 578–9.

Whittaker, Helène, 1993, "Numenius' Fragment 2 and the Literary Tradition," *Symbolae Osloenses* 68 (1): 96–9.

Whittaker, John, 1978, "Numenius and Alcinous on the First Principle," *Phoenix* 32 (2): 144–54.

Wick, Peter, 2004, "Jesus gegen Dionysos? Ein Beitrag zur Kontextualisierung des Johannesevangeliums," *Bib* 85 (2): 179–98.

Wieland, George, 2006, *The Significance of Salvation: A Study of Salvation Language in the Pastoral Epistles*, Paternoster Biblical Monographs, Milton Keynes: Paternoster.

Wifstrand, Albert W., 1922, *Von Kallimachos zu Nonnos. Metrisch-stilistische Untersuchungen zur späteren griechischen Epik und zu verwandten Gedichtgattungen*, Skrifter utgivna av Vetenskapssocieteten i Lund 16, Lund: Gleerup.

Wikander, Ola, 2013, "Old Testament Prototypes for the Hermetic *Trishagion* in *Poimandres* 31—and Support for an Old Conjecture," *GRBS* 53 (3): 579–90.

Wild, Robert A., 1981, *Water in the Cultic Worship of Isis and Sarapis*, EPRO 87, Leiden: Brill.

Wiles, M. F., 1970, "Origen as Biblical Scholar," in P. R. Ackroyd and C. F. Evans (eds.), *The Cambridge History of the Bible*, vol. 1: *From the Beginnings to Jerome*, 454–89, Cambridge: Cambridge University Press.

Wilkinson, Kevin W., 2009, "Palladas and the Age of Constantine," *JRS* 99: 36–60.

Wilkinson, Kevin W., 2010, "Palladas and the Foundation of Constantinople," *JRS* 100: 179–94.

Willers, Dietrich, 1992, "Dionysos und Christus—ein archäologisches Zeugnis zur 'Konfessionsangehörigkeit' des Nonnos," *MH* 49 (2): 141–51.

Willers, Dietrich, 1993, "Zur Begegnung von Heidentum und Christentum im spätantiken Ägypten," in *Begegnung von Heidentum und Christentum im spätantiken Ägypten*, 11–19, Riggisberger Berichte, Riggisberg: Abegg-Stiftung.

Williams, David S., 1992, *Stylometric Authorship Studies in Flavius Josephus and Related Literature*, Jewish Studies 12, Lewiston, NY: Mellen.

Willoughby, Harold R., 1929, *Pagan Regeneration: A Study of Mystery Initiations in the Graeco-Roman World*, Chicago: University of Chicago Press.

Wills, Lawrence M., 1995, *The Jewish Novel in the Ancient World*, Ithaca, NY: Cornell University Press.

Wills, Lawrence M., 2011, "Jewish Novellas in a Greek and Roman Age: Fiction and Identity," *JSJ* 42 (2): 141–65.

Wilson, Stephen G., 1979, *Luke and the Pastoral Epistles*, London: SPCK.

Wilson, Walter T., 1994, *The Mysteries of Righteousness: The Literary Composition and Genre of the* Sentences *of Pseudo-Phocylides*, TSAJ 40, Tübingen: Mohr-Siebeck.

Wilson, Walter T., 2005, *The Sentences of Pseudo-Phocylides*, CEJL, Berlin: de Gruyter.

Windisch, Hans, 1918, "Urchristentum und Hermesmystik," *Theologisch Tijdschrift* 52: 186–240.

Winer, George Benedict, 1892, *A Grammar of the Idiom of the New Testament*, 7th ed., Andover: Draper.

Winkler, John J., 1990, *The Constraints of Desire: The Anthropology of Sex and Gender in Ancient Greece*, New York: Routledge.

Winston, David, 1993, "Response to Runia and Sterling," *SPhiloA* 5: 141–6.

Winter, Michael M., 2012, "Interlopers Reunited: The Early Translators of Ben Sira," *JBL* 131 (2): 251–69.

Wittchow, Frank, 2001, *Exemplarisches Erzählen bei Ammianus Marcellinus: Episode, Exemplum, Anekdote*, BAlt 144, München: Saur.

Wlosok, Antonie, 1960, *Laktanz und die philosophische Gnosis. Untersuchungen zu Geschichte und Terminologie des gnostischen Erlösungsvorstellung*, Abhandlungen der Heidelberger Akademie der Wissenschaften, Philosophisch-Historische Klasse 1960/2, Heidelberg: Winter.

Wolter, Michael, 1988, *Die Pastoralbriefe als Paulustradition*, FRLANT 146, Göttingen: Vandenhoeck & Ruprecht.

Wood, Jordan Daniel, 2015, "Origen's Polemics in *Princ* 4.2.4: Scriptural Literalism as a Christo-Metaphysical Error," *VC* 69 (1): 30–69.

Woozley, Anthony, 2010, "Plato and the Need for Law," *Philosophical Quarterly* 60 (239): 373–95.

Woschitz, Karl Matthäus, 2005, *Parabiblica: Studien zur jüdischen Literatur in der hellenistisch-römischen Epoche. Tradierung – Vermittlung – Wandlung*, Theologie: Forschung und Wissenschaft 16, Wien: LIT.

Wyttenbach, Daniel, 1797, *Plutarchi Chæronensis Moralia*, vol. 4, pt. 2, Oxford: Clarendon.

Yamauchi, Edwin, 1980, *The Archaeology of New Testament Cities in Western Asia Minor*, Grand Rapids, MI: Baker.

Young, Dennis, 1998, *Theognis, Ps. Pythagoras, Ps. Phocylides, Chares, Anonymi Avlodia, Fragmentum teliambicum*, Bibliotheca scriptorum Graecorum et Romanorum Teubneriana, Stuttgart: Teubner.

Young, Edward J., 1957, *Thy Word Is Truth*, Grand Rapids, MI: Eerdmans.

Yunis, Harvey, 1988, "Law, Politics, and the *Graphe Paranomon* in Fourth-Century Athens," *GRBS* 29 (4): 361–82.

Zambon, Marco, 2002, *Porphyre et le Moyen-Platonisme*, Histoire des Doctrines de l'Antiquité Classique 27, Paris: Librairie Philosophique J. Vrin.

Zanni, Doukaina G., 2008, "Ambrosia, Nectar and Elaion in the Homeric Poems," in S. A. Paipetis (ed.), *Science and Technology in Homeric Epics*, 391–9, History of Mechanism and Machine Science 6, Dordrecht: Springer.

Zeller, D., 1995, "The Life and Death of the Soul in Philo of Alexandria: The Use and Origin of a Metaphor," *SPhiloA* 7: 19–55.

Ziebritzki, Henning, 1994, *Heiliger Geist und Weltseele: Das Problem der dritten Hypostase bei Origenes, Plotin und ihren Vorläufern*, BHT 84, Tübingen: Mohr-Siebeck.

Ziegler, Joseph, 1964, "Zwei Beiträge zu Sirach," *BZ* 8: 277–84.

Ziegler, Konrat, 1951, "Plutarchos (2)," *RE* 41.1: 636–962.

Zielinski, Th., 1905–6, "Hermes und die Hermetik," *ARW* 8 (3–4): 321–72; 9 (1): 25–60.

Ziolkowski, Jan M., 1990, "Classical Influences on Medieval Latin Views of Poetic Inspiration," in Peter Godman and Oswyn Murray (eds.), *Latin Poetry and the Classical Tradition: Essays in Medieval and Renaissance Literature*, 15–38, Oxford-Warburg Studies, Oxford: Clarendon.

Zivie-Coche, Christiane, 2002, *Sphinx: History of a Monument*, Ithaca, NY: Cornell University Press.

Zivie-Coche, Christiane, 2006, "Le Sphinx de Giza et le culte d'Harmachis," in Eugène Warmenbol (ed.), *Sphinx: Les gardiens de l'Égypte*, 55–69, Bruxelles: ING Belgique et Fonds Mercator.

Zöllig, August, 1902, *Die Inspirationslehre des Origenes*, Strassburger Theologische Studien 5, Freiburg: Herder.

Zusanek, Harald, 1998, *Die Nymphen: Untersuchungen zum dios-Begriff 2*, Frankfurt: Lang.

Index of Modern Authors

Index of References

Lightning Source UK Ltd.
Milton Keynes UK
UKHW022252080321
380005UK00003B/125